Exploring, OREGON'S Wild Areas

SECOND EDITION

Exploring OREGON'S Wild Areas

SECOND EDITION

A GUIDE FOR HIKERS, BACKPACKERS, CLIMBERS, X-C SKIERS,& PADDLERS

WILLIAM L. SULLIVAN

Research Consultant: The Oregon Natural Resources Council

THE
MOUNTAINEERS

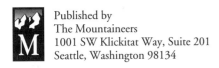

Published by
The Mountaineers
1001 SW Klickitat Way, Suite 201
Seattle, Washington 98134

Published simultaneously in Great Britain by Cordee, 3a DeMontfort Street, Leicester, England, LE1 7HD

First edition 1988. Second edition: first printing 1994, second printing 1995, revised 1997.

Edited by Meredith Waring
Maps by the author
All photographs by the author, except: page 73, Sherry Wellborn; pages 252 and 255, Wendell Wood.
Cover design by Watson Graphics
Book layout by Barbara Bash
Typesetting by The Mountaineers Books

Cover photograph: The Imnaha River near Eureka Bar in Hells Canyon (Area 54)
Frontispiece: Mount Hood from the Timberline Trail near McNeil Point (Area 2)

Library of Congress Cataloging in Publication Data
Sullivan, William L.
   Exploring Oregon's wild areas : a guide for hikers, backpackers, climbers, X-C skiers, and paddlers / William L. Sullivan. -- 2nd ed.
      p.   cm.
   Includes bibliographical references and index.
   ISBN 0-89886-386-4
      1. Outdoor recreation--Oregon--Guidebooks.   2. Wilderness areas--Oregon--Guidebooks.
3. Oregon--Guidebooks. I. Title.
GV191.42.O7S85   1994
796.5'09795--dc20   93-47684
                                                                                      CIP

CONTENTS

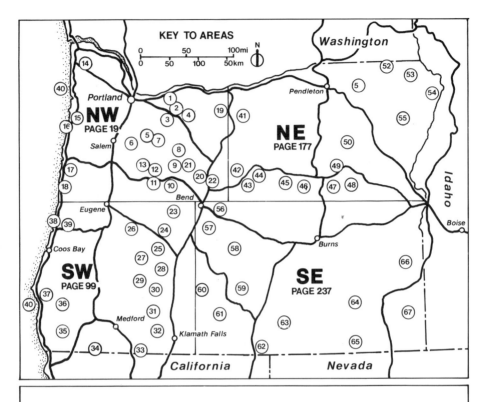

KEY TO AREAS

Washington

0 — 50 — 100mi
0 — 50 — 100 — 50km
N

14
40
Portland
NW PAGE 19
15
16
Salem
17
18
Eugene
38 39
Coos Bay
SW PAGE 99
37 36
40
Medford
35
34 33

1
2 4
3
19
41
5 7
6
8
13 12 9 21
11 10
Bend
23
26 24
25
27
28
29
30
31
32
Klamath Falls
62
California

Pendleton
52 53
5 54
55
NE PAGE 177
50
49
42 44
43 45 46 47 48
56
57
58
Burns
SE PAGE 237
59
60
61 63
64
65
66
67
Idaho
Boise
Nevada

KEY TO MAP SYMBOLS

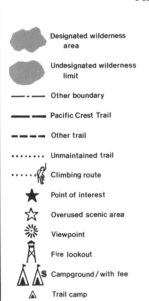

Designated wilderness area

Undesignated wilderness limit

—·— Other boundary

——— Pacific Crest Trail

— — — Other trail

········· Unmaintained trail

·····⚐ Climbing route

★ Point of interest

☆ Overused scenic area

☀ Viewpoint

Fire lookout

Campground / with fee

Trail camp

Shelter

Paved road

Gravel road

G Dirt road with gate / 4-wheel drive track

Freeway

99 U.S. highway

18 State or county road

5430 Forest Service road

Picnic area

Boat launch

Gasoline available

Food available

Scheduled bus service

Landing strip

Horse Loading facility

Forest Service station

Road with winter ski use

Trail with winter ski use

Nordic ski trail

P Sno-Park

Downhill ski area

Snowmobile area

Mountaineering site

Swamp

Meadow

Hill, slope, or mountain

Cliff

Seasonal stream / dry lake

Spring / rapids / falls

✗1320' Elevation in feet

Canyon Creek Meadows and Three Fingered Jack

INTRODUCTION

How can we love Oregon's fragile wilderness without loving it to death? If we intend to walk lightly on the land, we cannot all continue to beat dusty paths to Mount Jefferson's sorely trammeled Jeff Park, Mount Hood's Paradise Park, and the Three Sisters' Green Lakes Basin.

Oregon is chock full of alternative trips with both beauty and isolation. This guide describes more than 600 hikes and 130 cross-country ski tours, as well as prime spots for whitewater rafting, mountaineering, and even hang gliding.

The popular High Cascades wildernesses are all included, of course, but so are less crowded areas in four other major mountain ranges. And there's more: the deepest whitewater river canyons in the world. Fog-bound oceanshore rain forests. Winter hideaways at snowy lakes. Turquoise hot springs in stark deserts. Two areas of sand dunes. And thousands of miles of quiet trails.

HOW TO USE THIS BOOK

The Maps

A *locator map* following the Table of Contents identifies the book's sixty-seven areas by number and shows which quarter of the state each area is in. Turn to the appropriate *quadrant overview map* to find the best highway approach to an area.

Individual *area maps* use symbols identified in a key in the front matter. Note that solid gray areas denote wilderness designated by act of Congress. Undesignated wilderness—managed under quite different rules—is shown only by thin gray borders. Beyond the gray borders lies land unsuited for any kind of wilderness designation because of clearcuts, roads, private ownership, development, or insufficient size.

Area maps are only for orientation; topographical maps should always be used when exploring the wilderness. See the information blocks for which USGS-type map to carry.

Stars denote points of interest, but hollow stars indicate scenic spots already badly worn by overuse. Visitors heading for such fragile spots should tread lightly and plan to camp elsewhere.

The maps' north arrows always point to true north; magnetic north lies approximately 20° east of true north in Oregon. In the few instances where north is not at the top of the map, a square of gray shading helps draw attention to the north arrow.

Dirt roads shown with dashed lines are "ways"—unimproved tracks that are better suited for four-wheel-drive vehicles than for passenger cars. The maps do not show all the ways and roads. Particularly in southeast Oregon's desert country, backroads drivers may find the proliferation of unmarked ways confusing. Bureau of Land Management quadrangle maps are good insurance here (see Appendix C).

Long-distance recreation trails connecting many of the areas in this book are featured in the State Trail Plan Map in Appendix A.

The Information Blocks

Each entry begins with a synopsis of information about the area. The *location* tells the highway mileage and direction from major cities to the closest portion of a roadless area. The *size* reflects the approximate extent (in square miles) of all the roadless lands in each featured area. For state parks, the size is the total extent of park land. An area's *status* tells how many square miles have been designated by Congress as wilderness and the dates they were designated. Other less protective designations are also noted.

Next, each entry notes the roadless area's dominant types of *terrain,* as well as the highest and lowest *elevations* in feet. The *management* listing advises whether the national Forest Service (NF), the Bureau of Land Management (BLM), or some other agency administers the area.

These agencies can answer specific questions about road conditions, regulations, and permits. Their addresses and phone numbers appear in Appendix B.

Topographic maps, which show landforms by means of contour lines, are essential backup material for the maps in this book. The best topographic maps are listed first. Appendix C includes detailed information for ordering topographic maps.

The Text Descriptions

An area's *climate* information generally includes average snow levels, temperature ranges, and likeliest seasons to find mosquitoes, wildflowers, or huckleberries. Average annual precipitation reflects the total of rain and melted snow. All of these figures vary substantially from year to year. In addition, some of the data for remote areas are approximate, as they were extrapolated from weather station records. Wilderness visitors should always prepare for inclement weather.

All sections include descriptions of *plants and wildlife* and *geology.* However, only areas with a substantial history of human contact have *history* entries.

A FEW WILDERNESS RULES

The 1964 Wilderness Act defines wilderness as "an area where the earth and its community of life are untrammeled by man, where man himself is a visitor who does not remain." That law established strict rules that govern the thirty-seven Oregon areas Congress has thus far designated as wilderness. These rules include:

* No mechanical transport. This bans off-road vehicles (ORVs), motorcycles, bicycles, airplane drops, hang gliders, and helicopter landings—except for rescue or fire fighting.
* No new mining claims. Mining on pre-1984 claims, however, continues.
* No commercial enterprises. An exception currently allows some cattle grazing. Guides and outfitters may operate only under permit.
* No motorized equipment (such as generators or chainsaws).
* Fishing and hunting are permitted with a state license. Check with the Oregon Department of Fish and Wildlife for regulations.

Many designated wilderness areas have other restrictions as well. The most common "No's" are:

* Cutting, chopping, or clipping live or dead trees.
* Grazing, picketing, or tying saddle stock within 200 feet of a lake or stream.
* Discharging firearms within 150 yards of a campsite, or across any trail or body of water.
* Smoking while traveling.
* Traveling in groups larger than twelve.

In addition, some rules extend to all federal lands, wilderness or not:

* Collecting arrowheads or other cultural artifacts is a federal crime.
* Disturbing archaeological sites or pictographs is likewise a criminal offense (even making tracings or rubbings of pictographs can damage them).
* National Forests limit campers to fourteen days' stay at the same campsite in any calendar year.
* Permits are required to dig up plants on federal land.
* Rare plants and animals are sometimes protected by both federal and state law. Picking wildflowers may in fact be illegal.

HAZARDS IN THE WILDS

The Wilderness Act of 1964 insists a wilderness should offer outstanding opportunities for solitude. One backwoods hiker paraphrased this, suggesting a wilderness should offer outstanding opportunities for death.

Alas, I think the dangers of the wilderness have been overrated. Grizzly bears are extinct in Oregon, so there is no need to decorate backpacks with bear-warning bells. Oregon's black bears huff and scramble out of a hiker's way as fast as their little legs will take them—generally even when the hiker has accidentally passed mother bear's cubs. In a very few areas (notably the Wild Rogue Wilderness), bears have learned over the years to rip open the packs and coolers of careless campers at night for bacon, tuna, and sweets. Here a standard wilderness precaution will suffice: hang all food from a tree limb, at least 10 feet high and 5 feet away from the trunk. This will also keep food safe from the real scoundrels, chipmunks.

Likewise, rattlesnakes will disappoint the danger seeker. These reptiles are rare enough that most people will not see one in 1000 miles of wilderness hiking. What's more, the aggressive diamond-back species is not found in the state at all. Oregon's subspecies, *Crotalus viridis oreganus,* is a retiring sort, absolutely incapable of such spuriously attributed feats of daring as crawling into a sleeping bag for warmth.

These days, the most threatening beast in the woods is a microscopic protozoan by the name of *Giardia.* This pest, originally from Leningrad, has spread to some mountain streams in our country, where it can surprise the drinker of even cold, clear water with debilitating diarrhea and nausea. The symptoms appear in six to fifteen days and only abate after medical treatment. Some commercial filters and chemicals remove *Giardia,* though boiling water for ten minutes is the surest treatment. It's also possible to second-guess the little parasite. *Giardia* is spread only by mammals (often beavers), enters the water by defecation, and only moves downstream. Thus, water from a spring or a high mountain watershed unfrequented by mammals will have a lower risk of contamination.

Hikers in dry, grassy areas should check occasionally for ticks under their collars and cuffs. In Oregon only a handful of cases of Lyme disease have been reported. The ailment, carried by deer ticks, progressively affects the joints and nerves, so keep an eye on the site of any tick bite to make sure it doesn't develop the disease's characteristic bull's-eye-shaped sore (red with a white ring), followed within a month by a rash.

Of course, those who enter the wilderness without basic survival gear and skills are bringing hazard with them. Hypothermia is the number one killer in the wilds. It results from being wet and cold too long, and can be prevented by bringing proper clothing and shelter. Useful books and classes abound on preparation for hiking, backpacking, and climbing—with far more detail than this Introduction can possibly include. Be prepared for the worst and you will be able to enjoy the wilderness at its best.

Finally, errors in mileage, trail location, and the like are inevitable in any guidebook—especially when new roads and logging are constantly adding confusion. Despite all our efforts, the author, publisher, and research consultant cannot guarantee the accuracy of the information included here, or that the trips described are safe for everyone.

Without danger, wilderness would not be wild. Visitors in the wild are on their own, so pack some common sense and caution for safety's sake.

A WORD TO HIKERS

The easiest trips in each area are generally described first. Those who rarely hike should look for the nature trails, lakeshore paths, and short riverside hikes listed near the beginning of an area's *hiking* section. Remember that most mileages reflect the one-way length of a trail. Thus, a "1.4-mile trail to Twin Lakes" means a 2.8-mile round-trip hike. Also, the term "easy" is used only in relation to other hikes; someone who puffs climbing a few flights of stairs will not find a 2.8-mile walk easy at all.

And speaking of climbing, pay attention to the *elevation gains*—they warn of steep uphill trails. Many of the hike descriptions mention the elevation gain in feet, but even when they do not, the elevations shown on the maps make gains for most hikes calculable. A 1000-foot gain is an arduous uphill trudge for out-of-shape walkers, particularly if the climb is packed into less than 2 miles. A 2000-foot gain requires frequent rest stops even when hikers are in good condition. Hikers must be in very good shape—strong hearts and strong knees—to handle a 3000-foot elevation gain in a day. And only those in prime condition should tackle the 5000-foot climbs required by trails up Hat Point or South Sister.

A *car shuttle* allows a group with two cars to end their hike at a different trailhead. Drive both cars to the trip's end point, leave one there, and then drive in the other to the hike's starting point. A *key-swap hike* requires less driving but more careful planning. For this arrangement, two carloads of hikers walk the same trail, starting at opposite trailheads. When the two groups meet at a specified time at the trail's midpoint, they swap car keys for the drive home. Better yet, swap duplicate keys before leaving for the hike.

Advanced hikers may be interested in the *cross-country hiking routes* suggested for many areas. Bushwhacking, not to be confused with machete-style trail chopping, can be surprisingly easy and immensely rewarding. It's the only way to hike in Oregon's trailless desert country. And although off-trail travel is more difficult in the dense forests of western Oregon's wildernesses, one needn't bushwhack very far in such terrain before finding true isolation—even in an area billed as crowded. Perhaps the best way to walk lightly on the land is to walk where no one else has.

Cross-country hikers in particular should inform someone of their route before leaving. They should keep a topographic map and compass at hand, and have experience using them. Always carry survival gear.

All hikers—even those on short, well-marked trails—should bring a pack with the Ten Essentials:

1. Warm, water-repellent coat (or parka and extra shirt)
2. Drinking water
3. Extra food
4. Knife
5. Matches in waterproof container
6. Fire starter (butane lighter or candle)
7. First aid kit
8. Flashlight
9. Map (topographic, if possible)
10. Compass

Let someone know about the planned hike so that if it becomes necessary they can call the county sheriff's office to organize a search and rescue. Lost hikers should stay put and keep warm.

Trail mileages given in this book are approximate and may not agree with trail sign mileages (which are often incorrect). Likewise, official signs and maps often offer a confusion of names and numbers for the same trail. This guide generally avoids the debate by identifying trails according to their destination and starting point.

Road directions to trailheads are provided only when the map does not clearly show the route. When several obscure trailheads cluster together, complete car directions may be given to only one of them, with the understanding that drivers can then use the map to find the others.

Finally, remember a few courtesies:

• Step off the trail on the downhill side to let horses pass. Talking quietly to the horses can help prevent them from spooking.
• Leave no litter. Trailside orange peels and eggshells last for decades.
• Do not shortcut switchbacks.
• Divide large groups into independent hiking parties of twelve or fewer.
• Leave pets at home. A dog can dangerously anger bears, porcupines, and other wilderness users.
• Respect private land. This guide makes an effort to steer hikers clear of private property, but even designated wildernesses include some private inholdings.

A WORD TO BACKPACKERS

Wilderness campers face a serious challenge: leaving no trace of their camp. Choosing the right campsite is critical. Savvy campers will not pitch a tent over the wildflower meadow they came to see, but instead will choose a spot in the forest, and never in a hollow where rainwater will gather, making trenching a temptation. Likewise, never camp in a fragile alpine area, on a streambank, or within 100 feet of a lake. Choose a less delicate site on sand, snow, or bare pine needle duff. Best of all, bring a gallon's worth of water bottles per camper and pitch a dry camp, away from the water sources that attract camping overuse.

Permits are sometimes required to enter a wilderness area, but these are free and can generally be filled out at the trailhead. *For Mount Jefferson's Pamelia Lake trailhead and the Three Sisters' Obsidian trailhead, however, hikers must pick up a permit in advance at a ranger station.*

In addition, Trail Park permits are required to park at all trailheads in the Willamette National Forest, Deschutes National Forest, Wallowa-Whitman National Forest, and certain popular areas of the Siuslaw National Forest. In 1998, Trail Park permits will also be required in the Columbia Gorge National Scenic Area, Mount Hood National Forest, Siskiyou National Forest, and Winema National Forest. The permits cost $3 per car per day or $25 per year, and can be purchased at ranger stations or outdoor stores.

Campfires are banned in many of the wilderness areas' popular and fragile alpine areas. The truth is, open fires are a luxury the wilderness can no longer afford to provide. Instead, cook on a lightweight campstove using gas, alcohol, or butane. For warmth, wear more clothing. Even when an emergency requires a campfire, don't build a rock campfire ring; this needlessly blackens stones. Clear a circle of ground to mineral soil. Gather only small pieces of wood that can be broken off by hand; never hack limbs with a hatchet. After use, drown the fire, scatter the cold ashes, and restore the site.

Do not bury or burn garbage. Limit the trash to be packed out by bringing no canned or bottled foods, and by repackaging bulky foods into compact, lightweight bags or containers.

Never wash dishes or bathe with soap directly in a lake or stream. Carry water at least 200 feet away from the shore and wash there.

Bury human waste and toilet paper (or better, leaves) in a small hole dug at least 200 feet from water. Choose a site where no one would ever camp. Fill the hole with dirt and cover the spot with a natural-looking arrangement of rocks or sticks.

Lightweight backpacking gear includes a nylon tent, a backpacking stove, and dried food.

A WORD TO MOUNTAINEERS

This guide identifies mountaineering sites in seventeen areas across the state, including Mount Hood, the world's second most climbed snowpeak, and Smith Rock, a mecca for technical climbers with nearly 1000 named routes. In addition, *hiking* entries describe popular nontechnical climbs such as South Sister, Eagle Cap, and Mount McLoughlin.

Since available guidebooks discuss climbing techniques and safety and describe Oregon's technical climbs in detail, this book restricts itself to noting the chief attractions of each climbing area and the range of difficulty of the most important routes. The rating system used here, known as the Yosemite Decimal System, expresses the climb's overall difficulty first by a Roman numeral, then the climb's technical difficulty by a number from 1 to 5.13, and finally (when appropriate) the difficulty of available artificial aid by symbols from A1 to A5, as follows:

Overall Difficulty
(length of climb, degree of commitment)
   I – up to 2 hours
   II – up to a half day
   III – a full day
   IV – possibly requires a bivouac
   Oregon has no grade V or VI climbs

Technical Difficulty
(class of athletic skill needed)
   1 – hiking
   2 – scrambling over talus or through brush
   3 – steep slopes or exposed ridges
   4 – rope required
   5 – rope and protection required

   Class 5 climbs are broken down from 5.1 to 5.13 to indicate increasingly difficult pitches requiring rope and protection; climbs above 5.7 are demanding even for experts.

Artificial Aid Difficulty
   A1 – solid placements
   A2 – strenuous placements
   A3 – several marginal placements
   A4 – many marginal placements
   A5 – marginal protection throughout

   Thus, the east face of Smith Rock's Monkey Face, rated II-5.7-A3, requires up to a half day with advanced free-climbing skills and has several marginally secure aids.

   Climbers should refrain from adding new bolts to established routes, both to decrease clutter and to preserve a route's challenge.

A WORD TO CROSS-COUNTRY SKIERS

This guide covers most of Oregon's popular cross-country skiing areas, and many little-known spots as well. In the area maps, hatch marks along trails and unplowed roads indicate feasible winter routes for nordic skiers. Snowmobile-shaped symbols designate winter ORV staging areas; these have been included on the maps since other winter users may wish to avoid such areas.

   P symbols along highways represent plowed sno-park lots. From November 15 to April 30, cars parked in or near sno-park lots must display a valid permit or face a $10 fine. Since the permit only costs $9.50 per season (even less for daily permits), it pays to stop by a sporting goods store, ski shop, or Department of Motor Vehicles office to pick one up.

   In some high-use areas the Forest Service marks winter trails. ORV routes are signed with

The shelter at Gold Lake is one of five huts for Nordic skiers near Willamette Pass.

orange plastic diamonds, while cross-country ski trails have blue diamonds (or less visible oak diamonds, in designated wilderness areas).

Oregon's extremely variable snow conditions can produce delightful powder, heavy mush, and clattery ice all within a day's time. Waxless skis are usually the boards of choice.

Nordic skiers and snowshoers in Oregon need rain gear, plenty of warm clothing (wool is best), a rucksack with the Ten Essentials (see Introduction), a repair kit, and an insulated seating pad for rests. Never set out without a topographic map and compass. Wilderness exploration can be great fun in winter, but the need for caution and survival training is likewise great.

Avalanches, though infrequent in Oregon, may occur during or immediately after a snowstorm or high wind. Avoid slopes of more than 23 degrees—especially treeless slopes, since these may have a history as avalanche chutes. Also beware of frozen lakes. Particularly in the Cascades, heavy snows can insulate the water, preventing it from forming solid ice. Even when skiers succeed in crossing the snow-covered slush, those on foot may fall through.

For Oregon weather reports and road conditions, call (503) 238-8400; for the Bend area, call (503) 382-6922.

Finally, a few winter manners:

- Yield right of way to downhill skiers.
- Don't stop to rest in a ski track; step aside.
- Don't walk or snowshoe in a ski track; this ruins the smooth grooves.
- Leave pets at home.

A WORD TO BOATERS

This guide describes eight of Oregon's wildest whitewater river runs and numerous quiet spots for canoeing, sailing, or sailboarding.

The descriptions use a six-point scale to rate a rapids' difficulty for rafters, kayakers, and drift boaters:

class 1 – easy
class 2 – moderate
class 3 – dangerous; novices should consider lining or portaging boats
class 4 – very dangerous; novices should line or portage
class 5 – extremely dangerous; even experts should consider portaging
class 6 – unrunnable; portage boats

Those in decked canoes should add one point to the difficulty of the rapids. For open canoes, add two points.

Note that most of these rivers can only be run when water is high—but not too high. Suitable months for running rivers vary dramatically from year to year. Check with the Water Resources Data Center at (503) 249-0666 for daily updates of river levels.

Since float-boating concentrates visitor impact on the fragile camping beaches of wilderness rivers, it's important to follow the strictest no-trace camping guidelines:

- Cook on camp stoves. Those who require campfires must bring all of their own firewood, build the fire in a firepan they have brought, and then pack up both pan and ashes without a trace.
- Use toilets when provided. When they are not, do not bury toilet paper. Buried human waste decomposes within a few weeks, but paper remains for a year or more in riverbank soils, and can be exposed by wind or water. Burn the paper in a fire pan, if available, or pack it out in a plastic bag.

Proper boating skills and safety are essential on wilderness runs where escape or rescue is difficult. Check the references listed at the back of this book for information on these important subjects.

A WORD TO EQUESTRIANS

The role of horses in the wilderness is in transition. A few new routes have been added for horses, but more and more trails bear the sign "Hiker Only." The National Park Service at Crater Lake bans horses everywhere except on the Pacific Crest Trail, and allows no grazing.

As the no-trace ethic spreads, so have restrictions on saddle stock. Here's a list of guidelines that have grown into iron-clad rules in most wilderness areas:

- Allow no saddle stock within 200 feet of any stream or lake except for loading, unloading, watering, or traveling on a trail.
- Carry all the feed an animal will need. This cuts down on grazing.
- Bring no hay. (It spreads weed seeds.)
- Feed oats or hay pellets morning and evening from a nose bag, not from piles on the ground.
- Never tie stock to a tree, even temporarily. Tethers can girdle trees and hooves can dig circular pits.
- Hobble, don't picket stock. This disperses grazing damage.
- Do not build corrals or hitching racks.
- When breaking camp, fill in paw holes and scatter manure.

Gone are the days of campfires, big coffee pots, beans and bacon, and canvas tents. As equestrians limit their loads and their pack strings, their gear increasingly resembles that of the no-trace backpacker: lightweight nylon tents, lightweight campstoves, and freeze-dried food.

Many wilderness visitors who might once have used a pack horse now hire a llama. Llamas must be led on foot, since they can only carry a 60-pound pack. But llamas weigh a fifth as much as a horse, leave only deerlike pellets for droppings, and do a tenth of the damage to trails and meadows.

A FINAL WORD

Once Oregon was all wilderness from the Pacific to the Snake River. Now, only scattered islands of that great wilderness survive, and most of these still lack protection. Use this guide to discover the beautiful but fragile heritage that remains to show Oregon as it once was.

For the areas in this book, there is still time.

A NOTE ABOUT SAFETY

Safety is an important concern in all outdoor activities. No guidebook can alert you to every hazard or anticipate the limitations of every reader. Therefore, the descriptions of roads, trails, routes, and natural features in this book are not representations that a particular place or excursion will be safe for your party. When you follow any of the routes described in this book, you assume responsibility for your own safety. Under normal conditions, such excursions require the usual attention to traffic, road and trail conditions, weather, terrain, the capabilities of your party, and other factors. Keeping informed on current conditions and exercising common sense are the keys to a safe, enjoyable outing.

The Mountaineers

Opposite: *Mount Hood from Lost Lake*

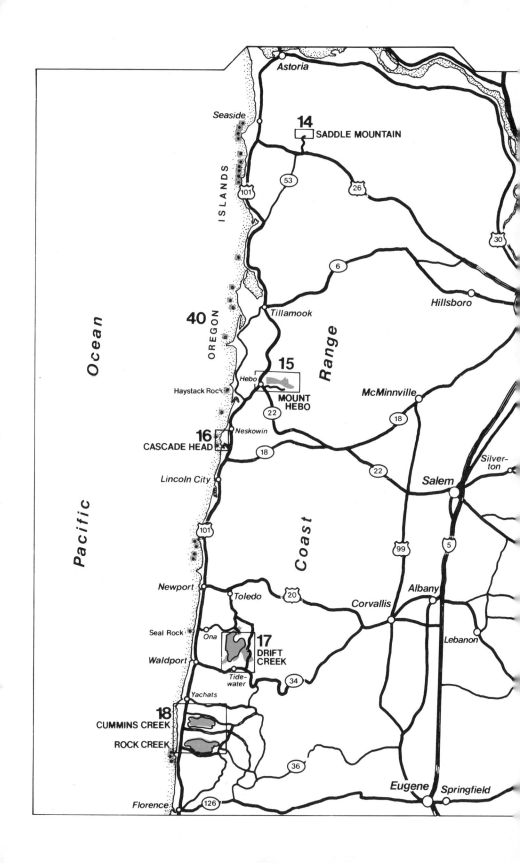

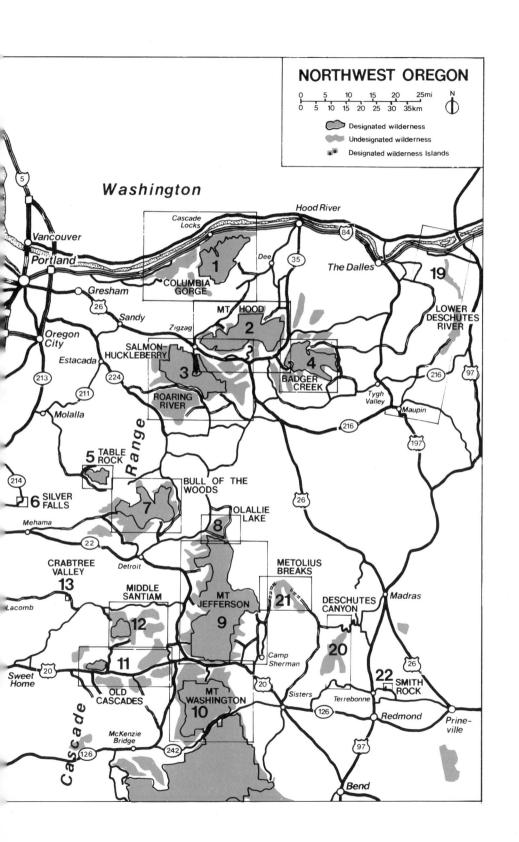

NORTHWEST OREGON

0   5   10   15   20   25mi
0   5   10   15   20   25   30   35km

N

Designated wilderness
Undesignated wilderness
Designated wilderness Islands

Washington

Vancouver
Portland
Gresham
Sandy
Oregon City
Estacada
Molalla
Mehama
Lacomb
Sweet Home
McKenzie Bridge

Cascade Locks
Hood River
Dee
The Dalles
Zigzag
Tygh Valley
Maupin
Detroit
Camp Sherman
Madras
Sisters
Terrebonne
Redmond
Prineville
Bend

Range
Cascade

1 COLUMBIA GORGE
2 MT HOOD
3 SALMON-HUCKLEBERRY / ROARING RIVER
4 BADGER CREEK
5 TABLE ROCK
6 SILVER FALLS
7
8 OLALLIE LAKE
9 MT JEFFERSON
10 MT WASHINGTON
11 OLD CASCADES
12 MIDDLE SANTIAM
13 CRABTREE VALLEY
19 LOWER DESCHUTES RIVER
20 DESCHUTES CANYON
21 METOLIUS BREAKS
22 SMITH ROCK

BULL OF THE WOODS

COLUMBIA GORGE

Location: 24 mi E of Portland
Size: 107 sq mi
Status: 62 sq mi designated wilderness (1984)
Terrain: Cliffs, densely forested canyons
Elevation: 100'–4960'
Management: Columbia Gorge National Scenic Area
Topographic maps: Forest Trails of the Columbia Gorge, Columbia Wilderness, PCT Northern Oregon Portion (USFS); Bridal Veil, Bonneville Dam, Hood River (Green Trails)

Several worlds collide in the Columbia Gorge. In the west, moss-covered rain forests cling to misty green cliffs. A few miles east, only scrub oaks dot a semi-arid scabland. And in between, a colonnade of more than twenty major waterfalls separates the alpine meadows of the Cascade Range from the mud flats of the Columbia River, nearly at sea level.

In the midst of these colliding ecosystems is the remarkable Columbia Wilderness. Although it lies a mere half-hour freeway drive from Portland and overlooks a busy transportation corridor along the Columbia, it remains delightfully wild, protected by a ribbon of breathtaking 3000-foot cliffs.

Climate

The annual rainfall varies from a soggy 150 inches in the Bull Run Watershed to 75 inches at Cascade Locks, and just 29 inches at Hood River on the eastern end of the Gorge. Summers, however, are dry throughout. Snow covers trails down to elevations of 3600 feet from December to May, but lower trails may be clear for hiking even in midwinter. Occasionally, winter ice storms drape the cliffs with icicles and coat trees and highways with silvery freezing rain, a result of warm Pacific clouds dropping rain through a layer of freezing air blown in from east of the mountains.

Plants and Wildlife

Between the dense Douglas fir and sword fern rain forests of the west and the open oak grasslands of the east, the Columbia Gorge hosts twelve plant species found nowhere else in the world, including six strictly confined to those wilderness lands. Look for rare plants and flowers on the rock walls of the Gorge's cool north-facing canyons, where even alpine wildflowers are often tricked into growing at sea level.

The California condors that Lewis and Clark reported here in 1805, attracted by the Columbia's salmon runs, are now gone, although bald eagles may yet be sighted.

The darling of the Gorge's many waterfalls is the water ouzel, a chubby little bluish gray bird that builds its mossy nests in the spray and spends its days walking along the bottom of rushing mountain streams, poking about for mosquito larvae with its deft little bill. When this robin-sized bird is not marching around underwater, it can be seen doing bobbing knee-bend exercises on creek rocks or whirring along just above the water with rapid, constant wingbeats. Though common throughout western North America, this dipper can live only where water runs wild and white.

Geology

The many layers of columnar basalt exposed in the cliffs of the Gorge are all part of the massive lava outpourings that inundated 50,000 square miles of eastern Washington, Eastern Oregon, and Idaho to a depth of up to a mile 10 to 17 million years ago. These rock floods—a result of the North American continent overriding the Pacific Ocean floor—surged down the ancient Columbia as far as the sea, pushing the river north to its present location. When the

Oneonta Gorge

crest of the Cascade Range then gradually warped upward, making those mountains ever higher, the Columbia kept pace by cutting its gorge deeper and deeper. The original surface of the lava flows is now a tilted and well-eroded upland, evident in the 2000-foot plateau above Multnomah Falls and the 4000-foot Benson Plateau. More recent volcanoes—Larch Mountain, Tanner Butte, and Mount Defiance—protrude above this general silhouette.

During the Ice Age twenty small glaciers formed on the Gorge's southern rim, carving the hanging amphitheaters that lie above many of the waterfalls. Much of the scenery of the Gorge, however, can be attributed to a series of monumental Ice Age floods of the Columbia River. These floods occurred when the continental ice sheet then covering Canada temporarily dammed the Clark Fork River in western Montana. The most recent such flood, 13,000 years ago, unleashed a body of water half the volume of Lake Michigan across eastern Washington and through the narrow Columbia Gorge. The flood denuded the Gorge to an elevation of 800 feet and undercut the cliffs, leaving the graceful waterfalls visible today.

THINGS TO DO

Hiking

The thorough trail network is very heavily used on weekends, particularly in the vicinity of Multnomah Falls and along Eagle Creek. The dramatic elevation gains on many trails (as much as 4000 feet) should be taken into consideration when planning trips.

Oregon's tallest waterfall, Multnomah Falls, has inspired a cluster of trails well suited to day hikes. Paths within roughly 0.5 mile of this noble 620-foot double cascade are paved to accommodate the frequent foot traffic. A good way to beat the crowds is to park at nearby Wahkeena Falls and take the 1.5-mile Perdition Trail, climbing a modest 800 feet to Multnomah Falls' top.

Long, slotlike Oneonta Gorge, though less well known than neighboring Multnomah Falls, has perhaps equal charm. A 3.7-mile loop trail peers down into this mossy chasm from its rim, but it can be more directly experienced by wading 0.5 mile up the narrow creekbed from the old Columbia River Highway bridge.

Half a dozen exhilarating day hikes switchback up to viewpoints of the Gorge. Angels Rest, atop the 6.4-mile trail between Wahkeena Falls and the Columbia Scenic Highway at Bridal Veil, is one of the most popular of these routes, with a moderate 1500-foot elevation gain. Nesmith Point, just west of elegant Elowah Falls, is an ambitious 3700-foot climb to a stunning view. Two viewpoint hikes climb through wildflower meadows: the 4.8-mile Ruckel Creek Trail from the Eagle Creek Campground, and the steep 3.3-mile path up Nick Eaton Ridge from the Herman Creek Campground. Both have loop options.

The spectacular Eagle Creek Trail features seven waterfalls, a high bridge, and one tunnel (which actually goes behind Tunnel Falls). Blasted out of the sheer cliffs in the 1910s, this trail is now very popular. A day trip can hardly do the trail justice; it is better seen on a two-day backpack, perhaps returning via the beautiful Benson Plateau or the quiet Tanner Creek or Herman Creek trails. Camping along the Eagle Creek Trail is restricted to designated sites; on summer weekends space can be tight.

Three long-distance trail routes cross the Columbia Wilderness. The 35.5-mile low-elevation Gorge Trail, between Bridal Veil and Wyeth, avoids the steep climbs found on many other trails and is snow-free year round. It is used primarily to connect other trails, but it makes good hiking from end to end. And because of the Gorge Trail's many trailheads along the Columbia River Highway, sections of the path make for accessible and undemanding day hikes.

A higher elevation trail winds 38 miles from 4056-foot Larch Mountain to 4960-foot Mount Defiance. Together with the low-elevation Gorge Trail, this route makes it possible to convert any of the area's 15 north–south trails into scenic loop hikes. Hiking the length of the high-elevation Gorge Trail is a challenging four-day backpack; the route zigzags across several steep canyons in the most remote part of the wilderness.

The third long-distance trail in the Gorge is the Pacific Crest Trail (PCT), which passes Wahtum Lake and crosses the 2-square-mile forested Benson Plateau. Those who just can't wait

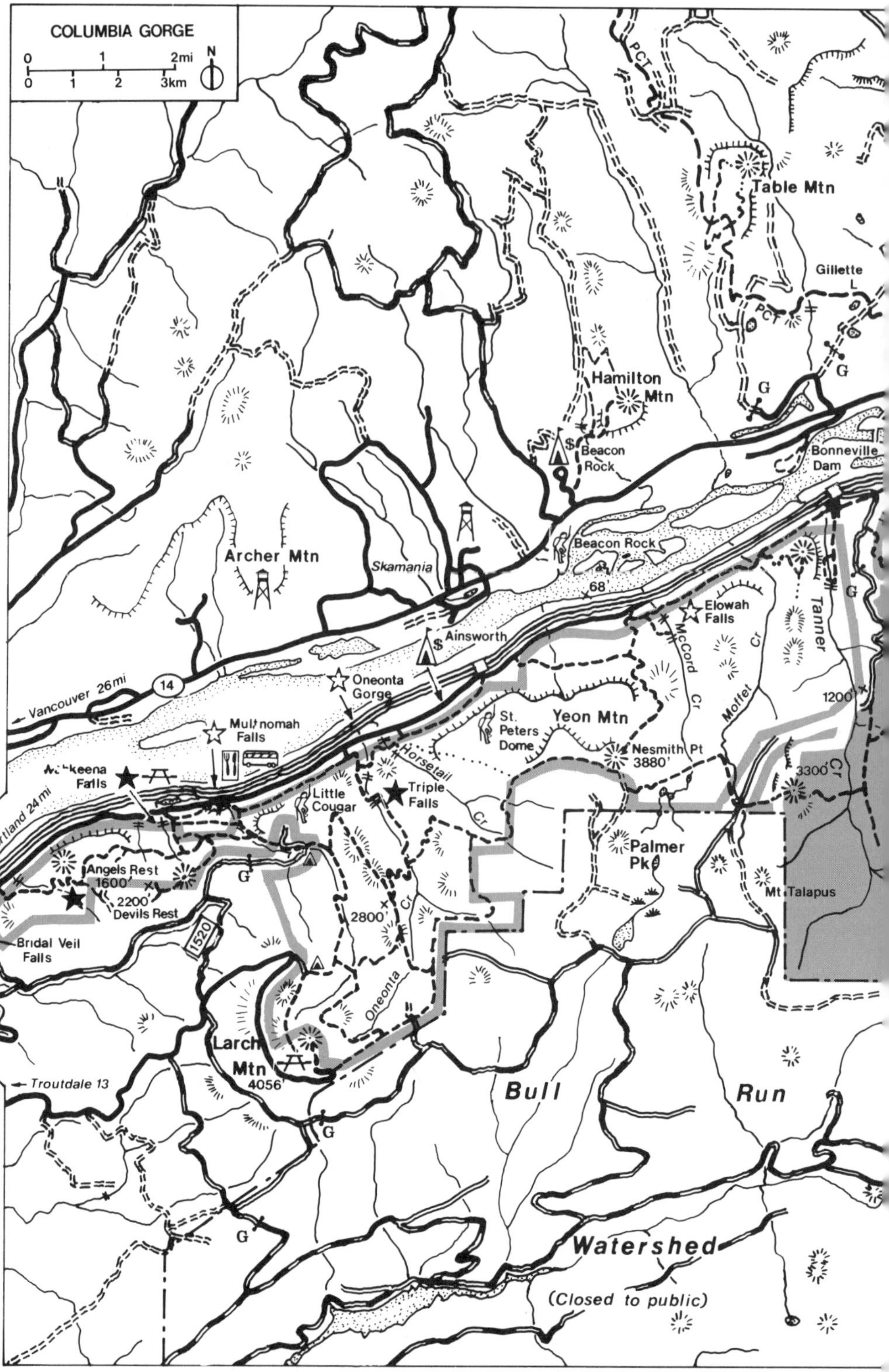

COLUMBIA GORGE

0   1   2mi   N
0   1   2   3km

Table Mtn

Gillette

G

PCT

G

Hamilton
Mtn

G

Bonneville
Dam

Beacon
Rock

Beacon Rock

Archer Mtn

Skamania

68'

Elowah
Falls

Tanner

1200'

Vancouver 26mi   14

Ainsworth

Oneonta
Gorge

St.
Peters
Dome

Yeon Mtn

McCord Cr

Moffet

Cr

3300'

G

Multnomah
Falls

Nesmith Pt
3880'

Wahkeena
Falls

Horsetail

Little
Cougar

Triple
Falls

Cr

Palmer
Pk

Portland 24 mi

Angels Rest
1600'

G

2800'

Mt Talapus

Bridal Veil
Falls

2200'
Devils Rest

1520

Oneonta

Cr

Larch
Mtn
4056'

G

Troutdale 13

Bull   Run

G

Watershed

(Closed to public)

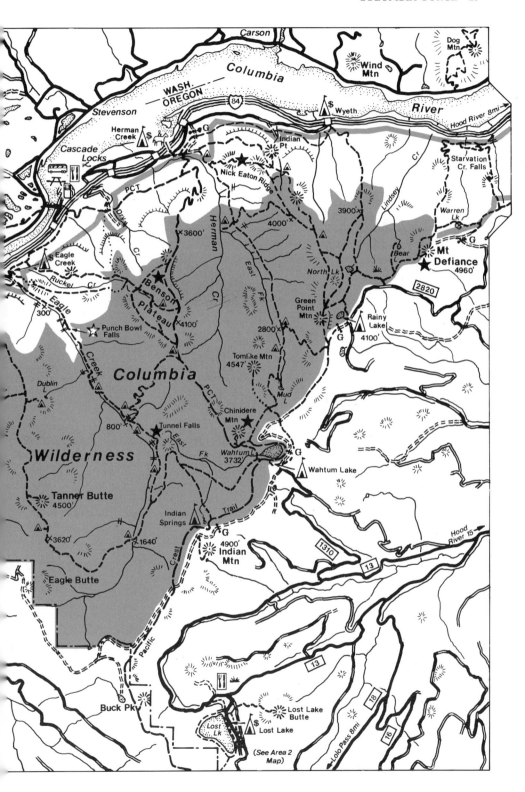

The Columbia Gorge from Indian Point, above Herman Creek

to see the summer display of alpine wildflowers will find them blooming as early as June along the Benson Plateau's northeast rim. Huckleberry afficionados can profitably prowl about Wahtum Lake in late August.

For those able to arrange a car shuttle between trailheads, Larch Mountain and Mount Defiance can be the starting points of dramatic, downhill day hikes. The Larch Mountain Trail drops 4000 feet in 6.7 miles to the Multnomah Falls Lodge. The Mount Defiance Trail loses fully 4800 feet elevation to Starvation Creek Falls in just 5.8 miles. Both mountains offer dramatic views of Mount Hood, Mount Adams, and Mount St. Helens.

Throughout the Columbia Gorge, hikers should remember that poison oak is common below 800 feet, that trailside cliffs make some paths inappropriate for unsupervised children, and that underbrush and steep slopes virtually prohibit cross-country travel. Only the wider, well-graded Herman Creek and Pacific Crest trails are recommended for horses or pack stock. The Bull Run Watershed to the south, the source of Portland's water supply, is closed to the public except specifically for travel on the PCT.

Climbing

The Columbia Gorge is a center for testing technical climbing skills. For starters, good conditioning hikes include the nearly 5000-foot climb from Starvation Creek Falls to Mount Defiance and the numerous trails up to the 4000-foot Benson Plateau. Then, 3 miles west of Bridal Veil Falls are Rooster Rock (a 200-foot pinnacle with routes varying in difficulty from level I-4 to II-5.6-A3) and Crown Point (a 700-foot bluff with routes of difficulty II-5.4 and III-5.6). The Pillars of Hercules, a group of 100-foot basalt towers immediately west of Bridal Veil, rate difficulty levels from I-5.2 to II-5.8.

Little Cougar, a small thumb of rotten rock at 1300-foot elevation 1 mile east of Multnomah Falls, is a level I-4 or I-5.4 climb, depending on the route taken. St. Peters Dome, 1 mile east of Ainsworth State Park, consists of similarly poor rock but requires level II-5.6 or III-5.6-A3 skills. It is a 200-foot thumb at 1525 feet and was unclimbed until 1940.

The greatest of all climbing challenges in the area is Beacon Rock, just across the Columbia from St. Peters Dome. This impressive 848-foot andesite monolith requires about five rope lengths of skilled climbing. Difficulty levels of II-5.6 to IV-5.11 are encountered on a total of forty-five named routes and variations.

2

MOUNT HOOD

Location: 34 mi E of Portland
Size: 115 sq mi
Status: 74 sq mi designated wilderness (1964, 1978)
Terrain: Glaciated peak, alpine meadows, forested slopes
Elevation: 1800'–11,240'
Management: Mount Hood NF
Topographic maps: Mount Hood (Geo-Graphics); Mount Hood Wilderness, PCT Northern
  Oregon Portion (USFS); Government Camp, Mount Hood (Green Trails)

Oregon's tallest peak dominates this popular wilderness. Hikers can meet alpine vistas of Hood from every path of the area's well-developed trail network. The dormant volcano's summit, ringed with eleven active glaciers, is the goal of 10,000 climbers a year.

But the peak is not the area's only attraction. The 38-mile Timberline Trail circles the mountain through a succession of stunning alpine meadows filled with flowers. Ramona, Tamanawas, and a dozen other waterfalls grace heavily forested river valleys. Zigzag Canyon is an impressive 1000-foot-deep gorge on the mountain's flank. And 5000-foot Zigzag Mountain, an 8-mile-long western spur of Hood, offers lakes and ridges of its own.

Climate

The area's 150 inches of annual precipitation come largely as snow between October and April. Skiers and snowshoers will find the snow drier, and the skies often bluer, on Hood's east and southeast slopes. Snow melts off lower trails (up to 4000 feet) by about June 1, and off higher trails (up to 7000 feet) by mid-July. July and August yield warm days and cold nights. Sudden storms can bring snowfall in any month—a fact that has led to climbing tragedies.

Plants and Wildlife

Dense Douglas fir forests blanket the wilderness' lower areas, with an understory of Oregon grape, huckleberry (ripe late August), salal, and rhododendron (blooms late May). Higher forests are of mountain hemlock, noble fir, and subalpine fir. Near timberline (6500 feet), gnarled whitebark pines frame meadows of blue lupine, red Indian paintbrush, beargrass plumes, penstemon, purple Cascade aster, and western Pasque flower ("old-man-of-the-mountain"). Profuse displays of white avalanche lilies decorate Paradise Park in July and Cairn Basin in August.

A bird checklist for Hood's south slope notes 132 species, from hummingbirds to bald eagles. Forty species of mammals live on the mountain's slopes, including black bear, mountain lion, and elk.

The whistling, squirrellike animals often met on Hood's rocky timberline slopes are pikas. Pikas (also known as rock rabbits) are round-eared, apparently tailless animals the size of guinea pigs. Colonies of pikas live at higher elevations than any other North American mammal, cutting and sun-drying bushels of grass to last them through nine snowbound months without hibernation. Yellow-bellied marmots also live in rockslides and whistle to each other for warning, but are much larger, resembling bushy-tailed beavers.

Geology

Mount Hood is the most recently active of all Oregon volcanoes. In the 1800s, four minor eruptions of steam, ash, and magma alarmed observers as far away as Portland. In 1907 glowing rock near the summit melted part of the White River Glacier, causing floods. Even today, climbers encounter hot rock, scalding steam vents, and a powerful sulfur smell in the depression south of the summit, between Steel Cliff and Crater Rock.

The volcano itself had its beginnings after the surrounding hills and rivers were in nearly their present form. Lava flows filled nearby river canyons, forcing the rivers aside. When the rivers eroded the softer rock around the hard lava, the original valleys were left as lava-topped ridges—an example of "reverse topography."

Mount Hood reached its greatest height, about 12,000 feet, just prior to the Ice Age. Then, glaciers removed the crater and much of the north slope. Barrett Spur and Cooper Spur remain to show the mountain's earlier dimensions, indicating the ancient crater was north of the present summit. Crater Rock, south of the summit, was long thought to be a remnant of the volcano's central plug. In fact, it is a recent side vent's lava dome, the creation of which smothered the Timberline Lodge area with cinder-and-mud avalanches just 2000 years ago.

History

Spotted in 1792 by a Lieutenant Broughton under explorer Vancouver's command, Mount Hood was named for British admiral Lord Hood. In 1845 Sam Barlow laid out Oregon's first road around the south base of Mount Hood, leading Oregon Trail wagons from The Dalles to Sandy over Barlow Pass. The route spared settlers the expense of a raft trip on the Columbia, but subjected them to the miseries of Laurel Hill, 3 miles west of Government Camp, a slope so steep wagons had to be skidded down with wheels removed.

A 4-mile section of the Barlow Road over Laurel Hill was rebuilt as a hiking and equestrian trail by the Civilian Conservation Corps in 1935. Other Depression-era work projects include the artistically designed Timberline Lodge and the Timberline Trail, with its scenic stone shelters.

THINGS TO DO

Hiking

The marvels of Mount Hood are so close to Portland that overuse is a real concern. The many meadows, with their wildflower displays and mountain views, have had to be protected by a complete ban on camping. Backpackers must seek out less fragile sites in forested areas—and even the forested "islands" in Elk Meadows and Elk Cove have been placed off-limits to tents or

Cast Lake and Mount Hood from Zigzag Mountain

fires. The small lakes of Zigzag Mountain, popular for their reflections of Mount Hood, are included in a general ban on camping within 200 feet of any lake's or stream's shoreline. Camping is not allowed within 500 feet of popular Ramona Falls, and fires are forbidden within 500 feet of McNeil Point, to save the gnarled dead wood at timberline for its own beauty.

This list of relatively crowded areas, however, also reads as a list of the wilderness area's top attractions, worth visiting by day hikers or careful backpackers.

Start with Ramona Falls, an easy, 4.5-mile loop hike from Road 100 through the sparse forest along the Sandy River to a mossy, 100-foot falls on a stair-stepped cliff of columnar basalt. A comparable, but less well known day hike on the east side of Mount Hood leads an easy 2 miles from Sherwood Campground to 100-foot Tamanawas Falls.

The prime hike through Hood's alpine meadows is the 37.6-mile Timberline Trail, a three- to five-day trip usually hiked clockwise around the mountain, so as to finish up at the showers and swimming pool (suit rentals available) at the classic old Timberline Lodge. Five unbridged creek crossings on the route can be hazardous in the high water of June and July snowmelt: Zigzag River, Sandy River, Muddy Fork, Eliot Branch, and White River. Water is lower in August and during the mornings.

No fewer than twenty-one trails lead up the flanks of Mount Hood to the Timberline Trail, making all manner of loop hikes and day trips possible. Many of these tributary trails ascend ridges that are scenic in their own right, notably Gnarl Ridge on Hood's east slope, the Hidden Lake Trail and Zigzag Canyon Trail on the mountain's southwest slope, and Cathedral Ridge, Vista Ridge, and The Pinnacle on Hood's north flank. All make excellent day trips for the fit hiker; distances average 3 to 5 miles one way with 2000-foot elevation gains.

Hikers who shy from such climbs can still sample the Timberline Trail's charms from two high-elevation trailheads. Timberline Lodge, set among wildflowers itself, is a good starting point for an easy 2.2-mile traverse to Zigzag Canyon, an impressive 1000-foot-deep erosional gash into Hood's volcanic scree. On the mountain's northeast flank, Cloud Cap Saddle Campground touches the Timberline Trail amidst 6000-foot elevation meadows; the popular meadow at Elk Cove is a 4-mile hike west.

The adventurous hiker can climb well above timberline to view Hood's glaciers close up at several points. By far the highest trail is 8514 feet up, at Cooper Spur, overlooking Eliot Glacier, 4 miles from Cloud Cap Saddle. A trail up from Timberline Lodge passes the Silcox Hut (a European-style hut with cafe and bunks) before petering out at the 8000-foot level. Yocum Ridge and the McNeil Point shelter are atop other high trails; Barrett Spur's viewpoint is a cross-country scramble above the Timberline Trail. Climbing beyond these points is technical, requiring special gear and climber registration.

West of Mount Hood, Zigzag Mountain is another popular hiking center, with four lakes, two lookout tower sites (West and East Zigzag), and six trailheads. The Devils Canyon trailhead provides the gentlest grades to the area's best viewpoints, West Zigzag (2.5 miles) and East Zigzag (4 miles). A popular 3.5-mile trail up Lost Creek climbs to Burnt Lake and a ridgetop view beyond. Even in winter the steep 0.9-mile path to Castle Canyon's rock formations is usually snow-free.

East of Hood, Elk Meadows is another popular destination because of its fine mountain view. From Highway 35, reach the meadow's three-sided shelter either up the 3.4-mile trail from the Clark Creek sno-park or along the heavily forested 6.2-mile Cold Spring Creek Trail from the Polallie picnic area. One of the best hikes for a foggy, viewless day is the 4.1-mile East Fork Hood River Trail, a level forest walk between Robin Hood and Sherwood campgrounds.

Most equestrian use in the wilderness begins at the horse-loading facilities at Riley Campground, west of Mount Hood. Signs mark the fragile or hazardous trails closed to pack and saddle stock: the non-Pacific Crest Trail portion of the Timberline Trail, Cathedral Ridge, Vista Ridge, Pinnacle Ridge, Elk Cove, Paradise Park Loop, Castle Canyon, Yocum Ridge, Burnt Lake, and the Sandy River portion of the Ramona Falls loop.

Climbing

First climbed in 1857, Mount Hood has become the second most climbed snowpeak in the world, after Japan's sacred Mount Fuji. Portland's outdoor club, the Mazamas, was organized in

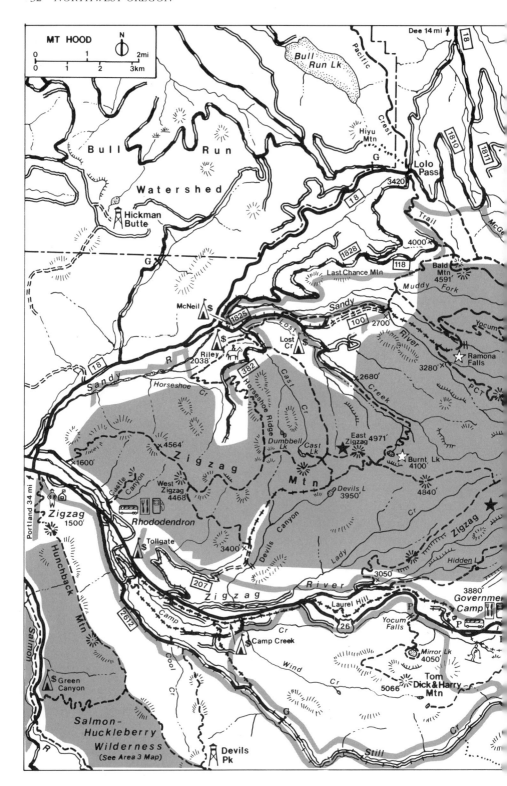

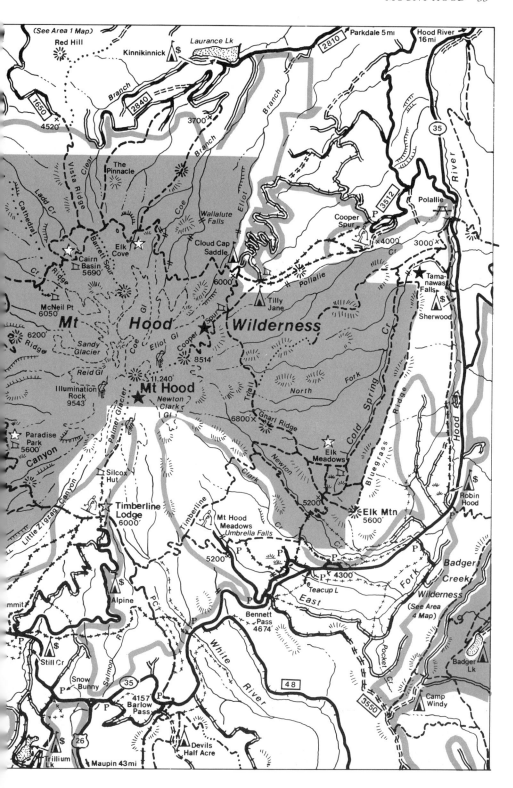

Tamanawas Falls

1894 by 193 climbers who convened on the summit in inclement weather. Hood has been scaled by a woman in high heels and by a man with no legs. Climber Gary Leech once raced from Timberline to the summit in 85 minutes.

But Hood is still a technical climb, over crevassed glaciers and loose, rotten rock. Lack of caution, and the area's volatile weather, have given Hood one of the highest accident rates of any peak in the country. An ice ax, crampons, and rope are essential; helmets are recommended. And all climbers must register either at Timberline Lodge or at Cloud Cap Inn.

The easiest and most popular route to the top, the South Side route, proceeds at a true 5° compass bearing from the Silcox Hut to the Hot Rocks, a geothermal area between Crater Rock and Steel Cliff. A snow hogback north of Crater Rock leads to the summit wall, where a large crevasse must be circumvented before continuing to the summit. The climb takes 4 to 10 hours, and is begun in the predawn dark to avoid the afternoon's slushy snow. A descent in poor visibility must be undertaken by compass; the tendency to return "straight down" often leads climbers southwest toward Zigzag Canyon.

The second most common summit route, also rated level I-2, ascends the 45° snow slope above the Cooper Spur viewpoint on the mountain's east face. Avalanches can be a hazard here.

There are twelve additional ascent routes varying in difficulty from I-3 to III-5.6.

Illumination Rock, a 9543-foot crag between the Reid and Zigzag glaciers southwest of Hood's summit, offers some interesting climbing topography. Five level I routes, of classes 4 to 5.4, explore the rock's pinnacles and a summit "skylight" hole.

Winter Sports

Mount Hood offers the largest selection of nordic ski routes in the state. Highways 26 and 35 are plowed in winter, providing access to five developed downhill ski areas and thirteen plowed sno-park lots. All of the downhill areas except Timberline Lodge rent cross-country skis.

From Timberline Lodge, nordic skiers can traverse 2.6 miles to the brink of Zigzag Canyon on the PCT, or choose one of three heavily used routes for the 4-mile glide down to Government Camp. From Government Camp, numerous short trails lace the level area between Multorpor Meadows and the snowed-under Still Creek Campground. More advanced skiers can tackle the 6.3-mile Yellowjacket Trail, traversing from the junction of Highway 26 and the Timberline Lodge Road to the White River sno-park on Highway 35.

The site of former Snow Bunny Lodge, now a snow play center, is the starting point for the many nordic routes on snowed-under roads around scenic Trillium Lake. The easiest trip is to Summit Meadows, north of Trillium Lake, where the graves of Barlow Road pioneers are marked by white crosses.

The winding, 2.4-mile section of old highway at Barlow Pass makes a pleasant ski route; the Giant Trees loop trail between the old and new highways explores an old-growth grove. Trailless exploration of the scenic White River Canyon is relatively easy from the White River sno-park on Highway 35.

Nordic ski routes from Bennett Pass head southeast along roads toward the Badger Creek Wilderness. From the parking lots of nearby Mount Hood Meadows, Elk Meadows makes a spectacular winter goal, but bring map and compass for safety on the 2.4-mile trail. Robin Hood Campground's sno-park offers good level skiing along the East Fork Hood River Trail, as well as on roads to the west, through Horsethief Meadows toward Bluegrass Ridge.

From the Cooper Spur Ski Area's sno-park, the challenging Cooper Spur Ski Trail climbs 1800 feet in 3 miles to the snowed-under Tilly Jane Campground; a return loop is possible via the 8.6-mile Cloud Cap Road.

Although there are no sno-parks on the west side of Mount Hood, the lower portion of Road 18 is typically snow-free, allowing access to good ski-touring country. Drive to the snow gate at McNeil Campground, then ski 5.7 miles east to beautiful Ramona Falls. Another trip from the snow gate tours 4 miles south up Road 382 into Horseshoe Canyon. In spring, when higher snow levels open Road 18 farther, drive to the snowline and continue on skis along Road 18 to Lolo Pass, where views open up in all directions. For a genuine challenge, ski the 9.2 miles back to McNeil Campground on Road 1828, around Last Chance Mountain.

3

SALMON-HUCKLEBERRY AND ROARING RIVER

Location: 32 mi SE of Portland
Size: 164 sq mi
Status: 70 sq mi designated wilderness (1984)
Terrain: Densely forested river canyons, ridges, lake basins
Elevation: 980'–5159'
Management: Mount Hood NF
Topographic maps: Salmon-Huckleberry Wilderness, PCT Northern Oregon Portion (USFS); Cherryville, Government Camp, Fish Creek Mountain, High Rock, Mount Wilson (Green Trails)

Less than an hour's drive from Portland, this spacious wilderness remains virtually undiscovered. Hidden here are the delightful subalpine lakes of the Rock Lakes Basin and the spectacular Salmon River canyon. Yet the area's greatest charms are subtler: fog-draped ridgecrests of ripe huckleberries and lonely whitewater canyons lined with mossy maples.

Climate

Trails below 2000 feet are usually snow-free in winter; ridge trails and the Pacific Crest Trail (PCT) remain under snow from November to May. Spring and fall rains account for a share of the area's 80-inch annual precipitation. Summers are generally clear and dry.

Plants and Wildlife

Major runs of steelhead, Chinook, and coho salmon return annually to the aptly named Salmon River. The Roaring River's thunderous torrent is home to hardy anadromous fish as well, while every stream and lake of size in the area supports brook trout and rainbow trout.

The fire lookout atop Devils Peak, though no longer in service, is open to hikers.

Black bear and mule deer rely on the area's extremely rugged, snowless lower canyons for winter range. The large, trailless upper Roaring River valley shelters several shy wildlife species, including cougar, badger, fisher, and marten. Listen for the flutelike call of the hermit thrush in June and July. Water ouzels whir along streams year round.

The dense western hemlock and Douglas fir forests of the canyon bottoms are interspersed with droopy-branched western red cedar and red alder. Creekside vine maple adds brilliant scarlet foliage in fall. Rare Alaska cedar can be found on the fringes of Salmon River Meadows.

Ridgetops are mostly open, decorated in June with the white plumes of beargrass. The area's famed huckleberries, once the goal of annual harvest treks by Indians and pioneers alike, are ripe in late August. The blue fruit is most abundant around Veda Lake, and on Indian Ridge, Huckleberry Mountain, Old Baldy, and Devils Peak.

Geology

The ridges of this area belong to the Old Cascades, a broad volcanic mountain range that erupted 10 million years before the High Cascades, and which now forms the rugged western foothills for those taller, snow-capped peaks. Devils Peak and Salmon Butte are probably remnants of once-tall volcanoes, but the erosive power of water and ice have reduced them to ridges. Broad, U-shaped glacial valleys, now filled with meadows and lakes, are recognizable at Rock Lakes, Squaw Lakes, Plaza Lake, and Serene Lake.

THINGS TO DO

Hiking

Two very easy day hikes with views of Mount Hood are the 1.2-mile trail into Mirror Lake (1 mile west of Government Camp) and the 1.2-mile Veda Lake Trail (8 miles south of Government Camp on Road 2613). The lower Salmon River trail, paralleling Road 2618 for 2.6 miles, makes another pleasant warm-up trip.

The Salmon River trail upriver of Green Canyon Campground traces a wilder canyon. The trail ambles amidst massive old-growth trees for the first 2 miles, then climbs several hundred feet above the river, traversing steep slopes with viewpoints. The roar audible from the second viewpoint (3.8 miles in) is caused by a series of hidden waterfalls; avoid the dangerous 0.2-mile scramble trail descending toward a slippery viewpoint. Backpackers can hike onward and upward to other trailheads (Kinzel Lake is 8.1 miles; Linney Creek, 8.8; Fir Tree, 14.5; and Mud Creek Road, 14.4).

The 7.7-mile Rock Basin loop trail offers the attractions of a High Cascades hike, without the crowds. The loop passes three subalpine lakes, a clifftop viewpoint, and Cache Meadow's small log shelter. Side trails from the loop plunge toward the Roaring River. To reach the trailhead at Frazier Turnaround (a primitive campground with no water) take Highway 224 southeast of Estacada 26 miles, turn left just after the bridge at Ripplebrook onto Road 57, turn left again after 8 miles onto Road 58, head left after another 7 miles onto Road 4610 past High Rock, then after 2 more miles, continue straight on Road 240 to its end. From the same trailhead, try the 1-mile jaunt down to Shellrock Lake, or hike the scenic abandoned road 4.8 miles to Shining Lake.

The Salmon-Huckleberry Wilderness has no fewer than five panoramic ridges with trails; most of these hikes begin with long climbs. The closest to Portland is Wildcat Mountain, a 5-mile trip (one way) gradually gaining 1800 feet up McIntyre Ridge to views of Hood. To find the trailhead, drive 11 miles east of Sandy on Highway 26 and turn right onto East Wildcat Creek Road for 4.1 miles; at forks always take the larger uphill road.

Two good routes ascend Huckleberry Mountain—the Boulder Ridge Trail from the parking area at the BLM's Wildwood Recreation Site, and the Bonanza Trail, which starts along Cheeney Creek and climbs past an old mine's tunnel. Park along paved Welches Road and walk across a Salmon River bridge 0.2 mile to the "trailhead," where parking is strictly forbidden.

The panorama from the lookout tower on Devils Peak is another worthy hiking goal; it can be reached either by the grueling 4.1-mile Cool Creek Trail from Road 2612, the 5.7-mile

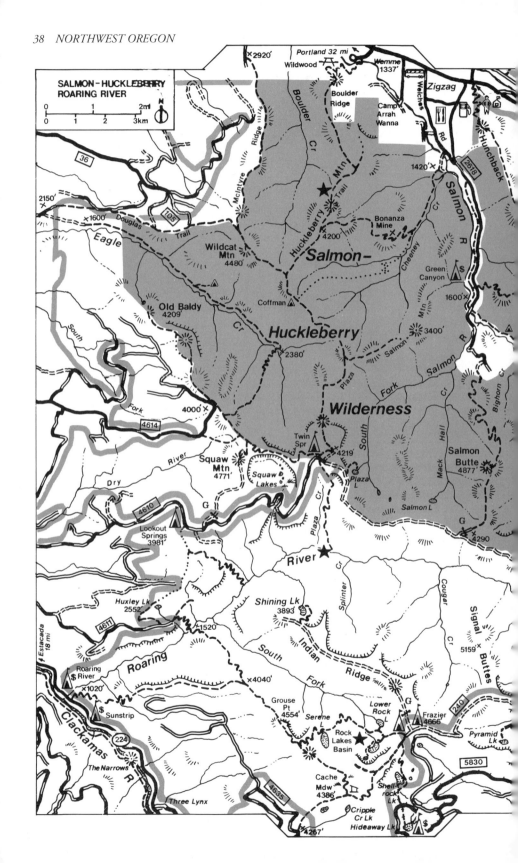

SALMON–HUCKLEBERRY
ROARING RIVER

0   1   2mi
0   1   2   3km

2920'
Portland 32 mi
Wildwood
Wemme
1337'
Zigzag
Weiches
Boulder
Ridge
Camp
Arrah
Wanna
1420'
2618
Hunchback
Boulder Cr
Mtn

36
2150'
1600'
Douglas
Trail
McIntyre
Ridge
Huckleberry Trail
Bonanza
Mine
4200'
Salmon–
Salmon R
Cheeney Cr
105
Eagle
Wildcat
Mtn
4480'
Green
Canyon
1600'
Old Baldy
4209'
Coffman
Huckleberry
3400'
South
Cr
2380'
Salmon Mtn
Salmon
Cr
Plaza
Fork
4000'
4614
River
Wilderness
Bighorn Cr
Dry
Fork
Squaw
Mtn
4771'
Squaw
Lakes
Twin
Spr
4219'
Plaza
L
Salmon
Butte
4877'
G
4610
Salmon L
Mack Hall Cr
Lookout
Springs
3981'
Plaza Cr
G
4290
River
Huxley Lk
2552'
4611
1520'
Shining Lk
3893'
Splinter Cr
Cougar Cr
Signal
Buttes
5159'
Estacada
18 mi
Roaring
South
Fork
Indian
Ridge
240
Roaring
River
1020'
4040'
Grouse
Pt
4554'
Serene
L
Lower
Rock
L
G
Frazier
4666'
Pyramid
Lk
Sunstrip
Clackamas R
224
Rock
Lakes
Basin
5830
The Narrows
Cache
Mdw
4386'
Shell
rock
Lk
Three Lynx
4635
4267'
Cripple Cr Lk
Hideaway Lk

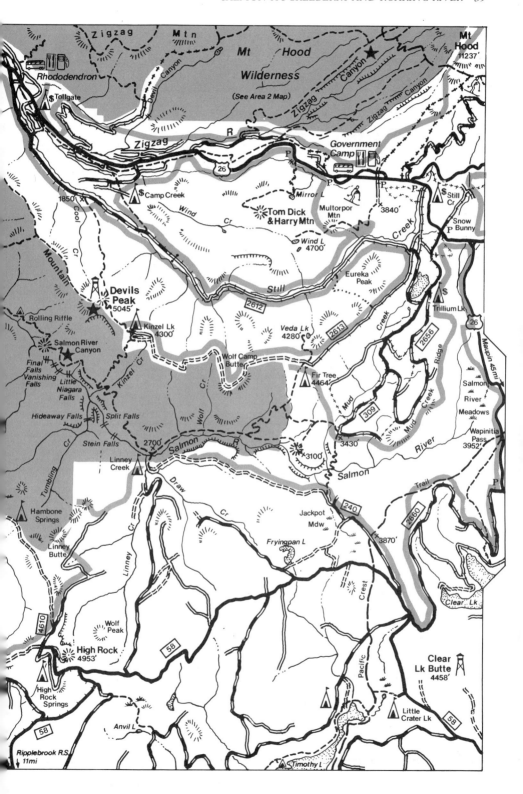

The Eagle Creek Trail in the Salmon-Huckleberry Wilderness

Green Canyon Trail from Road 2618, or the 8.1-mile Hunchback Ridge Trail from the Zigzag Ranger Station. Since all these routes gain over 3000 feet in elevation, it's tempting to take the easy 1.2-mile trail from near Kinzel Lake instead, even though this requires a bone-jarring 10-mile drive to the end of rutted dirt Road 2613.

The views from the open, rocky summit of Salmon Butte are reached by a woodsy 4.3-mile trail climbing 2800 feet from a spur near the end of Road 2618. Another ridgetop trail center is at primitive Twin Springs Campground; drive 6.5 miles southeast of Estacada on Highway 224, then turn left on Road 4610 for 18.4 miles. Twin Springs is atop The Plaza, a 1-square-mile plateau. Follow the Plaza Trail 1.4 miles north to the Sheepshead Rock viewpoint at the tip of The Plaza, then hike another 3.6 increasingly rugged miles northeast for the view of Salmon Mountain.

Roaring River is one of the wildest and most remote streams in northwest Oregon. Quiet trails switchback down from Twin Springs Campground (2.3 miles) and the end of Road 4611 (1.2 miles). No trails or easy bushwhacking routes follow the river itself through its rugged canyon.

The Eagle Creek Trail follows a rushing stream through a towering old-growth rain forest. A small meadow at 4.7 miles makes a logical stopping point for day hikers. A Mount Hood National Forest map is necessary to locate the trailhead, 19 miles east of Estacada.

Winter Sports

Three excellent cross-country skiing centers border the area. Most popular is the Snowbunny sno-park on Highway 26, from which a wide variety of tours are possible into the Trillium Lake Basin. Several short trips are described in the Mount Hood entry; longer tours follow Road 2613 for 5.5 miles to a view on the Veda Lake Trail, or prowl the roads and clearcuts along Mud Creek and Mud Creek Ridge. Numerous loop routes are possible by cross-country travel between roads; remember a compass and topographic map.

The second major nordic skiing area focuses on four sno-parks, located 0.5, 1.5, 2.7, and 4.4 miles south of Wapinitia Pass on Highway 26. The area features road tours around scenic Clear Lake and Frog Lake. A short, often overlooked trip is the 0.5-mile jaunt to spacious Salmon River Meadows, 1.6 miles north of Wapinitia Pass on Highway 26, but hidden from the road by trees.

The high country southeast of Roaring River offers solitude for cross-country skiers. This area begins near the Ripplebrook Ranger Station, 26 miles southeast of Estacada on Highway 224. Winter plowing extends as far as the Silvertip Work Center, 3 miles up Road 4630 from Ripplebrook, so after heavy midwinter snows, tours start there. It is 11.4 miles up Road 4635 to Cache Meadow, a worthy overnight trek for the prepared. When the snowline reaches 3000 feet in spring (call Ripplebrook Ranger Station, at 503-630-4256, for snow information), skiers can drive 8 miles east of Ripplebrook on Road 57, then turn left on Road 58 another 3 miles. From that point, tours on Roads 58 and 5830 extend to Shellrock Lake and High Rock.

4

BADGER CREEK

Location: 65 mi E of Portland, 44 mi SE of The Dalles
Size: 45 sq mi
Status: 36 sq mi designated wilderness (1984)
Terrain: Forested canyons
Elevation: 2100'–6525'
Management: Mount Hood NF
Topographic maps: Badger Creek Wilderness (USFS); Mount Hood, Flag Point (Green Trails)

Draped across the eastern foothills of Mount Hood, the Badger Creek canyonlands form the remarkable transition zone between High Cascade forest and Columbia Plateau steppe. The area's 80 miles of trails connect with the Mount Hood Wilderness nearby.

Climate

Lying to the east of the Cascade crest, Badger Creek is often sunny when western Oregon is suffering drizzle. Though the area measures just 12 miles end to end, annual precipitation ranges from 80 inches on the windy western ridges to 20 inches in the dry eastern lowlands. Snows close the lower trails from December to March. The ridges' relatively light winter snow-pack melts from the highest trails by mid-June. Afternoon thunderstorms occasionally interrupt hot summer days.

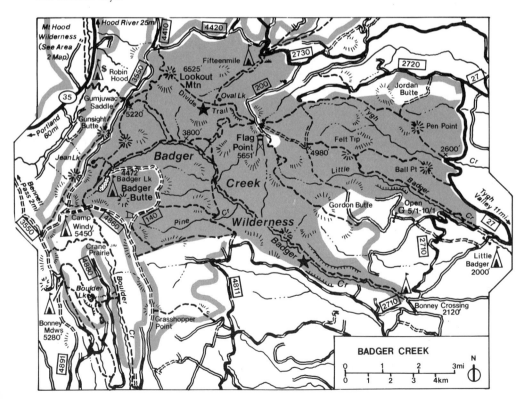

Plants and Wildlife

The higher elevations of Badger Creek share the alpine rock gardens and Hudsonian forests of Mount Hood, but the eastern lowlands exhibit a pine-oak biologic zone unique in Oregon wilderness. This open, parklike ecosystem of ponderosa pine and Oregon white oak extends only a short distance north and south of the Columbia River between Hood River and The Dalles.

Nowhere is the pine-oak zone's spring wildflower display as spectacular as on the School Canyon Trail, west from Road 27 over Ball Point. Tall, purple larkspur bloom in mid-April, with pink shooting star in damp areas. By late May, great fields of lupine turn the hillsides blue, splashed yellow at places by balsamroot. By July, white death camas and purple onion remain among the yellow, withered grass.

By late July the wildflowers of the pine-oak zone are gone, but the rock gardens of the alpine zone are at their peak. Amble along the Divide and Gunsight Butte trails for showy penstemon, Indian paintbrush, avalanche lilies, and stonecrop.

The Portland Audubon Society has compiled lists for Badger Creek showing 46 butterfly species, 101 lichens, and 157 birds—surprising diversity for such a compact area.

Geology

Volcanism from Mount Hood provided the raw material for the Badger Creek area. An Ice Age glacier scoured a curving, 2500-foot-deep, U-shaped valley from its cirque at Badger Lake down Badger Creek, leaving the dramatic cliffs below the Divide Trail. A second glacier cut the valley of Boulder Creek; its cirque lake, below Camp Windy, has filled with sediment to become Crane Prairie. Stream erosion since the Ice Age cut the precipitous, narrow gorges of lower Badger Creek and Little Badger Creek, leaving interesting badlands and pinnacles of more resistant rock.

THINGS TO DO

Hiking

The steep 2.4-mile route up from Robin Hood Campground on Highway 35 to Gumjuwac Saddle offers good views of Mount Hood during its 1700-foot climb—and brings the hiker to the intersection of four Badger Creek trails, all suitable for day hikes or longer treks.

Southeast of Gumjuwac Saddle, the Gunsight Trail parallels Road 3550 for 4.5 miles to the junction of Road 3550, following a ridgetop packed with rock gardens, interesting rock formations, and viewpoints. Due south of Gumjuwac Saddle is the 2.5-mile trail down to Badger Lake.

A trail heading east from Gumjuwac Saddle drops 1300 feet in 2.2 miles to the Badger Creek Trail; from there, Bonney Crossing Campground is an enchanting 9.9-mile backpack downstream, past old-growth Douglas fir, green-pooled cascades, and finally, oak-fringed cliffs. Yet another trail from Gumjuwac Saddle climbs 2.2 miles northeast to 6525-foot Lookout Mountain, the finest viewpoint in the area.

If you'd like to drive to the trail crossing at Gumjuwac Saddle, take Highway 35 around Mount Hood to between mileposts 70 and 71, go 3.8 miles east on Road 44, turn right for 4.7 miles on Road 4410, and turn right on dirt Road 3550 for 3.3 bumpy miles.

The northern portion of the Badger Creek Wilderness features a dramatic 3.7-mile portion of the Divide Trail between Lookout Mountain and Flag Point's staffed fire lookout. The path is a series of cliff-edge viewpoints, rock formations, and wildflower gardens. Reach it by driving as to Gumjuwac Saddle, but at the end of Road 4410 turn left 200 yards on Road 4420. An easy 1-mile abandoned road leads up to the spectacular viewpoint atop Lookout Mountain and to the Divide Trail.

To reach the trailhead to Crane Prairie, in the lovely valley of Boulder Creek, take Highway 35 to Bennett Pass, drive 4 horribly rough miles on Road 3550, and veer right on Road 4891 for 0.3 mile. Another mile down Road 4891 is Bonney Meadows Campground, which offers several trails, including the pleasant 1.7-mile day hike to Boulder Lake.

On the eastern edge of the wilderness, four trails set out through the unique pine-oak forest.

View east down Little Badger Creek's canyon from the Schoolhouse Trail

The 11.9-mile Badger Creek Trail to Badger Lake is more than a day hike, but worth it. The Little Badger Creek Trail fords its creek four times in the first 3 miles of its rugged canyon; crossings are easy except in early spring. Other trails climb to views at Ball Point and Pen Point. Access to the eastern Badger Creek trailheads is via Highway 197. At milepost 33, near Tygh Valley, turn west on Shadybrook Road for 1 mile. Then turn left on Fairgrounds Road for 1.1 mile and turn right on Badger Creek Road, which becomes Road 27.

Winter Sports

Cross-country skiers can follow Road 3550 from the sno-park at Bennett Pass toward a number of destinations: Bonney Meadows (5.8 miles), Gunsight Butte (7.2 miles), and Badger Lake (7.4 miles via the trail at Camp Windy).

5

TABLE ROCK

Location: 19 mi SE of Molalla, 50 mi S of Portland
Size: 9 sq mi
Status: 9 sq mi designated wilderness (1984)
Terrain: Forested ridges
Elevation: 1300'–4881'
Management: Salem District BLM
Topographic maps: Rooster Rock, Gawley Creek (USGS)

This pocket wilderness offers surprisingly quiet forest trails within a short drive of the populous Willamette Valley. Table Rock's basalt mesa is the area's high point, with a view worth the climb.

Climate

Summers are sunny, while other seasons are mild and wet (100 inches annual precipitation). Winter snows cover trails over 3000 feet from December to May.

Plants and Wildlife

The forests here are Douglas fir and western hemlock, with noble fir at higher elevations. Pink-blossomed rhododendron crowd upper slopes. The small, sparsely petaled Gorman's aster found on rockslides is a federally listed endangered species, as is Oregon sullivantia, a saxifrage of cliff seeps. White Clackamas iris, showy Washington lilies, and delicate calypso orchids are endangered primarily by indiscriminate flower pickers.

Blue huckleberries

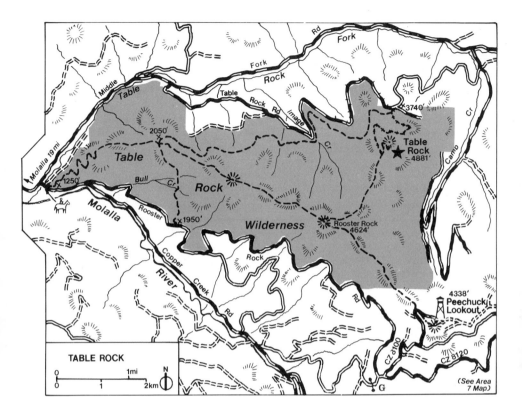

Geology

Fortress-shaped Table Rock is the remnant of a hard basalt lava flow that once capped the entire area. All local rocks date from the Old Cascades' eruptions 16 to 25 million years ago.

History

Table Rock was in the hunting grounds of the Northern Molalla, a small tribe confined to the rugged foothills between the Willamette Valley and the High Cascades. Because the Molalla spoke a Sahaptin language similar to that of the Nez Perce, they are thought to have been driven from an eastern Oregon homeland centuries ago to this unlikely range.

The east–west trail from the Molalla River to Peechuck Lookout is a remnant of a Molalla trail leading from the lowlands to Bull of the Woods and the High Cascades. Three archaeological sites, evidently Molalla camps, have been identified in the area.

THINGS TO DO

Hiking

Seldom are wilderness viewpoints as sweeping and accessible as the one atop Table Rock, a pleasant 2.3-mile hike away from the Table Rock Road. On its 1200-foot climb, the trail winds about the impressive columnar basalt cliffs of Table Rock's north face, then switchbacks up the gentler west slope. The panorama extends from Mount Rainier to the Three Sisters, including views into the Bull of the Woods Wilderness and the Willamette Valley.

Rooster Rock, an additional 1.5 miles by trail from Table Rock, affords lesser views, but protrudes from a scenic heather-topped ridge. The hiker who has planned a car shuttle can continue past Rooster Rock on this ridge to the Molalla River trailhead, an 8.8-mile trip in all. Peechuck fire lookout, a rare two-story stone structure from 1932, is another interesting goal.

Rooster Rock and Mount Jefferson

There are no reliable water sources on the area's trails. Equestrians will want to avoid the rough rock talus slope directly north of Table Rock.

All trailheads are reached via the town of Molalla, 30 miles south of Portland. Take Highway 211 east of Molalla 0.5 mile, turn south onto South Mathias Road for 0.4 mile, curve left onto South Feyrer Park Road for 1.6 miles, and turn right onto South Dickey Prairie Road. Follow this road past several jogs 5.3 miles to an unsigned junction, turn right across a Molalla River bridge, and follow a paved road 12.8 miles to a junction with Middle Fork Road. The low elevation Table Rock trailhead is a stone's throw to the east. To find the upper trailhead, take Middle Fork Road 2.6 miles and turn right on Table Rock Road for 5.6 miles.

Winter Sports

From December to March it is pleasant to drive to snowline on the Table Rock Road, park to one side, and ski up the road and Table Rock Trail to the base of Table Rock's ice-encrusted cliffs for the fine view. The distance varies from 2 to 4 miles, depending on the road's snow level.

6

SILVER FALLS

Location: 26 mi E of Salem
Size: 13 sq mi
Status: State park
Terrain: Forested gorge, waterfalls
Elevation: 760'–2400'
Management: State Parks and Recreation Department
Topographic maps: Silverton, Scotts Mills, Stayton NE, Drake Crossing (USGS)

Waterfalls are the specialty of this very popular state park. Trails lead through a steep-sided, scenic canyon past ten falls, five of which are over 100 feet tall. In three cases, trails actually lead through mossy caverns *behind* waterfalls. From May through September, expect to pay a parking fee.

Climate

The mild, wet weather of this relatively low elevation park allows hiking in any season. In fact, the falls are most spectacular in winter, when silvery icicles and snow add a delicate beauty missed by the summer crowds.

Plants and Wildlife

Dense Douglas fir forests and streambank maples shelter a lush undergrowth of ferns, Oregon grape, salal, and many forest wildflowers. Though most wildlife species shy away from the park's populous trails, look for robin-sized water ouzels dipping or flying along the creek. Hikers often marvel at the area's spectacular anthills, some 4 feet tall.

Geology

Silver Creek Canyon's cliffs are part of the Columbia River basalt flows that inundated this area about 15 million years ago, leveling the landscape. When the area was then tilted upward with the rising Cascade Range, Silver Creek cut through the resistant basalt. The basalt now forms the lips of the waterfalls. Many of the waterfalls' splash pools have eroded caverns into the soft rock beneath the basalt. Cylindrical indentations in the roofs of these canyons are "tree wells" left when the Columbia River lava flows surrounded tree trunks, which then burned.

Another feature of the basalt is its interesting six-sided columnar jointing. When basalt cools slowly, it cracks into a honeycomb of pillars perpendicular to the cooling surface. Look for these pillars in the cliffs.

History

The Silverton Fire, largest in Oregon history, burned this area in 1865. Silver Falls City, on the site of the present South Falls picnic area, was founded as a logging camp in 1888. Stumps attest to early logging activity.

The canyon trail ducks behind South Falls.

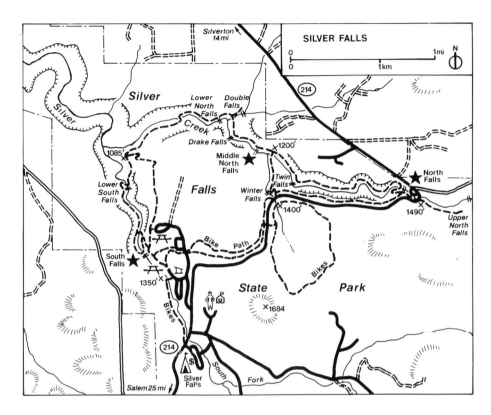

State park status came in 1931. The canyon trails, lodge, shelters, and highway overlooks were built by 200 Civilian Conservation Corps employees stationed near North Falls from 1935 to 1942.

THINGS TO DO

Hiking

Long, graceful waterfalls appear at nearly every bend along the beautiful 4.2-mile canyon trail from South to North Falls. Side trails create loop hike possibilities ranging in length from 0.7 to 7 miles. Dogs are not permitted on the canyon trails.

Most loop hikes begin at 177-foot South Falls, the tallest and most popular of the cascades. A paved, heavily used 0.7-mile loop winds through the cavern behind the waterfall, crosses a footbridge, and returns to the South Falls picnic area. A quieter 2.4-mile loop extends the shorter hike as far down the canyon as 93-foot Lower South Falls.

A 5.1-mile circuit of the canyon continues past Lower South Falls to Lower North, Double, Drake, and 106-foot Middle North falls before crossing a footbridge and climbing to the Highway 214 parking area above Winter Falls; from there a 1.6-mile hiking trail through a large Douglas fir forest parallels the highway back to the South Falls picnic area. The longest loop hike, 7 miles, follows the canyon from South Falls to 136-foot North Falls and returns on the trail near the highway.

A paved 4-mile bicycle path beginning at Silver Falls Campground is also hikable; it passes South Falls and prowls the forest above Winter Falls. Another 12.2 miles of hiking and equestrian trails begin at the hitching rails and horse-loading ramp at the southwest park entrance on Highway 214. This trail network consists primarily of logging roads maintained for recreation.

The most remote portion of the park is the lower 2.5 miles of Silver Creek Canyon, a trailless gorge with four rarely visited waterfalls.

7

BULL OF THE WOODS

Location: 68 mi SE of Portland, 64 mi E of Salem
Size: 80 sq mi
Status: 74 sq mi designated wilderness (1984, 1996)
Terrain: Densely forested mountain ridges, valleys
Elevation: 2000'–5710'
Management: Mount Hood NF, Willamette NF
Topographic maps: Bull of the Woods Wilderness (USFS), Battle Ax (Green Trails)

Hidden high in the Cascade foothills, the uncrowded Bull of the Woods Wilderness and its newly designated neighbor, the Opal Creek Wilderness, feature subalpine mountains and lakes amidst gigantic old-growth forests. At the center of the extensive trail network is the Bull of the Woods lookout tower, with its panoramic view. Bagby Hot Springs' cedar tubs provide a spot for a hot soak, while Sawmill Falls in the Opal Creek area is ideal for a chilly dip.

Climate

Trails below 3000 feet are usually snow-free from April into December; the highest trails are clear from June through October. Despite over 100 inches of annual precipitation, summers are sunny.

Plants and Wildlife

Bull of the Woods and adjacent Opal Creek comprise one of the last great old-growth forest reserves of western Oregon. Towering western hemlock and Douglas fir remain in the valleys, with a complex ecosystem of lichens, birds, insects, and mosses. Elegant white trilliums bloom in the deep forest in April, while tangles of rhododendrons erupt in pink blossom in early July.

Here the patient observer may sight a northern spotted owl, the huge, shy bird threatened by reductions in its old-growth habitat. By day the owl remains in its nest, high in the resprouted top of a broken conifer, or it may perch like an 18-inch-tall, earless statue on a branch near the trunk, where the owl's mottled, white-spotted feathers camouflage it perfectly against the tree's

The Bull of the Woods lookout tower

bark. At night, however, this owl glides through the forest on its 3.5-foot wingspan, catching wood rats, mice, and flying squirrels. In the dark it answers readily to its own recorded call, a high-pitched "hoo, hoo-hoo" (a human imitation will do). Then a flashlight held at the observer's eye level will reflect off the owl's dark eyes, revealing its location.

Five other species of owls share the area: the larger, ear-tufted great horned owl, the robin-sized screech owl, the day-hunting pygmy owl, the small saw-whet owl, and the dark-eyed flammulated owl. A good range for owling indeed!

Geology

Erosion has uncovered quartz veins containing small amounts of copper and silver in this section of the 16- to 25-million-year-old Old Cascades. A relic of the Elkhorn Mining District, which once brought a rush of prospectors to the area, survives in the historic Jawbone Flats mining camp near Opal Creek.

Ice Age glaciation carved the area's many bowl-shaped lake valleys. A vanished Ice Age glacier carved Elk Lake's basin and polished the smooth bedrock visible along the trail on the eastern slope of Battle Ax.

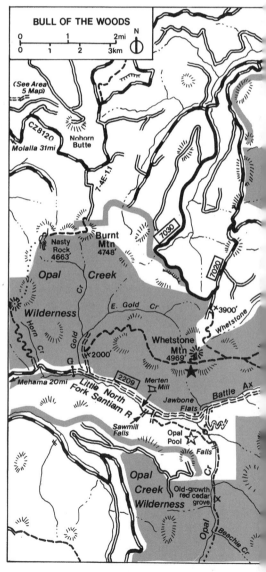

THINGS TO DO

Hiking

This wilderness has ample room for satisfying two- and three-day backpacking trips, yet it is small enough to be explored by day hikers as well.

The easy, 1.5-mile hike to Bagby Hot Springs, leading through a huge, old-growth forest, is the area's most popular day trip. Although the hot springs' shake-roofed bathhouse burned in 1979 when night bathers left a candle lit, the 8-foot cedar log tubs were too waterlogged to burn, and have been installed in an even larger bathhouse, built by volunteers. A resident ranger enforces a ban on camping extending from the trailhead to a quarter mile beyond the springs. Visit in midweek to avoid crowds.

To reach the hot springs' trail from Estacada, drive Highway 224 southeast 26 miles to the bridge by Ripplebrook Campground, veer right onto Road 46 for 3.6 miles, continue to the right on Road 63 another 3.5 miles, then turn left on Road 70 for 6 miles.

Pansy Lake is another rewarding, easy goal. A 1.2-mile trail traverses a towering grove of Douglas fir on the way to the swimmable lake in a forested cirque. The drive starts out the same as to the hot springs, but follows Road 63 for 5.6 miles before turning left onto Road 6340 for 7.8 miles; then turn right onto Road 6341 for 3.5 miles,.

Several outstanding, but more strenuous,

day hikes seek out viewpoints. Chief among these is Bull of the Woods, the only area peak still topped by a lookout tower. Here the view across beargrass-dotted meadows stretches from Mount Rainier to the Three Sisters. Staffed only in times of extreme fire danger, the tower also serves as an emergency shelter. The Pansy Basin Trail extends to the Bull of the Woods lookout, a 3.8-mile route in all, but the Bull of the Woods Trail from Road 6340 (past the Dickey Peaks) climbs 1200 feet less and is 0.5 mile shorter.

Two craggy peaks contend for the title of best viewpoint in the southern end of this wilderness: Battle Ax and Mount Beachie. To reach either, drive Highway 22 to Detroit, turn north for 4.4 miles on Breitenbush River Road 46, turn left onto Road 4696 for 0.8 mile, turn left onto Road 4697 for 4.7 steep miles, and turn left for 2 miserably rough miles to the Elk Lake Campground entrance. The 1-mile dirt track from the campground to the trailheads at Beachie Saddle is too rough for most vehicles; park and walk.

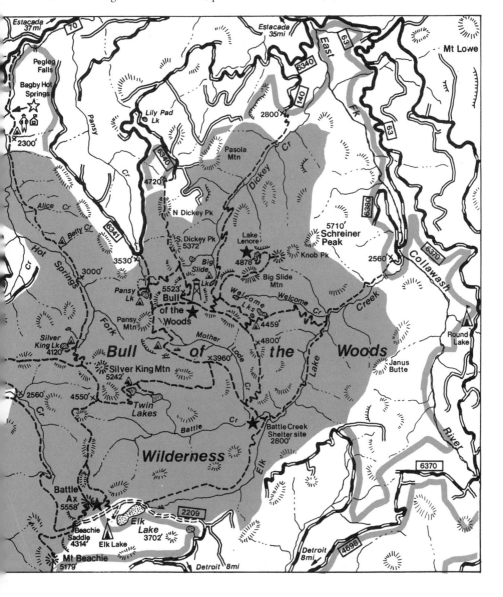

To the north from Beachie Saddle, a 1.6-mile trail switchbacks up to the clifftop views at Battle Ax's old lookout site, gaining 1200 feet elevation. The trail continues north, making a loop trail possible back to the Elk Lake Campground—a pleasant 6.5-mile hike in all.

To the southwest from Beachie Saddle, a 5.6-mile trail traverses to a lovely ridge topped by Mount Beachie, gaining just 900 feet to reach views of Elk Lake, Mount Jefferson, and beyond.

Whetstone Mountain, a former lookout site in the seldom visited western end of this wilderness, is the quietest viewpoint of all. The easiest route up, a 2.4-mile trail on the mountain's north flank, begins on Road 7020, 9 miles south of the Bagby Hot Springs trailhead.

A much more arduous trail up Whetstone Mountain, gaining 3000 feet in 4.5 miles, is the route of choice for some hikers because of its easier trailhead access from Salem. To reach it, drive 25 miles east of Salem on Highway 22 to Mehama, turn left on the Little North Fork Road for 15 paved miles, continue straight 1.3 miles on gravel, then fork left on Road 2209 for another 6 miles to a locked gate. Walk the mining road 0.5 mile past the gate and another 0.5 mile up Gold Creek to the trail.

For an easy tour of the newly designated Opal Creek Wilderness, park at the locked gate on Road 2209 and walk up this road amidst 700-year-old Douglas firs. After 2 miles you'll pass Merten Mill, a defunct sawmill with a campable meadow and a deep, swimmable pool at the base of a broad waterfall. After another 1.5 miles reach rustic Jawbone Flats, a collection of cabins built 1929–1932 and now deeded to the Friends of Opal Creek as an old-growth study center. Cross Battle Ax Creek and turn right 0.3 mile to Opal Pool's scenic gorge.

For a longer hike up Opal Creek, turn right just past Merten Mill, cross an old river bridge, and continue upstream on a trail built in 1991. It's 1.4 miles to an overlook of Opal Pool, another 0.6 mile to a bridge over Opal Creek, and an additional 1.4 miles, past waterfalls and 1000-year-old cedars, to where the trail peters out.

Another good old-growth forest walk follows an easy 4-mile trail from Elk Lake to the site of the former Battle Creek shelter, where two woodsy streams join.

Most of the small, scenic lakes in this wilderness are just far enough from trailheads to be the destinations of either very challenging day hikes or pleasant overnight trips. For instance, the Welcome Lakes are 5 miles in and 2000 feet up from the Road 6380 trailhead—a rugged 10-mile-round-trip day hike through old-growth forest. But the backpacker can pitch his tent near Upper Welcome Lake and still have energy left to hike another mile up to the Bull of the Woods lookout, or to prowl the interesting ridges and meadows along nearby trails.

Likewise, Big Slide Lake is 5 miles in and 1600 feet up the rhododendron-lined Dickey Creek Trail from Road 6340-140. A base camp at the lake will allow the backpacker to continue out Big Slide Mountain's ridge to Lake Lenore's clifftop cirque.

Another pretty lake destination is Silver King Lake. It's a 4.7-mile hike from Road 7020 along the Whetstone Mountain Trail's scenic ridgetop. Those who can arrange a short car shuttle can camp at the lake, then hike 7.7 miles down the Bagby Trail the second day through old-growth forest to Road 70, stopping at the hot springs for a dip on the way.

Finally, the Twin Lakes make a good hiking goal. Start out from Road 2209 near the Elk Lake Campground, climbing to a scenic ridgetop trail north of Battle Ax. Camp after 6.2 miles at Lower Twin Lake. The second day, either stroll 5.3 miles to an easy camp at the site of the former Battle Creek shelter, or hike 4 miles farther to Elk Lake.

Climbing

Nasty Rock and a small unnamed pinnacle to the southwest offer some technical rock pitches. Many of the routes on these remote volcanic crags are untested. The rugged, up-and-down 4-mile trail route to Nasty Rock begins off Road 2209, a mile before the road's gate.

Winter Sports

Though adjacent roads are unplowed in winter, skiers park at snowline on Road 2209 and ski to Elk Lake. In spring the trip is usually 3 to 4 miles one way, with Beachie Saddle a tempting additional 1.5-mile climb.

8

OLALLIE LAKE

Location: 80 mi SE of Portland, 69 mi E of Salem
Size: 36 sq mi
Status: 17 sq mi Forest Service scenic area, 14-sq-mi Indian reservation
Terrain: Forested, lake-dotted plateau
Elevation: 2100'–7215'
Management: Mount Hood NF, Confederated Tribes of Warm Springs
Topographic maps: Olallie Scenic Area, PCT Northern Oregon Portion (USFS); Olallie Butte (USGS); Breitenbush (Green Trails)

In the shadow of Mount Jefferson, this forested plateau of 200 lakes and ponds is one of the most accessible portions of the Cascade's high country. Short, nearly level trails from seven developed campgrounds along Skyline Road 4220 lead to the larger lakes, while the open, lodgepole pine forests invite easy cross-country hikes to more remote lakeside campsites.

Climate

A very heavy winter snowpack keeps most trails, and Road 4220, closed from about mid-October to the first of July. As lingering snow melts during the peak wildflower month of July,

Mount Jefferson from Olallie Lake

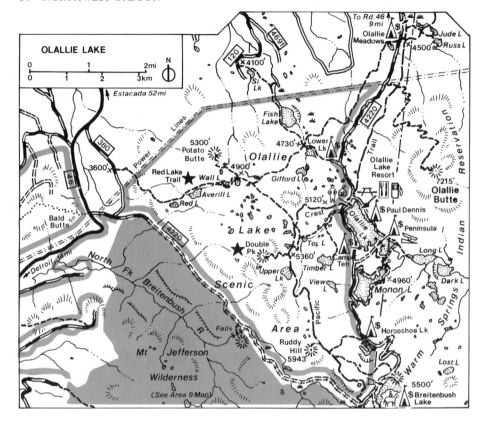

mosquitoes are so profuse that headnets are advisable. By late summer, cross-country hikers may stumble on ground-nesting yellowjackets.

Plants and Wildlife

Low huckleberry bushes provide a carpet beneath the forests of lodgepole pine and mountain hemlock. Watch for mink, otter, and eagles at the many fish-filled lakes.

Geology

This Cascade Range upland has been dotted by geologically recent cinder cones such as Olallie Butte and Potato Butte. A broad Ice Age glacial ice sheet left the many shallow lake basins. Look for glacier-polished bedrock at the north end of Monon Lake and along the Pacific Crest Trail (PCT) near Olallie Lake.

History

The Indians who once trekked here each fall to hunt deer and gather the abundant huckleberries named the largest lake *olallie*—the Chinook jargon word for berry. Seven bands of central Oregon Indians were granted the eastern portion of this area when the Warm Springs Indian Reservation was created by a treaty in 1855.

THINGS TO DO

Hiking

Short trails and frequent lakes make the area well suited for beginning backpackers and families with young hikers. A good day hike for children is the 0.8-mile Russ Lake Trail from wildflower-filled Olallie Meadows. Hiking the shore trails around Olallie or Monon lakes is also fun with children, and yields first-rate views of Olallie Butte and Mount Jefferson. It's 2.7 miles around Monon Lake, and 2.9 around Olallie Lake.

The pleasant 2.8-mile trail from Si Lake, past cliff-rimmed Fish Lake and 73-foot-deep Lower Lake, climbs 700 feet on its way to the Lower Lake Campground.

Good camping lakes appear at nearly every bend in the 5.8-mile Red Lake Trail between Road 380 and Olallie Lake. Worthwhile side trips from this east–west route are the 1-mile climbs to the viewpoints atop Potato Butte and Double Peak.

The most interesting section of the Pacific Crest Trail (PCT) here is the 6.1 miles between Olallie Lake guard station and Road 4220 just west of Breitenbush Lake. At either end, this section follows cliffs and ridges with good views.

Monon and Olallie lakes from the summit of Olallie Butte

Olallie Butte has the best view of all, from a trail climbing 2600 feet in 3.8 miles beginning at an unmarked trailhead under the southernmost of three sets of powerlines. This is Indian land, so disturb nothing along the route. The former lookout site not only overlooks the entire Olallie Lake area, it also offers an eye-level view of Mount Jefferson and a long look into central Oregon.

Hiking cross-country to trailless lakes is one way to avoid the crowds of the best hiking months, August and September. Beginners in the art of route-finding with map and compass can practice by bearing south from crowded Lower Lake to quiet Gifford Lake, or from Timber Lake to View Lake (the view is of Olallie Butte). Then try bushwhacking on compass bearings along the string of small lakes that form a 1-mile-diameter circle around the northern base of Double Peak. It is difficult to become hopelessly lost anywhere in the area, since a trail or road is never over a mile away.

Camping is prohibited within the Warm Springs Indian Reservation, except specifically at Breitenbush Lake. Anglers on reservation lands must have a state fishing license, tribal fishing permit, and a copy of the Warm Springs fishing regulations. Violations are subject to a $200 fine or ninety-day imprisonment.

To reach the Olallie Lake area from the north, follow Highway 224 and then paved Road 46 a total of 47.5 miles past Estacada. Turn left on paved Road 4690 for 8 miles, then turn right on gravel Road 4220 for 6 miles to Olallie Lake. Beyond Horseshoe Lake, Road 4220 becomes a very slow, badly rutted track, unsuited for trailer travel. The Fish Lake trailhead is only 6 miles from Highway 46; drive 3.4 miles up Road 4690, turn right on Road 4691, and follow signs.

Drivers approaching from Salem can take Highway 22 to Detroit, follow paved Road 46 for 17 miles, then turn right on treacherously rutted Road 4220 for 7.5 miles to Breitenbush Lake. Those without four-wheel drive should continue on paved Road 46 another 7 miles before turning right on Road 4690 toward Olallie Lake.

Winter Sports

Road 46, plowed in winter, allows cross-country ski access to the area's lakes via snowed-under Roads 4220 and 4690. Snowmobiles are allowed on these routes. The 7.5-mile distance to Breitenbush Lake makes an overnight trip in order, perhaps to one of the two shake-roofed, stone shelters beside the lake.

Boating

A resort at Olallie Lake rents rowboats, and Peninsula Campground offers a boat ramp. Motors are prohibited on all of the area's lakes.

9

MOUNT JEFFERSON

Location: 64 mi E of Salem, 37 mi NE of Bend
Size: 273 sq mi
Status: 174 sq mi designated wilderness (1968, 1984)
Terrain: Glaciated peak, forested ridges, lake basins
Elevation: 2400'–10,497'
Management: Willamette NF, Deschutes NF, Mount Hood NF, Confederated Tribes of Warm Springs
Topographic maps: Mount Jefferson, Santiam Pass Winter Recreation (Geo-Graphics); Mount Jefferson Wilderness, PCT Northern Oregon Portion (USFS); Mount Jefferson, Whitewater River (Green Trails)

Mount Jefferson ranks as Oregon's second-highest peak (after Mount Hood), and forms the centerpiece of Oregon's second most visited wilderness (after the Three Sisters).

The top attractions are 150 mountain lakes, ranging from heavily visited, half-square-mile Marion Lake to the delicate tarns of Jefferson Park's popular alpine wildflower meadows. Three Fingered Jack, an impressive 7841-foot crag, dominates the southern end of the wilderness with its own collection of alpine lakes and meadows.

Climate

Winter snows, commencing early in November, total from 250 to 700 inches at Santiam Pass. The spring melt typically opens trails up to 3500 feet elevation by mid-May, up to 4500 feet by mid-June, up to 5500 feet by mid-July, and up to 6500 feet by August 1. Mosquitoes are troublesome for two to three weeks following the final snow melt in each region.

Storms occasionally interrupt clear, dry summer weather. The eastern slopes, with 40 inches annual precipitation, are often sunny even when the western slopes, with 100 inches precipitation, are lost in clouds.

Plants and Wildlife

Deer, elk, black bear, and coyotes are numerous enough to be seen frequently. Bald eagles can be spotted fishing in the lakes.

The area's lower western valleys shelter old-growth Douglas fir forests. Spire-shaped subalpine fir and mountain hemlock cluster at higher elevations. Descending the area's drier eastern slopes is a remarkably compact sequence of forest zones, from mountain hemlock to lodgepole pine, and finally to the long-needled ponderosa pine of the Metolius Valley.

Fields of blue lupine and red Indian paintbrush attract day hikers to Canyon Creek Meadows, Jefferson Park, the Eight Lakes Basin, and the Santiam Lake area in late July.

Also in July, the white, 4-foot-tall plumes of beargrass may be profuse along ridges, on slopes, and in lodgepole pine forests. This bunchgrasslike plant fills the wilderness with its fragrant blooms about every third year, mysteriously choosing not to flower at all in other years. An unlikely looking lily family member, beargrass has blooms consisting of hundreds of tiny, six-petaled flowers. Bears unearth and eat the plant's succulent root, which, when boiled, is said to make a soap substitute. Indians gathered the plant's 2-foot-long leaves and wove them into useful baskets—a craft that wilderness hikers today can practice to while away an evening.

Geology

Mount Jefferson and Three Fingered Jack are both heavily eroded remnants of apparently extinct volcanoes. On Three Fingered Jack, only the hard lava plug, or central core, survives, flanked by ridges of the old volcano's subsidiary lava dikes. Mount Jefferson is also topped by a lava spire, but it is not the mountain's ancient plug. Glaciation has removed the western third of the mountain, including the ancient summit. The current summit rock was once a flank lava flow.

Geologically recent cinder cones (including Pyramid Butte, South Cinder Peak, and Maxwell Butte) and two large 6500-year-old lava flows 6 miles southeast of Mount Jefferson prove that the area is not volcanically dead.

History

Lewis and Clark sighted Mount Jefferson from the mouth of the Willamette River in 1806 and named it after the president who had sent them on their expedition. Three Fingered Jack apparently won its name because its summit spires reminded pioneers of a renowned, mutilated cohort of California Gold Rush bandit Joaquin Murietta.

Two failed transportation routes across the Cascade Range left their mark on the wilderness here. Minto Mountain and Minto Lake recall Salem pioneer John Minto, who in the 1870s urged in vain that a wagon road be built over Minto Pass.

The designated wilderness boundary between Santiam Pass and Lost Lake follows a bit of railroad grade built in the 1880s by entrepreneur Colonel T. Egenton Hogg. Hogg dreamed of a transcontinental line from Corvallis east, but his London financiers doubted a crossing of Santiam Pass was feasible. Undaunted, he ordered Chinese laborers to build 11 miles of grade, lay 300 feet of track, and pack a disassembled boxcar to the site. Mules pulled the car across the pass, allowing Hogg to tell his investors, straight-faced, that his train had already crossed the Cascades. The grade is still hikable from Santiam Lodge part way around the sheer cliffs of Hogg Rock.

Mount Jefferson from Jefferson Park

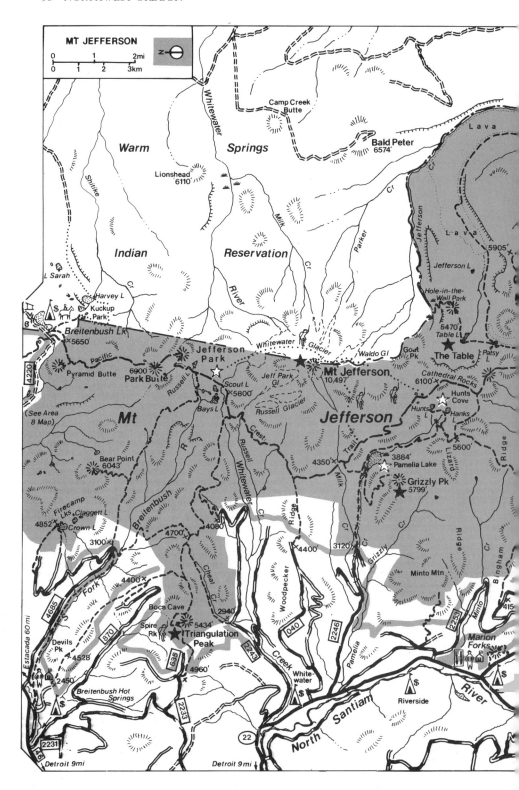

THINGS TO DO

Hiking

With 200 miles of trails, the heavily used Mount Jefferson area offers a dazzling variety of trek options. The open high country and off-trail lakes invite cross-country exploration as well.

Trail Park permits ($3 a day or $25 a year) are required for cars at all trailheads, even in the adjacent national forests. In addition, visitors must fill out free permits before entering the wilderness. Unlimited entry permits can be filled out at every trailhead except Pamelia Lake, where visitors must bring a permit that they obtained in advance from the Detroit Ranger Station. Only 20 of these permits are issued per day. Call (503) 854-3366 for details.

Camping is banned altogether on Marion Lake's northwest peninsula, on the peninsulas of Scout and Bays lakes, and within 100 feet of the high water mark of Marion, Pamelia, Hanks, and Hunts lakes. Campfires are banned within 100 feet of any water source. Livestock may not be tethered or picketed within 200 feet of any body of water. Wilderness rangers patrol the area. Camping is also banned within the Warm Springs Indian Reservation except at Breitenbush Lake. Hikers entering the reservation need written permission from the Confederated Tribes.

Among the easiest and most rewarding day hikes is the 2.2-mile trail from Road 2246 along a splashing creek under towering Douglas firs to Pamelia Lake. In early June the lake is ringed with pink rhododendron blooms. The area's best mountain view is 2.8 miles farther, at the old lookout site atop Grizzly Peak, 1900 feet above the lake and breathtakingly close to Mount Jefferson.

Marion Lake is an easy 2.5-mile walk from Road 2255 along a wide and occasionally dusty path. Hikers can pack in inflatable boats or light canoes to sail the 360-acre, 180-foot-deep lake. Fishing is prohibited in inlet streams and in the outlet creek as far as massive Marion Falls.

Square Lake, nestled in the forest at the foot of Three Fingered Jack, is an easy 2-mile day hike either from the Pacific Crest Trail's Santiam Pass trailhead on Highway 20 or from the Round Lake Campground.

Wildflowers and a close-up view of Three Fingered Jack highlight the 2-mile walk into Canyon Creek Meadows. The trail begins at the Jack Lake Campground at the end of Road 1234; a 2.3-mile trail along Canyon Creek makes a loop trip possible past that creek's pair of 20-foot falls. From the meadows, an additional 1.5-mile track leads steeply up a glacial moraine, past an ice-filled cirque lake, to a viewpoint saddle overtowered by Three Fingered Jack's summit pinnacles.

The fire lookout structures that once topped five peaks in this wilderness have been removed, but their panoramic views remain, an enticing goal for invigorating day hikes. Bear Point's view of Mount Jefferson is 3.8 miles away, and 2900 feet up, from Road 4685, which joins Road 46 a mile east of Breitenbush Hot Springs.

Triangulation Peak is surrounded by several interesting rock spires and a cave. The huge mouth of Boca Cave, a protected archaeological site, can be reached by scrambling several hundred yards down the rugged east side of the summit. Triangulation Peak is an easy 2.1-mile walk from the junction of Roads 2233 and 635, but the Cheat Creek trailhead on Whitewater Creek Road 2243 is easier to find, and its 6.3-mile route passes a lovely meadow and scenic ridge during its 2500-foot climb to the peak.

Marion Mountain, the area's lowest lookout site, is a 2.8-mile side trip up from Marion Lake, or a 4.2-mile hike from the Camp Pioneer trailhead on Road 2261. Maxwell Butte, a cinder cone overlooking the Santiam Pass area, is 4.8 miles up from Road 080, off Highway 22; at the dry trail's midpoint, Twin Lakes offer an irresistible swimming opportunity.

Another viewpoint worth the hike involves following the Pacific Crest Trail (PCT) 5.3 miles from Santiam Pass to Three Fingered Jack. After a 1600-foot climb the PCT crests a ridge with views south along the Cascades, then traverses almost directly below Three Fingered Jack's sheer west face.

Many of the wilderness's most spectacular areas are reached either by very long day hikes or by leisurely backpacking trips. The best example is Jefferson Park, a 1-square-mile plain of lush wildflowers and swimmable alpine lakes set so close to Mount Jefferson the snowy mountain seems to fill the sky.

Skiing the Pacific Crest Trail to Three Fingered Jack

Three routes reach Jefferson Park. The easiest trail climbs 5.1 miles from Whitewater Creek Road 2243 along a pretty ridge. The PCT also reaches Jefferson Park, climbing to breathtaking viewpoints on Park Butte's 6900-foot ridge; the 5.6-mile route begins at Skyline Road 4220 near Breitenbush Lake. A third, much less used route to Jefferson Park climbs 6.2 miles along the South Breitenbush Trail from Road 4685. Because Jefferson Park's alpine flora is so fragile, backpackers are urged to make low-impact camps in the area's sparsely visited, wooded edges, away from lakes.

Hunts Cove is a similar but much smaller alpine basin on the south side of Mount Jefferson. The two main lakes, Hunts and Hanks lakes, are 6.2 miles up from Road 2248 via Pamelia Lake. Backpackers based at Hunts Cove can climb to the PCT and prowl the interesting crags of Cathedral Rocks.

Duffy, Mowich, and Santiam lakes lie in a plateau of open lodgepole pine forests and wild-flower meadows at the foot of Three Fingered Jack. From Road 2267, a 3.5-mile trail through the dry forest along the North Fork Santiam River will reach Duffy Lake; Mowich Lake, with its large island, is another mile. Santiam Lake is a 5.1-mile walk from Highway 20 at Santiam Pass (or start at Santiam Lodge, and avoid the dusty PCT).

Just 1.8 miles past Mowich Lake is the Eight Lakes Basin, a patchwork of meadows and forest renowned for its wildflowers, pretty lakes, and July mosquitoes. The five nearest trailheads are from 6.8 to 8.6 miles distant; a car shuttle would allow backpackers to see a different trail on the trip out.

Trails on the east side of the wilderness are often sunnier but are much less used because of the longer gravel road access. The Bear Valley Trail from Road 1235 gains 2000 feet on its 5.2-mile route to Rockpile Lake, where there are views and alpine rock gardens. For a 13-mile loop, return from the lake by heading south on the PCT and keeping left past Minto Lake.

Carl Lake, a forest-rimmed rock basin, is 5 miles up the Cabot Creek Trail from Road 1230. Hike 2.1 miles past Carl Lake to reach the sweeping viewpoint atop South Cinder Peak.

Table Lake lies at the center of a fascinating, rarely visited landscape of wildflower-filled mesas, sudden canyons, cinder cones, and lava flows. Backpack to Table Lake via Carl Lake (10 miles from Road 1230), via the long uphill climb of Sugarpine Ridge (10.5 miles from Road 1292), or on the Jefferson Lake Trail, skirting a lava flow (10.1 miles from Road 1292).

Another rewarding, longer backpack is the 20-mile circuit around Three Fingered Jack, following the Pacific Crest Trail from Santiam Pass and returning via Jack and Square lakes; plan to take three days.

For an even greater challenge, try the 36-mile stretch of Pacific Crest Trail south of Breitenbush Lake. After crossing Jefferson Park and skirting halfway around Mount Jefferson, the wide, well-graded PCT follows a high, scenic ridgecrest south 10 miles to Minto Pass, passing lots of viewpoints, but no water. Then the PCT climbs high along the side of Three Fingered Jack before dropping to Santiam Pass—a spectacular three- to six-day hike.

Climbing

Mount Jefferson is the most difficult to scale of Oregon's Cascade peaks, both because of the relentless, 4000- to 6000-foot elevation gains required from base camps and because of the 400-foot summit pinnacle of crumbly lava, a class 4 climb in itself.

A dozen routes ascend as far as the summit pinnacle, with difficulties ranging from I-2 to III-5.2. The three easiest are from Jefferson Park across Whitewater Glacier to the ridge south of that glacier, from Pamelia Lake straight up the mountain's southwest ridge, and from the Pacific Crest Trail above Hunts Lake directly toward the summit.

In the 19th century Mount Jefferson was believed unclimbable. A reputed first ascent in 1888 probably did not reach the summit. When a group led by Salem lawyer Charles E. Robin really did scale the peak in 1899 but found that their photographer had put in his film backward, skeptics drove Robin to climb it again a week later.

Three Fingered Jack, though much lower and easier, was first climbed on Labor Day 1923 by six Bend boys, four of whom had been first to the top of Mount Washington the previous weekend.

A popular, level I-4 route follows a well-defined climbers' trail up the south ridge, passes to the east of a gendarme spire at 7600 feet, and continues 300 feet to a rough, 40-foot recessed wall in the summit block.

The West Face Direct route is a level II-5.6-A1 climb, while a northeast route, above Canyon Creek Meadows, is rated III-5.4. Both cross dangerously rotten rock.

Winter Sports

Santiam Pass typically has enough snow to ski by late November. Starting from the sno-park near Santiam Lodge, a marked trail leads 0.5 miles through the woods to the PCT trailhead. From there, Square Lake is a nice 2.2-mile goal, with views of Three Fingered Jack across the frozen lake. The PCT toward Three Fingered Jack climbs steadily, requiring downhill skiing skills on the return. The 3.6-mile trail from the Santiam Lodge sno-park to Lower Berley Lake crosses pleasant, rolling terrain, and can be combined with the PCT to form a loop.

Map and compass are essential on all wilderness trail routes. Consult the Mount Washington entry for ski tours south from Santiam Pass.

The Maxwell sno-park on Road 080 is the starting point for several marked loops, as well as a level 3-mile tour to Fay Lake (which passes Big Meadows, a large open area good for exploring) and a 2.6-mile climb to Twin Lakes (with Maxwell Butte a goal for the hardy).

When the snow level drops to 4000 feet, the 1-mile road along the shore of Lost Lake is popular with beginners. After December, routes lower in the North Santiam River canyon become skiable. Marion Lake and Pamelia Lake are both dramatic goals. In midwinter, when the access roads are snowed in all the way down to Highway 22, Pamelia Lake is 6 miles away and Marion Lake is 8. By March the snow melts off these access roads and shortens the ski trip to these lakes. Spring brings sunny, shirt-sleeved skiing weather.

MOUNT WASHINGTON

Location: 70 mi E of Eugene, 31 mi W of Bend
Size: 111 sq mi
Status: 82 sq mi designated wilderness (1964, 1984)
Terrain: Lava plains, high forest, peak
Elevation: 2800'–7794'
Management: Deschutes NF, Willamette NF
Topographic maps: Mount Washington, Santiam Pass Winter Recreation (Geo-Graphics); Mount Washington Wilderness, PCT Northern Oregon Portion (USFS)

The Patjens Lakes and Mount Washington

Sometimes called the Black Wilderness because of its 38 square miles of rugged lava flows, the Mount Washington area also features sweeping forests and scores of small lakes. Mountain vistas are everywhere, not only of Mount Washington's craggy spire, but of a half dozen snowpeaks in the adjacent Three Sisters and Mount Jefferson areas.

Climate

Santiam Pass, with an average snowfall of 250 to 700 inches, is plowed throughout winter. Highway 242 over McKenzie Pass is closed from November or December to May or June. Trails are clear of snow from mid-June to mid-October. Summers are warm and dry.

Plants and Wildlife

The barren lava fields support little more than an occasional "bonsai" whitebark pine. But the high plains surrounding the lava are evenly covered by mountain hemlock and true fir on the west and by lodgepole and ponderosa pine on the east. Blacktailed deer wintering in the Old Cascades and mule deer wintering in the Metolius Valley often make Mount Washington their summer range.

Geology

At least 125 eruptive centers have produced cinder cones and basalt lava flows in this area since the Ice Age—an average of one major eruption every century. The most recent flow, 1300 years old, streamed 12 miles from Belknap Crater's flank to divert the McKenzie River south of Koosah Falls.

Clear Lake was formed when a lava flow from a cone south of Sand Mountain succeeded in damming the McKenzie River and drowning a forest. The lake's water is so cold and clear that the branchless forest can still be seen as much as 100 feet below the lake surface, a source of fascination for boaters (no motors permitted) and wet-suited scuba divers. Radiocarbon dating of the wood indicates the lake and lava flow are 3000 years old.

The intensely jumbled, almost uncrossable surface of the area's lava resulted from the cooled crust of molten flows being broken up by lava continuing to flow under-

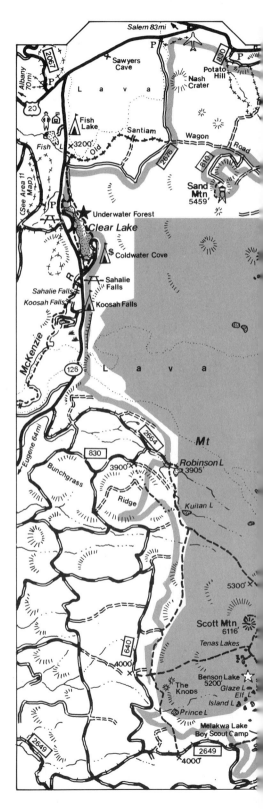

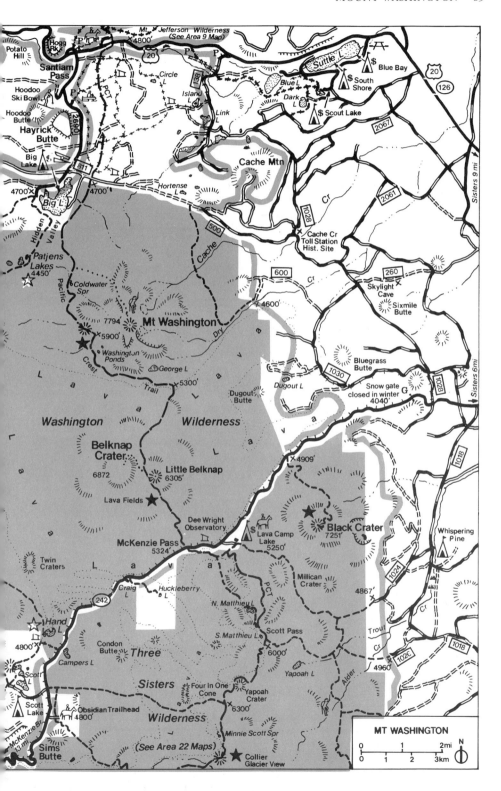

Mt Jefferson Wilderness
(See Area 9 Map)

Potato Hill
Hogg Rk
Santiam Pass
Hoodoo Ski Bowl
Hoodoo Butte
Hayrick Butte
Big Lake
4700'
Big L

Circle L
Island L
Link L

Suttle L
Blue Bay
South Shore
Blue L
Dark L
Scout Lake

Cache Mtn
Hortense L

Hidden Valley
Patjens Lakes 4450'
Coldwater Spr
Pacific
7794
5900'
Mt Washington
Washington Ponds
George L
5300'
Crest
Trail

Cache
500
600
4600'
Dry

Cache Cr Toll Station Hist. Site

Skylight Cave
Sixmile Butte

Bluegrass Butte
1030

Dugout L
Dugout Butte

Snow gate closed in winter 4040'

Washington
Wilderness

Belknap Crater
6872
Little Belknap
6305'
Lava Fields

Lava
L
a
v
a

4909'

1018

Black Crater
7251'

Whispering Pine

Dee Wright Observatory
McKenzie Pass 5324'
Lava Camp Lake 5250'

Twin Craters

Craig L
Huckleberry L

N. Matthieu L

Millican Crater
4867'

1024

242

Hand L
4800'

Condon Butte
Campers L
Three

Scott L
Scott Lake

McKenzie Br 3 mi

Sims Butte

Obsidian Trailhead 4800'

Sisters

Four In One Cone
6300'

Minnie Scott Spr

Wilderness

(See Area 22 Maps)

S. Matthieu L
Scott Pass
6000'

Yapoah L
Yapoah Crater

Trout

PCT

Alder

4960'

1020
1018

Collier Glacier View

Sisters 9 mi
Sisters 6 mi

20
126
2067
2061
1028
260
1028

MT WASHINGTON
0   1   2mi
0   1   2   3km
N

A mile from the snowed-under McKenzie Pass Highway, the Hand Lake shelter makes a good stop for skiers who plan to cross the pass in two days.

neath. Where molten lava flowed out from under an intact crust, lava tubes, such as Sawyer's Cave and Skylight Cave formed. Permanent ice and smooth lava stalactites can be seen in these long caves and in the collapsed lava tubes filling the summit crater of Little Belknap.

Though at least 100,000 years older than Belknap Crater, Mount Washington began as a similarly broad shield volcano. It went on to add a cone as large and symmetrical as any of the Three Sisters, but then was stripped to its central lava plug by glaciation.

History

The Santiam Wagon Road, built in 1866 to allow the grazing of Willamette Valley livestock in central Oregon, can still be traced between Fish Lake and the 1896 Cache Creek Toll Station site.

On a cinder cone along that route, the Sand Mountain fire lookout tower burned in 1968, but was rebuilt in 1990 by volunteers who staff the tower in summers and welcome visitors. A 1.3-mile loop trail passes the tower and tours the cinder cone's rim.

Around 1871, John Craig built a wagon route over McKenzie Pass, arduously chipping and leveling a lava roadbed still visible in the rugged basalt flows around Hand Lake and near Dee Wright Observatory at McKenzie Pass. Craig contracted to carry mail across his wagon road through the winter on skis. In an 1877 storm he froze to death in a cabin at Craig Lake. Since the 1930s, an annual John Templeton Craig ski tour and ski race has carried specially marked mail on the 22-mile route across McKenzie Pass each April.

THINGS TO DO

Hiking

Free, unlimited wilderness entry permits are available at all trailheads, but to park your car you'll need to pick up a *Trail Park permit ($3/day or $25/year) in advance from a ranger station or* *outdoor store.* Since the area lacks running water, campers should plan on purifying lake water.

The most popular day hike is the 0.5-mile walk through wildflower meadows from Highway 242 to the Hand Lake shelter. For a longer hike, continue 1.5 miles to photogenic Scott Lake.

Another very heavily used trail climbs 400 feet in 1.4 miles from the Scott Lake Campground to Benson Lake, a deep, blue jewel partly rimmed by cliffs. One mile past Benson Lake are the similarly scenic and popular Tenas Lakes. Hikers seeking solitude should head for one of the many off-trail lakes in this area. Bring a compass.

The Patjens Lakes, with wildflower meadows and reflections of Mount Washington, are on a 6-mile loop through rolling forest from the end of paved Road 2690 at Big Lake. An equally swimmable, but far less visited lake is Robinson Lake, on an easy 0.3-mile trail from Road 2664.

Day hikers often follow the Pacific Crest Trail south from Lava Camp Lake Campground to South Matthieu Lake, then take the abandoned Skyline Trail back via North Matthieu Lake, a 6-mile loop through both lava and forest.

The lava fields at McKenzie Pass are so impressively rugged that many visitors only hike the paved 0.5-mile Lava River nature trail around the Dee Wright Observatory's basalt-block hut. But the Pacific Crest Trail (PCT) climbs on a very good grade from a nearby trailhead through the heart of the lava's spectacular barrens. The panoramic view atop Little Belknap is 2.6 miles via a short spur trail. From the spur trail, Belknap Crater's three distinct summit craters are an additional 0.7-mile cross-country climb, mostly through forest.

Another good view, atop shield-shaped, forested Scott Mountain, is reachable from seven different trailheads. The best view of the Three Sisters is at Black Crater, on a trail climbing 2400 feet in 4 miles from Highway 242.

The PCT leads to views up and down the Cascades from wildflower meadows on Mount Washington's shoulder. Carry water on this dry, 12.4-mile section of the PCT north from McKenzie Pass to Road 811.

Cross-country hiking, though impractical on lava, is pleasant both through the open forest and along the beachlike cinder strips separating lava flows from forest.

Climbing

Mount Washington's eroded lava plug offers several technical climbs. To take the level I-4 North Ridge route, pioneered by six boys from Bend in 1923, follow the PCT 2 miles south of Road 811. Follow tree blazes cross-country to the mountain's north ridge, then hike up the ridge to a small saddle at the base of the summit pinnacle. West of the saddle 25 feet, ascend a 30-foot chimney, then climb 30 feet upwards and to the left on the rough, rotten rock of the "nose." Atop the nose, a steep hike leads to an additional 20-foot chimney and the summit.

A dozen additional climbing routes increase in difficulty to the foolishly dangerous, level III-5.7 East Face Direct and the west face's level II-5.8 Chimney of Space.

Winter Sports

Santiam Pass is a major nordic skiing center, while McKenzie Pass offers a few longer, more remote trips. See area 9, Mount Jefferson, for routes north of Santiam Pass.

A network of marked cross-country ski trails converges at the Ray Benson sno-park on Big Lake Road 2690. Three shelters make easy goals in the rolling terrain, with mountain views due to clearcuts and a 1967 fire. Nordic routes occasionally cross or parallel marked snowmobile routes. Cross-country ski rentals, lessons, and groomed trails are available for a fee at Hoodoo Ski Bowl nearby.

Another marked nordic route climbs 1000 feet in 3 miles from the Road 830 sno-park to the view atop Potato Hill. A 4-mile loop trail south of Potato Hill requires less of a climb.

The generally unplowed side roads from Highway 126 are skiable, especially Road 2664 to Robinson Lake (4 miles one way), and Road 2649 to Melakwa Lake (10 miles one way).

McKenzie Pass is typically plowed only a week or so past the first snowfall, usually in November. Once the snow gates are closed, tourers must hike and/or ski 7 miles from the east gate and a full 15 miles from the westside gate at White Branch camp. Those prepared for a snow camp will find the 18-mile crossing of McKenzie Pass unparalleled in scenic splendor.

11

OLD CASCADES

Location: 45 mi E of Albany
Size: 74 sq mi
Status: 8 sq mi designated wilderness (1984)
Terrain: Densely forested ridges, ridgetop meadows, rock pinnacles
Elevation: 1230'–5830'
Management: Willamette NF
Topographic maps: Menagerie Wilderness (USFS); Upper Soda, Harter Mountain, Echo
Mountain, Cascadia (USGS); Santiam Pass Winter Recreation (Geo-Graphics)

Six separate roadless areas along Highway 20 remain to show the scale of the wild forests that once blanketed the western foothills of the Cascade Range. Here are broad ridges, subalpine meadows, and views of the High Cascades' snowpeaks, all within an hour's drive of the Willamette Valley.

Climate

The area's 80 annual inches of precipitation come as snow from December through March, and rain in spring and fall. Trails up to 4000 feet are usually clear of snow by May.

Plants and Wildlife

The Old Cascade's remarkable botanic diversity is best seen in early summer on the Echo Mountain–Iron Mountain ridge. A study of this site found sixty plant species that are rare or unusual in the western Cascades, including spectacular penstemon and other wildflowers. Nowhere in Oregon are there more varieties of conifers in such a compact area—seventeen species, from water-loving western red cedar to drought-tolerant juniper and rare alpine Alaska cedar.

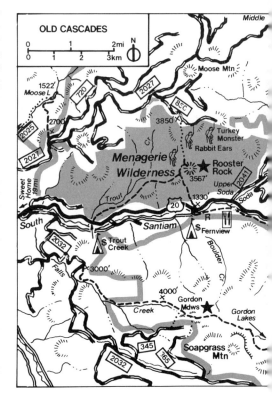

Lower elevation areas of the Old Cascades include pockets of old-growth western hemlock and Douglas fir; higher elevations are dominated by flexible-limbed, snow-resistant Pacific silver fir and noble fir. Stumps in a 1986 clearcut 3 miles south of House Rock Campground indicate the area once held Oregon's oldest trees.

Fishing is banned in Hackleman Creek to protect that stream's unique strain of cutthroat trout.

Geology

The Old Cascades are a chain of volcanoes predating the peaks of the High Cascades by 10 million years. It was the Old Cascades that originally made Eastern Oregon the semiarid area it is today and that filled ancient inland seas with rhyolite ash, preserving the John Day area's famous fossils.

Time and erosion have reduced the Old Cascades' once-tall volcanic cones to a dissected canyonland, studded with the cliffs and pinnacles of resistant lava intrusions. The Menagerie is a collection of two dozen such rock spires, including three natural arches and a 300-foot tower called Turkey Monster.

History

The Santiam band of Kalapuya Indians once had a summer hunting and gathering camp at House Rock. White settlers built the Santiam Wagon Road through the area between Albany and central Oregon in 1861–68. The state purchased the heavily used toll route in 1927. Construction of Highway 20 largely bypassed the old wagon route, now being developed as a hiker/equestrian trail between Fernview Campground and Santiam Pass.

THINGS TO DO

Hiking

All six of the Old Cascades areas have good hiking trails. In the east, the 4-mile Crescent Mountain Trail crosses broad, grassy slopes of alpine wildflowers on its 2000-foot climb to an excellent viewpoint. The first 1.2 miles to Maude Creek make a less strenuous, but also rewarding walk.

Two trails climb through the forests and wildflower meadows near Iron Mountain's dramatic cliffs: the crowded and steep 1.7-mile Iron Mountain Trail from Road 15 near Tombstone Pass, and the quieter, more scenic 3.3-mile Cone Peak Trail from Tombstone Prairie. Iron Mountain's lookout building was blown off the peak by a 1976 winter storm. The Forest Service repaired the structure and returned it by helicopter. It is one of only three remaining lookouts in the Willamette National Forest staffed each summer. An outstanding cross-country hiking route follows the ridge from Cone Peak past Echo Mountain to North Peak.

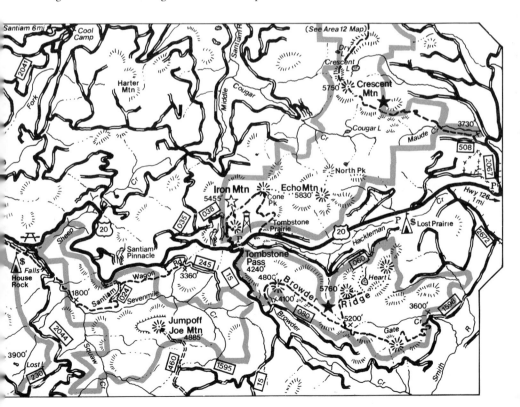

Iron Mountain from the Cone Peak Trail's wildflower meadows

Two trails lead to the fern meadows of Browder Ridge: the 4.5-mile Browder Ridge Trail from Road 080 and the lovely 3.1-mile Gate Creek Trail from Road 1598. Where the routes join, take a faint spur trail 1 mile north and bushwhack up a meadow to the ridge's panoramic high point.

The old Santiam Wagon Road, occasionally overgrown by young hemlock and cedar, is easily hiked and makes an interesting historical route. Old mileposts and signs should be left undisturbed. Find the unmarked Sevenmile Creek segment of the wagon trail by walking along either Road 024, 6 miles east of House Rock Campground via Highway 20, or along Road 245, 3 miles west of Tombstone Pass.

An easier-to-find section of the old wagon route is part of House Rock Campground's marked trail network. Follow the wagon trail 0.6 miles east from the campground to a waterfall on the South Santiam River, or explore the old route west from the campground 1.5 miles to a private property boundary.

The weird rock pinnacles of The Menagerie can be reached by two trails from Highway 20, both of which climb 2200 feet through Douglas fir forests. The 3.3-mile Trout Creek Trail begins near the Trout Creek Campground entrance, while the steep, 2.1-mile Rooster Rock Trail starts near the Fernview Campground entrance. From the viewpoint beside Rooster Rock's spire, a rough climber's path contours onward to Rabbit Ears' twin towers.

The wildflowers of Gordon Meadows are a good hiking goal. The brushy meadows are 4.3 miles through the old-growth forests of the Falls Creek Trail from Road 2032, or 3.6 miles from Road 230, past scenic Gordon Lakes and the cliffs of Soapgrass Mountain.

Moose Lake, snow-free most winters, is particularly pretty in spring, when the moss of Moose Creek's boulder-strewn rapids glows a brilliant green. Reach the steep, 1-mile Moose Lake Trail by turning off Highway 20 onto the Moose Creek Road, 2.5 miles east of Cascadia. Promptly turn right on Road 2027 for 5.5 miles, fork left onto Road 720 for 0.2 mile, and park at a wide spot in the road to find the trailhead.

Climbing

The two dozen spires of The Menagerie provide popular technical climbing challenges. Rooster Rock's old lookout site can be reached with class 5.4 skills; three other routes up that crag range in difficulty to level II-5.8. Nearby are Roosters Tail, Chicken Rock, and Hen Rock, with routes of similar difficulty.

Clustered a mile north of Rooster Rock, but composed of slightly lower-quality rock, are two natural arches (Big Arch is a level II-5.7-A1 climb) and six additional spires, including 265-foot South Rabbit Ear (a III-5.7 climb) and North Rabbit Ear (III-5.7-A2).

A dozen other crags and spires dot the slope above Keith Creek, 0.5 mile east of Rabbit Ears. The first of these is Turkey Monster, unclimbed until 1966. This 300-foot column has level III-5.6-A3 and IV-5.7-A3 routes. Other difficult spires include The Porpoise (I-5.8) and The Bridge (II-5.9).

Elsewhere in the area, the Santiam Pinnacle, above Highway 20, offers four routes of level I-4 to II-5.6 difficulty. And although a trail ascends Iron Mountain's west slope, the 400-foot cliff on the south face is a level I-5.6 climb.

Winter Sports

Plowed Highway 20 provides access to some cross-country ski opportunities on trails and side roads in the Tombstone Pass area. Skiable snow can be expected in January and February. Beginners often practice on Tombstone Prairie. Sno-parks at Lost Prairie and Lava Lake Road 2067 provide a half dozen marked tours and loops.

12

MIDDLE SANTIAM RIVER

Location: 56 mi E of Albany
Size: 40 sq mi (including the Pyramids)
Status: 13 sq mi designated wilderness (1984)
Terrain: Densely forested river valley, rocky peaks
Elevation: 1300'–5618'
Management: Willamette NF
Topographic maps: Middle Santiam Wilderness, Chimney Peak, Coffin Mountain, Echo Mountain, Harter Mountain, Quartzville (USGS); Detroit (Green Trails)

Hidden along the remote headwaters of the Middle Santiam River is one of Oregon's largest low-elevation old-growth forests. Great Douglas firs, western hemlocks, and western red cedars tower above the steep, mist-shrouded valley, where the green-pooled river cascades between mossy banks.

Climate

Though the river's canyon seldom sees snow, access roads and trails cross higher elevations, and are blocked from about December through March. Annual rainfall averages 80 inches; only summers are reliably dry.

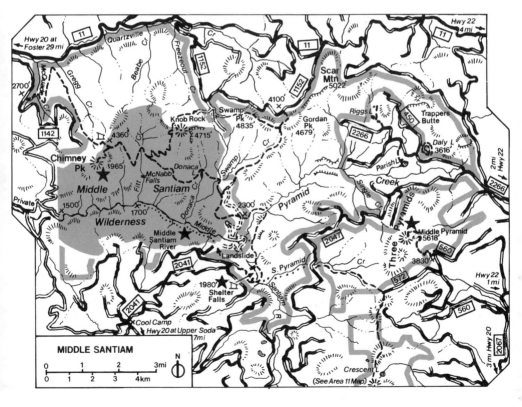

Plants and Wildlife

Pockets of extremely old forest (over 450 years) throughout the area form a spectacular 200-foot-high canopy above a shady world of rhododendrons, lichen-covered snags, and huge rotting logs. Old-growth forests, now rare in Oregon, are the optimum habitat for 137 vertebrate species, including the spotted owl and eighty-five other types of birds.

Fallen old-growth trees across the Middle Santiam River create the river's silt-free, gravel-bottomed pools, the spawning sites of a third of the Santiam drainage's Chinook salmon.

The Pyramids host higher-elevation plant species: wildflowers in subalpine meadows and old-growth noble fir.

Geology

In the east, the Three Pyramids are relatively recent volcanoes associated with the High Cascades. The remainder of the area consists of ancient, heavily eroded Old Cascades volcanics. Chimney Peak is an Old Cascades lava plug. Traces of gold and silver brought prospectors to Quartzville Creek in the 19th century.

Cliffs left by immense landslides extend from Scar Mountain to Knob Rock. One of these ancient slides dammed Donaca Lake. A recent 100-acre slump closed Road 2041 0.5 mile from

The McQuade Creek shelter near Chimney Peak

the Middle Santiam River bridge. The area's steep, unstable clay soils make road construction so expensive that many of the unroaded old-growth forests could only be cut at a net loss.

THINGS TO DO

Hiking

In the east, forest-rimmed Daly, Parish, and Riggs lakes are each at the end of easy 0.5-mile trails suitable for day hikes with children. The trails are reached via Road 2266, which joins Highway 22 about 8 miles north of the Highway 20 junction.

Viewpoints and alpine rock gardens at the summit of Middle Pyramid are the climax of a more challenging 2.1-mile, uphill trail from Road 560. Get there via Lava Lake Road 2067, which meets Highway 22 about 4.8 miles north of the Y junction with Highway 20.

Chimney Peak, site of a former fire lookout, commands views across valley after valley of old-growth forests. The 6.1-mile McQuade Creek Trail leads to the peak, through deep forest and past a well-preserved shelter. The trail ends 100 yards below the summit; the final climb is a tricky scramble requiring caution and both hands. To find the McQuade Creek trailhead, turn north from Highway 20 onto the Quartzville Road 4 miles east of Sweet Home. After 24.7

miles, cross a bridge to a three-way fork. Keep right on Road 11 for 2.6 miles and turn right on Road 1142 for 4 miles.

The best sampler of the Middle Santiam, however, is the 11.4-mile trail from a spur of Road 2041. This path descends 0.8 mile to a log crossing of the Middle Santiam River a few hundred yards upstream from Shedd Camp shelter and a large waterfall pool with a sandy beach. Then the trail contours above the river 2.6 miles, crosses Pyramid Creek, climbs 0.9 mile to an abandoned portion of Road 2041, and continues 2.5 miles to little, blue-green Donaca Lake. Backpackers will be able to camp at the lake and continue 5.5 miles to Chimney Peak, or perhaps take side trails up to Gordan Peak or the viewpoint at Knob Rock.

A cross-country route to the Middle Santiam River begins at the landslide that now ends Road 2041. Adventurers can take a sharp forested ridge from the slide down to the river and follow the river's south bank downstream 3 miles. Flats along the river feature towering Douglas firs, mossy big-leaf maples, and frequent glimpses of Chimney Peak and the Pyramids. West of Fitt Creek the canyon becomes too narrow even for bushwhackers.

To reach the trailheads on Road 2041, drive 25 miles east of Sweet Home on Highway 20, turn left onto Soda Fork Road 2041, and follow this road carefully 8 miles up to a pass at Cool Camp, where five roads meet. Then continue on Road 2041 downhill another 4.5 miles to a hairpin curve. The Chimney Peak Trail (to Donaca Lake) is to the right at the end of spur Road 646.

13

CRABTREE VALLEY

Location: 42 mi E of Albany
Size: 2 sq mi
Status: Proposed outstanding natural area
Terrain: Old-growth forest valley
Elevation: 2850'–4443'
Management: Salem District BLM
Topographic map: Yellowstone Mountain (USGS)

Oregon's oldest trees—perhaps 1000 years old—grow undisturbed in this secluded western Cascades valley.

Climate

Snow typically blocks the roads from December to April. Annual precipitation is 100 inches.

Plants and Wildlife

Crabtree Valley's claim to Oregon's oldest trees remains unproven, since the very largest trunks are too wide for growth rings to be counted by the usual method, drilling out a core sample with an incremental borer. King Tut, a monumental Douglas fir, is a prime suspect for 1000-year honors. The majority of the Douglas fir, western hemlock, and western red cedar forming a canopy across the valley are at least 500 years old.

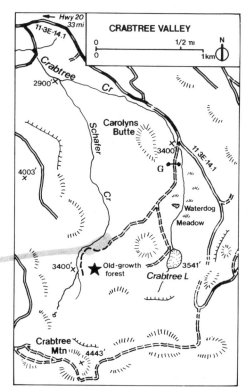

Even before the advent of logging, western Cascades forests rarely lived 200 years before being overswept by fire. But Crabtree Valley's ring of glacier-carved palisades has served as a natural firebreak. The valley was preserved from logging when a 1985 land swap transferred a square mile of private land to the Bureau of Land Management.

THINGS TO DO

Hiking

The valley lends itself to short, cross-country trips. Crabtree Lake, Waterdog Meadow, or cascading Schafer Creek may be the destinations, but the huge old-growth forests on either hand are always the real goal. Fall mushrooms provide another good excuse to roam these grand woods.

To find Crabtree Valley, drive 4 miles east of Sweet Home on Highway 20, turn north at a sign for Quartzville, and drive 20.5 paved miles on what becomes the Quartzville Access Road along Green Peter Reservoir. At this point, watch the odometer carefully; the BLM's road network is not user-friendly. Three miles past the reservoir's end, turn left onto Yellowstone

Trillium

Access Road (11-3E-35.1) for 1.9 miles. Then turn left onto Yellowstone B Road (11-3E-27) for 3 miles, turn right on Road 11-3E-33 for 4.9 miles, turn right onto Road 11-3E-17 for 0.8 mile, turn left onto Kiote Creek Road (11-3E-8) for 1.5 miles, turn right onto K-Line Road (11-3E-14.1) for 1.2 miles, and finally turn right onto Road 11-3E-16.1 for 0.4 mile to a gate and parking area. Crabtree Lake is a 0.7-mile walk beyond.

The BLM Salem District's Santiam Planning Unit Transportation Map, showing the entire maze of logging roads between Lacomb and Crabtree Valley, is a good $1 investment.

14

SADDLE MOUNTAIN

Location: 73 mi NW of Portland, 21 mi W of Seaside
Size: 4 sq mi
Status: State park
Terrain: Meadow-topped mountain
Elevation: 900'–3283'
Management: State Parks and Recreation Department
Topographic map: Saddle Mountain (USGS)

From the summit of this saddle-shaped mountain, highest point in the northern Oregon Coast Range, views sweep from Mount Rainier to the Columbia River and ships far out to sea.

Climate

The area's mossy rain forest results from over 120 inches annual precipitation. Storms briefly cover the peak with snow and ice in midwinter.

Plants and Wildlife

Saddle Mountain features 301 identified species of flora, some of which have chosen this singular, tall peak as their sole Coast Range habitat. Trilliums and pink coast fawn lilies spangle the lower slopes in April and May. Summit wildflower displays peak in mid-June. Patterson's bittercress, a delicate, pink-petaled mustard, is known only on Saddle Mountain and nearby Onion Peak.

Herds of up to seventy elk have been sighted on the peak. The Sitka spruce and western hemlock rain forest about the mountain's base is regrowing from 1920s logging and fires in 1936 and 1939.

Oregon grape

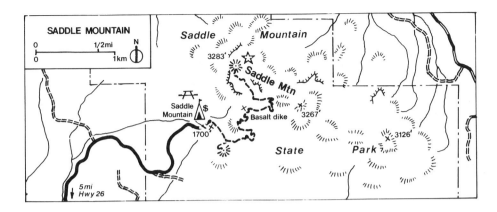

Geology

Saddle Mountain erupted as a sea-floor volcano about 20 million years ago. Lumpy, "pillow basalt" lavas exposed around the mountain are typical of underwater flows, much like the flows forming many Oregon coastal headlands. Later, basalt oozed into cracks in the Saddle Mountain volcano, forming resistant, wall-like dikes. One dike along the summit trail fractured hexagonally due to slow cooling; it now resembles an immense stack of cordwood. The Coast Range has been rising from the sea floor for 35 million years.

THINGS TO DO

Hiking

The exhilarating 3-mile summit trail traverses 0.6 mile through dense forest, then switchbacks up to a cliff-edged saddle before crossing meadows to the taller of the mountain's two peaks, the former site of a fire lookout cabin. Bring binoculars to spot the Olympic Mountains and Astoria's Columbia River Bridge.

The park's paved 7-mile access road turns off Highway 26 near milepost 10, 66 miles from Portland.

Edible pink salmonberry

15

MOUNT HEBO

Location: 20 mi S of Tillamook, 26 mi N of Lincoln City
Size: 24 sq mi
Status: Undesignated wilderness
Terrain: Flat-topped mountain, steep forested flanks, lakes
Elevation: 200'–3176'
Management: Siuslaw NF
Topographic maps: Niagara Creek, Hebo, Blaine, Beaver (USGS)

The mossy forests ringing this broad peak harbor a pair of waterfalls and three lakes, rarities in the Coast Range.

Climate

Over 100 inches of annual precipitation sustain Mount Hebo's rain forest. Snow caps the summit briefly after winter storms.

Plants and Wildlife

Early summer wildflowers, thimbleberry, and bracken fern carpet the summit meadows, home to the rare silverspot butterfly. At lower elevations, Douglas fir, Sitka spruce, and alder dominate a green world of moss, sourgrass, sword fern, and trilliums.

Geology

Mount Hebo's flat top is the remains of a sill, a band of lava squeezed between layers of sea-floor rock 20 million years ago. Subsequent uplifting of the Coast Range made this erosion-resistant basalt a plateau.

History

Tillamook settlers seeking a route to the Willamette Valley used an Indian trail across Mount Hebo from 1854 to 1882. A portion of the route was restored in 1984 as the Pioneer-Indian Trail. Following massive fires in 1853 and 1910, the Forest Service replanted 12 square miles with Douglas fir in 1912, one of the earliest Oregon reforestation projects. A World War II radar installation was removed from the west summit in the 1980s, but a small military reservation remains on the slightly taller east summit, near primitive Mount Hebo Campground.

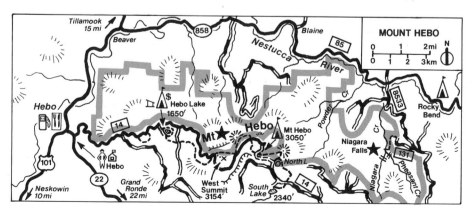

Skunk cabbage blooming at Hebo Lake

THINGS TO DO

Hiking

A 1-mile trail descends from Road 131 to a footbridge at the base of two waterfalls: Niagara Creek's 100-foot plunge and neighboring Pheasant Creek's 80-foot fan.

An even easier, all-accessible path loops 0.5 mile around Hebo Lake from the Hebo Lake Campground, just off Road 14. The campground itself is closed to cars from November to mid-April.

For a more substantial hike, try the 8-mile Pioneer-Indian Trail. Starting at Hebo Lake, this route climbs 1200 feet in 2.9 miles to a crossing of paved Road 14. At this point an unofficial side trail to the right climbs steeply 0.2 mile to a panoramic view atop Mount Hebo's west summit. The main trail contours 2.4 miles through meadows to a junction near Mount Hebo Campground, switchbacks 1 mile down to brush-lined North Lake, and ambles 1.7 miles to a campsite at South Lake.

The Hebo Plantation Trail, a 0.7-mile loop from Road 14 west of Hebo Lake, was built by the Civilian Conservation Corps in the 1930s to showcase reforestation methods.

16

CASCADE HEAD

Location: 7 mi N of Lincoln City, 56 mi W of Salem
Size: 10 sq mi
Status: Scenic-research area; islands are designated wilderness
Terrain: Clifftop meadows, rain forest
Elevation: 0'–1783'
Management: The Nature Conservancy, Siuslaw NF
Topographic map: Neskowin (USGS)

Surf-pounded cliffs surround the wildflower meadows on Cascade Head's steep headland. Craggy islands crowded with birds dot the sea. On either hand, 20 miles of beaches and headlands diminish into blue silhouettes. Yet just behind the meadows lie dark green rain forests of dense salal and Sitka spruce, where it is easy to imagine oneself far from the ocean.

Climate

Rain falls at Cascade Head on more than 180 days per year. Cool fog shrouds the headland most of the summer, particularly when temperatures in the Willamette Valley are high. Fog drip brings the annual precipitation to over 100 inches in the forests, although rainfall only totals 69 inches on the beach. Winters are snowless; fall and spring have the most clear days.

Plants and Wildlife

The area's many offshore crags, roosting sites for a multitude of sea birds, are part of the Oregon Islands Wilderness (see area 40, Oregon Islands). Sea lions are usually lounging on the inaccessible beaches below the cliffs of Harts Cove. Cascade Head is also an ideal lookout from which to spot the spouts of migrating gray whales from December to May. Cascade Head's meadow is one of only three locations worldwide that supports a stable population of the threatened, orange-and-brown mottled, Oregon silverspot butterfly.

The headland meadows are filled with summer asters and Indian paintbrush reminiscent of an alpine environment. Several species of these wildflowers grow only in the windswept meadows of coastal headlands. Wind has sculpted the oceanfront Sitka spruce into a waist-high mat, but only a short distance inland, Sitka spruce grow as much as 7 feet thick and 240 feet tall. The mossy western hemlock and Sitka spruce rain forest has one of the fastest growth rates and one of the highest biomass-per-acre ratios of any area in the world. At its densest, the forest has 24 square meters of leaf surface for every square meter of sunlight.

The Cascade Head Experimental Forest, a research facility overseeing National Forest land on the headland, pioneered Northwest forestry's clearcutting and herbicide-spraying techniques.

Geology

The rocks here formed on the sea floor about 50 million years ago when sand and mud became interlayered with submarine basalt lava flows. As the Coast Range rose from the sea, areas with exposed mudstone and soft sandstone quickly eroded to create low beaches; Cascade Head's much more resistant basalt, however, remained as a headland.

THINGS TO DO

Hiking

The most popular trail is the 2-mile Nature Conservancy path from Three Rocks Road to Cascade Head. After 0.5 mile through a lush forest of sword ferns, salmonberry (edible orange berries in June), and red alder, the route breaks out into steep meadows with breathtaking views across the Salmon River estuary and offshore islands. The fragile flora of the headland's low, final bluff is protected by a fence; do not leave the main trail at any point. The Nature Conservancy purchased the headland's tip in 1967. Dogs are banned, and the upper part of the trail is closed January 1 to July 15 to protect the threatened silverspot butterfly.

To reach this beautiful but overused trail, drive 1 mile north on Highway 101 from the junction with Highway 18. Turn left on Three Rocks Road for 2.2 miles and turn right on Savage Road for 0.5 mile.

A less-used upper trailhead, accessing both this trail and the Harts Cove trail, is open from July 16 to December 31 each year. To find it, drive 4 miles south of the Highway 18 junction on Highway 101. At the crest of a hill, turn left on Road 1861 for 3.3 miles.

Harts Cove is a cliff-rimmed bay where the crashing of the surf competes with the barks of sea lions, the cries of sea gulls, and the rush of Chitwood Creek's waterfall. The 2.6-mile downhill trail to the meadow overlooking the cove is far less used than the better-known Cascade Head trails. After wet weather, these paths can be too muddy for tennis shoes.

Except on Cascade Head's meadow, cross-country hiking is generally impractical because of dense salal bushes, a plant whose tough-skinned, dark blue berries were used by pioneers for preserves. Seaside cliffs prevent all access to the headland's few rocky beaches.

For a woodsy hike away from the roar of the sea, try the "other" Cascade Head Trail (not shown on map) that crosses this headland a few miles inland, through dense forest. This new trail starts at the junction of Three Rocks Road and Highway 101, climbs 1000 feet in 3.5 miles to a crossing of Road 1861, and descends 2.5 miles to Highway 101, 2 miles south of Neskowin.

Mouth of the Salmon River from Cascade Head

17

DRIFT CREEK

Location: 12 mi E of Waldport, 57 mi W of Corvallis
Size: 18 sq mi
Status: 9 sq mi designated wilderness (1984)
Terrain: Steep valleys, rain forest
Elevation: 80'–2100'
Management: Siuslaw NF
Topographic maps: Tidewater, Hellion Rapids (USGS)

Drift Creek features the Coast Range's largest remaining stands of old-growth rain forest. The rock-strewn creek's steep-sided canyon gives the area a mountainous feel, although it is actually close to tidewater.

Climate

Temperatures are mild year round. Heavy rainfall can be expected from fall through spring (74 inches annually in the west, 120 inches at Table Mountain). Winter snow is rare even at high elevations.

Plants and Wildlife

Sitka spruce and western hemlock trees grow 7 feet thick many places in the area, particularly along the northern portion of the Horse Creek Trail. Creekbanks are overhung with bigleaf maple trees, their spreading branches cushioned by a 6-inch-deep layer of moss and licorice ferns.

In summer look for edible berries in the rain forest undergrowth: orange salmonberry, red thimbleberry, blue and red huckleberry, and dark blue salal. Sour grass, or oxalis, is edible in small quantities and tart as a lemon. Its shamrock-shaped leaves often carpet the forest floor. Swampy areas brighten in April with the huge yellow spathes of skunk cabbage. Disturbed hillsides sprout 6-foot-tall spires of red and white foxglove throughout summer.

Several pairs of northern spotted owls and bald eagles, both endangered in Oregon, nest in the old-growth forest. It is not uncommon to find evidence of Roosevelt elk or black bear.

Though Drift Creek is not ranked as a river, it supports river-sized runs of native fish. Chinook salmon, coho salmon, steelhead, and cutthroat trout return each fall, while a much smaller Chinook run comes in spring. Hatchery fish have never been stocked.

Geology

This area's crumbly sandstone and siltstone weather to slippery clay, making roads and trails susceptible to landslides. The rock began as oceanic deposits of mud and sand; the rise of the Coast Range lifted this section of sea floor from the waves.

History

Drift Creek was once the hunting and gathering grounds of the Waldport Bay–based Alsea Indians. Some meadows show the attempts of failed, pre-World War II homesteads.

THINGS TO DO

Hiking

Three paths descend through forest to the shady, green banks of Drift Creek. The trails can be connected by wading 20-foot-wide Drift Creek in summer or fall, when it is only knee-deep.

The southern part of the Horse Creek Trail loses over 1200 feet on its 2-mile route to the creek. The Harris Ranch Trail drops 1000 feet in 2 miles to a large, campable creekside meadow. A path along the creek, requiring two fords, makes a pleasant 5.5-mile trip for those who can shuttle cars between the southern Horse Creek and Harris Ranch trailheads.

The third route to Drift Creek, the 3-mile-long northern portion of the Horse Creek Trail, traverses spectacular old-growth forest. Hikers starting on this trail usually return the way they came, since a car shuttle to the southern end of the Horse Creek Trail requires a 23-mile drive on gravel roads over Table Mountain. Good campsites are on either side of Drift Creek at the Horse Creek Trail crossing.

An angler's trail scrambles along the north bank of Drift Creek from the Horse Creek Trail, crossing as far as a campable site across from the mouth of Boulder Creek. Bushwhacking along other creeks and ridges is just difficult enough to ensure solitude.

Drift Creek

Reach the northern Horse Creek trailhead from Highway 101 by turning inland on North Beaver Creek Road at Ona Beach State Park, just north of Seal Rock. After 3.8 miles, turn right onto North Elkhorn Road 51. After 6 more miles, turn left on Road 50 for 1.3 miles, then turn right onto Road 5087 for 3.4 miles to the marked trailhead.

For the southern trailheads, drive 7.4 miles east of Waldport on Highway 34 and turn left on Risley Creek Road 3446.

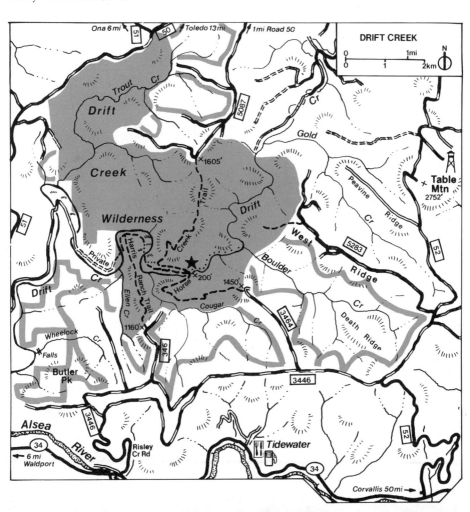

18

CUMMINS CREEK AND ROCK CREEK

Location: 15 mi N of Florence
Size: 26 sq mi
Status: Designated wilderness (1984)
Terrain: Steep valleys, coastal rain forest
Elevation: 0'–2300'
Management: Siuslaw NF
Topographic maps: Yachats, Heceta Head, Cummins Peak, Cannibal Mountain (USGS)

A stone shelter from the 1930s overlooks Cape Perpetua's rugged coastline.

On this wild stretch of coast, pristine rain forest canyons pour half a dozen clear creeks between the cliff-tipped headlands of 2000-foot-tall ridges. Here, hikers can prowl an old-growth forest, study tide pools, or picnic on a secluded beach.

Climate

Rainfall varies from 80 inches annually on the beach to over 100 inches in the interior. Cool fogs line the coast and fill the valleys most of summer. Winters are snowless; fall and spring have the most clear days.

Plants and Wildlife

The ridge between Rock Creek and Big Creek is one of only three locations worldwide to support a stable population of the threatened, mottled orange-and-brown Oregon silverspot butterfly. Cape Perpetua is a popular lookout from which to spot the spouts of migrating gray whales from December to May. Low tides expose sea urchins, sea anemones, and other marine tide-pool life on the rocky coastline between the Devils Churn and Captain Cook Point.

Sitka spruce as large as 9 feet in diameter dominate the valley slopes within 2 miles of the ocean. Farther inland the forest gradually shifts to old-growth Douglas fir. Undergrowth of rhododendron (blooms in May), salal, sword fern, and salmonberry is so dense that even shade-tolerant western hemlock seedlings often must sprout atop rotting old-growth "nursery logs" to survive. Creeks are generally overhung with red alder and mossy bigleaf maple. Wildflowers include yellow monkey flower, purple aster, white candy flower, and the tall red spires of foxglove. Wild lily of the valley carpets the forest with heart-shaped leaves.

The area supports larger native runs of salmon, steelhead, and cutthroat trout than any other similar-sized watershed in Oregon. A fish count in late June 1979 found an average of fifty coho salmon per 100 feet on the lower 2 miles of Cummins Creek.

Geology

The area's basalt bedrock began as undersea lava flows. As upfaulting lifted the Coast Range from the ocean, creeks eroded the face of the fault block into steep, shallow-soiled canyons. Small oceanfront fractures have been widened by wave action into slot-shaped spouting horns and the Devils Churn.

History

Excavation of middens (shell piles) near the cape's tide pools show that humans have camped here to gather mussels for 6000 years—a tradition carried on by the Alsea tribe until the 1870s.

Explorer Captain Cook, sailing against stormy seas near here on March 11, 1778, complained that the same cape had been in sight to the north for five days. He named the perpetual landmark Cape Perpetua, in part because March 11 is St. Perpetua's holy day.

THINGS TO DO

Hiking

Five trails suitable for day hikes originate at the Cape Perpetua Visitor Center. The most heavily used of these are paved, and several are equipped with interpretive signs. An 0.8-mile loop visits tide pools, shell middens, and Cook Chasm's spouting horn (an optional 0.8-mile loop continues to the Devils Churn). A 1.5-mile trail climbs 700 feet to a viewpoint at a 1938 stone shelter atop Cape Perpetua. A 1-mile trail follows the south bank of Cape Creek, past the Perpetua Campground, to a giant spruce tree. A more ambitious 5.5-mile loop follows the Oregon Coast Trail south from the Visitor Center, utilizing a pioneer wagon road, ascends quiet Gwynn Creek's valley, and returns along a ridge with ocean views.

A lovely, unofficial trail along Cummins Creek emerges at intervals from lush, valley-bottom rain forest to pass creekside gravel bars ideal for picnics. To start, turn off Highway 101 immediately north of Neptune State Park at a sign reading, "Cummins Creek Trailhead ¼ mile." The trailhead is a barricade blocking Road 1030. Hike up the abandoned road 250 yards and take an unmarked spur to the right; after another 250 yards this path splits again, with the right fork soon ending at the creek and the left fork leading 0.6 mile upstream before petering out at a

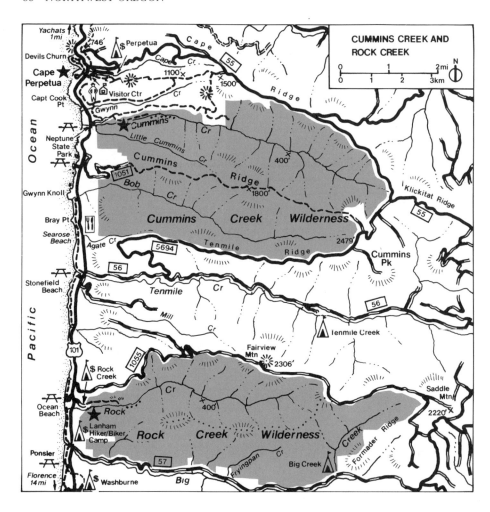

creek crossing. To hike the official Cummins Creek Trail (and to make a loop), walk up abandoned Road 1030 through deep forest for 2.3 miles. Then turn left on a 1-mile trail that climbs past several viewpoints to a ridgetop junction. Head left 3.6 miles on the Gwynn Creek Trail and finally turn left on a 0.3-mile connector trail back to your car.

A 6.2-mile trail exploring the old-growth Sitka spruce forest on Cummins Ridge begins at the barricaded end of Road 1051. Hike the abandoned road 3.5 miles along the ridgetop and continue on a newly built ridgecrest trail to Road 515, a short spur of Road 5690.

Hikers heading up Rock Creek start at the far end of the Rock Creek Campground and walk east along a 0.5-mile trail to a meadow that was once the site of a homestead. Here the impromptu trail becomes a bushwhacking route. To continue, walk up the middle of the chilly (average 56°F) creek in tennis shoes.

A 5-mile-long elk trail traces the Rock Creek–Big Creek Divide from a saddle on Road 1055. Ridgetop meadows allow views of the valley forests on either hand.

The Oregon Coast Trail is being developed along the length of this shore. In the south, a 4-mile loop from Washburne Campground follows China Creek to a meadow, crosses Highway 101 as the Hobbit Trail, and returns along the beach. In the north, a planned 1.7-mile section of trail will extend from Cape Perpetua down toward Yachats.

19

LOWER DESCHUTES RIVER

Location: 14 mi E of The Dalles
Size: 38 sq mi
Status: Federal wild and scenic river
Terrain: Rimrock-lined river canyon
Elevation: 150'–2500'
Management: Prineville District BLM, Oregon Parks and Recreation Department
Topographic maps: Wishram, Emerson, Locust Grove, Erskine, Summit Ridge, Sinamox, Sherars Bridge, Maupin (USGS)

Roaring whitewater and cliff-rimmed canyons highlight the final 51 miles of the Deschutes River, popular for two-day float trips.

Climate

With just 10 inches of annual precipitation, the area boasts reliable sunshine. Summers are hot, but frost is common at night and throughout winter.

Plants and Wildlife

Sagebrush dominates this canyonland. Mule deer, coyotes, and rattlesnakes are common. The river's famous steelhead include a native Deschutes strain (6 to 8 pounds), which swim up the river from June to September, and a Clearwater River strain (up to 22 pounds), which visit the cool Deschutes seeking respite from the warmer Columbia River on their way to spawning grounds in Idaho.

Geology

The canyon walls are layered with 25- to 100-foot-thick lava flows belonging to the 13- to 16-million-year-old Columbia River basalts.

History

Warm Springs Indians maintain a centuries-old tradition by dipnetting migrating salmon each spring and fall from rickety wooden platforms overhanging 15-foot Sherars Falls. Explorer Peter Skene Ogden lost five horses through an Indian bridge at the falls in 1826. A toll bridge built there in 1860 connected The Dalles with the rich Canyon City gold fields in central Oregon. The old county bridge at Freebridge was apparently dynamited in 1912 by competing toll-bridge owners.

Although an 1855 Army engineering survey reported that a railroad grade was impossible along the lower Deschutes, rivalry between railroad magnates James Hill and Edward Harriman resulted in *two* rail lines being built up the "impossible" canyon to Bend in 1909–1911. Hill's Oregon Trunk Railway remains on the west bank; track has been removed from the east-bank grade, now a bike path.

THINGS TO DO

Hiking

The best trails start at Deschutes River State Park. For a 4.2-mile loop, hike the riverbank path to Moody Rapids, climb to a viewpoint at Ferry Springs, and return on a portion of a historic wagon road. The old railroad grade, converted to a mountain bike path, leads 12 miles from the park to Harris Canyon, and continues as an undeveloped route to Macks Canyon Campground. Backpacking campsites are plentiful along the river, but stays are limited to four nights, campfires are all but prohibited, and private land can block access, especially south of

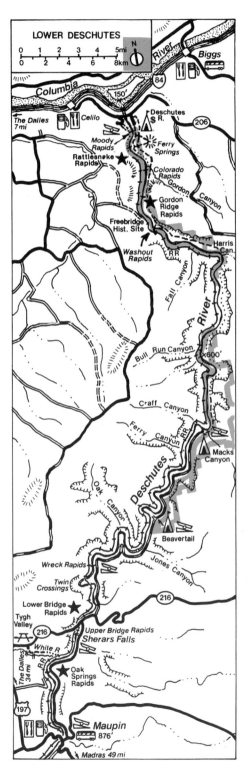

LOWER DESCHUTES

0 1 2 3 4 5mi
0   2   4   6   8km

N

Freebridge (on the west bank) and Harris Canyon (on the east). Anglers are urged to use barbless hooks and to release all native fish.

An easy 0.3-mile trail from the Tygh Valley picnic area on Highway 216 visits three colossal White River waterfalls; a bushwhacking route continues downstream 2.2 miles (beware of poison oak) to the Deschutes.

Boating

The popular 51-mile drift trip from Maupin to the Columbia River encounters three thrilling class 4 rapids, dozens of lesser riffles, and one impassable falls.

Four miles below the Maupin City Park boat ramp, class 4 Oak Springs Rapids splits the river into three channels; stop to look it over, then avoid the right-hand channel. After another 3.5 miles, all craft *must* portage around unnavigable Sherars Falls. Just 150

yards beyond the portage, boaters are faced with class 3 Upper Bridge Rapids and, in another 0.2 mile, the dangerous Lower Bridge Rapids. Scout this class 4+ whitewater from the right bank, then paddle hard to stay in the smaller, right-hand channel.

Downriver 3.6 miles, class 3 Wreck Rapids introduce a 34-mile stretch of calmer water with a steady 5-mile-per-hour current, past some of the canyon's most spectacular basalt rimrock.

The pace picks up for the river's final 6 miles. First comes Gordon Ridge Rapids, a long, class 2+ ride with outcroppings of columnar basalt in midriver. Scouting is required. A mile and a half downstream comes class 3 Colorado Rapids, with a treacherous standing wave and suckhole on the left-hand side. Class 4 Rattlesnake Rapids are only 1.2 miles farther. Three drownings testify to the danger of this narrows, where boaters must thread their way between rocks on the river's left side and a gigantic suckhole in the river's middle. Two miles farther on, the class 2 Moody Rapids delivers boaters to the backwater of The Dalles Dam.

All boaters must carry a Deschutes River boater pass, available at local sporting goods stores. Fishing is prohibited from any floating device in the river. Campfires are permitted only in fire pans, and only from October 16 to May 31. Campsites between Macks Canyon and Deschutes River State Park Campground have a four-night stay limit; maximum group size is sixteen. No camping is allowed on islands. Boaters can recognize the beginning of private, off-limits shorefront by watching for posts marked with circles; posts with triangles signal the return to public lands.

Lower Deschutes float trips are often coupled with the two-day, 45-mile drift of the central Deschutes River, from the Highway 26 bridge near Warm Springs to the boat landing at Maupin. Jet boats and motors are banned on the portion of the river bordering the Warm Springs Indian Reservation and are restricted elsewhere.

The Deschutes River curves past Gordon Canyon, between Colorado Rapids and Rattlesnake Rapids.

20

DESCHUTES CANYON

Location: 32 mi N of Bend
Size: 29 sq mi
Status: Undesignated wilderness
Terrain: Cliff-lined canyons, desert plateaus
Elevation: 1945'–2950'
Management: Crooked River National Grassland, Prineville District BLM
Topographic maps: Central Oregon (BLM); Steelhead Falls, Squaw Back Ridge, Round Butte Dam (USGS)

The Deschutes River roars through this seldom visited, 700-foot-deep canyon, beneath sagebrush mesas with views of the High Cascade snowpeaks.

Climate

Sunshine is the rule in this steppe, which gets less than 10 inches of annual rainfall. Summers are hot, but frost is common at night and in winter.

Plants and Wildlife

Heavy grazing on the tablelands has converted a historic grassland to sagebrush, cheatgrass, and tumbleweed. The steep canyons and The Island north of Cove Palisades Park, however, preserve native bunchgrasses. The river itself creates a narrow oasis dotted with ponderosa pine and vine maple. Coyote and mule deer abound.

Geology

The canyon's layer cake–style cliffs consist of 13- to 16-million-year-old Columbia River basalt lava flows. These lavas erupted from fissures near Hells Canyon, burying most of northern Oregon and eastern Washington, in places 5000 feet deep. Slow cooling allowed the basalt to fracture into a distinctive pattern of hexagonal pillars. The slopes between cliff layers, sometimes eroded into multicolored pinnacles, are composed of volcanic ash, gravel, and soil that accumulated between the devastating basalt floods, which were often 100,000 years apart.

Deschutes Canyon with the Three Sisters on the horizon

The Deschutes Arm of Lake Billy Chinook

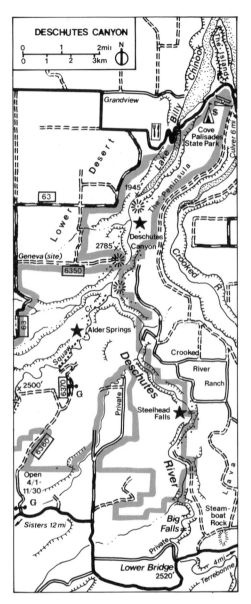

THINGS TO DO

Hiking

Cross-country hiking is easy; views are best along the rims of the open tablelands. Hardy hikers will find the rimrock broken in many places, allowing steep hiking on deer trails into the canyon itself. The canyon bottom is more easily reached by boat at the head of the Lake Billy Chinook reservoir.

To the south, massive Steelhead Falls is a 0.5-mile hike from poorly marked dirt roads. Roads in the extensive Crooked River Ranch subdivision north and east of Steelhead Falls are open to public use.

To the southwest, dirt Roads 6360 and 6370 descend to Squaw Creek, a linear oasis of quaking aspen and wildflowers in a cliff-rimmed canyon. A rewarding 2.4-mile walk from Road 6370 follows Squaw Creek to the hidden natural amphitheater at Alder Springs, walled with striped cliffs. For this hike, turn off Road 6360 to the gate announcing the private Alder Springs Ranch. Park here and walk 1.4 miles farther down the road to Squaw Creek. This county road is open to the public. Be careful to avoid a private spur road to the right at a large juniper tree. Cross the creek on stepping-stones, climb up through a break in the rimrock on the far side, and hike cross-country downstream 1 mile to Alder Springs. (Stay on the *north* side of the creek to avoid private land.) The remote canyon abyss where Squaw Creek and the Deschutes River join lies a difficult 1.5-mile scramble downstream. While Squaw Creek can be forded nearly everywhere, the raging Deschutes River is nowhere crossable.

Another cross-country hiking option is to drive Road 6360 to its ford of Squaw Creek and to hike 2.5 miles upstream to the end of public land. This canyon route requires some wading but features petroglyphs (don't touch!) and caves.

To find Road 6360, turn north off the Sisters-Redmond highway onto Goodrich Road (4.5 miles from Sisters), follow this paved route 8 miles, and turn left beside a hayfield onto marked Road 6360. To protect Roads 6360 and 6370 from tire damage, they're closed by gates during the wetter winter months, December 1 to March 31.

To explore The Island's otherworldly, 2.4-mile-long plateau, park at the Crooker River Petroglyph pullout at a pass in Cove Palisades Park, cross the road to the park's dump, and take an unmarked path to the right.

Boating

Big Falls and Steelhead Falls stop all whitewater boating on the Deschutes. Kayaks carried to the base of Steelhead Falls face 7.5 miles of apparently runnable rapids.

21

METOLIUS BREAKS

Location: 45 mi N of Bend, 32 mi W of Madras
Size: 17 sq mi
Status: Undesignated wilderness
Terrain: Steep, forested river canyon
Elevation: 2000'–5050'
Management: Deschutes NF
Topographic maps: Whitewater River (Green Trails); Shitike Butte, Prairie Farm, Fly Creek (USGS)

The Metolius is the most magical of all Oregon rivers. From the arid base of Black Butte it springs fully grown, at an identical temperature and volume year round, then slides swiftly through 29 miles of rugged canyons before vanishing into the backwaters of the Lake Billy Chinook reservoir. The Metolius Breaks are the wilderness canyon slopes of the remote lower river.

Climate

Though mostly sunny and dry (20 inches annual precipitation), the area receives snow from about December to February. Snow lingers on Green Ridge till April.

Plants and Wildlife

Orange-trunked ponderosa pine and autumn-red vine maple flank the river. Bitterbrush and rabbit brush (bright yellow blooms in fall) form a sparse ground cover. On the eastern ridges, gnarled juniper are the only trees.

The river's name comes from the Warm Springs Indian *Mpto-ly-as,* white fish. The light-fleshed salmon which prompted this name are gone; however, introduced Kokanee salmon and abundant hatchery trout attract eagles, bears, and other anglers.

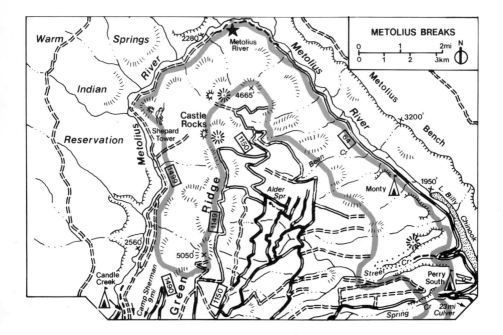

The Metolius River from the river trail

Geology

Green Ridge, a 16-mile-long, 2500-foot-tall fault scarp, gave rise to Black Butte's volcanic cone on the south and displaced the Metolius River to the north. Later Columbia River basalt flows created the adjacent Metolius Bench tablelands, with their dramatic rimrock.

THINGS TO DO

Hiking

A 1.5-mile trail in the heart of the area traverses a dense forest along the rushing Metolius River. The trail's eastern terminus is the end of Road 64, reached by driving west from Madras

through Cove Palisades State Park and Grandview. If you're coming from Sisters, drive 5 miles west on Highway 20, turn north onto Road 11 for 18 miles, turn right onto Road 1170 for 5 miles, and then take Road 64 to the left for 12 miles. The western trailhead can only be reached by high-clearance vehicles. To find it, take Highway 20 east of Santiam Pass 10 miles, go north on paved Road 14 for 13 miles to Lower Bridge Campground, then continue north on badly rutted dirt Road 1499 for 10 miles to its end.

Excellent views of Mount Jefferson and the craggy Castle Rocks await cross-country hikers willing to scale the persistent slopes of Green Ridge. The open forest presents no obstacle.

A nice hike in the east of the area follows an unmarked 0.5-mile-long trail up Street Creek. To find Street Creek, drive 2 miles past Perry South Campground on Road 64 to a sign reading, "Monty Campground 3 miles." From here the trail follows the creek's north bank. At trail's end, adventurous hikers can bushwhack another 1.5 miles upstream past ash formations and a cave, hike north up a side canyon, and walk east along the rimrock's edge to a viewpoint.

The Metolius River forms the southern boundary of the Warm Springs Indian Reservation. Entry to tribal lands is completely prohibited here.

Climbing

Shepard Tower of the Metolius, 0.5 mile uphill from Road 1499 (14.5 miles north of Camp Sherman) offers four routes via chimneys and ledges. Difficulty levels are I-3 to I-5.4.

Boating

Clear, deep, and cold (46°F year round), the Metolius races along at between 5 and 10 miles per hour, providing plenty of white-water thrills. In 26 miles of free-flowing water between Riverside Campground (1.5 miles south of Camp Sherman) and Lake Billy Chinook, the only unnavigable hazard is Wizard Falls, 6.5 miles from the start. A bridge immediately before the falls signals the portage. The last bridge across the river, Lower Bridge, is at river mile 9. The Confederated Tribes of Warm Springs discourage boating beyond this point because the river borders the reservation here; to avoid trespassing, do not land on the left bank. Those who continue usually take out at Monty Campground, since the next public boat landing (at Perry South Campground) requires a 3.5-mile paddle across the reservoir.

22

SMITH ROCK

Location: 8 mi N of Redmond
Size: 1 sq mi
Status: State park
Terrain: River peninsula with rock formations
Elevation: 2620'–3500'
Management: Oregon State Parks and Recreation Department
Topographic maps: Redmond, Opal City, O'Neil, Gray Butte (USGS)

The orange rock walls and pinnacles of Smith Rock tower above an oasislike river bend at the edge of central Oregon's sagebrush plains. The spectacular formation is both a reliably rainless hiking destination and the best technical rock climbing site in Oregon.

Climate

With just 8.5 inches of annual precipitation, Smith Rock is usually sunny even when the trails of the High Cascades are beset with rain or snow. Midwinter brings a few dustings of snow, and midsummer brings blazing heat.

Plants and Wildlife

Visit in spring for high-desert wildflowers. Admire but do not pick the riverbank's wild asparagus and wild onions. Climbers should take pains not to disturb birds of prey nesting on the crags.

Geology

The western vanguard of the Ochoco Mountains, Smith Rock is formed of welded rhyolite ash. This ash erupted from the Old Cascades, settled in a large inland sea, and fused to form rock by heat and pressure. More-recent lava flows pushed the Crooked River up against Smith Rock and left the plains and basalt rimrock of the river's south shore.

THINGS TO DO

Hiking

Start by hiking from the picnic area 0.5 mile down a service road to a footbridge across the Crooked River. Here hikers have several options. For an easy walk, turn left on the popular 2.8-mile riverbank trail. This route meanders below orange cliffs, with side trails leading up to Asterisk Pass and (at the 2.1-mile mark) to Monkey Face, a 350-foot rock monolith topped by a remarkable natural sculpture of a monkey's head. The tower's base offers a good view of the rock climbers usually found there, but also yields a view across central Oregon to the Cascade snowpeaks.

For a tougher 5.3-mile loop from the Crooked River footbridge, turn right and climb four steep flights of stairs up Misery Ridge. Here the path grows faint, but contour to the right past an overlook of Monkey Face, follow the ridgecrest 1.5 miles to Burma Road, and turn right on a trail back down to the river.

To reach the park, turn east off Highway 97 at Terrebonne, 6 miles north of Redmond, and follow state park signs 3 miles, past Juniper Junction, a shop known for its refreshing huckleberry ice cream.

Climbing

With more than 3 miles of rock faces and nearly 1000 named routes, Smith Rock ranks first among Oregon's technical climbing sites, with routes up to level IV-5.12. Good weather and easy access add to the area's popularity.

Tall as a thirty-story building, Monkey Face is Smith Rock's most famous climbing challenge.

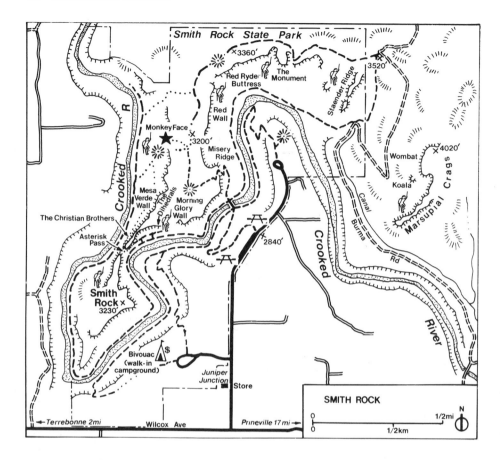

Heavy use, however, has necessitated several rules. Stay on established trails as much possible. Camouflage permanent anchors. Camp only in the designated bivouac area. Campfires are prohibited.

Large climbing classes and search-and-rescue practice groups should strive to minimize their impact by climbing in beginner areas. The 30-foot basalt rimrock cliffs on the opposite shore of the river from The Monument are easily accessible and offer technical pitches. Beginners intent on trying rhyolite will find a good practice boulder (named "Rope de Dope") on the riverbank opposite Morning Glory Wall.

The area's most spectacular challenge is Monkey Face, a 350-foot tower overhanging on all sides, first climbed on January 1, 1960. There are 27 routes and variations, including the level II-5.11 Monkey Space route behind the monkey's head, and the level II-5.7-A1 Pioneer Route past Panic Point, on the monkey's Mouth Cave.

Other major climbing areas include Picnic Lunch Wall (twenty-four routes), Morning Glory Wall (fifty-six routes), The Dihedrals (fifty-two routes), The Christian Brothers (forty-three routes), Smith Rock promontory (forty-three routes), Mesa Verde Wall (twenty-three routes), Red Wall (twenty-six routes), Red Ryder Buttress (six routes), Staender Ridge (six routes), and Marsupial Crags (thirty-one routes).

Opposite: *Broken Top from the Green Lakes*

SOUTHWEST OREGON

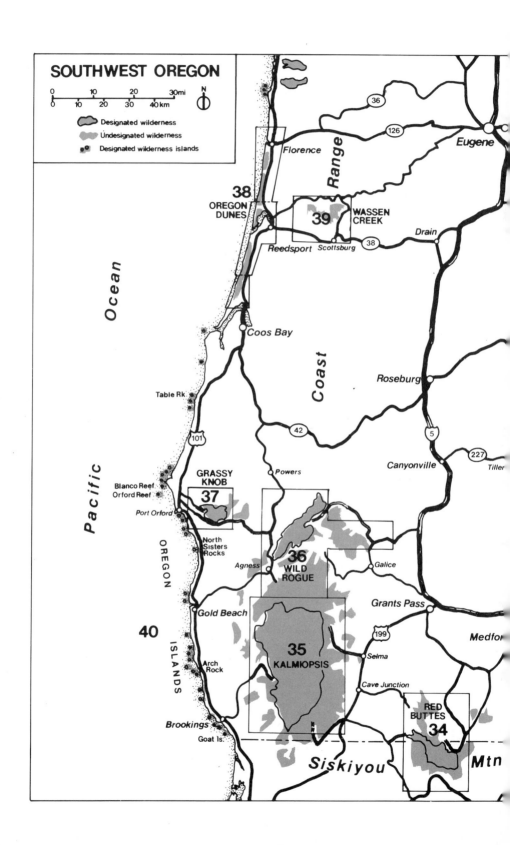

SOUTHWEST OREGON

0　　　10　　　20　　　30mi
0　　10　　20　　30　　40km

N

⬭ Designated wilderness
▨ Undesignated wilderness
•● Designated wilderness islands

Ocean

Pacific

Range

Florence

38
OREGON
DUNES

39 WASSEN
CREEK

Drain

Reedsport   Scottsburg

Coos Bay

Coast

Roseburg

Table Rk

101

42

Powers

Canyonville

Tiller

**GRASSY
KNOB**

Blanco Reef
Orford Reef

37

Port Orford

North
Sisters
Rocks

Agness

36
WILD
ROGUE

Galice

Grants Pass

40

Gold Beach

35
KALMIOPSIS

199

Selma

Medfor

Arch
Rock

Cave Junction

**RED
BUTTES**
34

Brookings

Goat Is.

Siskiyou

Mtn

OREGON

ISLANDS

Eugene

36

126

38

5

227

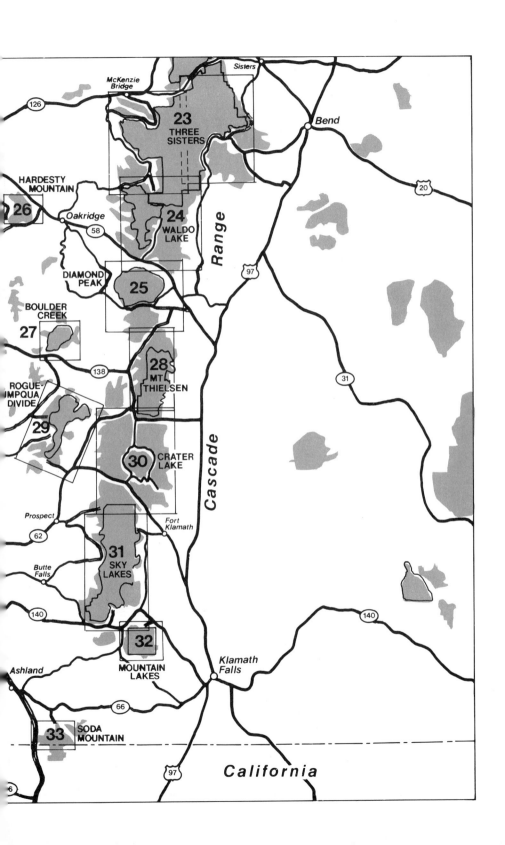

23

THREE SISTERS

Location: 52 mi E of Eugene, 26 mi W of Bend
Size: 572 sq mi, including Century Lakes, Chucksney Mountain, and Macduff Peak
Status: 443 sq mi designated wilderness (1964, 1978, 1984)
Terrain: Snowpeaks, lava, forests, lakes, valleys
Elevation: 1850'–10,358'
Management: Deschutes NF, Willamette NF
Topographic maps: Three Sisters (Geo-Graphics), Three Sisters Wilderness, PCT Northern Oregon Portion (USFS)

A cluster of glacier-clad volcanoes highlights Oregon's most visited wilderness. This large area contains four very different geographic zones.

In the alpine region ringing the Three Sisters and craggy Broken Top, wildflower meadows alternate with lava formations. But to the south, the Cascade crest is a rolling forest of pine and mountain hemlock with hundreds of lakes. To the west, foggy, low-elevation canyons brim with old-growth Douglas fir. To the southeast, sparse forests of lodgepole pine and beargrass carpet arid lands beyond the Century Lakes.

Teardrop Pool, in South Sister's summit crater

Climate

Winter snow in the uplands drifts to depths of up to 20 feet. In the east the snow falls dry, providing the state's best powder skiing. Even the lowest trails remain blocked by snow until May; trails to 5000 feet are clear by about mid-June and trails at 6500 feet are usually clear by August, though snowstorms can occur in any month.

The area's western slopes receive 90 inches of annual precipitation, but the eastern slopes receive just 20 inches a year. The Mink Lake and Horse Lake basins especially are plagued by mosquitoes in July and early August.

Plants and Wildlife

The area's size makes it a refuge for large, shy animals such as wolverine, mink, cougar, and bald eagle. Geographic diversity makes the area home to more plant species than any other Oregon wilderness.

Subalpine wildflower displays in July and early August include blue lupine and red Indian paintbrush. Snowmelt zones teem with white avalanche lily, marsh marigolds, and fuzzy Pasque flower. Wet areas have red elephant head, shooting star, yellow monkey flower, columbine, and larkspur. Drier fields host fuzzy cat's-ears and wild sunflower.

Pink rhododendron displays brighten the lower western slopes in early June. Ripe wild huckleberries line forest trails through 5000 to 6500 feet in late August.

Geology

Although a 1925 theory claimed the taller peaks were remnants of an exploded super-volcano, Mount Multnomah, more recent study shows the mountains formed separately, all within the past 100,000 years, along the High Cascades fault zone.

The oldest peaks in the group are North Sister, which has lost a third of its bulk to glacial erosion, leaving its central plug as a summit spire, and Broken Top, eroded so severely it offers a good cutaway view of a composite volcano's interior structure—alternating red and black bands of cinder and lava. Broken Top's violent past has left the area strewn with interesting, drop-shaped "lava bombs," football-sized bits of exploded magma that cooled in flight.

Middle Sister's Collier Glacier was once the state's largest, but a 1-mile retreat since 1900 has transferred the honor to South Sister's Prouty Glacier. South Sister is geologically young enough to have kept its uneroded conical shape. Its summit crater cups the state's highest lake, Teardrop Pool. Mount Bachelor, another "youthful" volcano, harbors inner fires that create small snow wells on the mountain's north slope, a hazard for skiers.

Some 15,000 years ago Collier Cone erupted directly in the path of the mighty Collier Glacier, commencing a battle of fire and ice. One of the cone's fresh-looking lava flows traced the White Branch valley for 8.5 miles, damming Linton Lake.

Flows of glassy, black obsidian are exposed both below Sunshine, near North Sister, and at Green Lakes, near South Sister. Another kind of high-silica-content eruption formed the frothy, lighter-than-water pumice of Rock Mesa. A California company's mining claim on Rock Mesa's pumice, which would have converted this prominent wilderness feature to cat litter, ended with a $2 million buyout by Congress in 1983.

Ice Age glaciers formed the steep, U-shaped valleys of the South Fork McKenzie River and Separation Creek. Sand-pile moraines left by retreating glaciers dammed most alpine lakes.

History

Once a popular autumn camp for Indians, the area provided huckleberries, venison, obsidian for arrowheads, and beargrass for basketry. Antler-shaped petroglyphs across the Cascade Lakes Highway from the east end of Devils Lake are federally protected.

Many place names in the area recall Chinook jargon, an Indian trade language once widely used by Indians and settlers of the Oregon frontier. Hikers can cross Skookum (powerful) Creek, camp in Olallie (berry) Meadows, climb Koosah (sky) Mountain, and spot Cultus (worthless) Lake.

Visitors to the area sometimes smile at the Three Sisters' "family" of lesser peaks: the Little Brother, The Husband, and The Wife. Few realize there are also a Chinook aunt and uncle

(Kwolh Butte and Tot Mountain) hiding behind Mount Bachelor. Other Chinook names in the area are Tipsoo (grassy) Butte, Hiyu (big) Ridge, Moolack (elk) Mountain, Kokostick (woodpecker) Butte, Talapus (coyote) Butte, and Sahalie (upper) Falls.

THINGS TO DO

Hiking (East Map)

Trail Park permits ($3 per car per day or $25 a year) are required to park at all trailheads in the area. Free wilderness permits can be filled out conveniently at all of the trailheads except the Obsidian Trailhead near North Sister's Sunshine area. To limit crowds in that popular area, permits for the Obsidian Trailhead are only issued for 20 groups a day, and the permits must be obtained in advance from the McKenzie Ranger Station. Call (541) 822-3381 for details.

The Three Sisters' popularity has brought other restrictions as well. In the Sunshine area, all campfires are banned and tents must be more than 100 feet from any water source or trail. Campfires are likewise taboo within a quarter mile of Husband or Eileen lakes and within 0.5 mile of other popular pools: Camp Lake, the three Green Lakes, the four Chambers Lakes, and Moraine Lake. In some high-use areas, camping is only allowed at sites marked by a post. To avoid crowds, plan your visit in fall or in the middle of the week, or try striking off cross-country by compass; it's not hard through the high country.

Two of the area's easiest hikes are the 0.5-mile walk to feathery Proxy Falls and the 1.4-mile, relatively level trail to Linton Lake. Both paths start from Highway 242 west of McKenzie Pass. For an easy hike near Sisters, take the 1.5-mile trail to 30-foot Squaw Creek Falls from a spur of Road 1514.

The very popular 4.8-mile, uphill path to Sunshine Meadow begins at the Obsidian trailhead on Highway 242. Day hikers should not miss the loop past Obsidian Cliffs and Obsidian Falls. Following the Pacific Crest Trail (PCT) either direction from Sunshine makes for memorable backpacking trips. Two miles north, the PCT crosses lava to Collier Cone and a viewpoint of the huge Collier Glacier. Five miles south of Sunshine, side trails of the PCT reach Linton Meadow, nestled between Middle Sister and the crags of The Husband.

The 7000-foot-high Chambers Lakes, surrounded by the glaciers of Middle and South Sister, often have drifting ice throughout summer. Wind-gnarled whitebark pines are the only trees. The dramatic lakes are 7.1 miles from the Pole Creek trailhead at the end of Road 1524. From the town of Sisters, drive west 1.4 miles on Highway 242, then turn left onto Road 15 for 5 miles to Road 1524.

Park Meadow features views of four mountains. Nearby, easy cross-country hikes lead to other wildflower havens higher on the slopes of Broken Top and South Sister. Park Meadow is an almost level 4.9 miles from the end of pavement on Road 16, a road that begins as Elm Street in downtown Sisters.

Cliff-edged Tam McArthur Rim rises from the lodgepole pine forests of central Oregon. A 2.5-mile trail climbs from the turnoff to Driftwood Campground on Road 16 to a dramatic rim viewpoint, where snow lingers through August. From there, the rim's above-timberline crest lures hikers on toward Broken Hand and increasingly grand views.

A dozen popular campgrounds and trailheads line the Cascade Lakes Highway. Opposite the turnoff to Mount Bachelor on this route is the trail to Tumalo Mountain, a 1.4-mile track climbing 1400 feet up the conical, sparsely forested butte to a former fire lookout site.

The most heavily used trail in the area, and one of the most scenic, climbs 4.2 miles from Sparks Lake to the Green Lake Basin at the foot of South Sister. The route follows Fall Creek around a blocky lava flow to the high lakes—which really are green, colored by finely ground silt from nearby Lewis Glacier. Open campfires are banned within 0.5 mile of Green Lakes.

A more nearly level route into the Green Lakes is available once August snowmelt opens Road 370 from Todd Lake to the Crater Ditch trailhead. The 4.8-mile Ditch Trail from spur Road 380 contours around Broken Top, offering viewpoints at every turn. A worthwhile cross-country trip from the same trailhead follows Crater Creek up to its head at an ice-filled lake inside Broken Top's ruined crater.

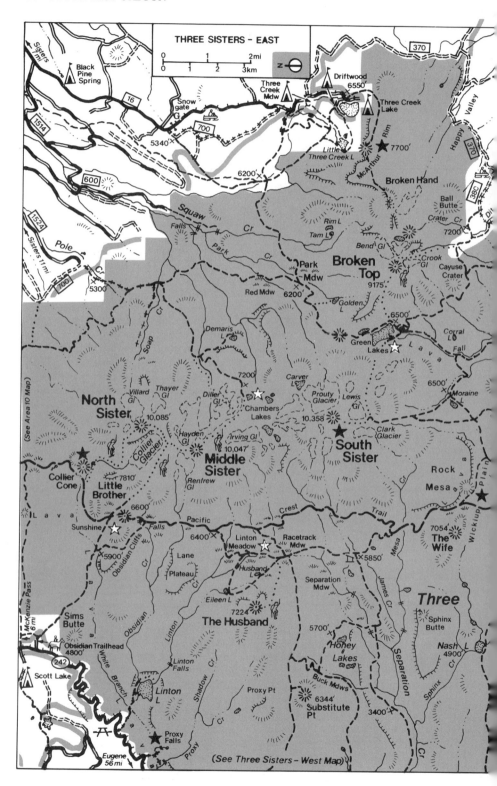

THREE SISTERS - EAST

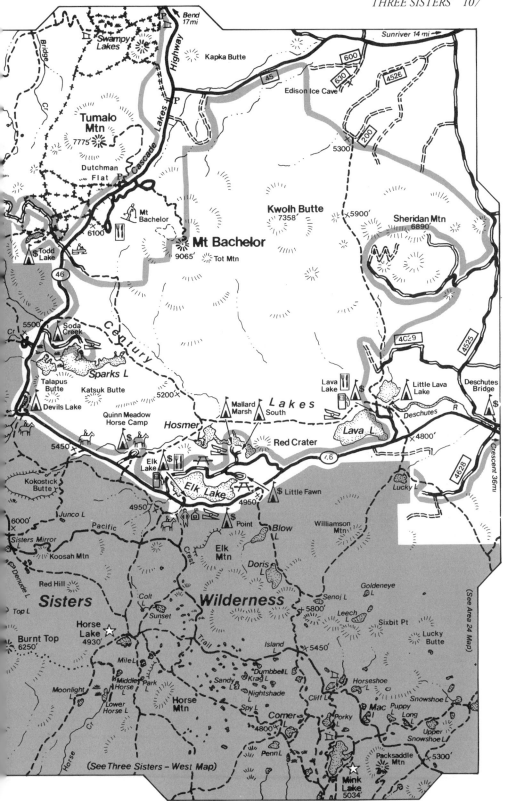

Bend
17 mi

Swampy
Lakes

Kapka Butte

Sunriver 14 mi →

600

45

630

452E

Edison Ice Cave

Tumalo
Mtn

7775'

200

5300

Dutchman
Flat

Kwolh Butte

7358'

×5900'

Sheridan Mtn
6890'

Mt
Bachelor

×
6100

Mt Bachelor

9065'

Tot Mtn

Todd
Lake

46

Century

4C29

4525

Cr

5500
×

Soda
Creek

Sparks L

Talapus
Butte

Katsuk Butte

5200'×

Lakes

Lava
Lake

Little Lava
Lake

Deschutes
Bridge

Devils Lake

Quinn Meadow
Horse Camp

Mallard
Marsh

South

Hosmer

Lava L

Deschutes

×4800'

R

5450

Elk
Lake

Red Crater

4.6

Crescent 36mi

4628

Kokostick
Butte

Junco L

Pacific

Elk
Lake

4950

4950

Little Fawn

Lucky L

6000'
×
Sisters Mirror

Point

Blow
L

Williamson
Mtn

Koosah Mtn

Crest

Elk
Mtn

Doris
L

Goldeneye
L

Red Hill

Senoj L

Leech
L

Sixbit Pt

Lucky
Butte

Sisters

Colt
L

Wilderness

5800

Top L

Sunset
L

Island
L

×5450

Horse
Lake
4930'

Burnt Top
6250'

Trail

Mile L

Dumbbell L

Krag L

Horseshoe

Middle
Horse
L

Park
L

Sandy
L

Nightshade

Cliff L

Snowshoe L

Moonlight
L

Lower
Horse L

Horse
Mtn

Spy L

Mac

Puppy

Long

Corner

Porky

4800'

Upper
Snowshoe L

Penn L

Packsaddle
Mtn

5300'

Horse
Cr

(See Three Sisters - West Map)

Mink
Lake
5034'

(See Area 24 Map)

Scaling South Sister may sound too ambitious for a hike, but in fact Oregon's third-tallest mountain requires no technical climbing skills or equipment. The hike gains 4900 feet in 5.5 miles to the view of a lifetime. Begin at the Devils Lake Campground and head directly for the summit. The unofficial trail peters out at the edge of Lewis Glacier, but hiking is easy on snow and steep cinder slopes from there to the summit. Do not attempt the trip in anything less than perfect weather. A good consolation goal is Moraine Lake, surrounded by an ancient, sandy glacial terminus.

South Sister rises like a wall from the edge of Wickiup Plain, a square mile of cinders and bunchgrass located 2 miles by trail from Devils Lake. LeConte Crater, a perfect little cinder cone at the plain's upper edge, makes a fun climb. The scenic plain has no water, so the meadows a mile farther west, at Sisters Mirror Lake, see heavy camping use. This area is quite fragile; explore the interesting surrounding terrain for campsites well away from trailside lakes.

Horse Lake, an easy 3.3-mile hike west of the Cascade Lakes Highway at Elk Lake, is the most heavily visited of a broad basin of lakes. Trails radiate from Horse Lake toward dozens of more peaceful lake destinations, though the forested lakeshores in this area lack views of snowpeaks.

Mink Lake is the largest of another cluster of forest-rimmed lakes. A popular 8.6-mile route to Mink Lake begins a mile south of Elk Lake. Expect crowds at the narrow gravel beach of Blow Lake, 1 mile along this trail, and at 90-acre Doris Lake, 1.4 miles farther. At a junction 5.4 miles from the trailhead, the PCT leads to other heavily used lakes: Mac, Horseshoe, Cliff, Island, and Dumbbell. Lake lovers can easily find solitude at the hundreds of quieter lakes nearby.

Equestrians should keep in mind that hitching, tethering, or picketing pack or saddle stock is banned within 200 feet of any lake, stream, or shelter in the designated wilderness.

Trails in the Century Lakes area, often used by equestrians, are also suitable for hikers. The 8-mile route from Quinn Meadow Horse Camp to Soda Creek Campground passes Hosmer Lake, then dives back into the dry, lodgepole pine forest toward Sparks Lake. Trails from Hosmer Lake to Lava Lake, and from Lava Lake east, traverse unbroken forests of lodgepole pine, beargrass, and cinders. Carry water. Even the briefest cross-country travel in this 54-square-mile roadless area provides complete solitude. Explorers may search here for undiscovered lava tube caves.

The PCT offers a long-distance route the length of the Three Sisters Wilderness: 52 miles from McKenzie Pass to Taylor Burn Road 600. Another rewarding long-distance challenge is the 44.1-mile hike around the Three Sisters, which follows 19.1 miles of the PCT's most scenic section.

Hiking (West Map)

An often overlooked hike in this area is the 1-mile Rainbow Falls Viewpoint Trail. To find

South Sister from Wickiup Plain

it, drive 3 miles east of the McKenzie Bridge Ranger Station on Highway 126 and turn right on Road 2643 for 6.5 miles.

Substitute Point's abandoned lookout site is the goal of another good viewpoint hike, through 5 miles of forest from the Foley Ridge trailhead. Linton Meadows and the PCT are 4.5 miles past Substitute Point (Buck Meadows and the Honey Lakes are even closer), offering good backpacking goals. To start, drive 3.5 miles past Rainbow Falls on Road 2643, then turn left on Road 485.

Several day hikes in the Olallie Ridge Research Natural Area begin at Horsepasture Saddle. To find the trailhead, drive to the east end of the bridge in McKenzie Bridge, turn onto Horse Creek Road for 1.7 miles, and turn right onto Road 1993 for 8.6 paved miles. A path from the saddle climbs 1100 feet in 1.3 miles to a first-rate viewpoint atop Horsepasture Mountain. A 5-mile trail northwest from the saddle follows a ridge down 1800 feet before rejoining Road 1993. A 4.5-mile hike west from the saddle traverses ridgetop meadows to Macduff Peak. Finally, a delightful 6-mile segment of the Olallie Trail leads southeast from Horsepasture Saddle, past viewpoints at Taylor Castle and Lamb Butte, to Road 1993 near Pat Creek.

Olallie Meadows and Olallie Mountain are both 3.5-mile day hikes (one way) away from Road 1993. The Olallie Trail continues east of Olallie Meadows 10.7 miles through forest to Horse Lake.

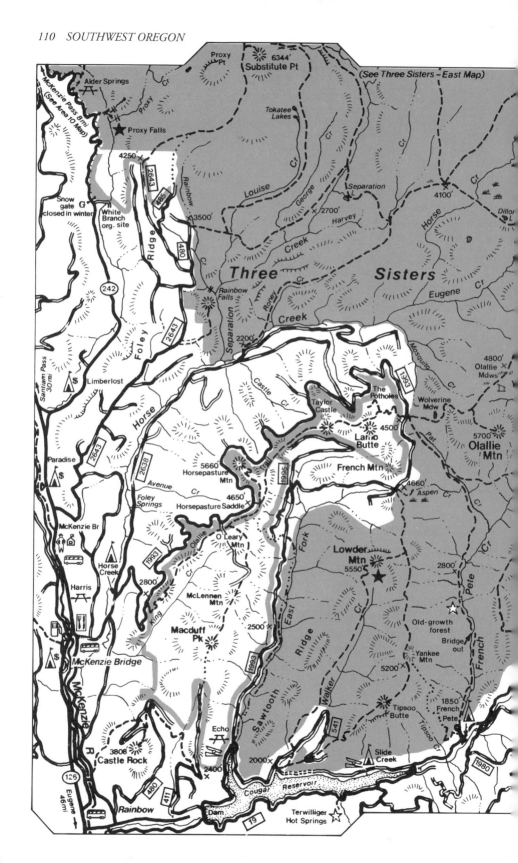

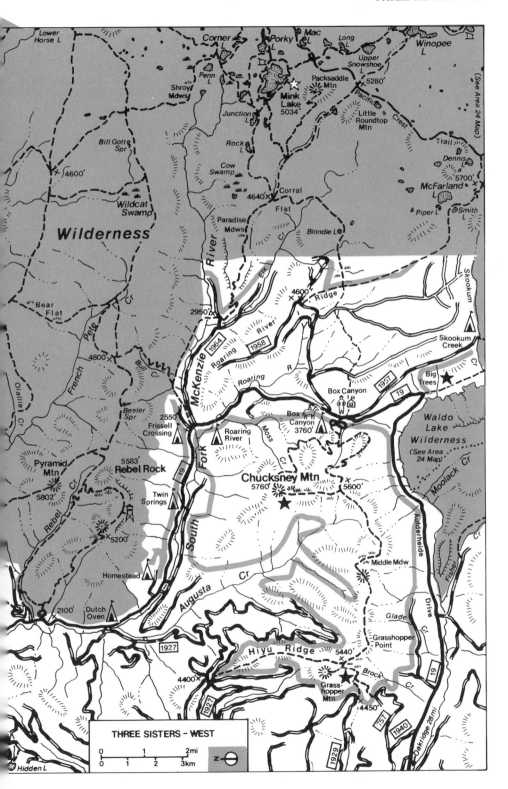

THREE SISTERS - WEST

French Pete Creek

Castle Rock, an abandoned fire lookout site, has a panoramic view of the McKenzie Valley. From the end of Road 480, a well-maintained 1-mile trail leads to the top, and two trails lead downhill to lower trailheads.

The meadow on Lowder Mountain's tablelike summit offers eye-level views of the High Cascades. Several trails lead there. The 2.8-mile route from Road 1993 is easiest. The Walker Creek Trail is a 6.5-mile climb.

Terwilliger Hot Springs is a good place to wash off trail dust. An easy 0.5-mile path leads to an old-growth forest canyon with a string of crowded natural hot pools (closed after dark). Parked cars mark the trailhead beside Cougar Reservoir on the paved Aufderheide Drive (Road 19).

The popular French Pete Creek Trail winds through a forest of massive old-growth Douglas fir. Day hikers starting from the French Pete trailhead on Road 19 usually turn back at the 3-mile mark, where a missing bridge demands a cold wade or an iffy crossing on wiggly logs. A car-shuttle option is to start at Road 1993 and descend Pat and French Pete creeks 9.8 miles to Road 19.

The Rebel Rock Trail climbs 3200 feet in 4.8 miles from Road 19 to a viewpoint and a cliff-edge lookout building (a mile west of Rebel Rock's trailless summit). An easier trip is the 1.1-mile walk up the adjacent Rebel Creek Trail to its second bridge amid 400-year-old Douglas firs. Or connect both trails with a strenuous 12.3-mile loop.

Two 7.8-mile routes lead backpackers to the popular Mink Lake area. The heavily used Elk Creek Trail switchbacks uphill 1700 feet in its first 2 miles from Road 1964. The lesser-known Crossing Way Trail, along Roaring River Ridge from Road 1958, avoids the initial, grueling climb. The two trails join at Corral Flat.

Chucksney Mountain boasts long ridgetop meadows with sweeping views. A 10.3-mile loop trail along this scenic ridgecrest climbs 2000 feet from Box Canyon Horse Campground on Road 19. With a car shuttle, hikers can continue 5 easy miles from the end of the loop to Grasshopper Mountain's meadows.

Grasshopper Mountain can also be the goal of two shorter hikes, either along Hiyu Ridge 4 miles from Road 1927, or up the 1.4-mile trail from Road 1929. To reach the Road

1929 trailhead, drive 13 miles from Westfir (near Oakridge) on Road 19, turn left on Road 1926 for 3 miles, then turn right on Road 1927 for 2.1 miles, and finally turn right on Road 1929 for 5.5 miles.

Winter Sports

Powder snow and panoramic scenery make the Dutchman Flat–Swampy Lakes area near Mount Bachelor ideal for nordic skiing. Highway 46 is plowed in winter to the Mount Bachelor ski resort, where cross-country ski rentals are available. Just across the highway, the Dutchman Flat sno-park has an extensive network of easy, marked trails through meadow and forest. Loop trips range from 1.4 to 8 miles. Snowmobiles are allowed in certain areas, notably Road 370 and the unplowed portion of the Cascade Lakes Highway.

Closer to Bend on the Cascade Lakes Highway, the Swampy Lakes and Meissner sno-parks access an even larger nordic ski trail network, with eight rustic shelters serving as fun destinations and emergency refuges.

Popular trips from the Swampy Lakes sno-park include the easy 4.4-mile loop to the Swampy Lakes shelter, the 6.2-mile Emil Nordeen shelter loop, and a 9-mile loop to the Swede Ridge shelter. The South Fork Trail descends to the Skyliner sno-park, a smaller nordic center accessed by driving west of Bend on Galveston Street. An 8-mile trail connects the Dutchman Flat and Swampy Lakes sno-parks, climbing through forest behind Tumalo Mountain.

Strong skiers can climb 1400 feet up Tumalo Mountain to an outstanding view. Ski directly up the cone-shaped mountain (any side will do) and telemark down through the sparse forest. The open high country between Broken Top and Tam McArthur Rim invites longer, cross-country tours. Spectacular Broken Top Crater is 6 miles from Dutchman Flat via the snowed-over Crater Creek Ditch; McArthur Rim is 8 miles. Carry a compass and emergency gear.

Road 16 from Sisters is plowed in winter as far as a snow gate, from which point Three Creek Lake is a 4.9-mile glide up the snowy road and Park Meadow is a 6-mile trek into the wilderness. In May or June, cars ascend unplowed Roads 15 and 1524 to the Pole Creek trailhead, where dramatic (but unmarked) ski tours to Soap Creek's meadows below North Sister begin.

Ski tours in the McKenzie Pass area are described in area 10, Mount Washington, but the Three Sisters maps cover two additional easy trips on Highway 242. Park at the White Branch snow gate, where plowing ends, and ski 2.5 miles to see the ice cascades of the 0.5-mile Proxy Falls Trail, or ski 4 miles to the 1.4-mile Linton Lake Trail.

Climbing

The Three Sisters and Broken Top are popular with climbers chiefly because of the very scenic setting. The rock itself is crumbly and the technical challenge is not great. Solo climbers have scaled all four peaks consecutively in a single day. The area's changeable weather and novice climbers account for an above-average mountain rescue rate.

North Sister is trickiest. For the easiest route (level I-4), hike from Sunshine to the col between Middle and North Sister. Follow the ridge toward North Sister, passing several gendarmes on the west at the 9500-foot-level. Skirt steep scree and snow slopes to the western base of the crown-shaped summit pinnacle, then scramble up a steep chute to the top.

Of North Sister's eight additional routes, the two most difficult (levels II-5.2 and III-5.2) ascend the east face's couloir and arête. They have only been done in winter.

Middle Sister is frequently climbed from Sunshine, via the col toward North Sister. An equally easy (I-2) route ascends the south flank's scree slopes. Level II-5.2 and II-5.0 routes scale the east face glaciers' headwalls.

Broken Top is a level I-3 climb, either from Green Lakes (via the peak's northwest ridge to a crumbly pinnacle), or from Crater Creek Ditch (ascending the Crook Glacier to the crater rim's lowest notch). The north face requires level II-5.2 skills.

The Husband, via the south ridge, is a I-3 climb.

24

WALDO LAKE

Location: 59 mi SE of Eugene, 43 mi SW of Bend
Size: 148 sq mi, including Maiden Peak
Status: 58 sq mi designated wilderness (1984)
Terrain: Lake-dotted upland forests
Elevation: 2480'–7818'
Management: Deschutes NF, Willamette NF
Topographic maps: Waldo Lake Wilderness, PCT Oregon Central Portion (USFS); Three Sisters, Willamette Pass X-C Ski Trails (Geo-Graphics)

Sailboats ply Oregon's second-largest natural body of water, a brilliant blue lake so pure and clear that fish are visible 100 feet below the surface. The forests rimming Waldo Lake shelter hundreds of smaller lakes and a thorough trail network.

Climate

Snowfall from November to April accounts for most of the area's 60–75 inches of annual precipitation. Trails are clear of snow in late June. Headnets or repellent are necessary from early July to early August, when mosquitoes are plentiful.

Plants and Wildlife

Only two species of moss survive in Waldo Lake's renowned clear water, in part because the lake has no inlet to bring nutrients for plant life, and partly because of natural arsenic at levels hazardous to plants, but not to fish or humans.

The Charlton Butte–Cultus Lake area is frequented by bald eagles and osprey, which often roost at Crane Prairie Reservoir (a viewing blind is near Quinn River Campground). The Maiden Peak area, with the Pacific Northwest's largest stands of mountain hemlock, provides known habitat for the shy wolverine, which is threatened in Oregon. The meadows and high ridges west of Waldo Lake support a large Roosevelt elk herd. Black bear, cougar, bobcat, fisher, and marten are found throughout the area.

The forests of the Taylor Burn area were burned by a sheepman at the turn of the century to encourage grass growth, but the result was a vast, even-aged stand of fire-resistant lodgepole pine.

Geology

The lake basins resulted from sheet glaciation in the Ice Age. Maiden Peak, Charlton Butte, The Twins, and Cultus Mountain are the largest of the many geologically recent volcanoes in the east of the area. Irish Mountain is an older, heavily eroded volcanic plug.

History

Salem Judge John B. Waldo (1844–1907) and four companions were the first white men to travel the length of Oregon's Cascade Range from Willamette Pass to Mount Shasta, in 1888. Klovdahl Bay is named for an engineer whose small, abandoned dam and tunnel would have tapped Waldo Lake for irrigation and power.

THINGS TO DO

Hiking

Two of the most popular 0.5-mile hikes are to Betty Lake (from Waldo Lake Road 5897) and to Upper and Lower Marilyn Lakes (via any of four paths off Road 500). Both trips lead to views of Diamond Peak across the lakes.

The Rosary Lakes nestle in a forest basin at the foot of Maiden Peak. A 2.7-mile section of

Salt Creek, the outlet of Gold Lake

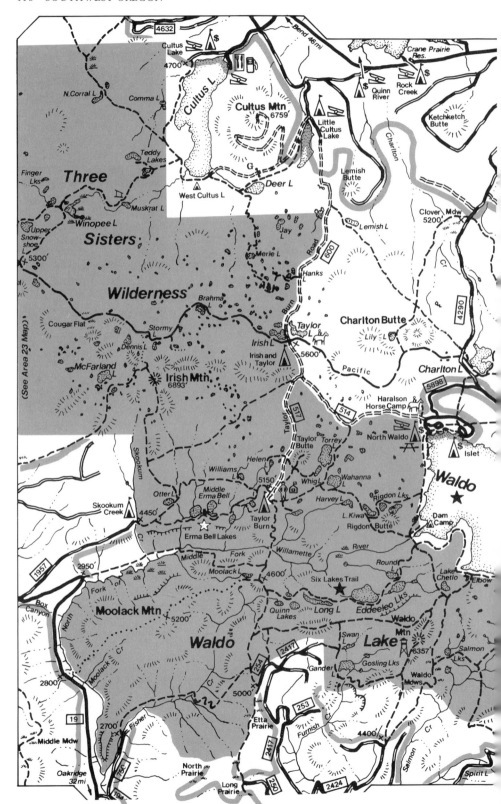

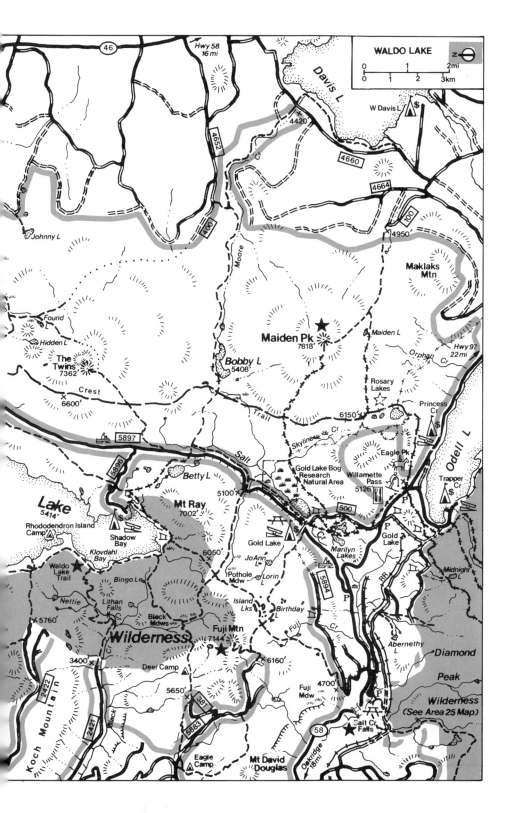

the Pacific Crest Trail (PCT) from Willamette Pass leads to large Lower Rosary Lake, traversing an old-growth forest with glimpses of Odell Lake.

Several short hikes sample Waldo Lake's shoreline. It's 1.7 miles from Shadow Bay Campground to South Waldo shelter's meadow. From North Waldo Campground, a 3-mile hike reaches the lake outlet, one of the heads of the Willamette River. The trail traverses deep woods and passes a sandy beach after 2.3 miles. On hot days the chilly water and whitecapped waves invite swimming.

Another hike from North Waldo Campground heads to the Rigdon Lakes. They're 2.4 miles away and are flanked by a little rocky-topped butte with a good view.

Lily Lake is an easy 2.4 miles, mostly on the Pacific Crest Trail, from Road 4290. The route passes lily-pad ponds in the lodgepole forest below Charlton Butte. Minimally maintained trails east of the butte provide a loop-trip option.

Cultus Lake is big, but one can hike halfway around as a day trip. It's 3.7 miles from Cultus Lake Campground to West Cultus Lake trail camp; those who plan a boat shuttle need only hike one way.

A waterfall connects popular, huckleberry-rimmed Middle Erma Bell Lake with its deep blue partner, Lower Erma Bell Lake. They're 1.7 and 2.1 miles along a nearly level trail from Skookum Creek Campground. Road access is via Oakridge; drive to Westfir and 32 miles beyond on Road 19 to the Skookum Creek turnoff.

Gander Lake, near Swan Lake and the Goslings, usually offers a rickety raft or two for impromptu boaters. The downhill 1.2-mile trail to Gander Lake begins at the end of Road 2417. Follow paved Salmon Creek Road (Road 24) east of Oakridge 11 miles and fork left onto Road 2417 for 7.2 miles.

Waldo Mountain's fire lookout and viewpoint climax a 2.9-mile trail that climbs 1900 feet. Drive to the trailhead as for Gander Lake, but turn off Road 2417 (onto Road 2424) after 6 miles. From the same trailhead, a much less strenuous 2.5-mile path leads to Waldo Meadows' wildflowers and the nearby Salmon Lakes.

Black Creek's impressive 2000-foot-deep canyon is the start of a day hike with variety. After climbing past Lithan Falls, the 3.8-mile Black Creek Trail takes hikers to a good picnic spot on Waldo Lake's Klovdahl Bay. To reach the trailhead, follow Salmon Creek Road 24 from Oakridge for 14.2 miles, then continue straight on Road 2421 to its end.

Interesting cinder formations and a view from Mount Hood to Mount Thielsen are the rewards at the former lookout site atop conical Maiden Peak. The 5.8-mile trail gains 2800 feet at a good grade from Road 500, 0.5 mile south of Gold Lake Campground. A next-best viewpoint hike, to The Twins' double summit, requires only a 3.3-mile hike (one way), gaining 1600 feet from Road 5897.

Fuji Mountain is a cliff-topped old lookout site with an impressive view. A 1.5-mile trail reaches the peak from gravel Road 5883 (which joins Highway 58 approximately 15 miles east of Oakridge), but many hikers prefer the 5.6-mile Fuji Mountain Trail from paved Waldo Lake Road 5897 near Gold Lake.

Two loop hikes prowl the forest east of Fuji Mountain, starting at paved Road 5897: the 9.7-mile trip from Gold Lake to Island Lakes, and the 9.5-mile circuit of Mount Ray past the South Waldo shelter.

Irish Mountain has no trail to its summit, but the PCT skirts the popular lakes around its base. The foot of the mountain is a 4-mile day hike on the PCT from the Taylor Burn Road.

Extending deep into the wilderness, the Taylor Burn Road (numbered 600, 514, and 517) is a series of deep mudholes when wet, and a rugged, high-centering track when dry. Vehicles able to survive 7 miles on this road can reach Taylor Burn Campground. From there, short hikes through the lodgepole pine forest lead to Wahanna, Upper Erma Bell, and half a dozen other lakes.

Many people enjoy hiking—or jogging or mountain biking—the level, scenic 20.2 miles around Waldo Lake in a single day. If 14.6 miles sounds better, plan a car shuttle between Shadow Bay and the North Waldo Campground. Shorten the trip further by arranging to meet a boat at Klovdahl Bay or the lake's outlet.

The Six Lakes Trail is another first-rate long-distance trail. Backpack from North Waldo Campground to the six forest-rimmed lakes. Camp, then either hike back via Taylor Burn and the Rigdon Lakes, or press on to a prearranged car shuttle; Road 254 is closest, but quiet trails through old-growth forest also lead down either Fisher Creek or the North Fork of the Middle Fork Willamette River to paved Aufderheide Drive (Road 19).

Winter Sports

Though snow at Willamette Pass is often wet, an abundance of trails and scenery make the area very popular. The Gold Lake sno-park is a nordic ski patrol base. The Willamette Pass ski resort has ski rentals.

A good beginner trip follows level, 2.2-mile-long Road 500 from the Gold Lake sno-park to Gold Lake. Return via any of the Marilyn Lakes trails. Caution: The insulation of heavy snows prevents thick ice from forming on lakes. Because skis distribute weight, skiers can sometimes cross snow-covered lakes, but it's not worth the risk.

Other easy trips explore the marked network of short loop trails through the forest just south of the Gold Lake sno-park. Three good goals are the Westview shelter (0.8 mile), the Bechtel shelter (2.1 miles), and Midnight Lake (2.7 miles).

The Salt Creek Falls sno-park is at the top of a 286-foot waterfall, Oregon's second tallest. From here, ski 0.5 mile back to Highway 58, cross it, and climb 1500 feet in 4 miles on

Cross-country skier

Road 5894 to the Fuji Mountain shelter, with its grand view of Diamond Peak.

The scenic basin of the Rosary Lakes is 3 miles from Willamette Pass, climbing gently on the PCT. Strong skiers can continue from Rosary Lakes to Maiden Lake, or make an 11-mile loop trip around Eagle Peak past Gold Lake. A chairlift to the top of Eagle Peak makes a number of mostly downhill tours possible.

Ready for an overnight trip? Try the 8.9-mile trek into South Waldo shelter from the Gold Lake sno-park (via Gold Lake and Betty Lake). For an even greater challenge, ski to the view atop Maiden Peak. The 7.3-mile trail there via Road 500 gains 2800 feet, and traverses some steep, possibly icy slopes.

See area 25, Diamond Peak, for tours into the Diamond Peak Wilderness.

Boating

In the still of the morning, canoeists can watch fish as much as 100 feet below the surface of 417-foot-deep, 10-square-mile Waldo Lake. From about 11:00 A.M. to sunset, a steady southwest wind fills the sails of sailboats and creates sizable waves that keep canoeists close to shore. Choppy water can obscure rock reefs near North Waldo and Shadow Bay.

Waldo, Davis, Odell, and Little Cultus lakes have 10-mile-per-hour limits for powerboats; motorized trolling is banned on Davis Lake. Cultus Lake, with no speed limit, is abuzz with waterskiers. Motors are prohibited on all other lakes.

25

DIAMOND PEAK

Location: 62 mi SE of Eugene, 64 mi SW of Bend
Size: 126 sq mi, including Cowhorn Mountain
Status: 82 sq mi designated wilderness (1964, 1984)
Terrain: Snowpeak, forested uplands, lakes
Elevation: 4240'–8744'
Management: Deschutes NF, Willamette NF
Topographic maps: Diamond Peak Wilderness (Imus Geographics); Willamette Pass X-C Ski Trails (Geo-Graphics); Diamond Peak Wilderness, PCT Central Oregon Portion, Rogue-Umpqua Divide and Oregon Cascades Recreation Area (USFS)

Diamond Peak is but one of the summits rising above this area's broad forests. Four other crags top 7000 feet, each surrounded by its own scenic lakes and trails.

Climate

Snowfall from November through April accounts for much of the area's annual precipitation, which totals 80 inches in the west and 40 inches in the east. Most trails are snow-free by mid-June, but hikers must cross snowfields on the Pacific Crest Trail (PCT) over Cowhorn Mountain and Diamond Peak until about August 1. Mosquitoes are a quite a problem from early July to early August.

Plants and Wildlife

Alpine scree slopes are habitat for pikas and marmots. They also provide footholds for lupine, penstemon, and heather. Dense mountain hemlock forests surround the peaks, leaving few openings for meadows. Lower forests are dominated by lodgepole pine and beargrass in the east, and by Douglas fir, rhododendrons, and huckleberries in the west. Roosevelt elk are common until the first snows.

Geology

The tallest peaks are the eroded remnants of extinct, pre–Ice Age volcanoes. Odell Lake and Crescent Lake fill the U-shaped gouges left by glaciers, showing the ancient ice rivers' width and direction of flow eastward from the Cascade passes.

History

John Diamond first climbed and named Diamond Peak in 1852 while trying to open an Oregon Trail shortcut through the Cascades. The Lost Wagon Train of 1853 set out from Pennsylvania toward Diamond's cutoff the following year, and after much trouble deciding which of the Cascade peaks was Diamond's landmark, followed his sporadic blazes to Emigrant Pass, arduously hewing a trail through the dense forest. There, in mid-October, the 1500 starving pioneers despaired at the sight of the immense, trailless forests ahead. A rescue party convinced many of them to abandon their wagons, then led them to the Willamette Valley, where they doubled Lane County's population.

THINGS TO DO

Hiking

For a waterfall hike, start at the Salt Creek Falls picnic area off Highway 58 (5 miles west of Willamette Pass). Salt Creek Falls, Oregon's second-tallest cascade, drops 286 feet from here. Cross a footbridge and take a 3.4-mile loop trail to lacy, 100-foot Diamond Creek Falls. For a longer hike, continue up the Fall Creek Trail past several more falls 2.3 miles to huckleberry-rimmed Vivian Lake, with a reflection of Mount Yoran's monolith.

From Willamette Pass, an easy, 3.3-mile segment of the PCT leads through old-growth forest above Odell Lake to tree-rimmed Midnight Lake. Nearby, a trailhead opposite the Trapper Creek Campground serves as a starting point for two popular, ambitious day hikes to lakes with fine views of Diamond Peak. Yoran Lake is 4.3 miles on a steady uphill grade through forest, and Diamond View Lake is 5.5 miles up the Trapper Creek trail.

Fawn Lake is also a popular destination, 3.8 trail miles from Odell Lake Lodge or 3.4 trail miles from the Crescent Lake Campground entrance. Worthwhile side trips lead 1.4 miles to shallow Stag Lake, at the foot of Lakeview Mountain's impressive cliffs, and 1.8 miles up to little Saddle Lake.

Trails fan out from Crescent Lake and Summit Lake to dozens of quiet lakes among the pines. The Windy Lake group is 3.9 miles from Road 60 at Crescent Lake; the Bingham Lake cluster is 3 miles from Road 60.

The PCT climbs unusually high over Diamond Peak and Cowhorn Mountain to sweeping vistas on above-timberline slopes. On Cowhorn Mountain, the PCT nearly crests the craggy summit, 3.5 miles from Windigo Pass. The PCT's best viewpoints

Sawtooth Mountain from Indigo Lake

on Diamond Peak are 6 miles from Emigrant Pass—a long but rewarding day hike. Really energetic hikers can follow the PCT to timberline, then climb Diamond Peak's smooth southern ridge cross-country to the exhilarating summit view. The 12-mile round-trip climb requires no technical skills, only stamina.

Sawtooth Mountain overtowers a scenic, less visited network of trails. From Timpanogas Campground, hike 1.9 miles to developed trail campsites at Indigo Lake, directly below the mountain's cliffs. For an 8.9-mile loop around Sawtooth Mountain, turn left just before Indigo Lake and then keep right; this loop comes within an easy 0.4-mile bushwhack of the mountain's panoramic summit. For a backpackable 11-mile loop, hike around Timpanogas Lake, climb to the Windy Pass Trail, and keep right, returning past Indigo Lake; this loop comes within an 0.4-mile bushwhack of Cowhorn Mountain's top.

To reach the Sawtooth Mountain area from Oakridge, follow Highway 58 a mile east of town, turn right at a sign for Hills Creek Reservoir, follow paved Road 21 for 31.2 miles, head left on Road 2154, and follow signs for Timpanogas Lake (9.3 miles).

Hidden on the less visited west side of Diamond Peak are a collection of good day hikes—and prime huckleberry picking in late August. Some of the area's best wildflower meadows border Blue Lake (1 mile) and Happy Lake (3 miles) along an up-and-down trail from Road 2149.

The former lookout site atop Hemlock Butte offers a panoramic view of Mount Yoran and Diamond Peak, and requires only a 0.5-mile hike from Road 23. But for mountain views, few trails can match the 4-mile path from Road 23 to Divide Lake. The route passes narrow Notch Lake in a forest, then switchbacks up a ridge to a timberline valley of tiny lakes below Mount Yoran's sheer face.

Trailheads on the west side of Diamond Peak are reached via Oakridge. Follow Highway 58 a

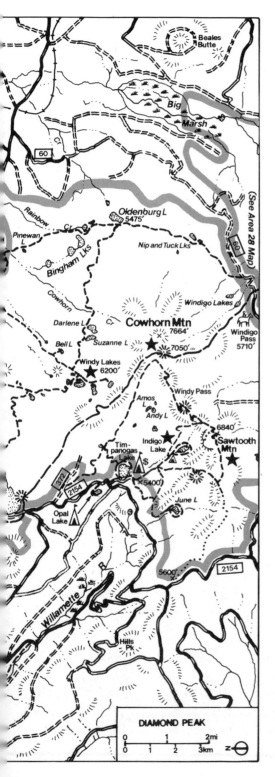

mile east of town, turn right at a sign for Hills Creek Reservoir for 0.5 mile to an intersection, and go straight on Road 23.

Long-distance hikers often choose the scenic, 28.7-mile section of the PCT from Willamette Pass to Windigo Pass, but there are other good routes as well. Most spectacular is the 29-mile circuit of Diamond Peak, passing Divide Lake and Diamond Rockpile.

Cross-country hiking is not difficult in the high, open forests, and is especially rewarding in the lake-dotted forests between Yoran Lake and Willamette Pass, where trailside lakes are overused.

Climbing

Diamond Peak's smooth scree ridges make it a hike rather than a technical climb; neighboring Mount Yoran requires level I-3 skills.

Winter Sports

A network of cross-country trails centers on the nordic ski patrol shelter at the Gold Lake sno-park. Tours north of this area are described in area 24, Waldo Lake. To the south, the well-traveled PCT leads 2.7 miles at a gentle grade through forest to Midnight Lake; several return loops are possible. The unmarked 6.3-mile trail to Yoran Lake and the 7.1-mile trail to Diamond View Lake are for skiers with route-finding skills and emergency gear.

Fawn Lake is a very popular, intermediate-level goal. One trail there climbs 3.8 miles from Odell Lake Lodge (ski rentals available); a route from the Crescent Lake sno-park makes the climb in 3.4 miles. A longer trip to Stag Lake is worth the extra 1.4 miles.

Skiers should avoid the tempting railroad grade along Odell Lake because of frequent high-speed trains; safer tours along Odell Lake follow forest roads above Sunset Cove.

Boating

High-elevation, 500-acre Summit Lake not only has a postcard view of Diamond Peak, it offers reliable afternoon breezes for sailboaters and an interesting shoreline for canoeists. Motors are permitted, but a 10 mile-per-hour limit prevails, and a rough dirt access road prevents crowds.

26

HARDESTY MOUNTAIN

Location: 25 mi SE of Eugene
Size: 22 sq mi
Status: Undesignated wilderness
Terrain: Densely forested valleys, ridges
Elevation: 940'–4616'
Management: Willamette NF, Umpqua NF
Topographic map: Mount June (USGS)

Soothing shades of green—moss, sword ferns, vanilla leaf—line the trails of Hardesty Mountain, where hiking is available year round, only 30 minutes from Eugene.

Climate

Typically the ridges here are snow-free by March, and lower trails are open year round. Rain accounts for the area's 55 inches of annual precipitation. Nearby Mount June was named to commemorate one year when snow lingered there until that month.

Plants and Wildlife

In the area's lush old-growth forests of Douglas fir, western red cedar, and bigleaf maple, watch for the rare Pacific giant salamander. Shiny, 7 to 12 inches long, they are easily distinguished from the orange-bellied, rough-skinned newts common in western Oregon. Also look for delicate calypso orchids on the forest floor in May and showy Washington lilies and beargrass on ridges in June. Spotted owls and osprey nest here; bald eagle nesting sites at times necessitate rerouting of trails.

Mount June from Sawtooth Rock

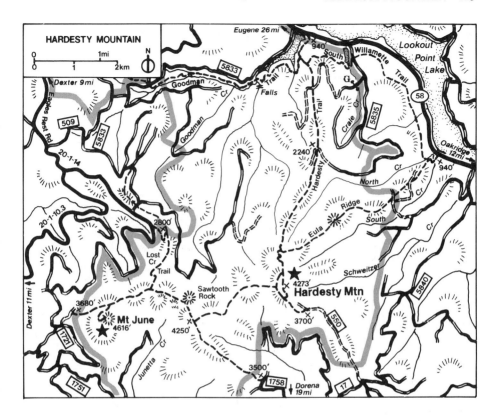

Geology

Though dense forest obscures most rocks, the outcropping atop Mount June reveals volcanic andesite typical of the Old Cascades, 16 to 25 million years old.

History

The Civilian Conservation Corps built most of the area's trails during 1933–38 to access lookout towers on Hardesty Mountain and Mount June. Foundations of the towers remain.

THINGS TO DO

Hiking

Three hikes begin at the well-marked parking area near milepost 21 of Highway 58. For a good kids' hike, walk up the Hardesty Trail 0.2 mile and turn right on the Goodman Trail. This path contours 1.8 miles to a small waterfall and log footbridge, continues 2.2 miles through towering old-growth woods to a crossing of Road 5833, and continues as the 2.5-mile Eagles Rest Trail, climbing past the Ash Swale shelter and crossing paved Eagles Rest Road before reaching Eagles Rest's 3022-foot summit viewpoint.

For a low-elevation walk from the same trailhead, 0.3 mile up the Hardesty Trail turn left on the South Willamette Trail and hike for 3.9 miles.

The Hardesty Trail itself gains 3300 feet in 5 steep miles to a partly overgrown lookout site. For a loop, return on the even steeper, 4.2-mile Eula Ridge Trail. An easier, 0.9-mile route to Hardesty Mountain's summit begins on Road 550, an unimproved spur of Patterson Mountain Road 5840.

Mount June, an even loftier former lookout site than Hardesty Mountain, commands a much better view that stretches from Mount Jefferson to Mount Thielsen. A 1.2-mile trail switchbacks to Mount June's cliff-edged summit meadow. For a longer hike, continue eastward along meadow-topped Sawtooth Ridge on a trail lined with wildflowers, viewpoints, and rock spires. Hardesty Mountain is 3.1 miles past Mount June on this scenic route.

To reach Mount June, drive 11.4 miles east from Interstate 5 on Highway 58 to Dexter Dam and turn south at a sign for Lost Creek. After 3.7 miles, turn left across a somewhat hidden bridge onto the signed Eagles Rest Road. Follow this paved, one-lane route 7.8 miles to a fork. Keep left, following a hiker-symbol pointer, and after another 1 mile reach a sign on the left identifying the Lost Creek Trail. This pleasant path does lead to the top of Mount June in 4 miles; however, those seeking the easier 1.2-mile trail to Mount June's summit should continue 5.1 miles farther on this road, which soon turns to gravel. At the far edge of a fenced tree plantation, turn left on Road 1721 for 0.1 mile, then turn left on Road 941 for 0.4 mile to the Mount June trailhead.

Falls along the Goodman Trail

27

BOULDER CREEK

Location: 47 mi E of Roseburg
Size: 33 sq mi
Status: 30 sq mi designated wilderness (1984)
Terrain: Steep, forested valley
Elevation: 1600'–5600'
Management: Umpqua NF
Topographic map: Boulder Creek Wilderness (USFS)

Boulder Creek's swimmable pools and small waterfalls are the center of a broad, steep valley of old-growth forests. Prominent rock spires provide technical climbing practice.

Climate

Lower trails are snow-free and hikable all year. Winter and spring rains swell Boulder Creek, requiring knee-deep wading on trail fords. The area's annual precipitation is 60 inches.

Plants and Wildlife

Pine Bench features an old-growth ponderosa pine forest with grassy openings, unusual so far west of the Cascade summit. Elsewhere, the forest is an interesting mix of gigantic

Beargrass

sugar pine, Douglas fir, western hemlock, droopy incense cedar, and gnarled yew. The rugged valleys are home to an estimated thirty black bear and 100 Roosevelt elk; both species are shy.

Geology

Eagle Rock and other spires of the Umpqua Rocks are eroded remnants of 30-million-year-old Old Cascades volcanoes. The scenic columnar basalt rimrock lining the North Umpqua River and Pine Bench is only a few thousand years old, part of a High Cascades lava flow that originated 20 miles up the North Umpqua River valley.

History

Several caves in the area preserve evidence of Indian camps. Arrowheads and other artifacts are federally protected.

THINGS TO DO

Hiking

The popular 2-mile trail to Pine Bench provides a good introduction to this area's variety. Near the trail's start, wildflower meadows at sulphurous Soda Springs have views of the North Umpqua's basalt cliffs. Farther on, rhododendrons bloom in May in an old-growth Douglas fir forest. At Pine Bench, the ponderosa grasslands sprout with Indian pipe and other saprophytes each fall. Head west from the Pine Bench campsite area 100 feet to find a spring; climb out on rocks nearby for a breathtaking view of Boulder Creek's canyon.

To reach the Soda Springs trailhead, turn off Highway 138 onto paved Medicine Creek Road 4775 (8 miles east of the Dry Creek Store). Immediately turn left onto the Soda Springs Dam access road and follow this track for 1.2 miles, crossing a narrow bridge over the river to the trailhead.

For a longer day hike, continue north from Pine Bench 1.5 miles on the Boulder Creek Trail to a good swimming hole at the trail's first crossing of Boulder Creek. For a good backpacking trip, cross the creek here (a knee-deep wade), then continue upstream another 2.5 miles, past good campsites and 3 easy creek crossings, to the forks of Boulder Creek. From there the trail climbs a ridge 4 miles to Road 3810 near Bear Camp.

Two of the area's best viewpoints are Mizell Point and Illahee Rock. The 1.2-mile route to Mizell Point follows the faint Perry Butte Stub Trail from a spur of paved Road 4775 up and down to the viewpoint's 200-yard side trail along a rocky ridge.

To find the 0.4-mile trail to the lookout tower atop Illahee Rock, drive Highway 138 to the Dry Creek Store, turn north on Road 4760 for 7 miles, turn right 1 mile on Road 100, and take a spur to the left. The nearby Grassy Ranch Trail contours 1.5 miles to Wild Rose Point, through meadows filled with rare Washington lilies each June.

A nearly level hike beneath Eagle Rock's crags follows a 2.5-mile portion of the North Umpqua River Trail from the Highway 138 river bridge near Eagle Rock Campground to the Soda Springs Dam access road (off Road 4775).

Backpackers and equestrians can tackle the entire 77.5-mile North Umpqua River Trail from Idleyld Park (23 miles east of Roseburg on Highway 138) to Maidu Lake in the Mount Thielsen Wilderness (area 28).

Climbing

Eagle Rock is the largest of a cluster of rarely visited andesite crags with challenging technical climbs. Eagle Rock was first climbed in 1958 via the northern Madrone Tree route (level I-5.2-A2). The 400-foot South Face cliffs present a level II-5.6 challenge.

Old Man Rock, rated I-5.4-A1, remained unclimbed until 1963. The spire directly north of it, Old Woman, has I-5.2 and I-5.6 routes. Other crags in the area are easier, including prominent Rattlesnake Rock (I-3).

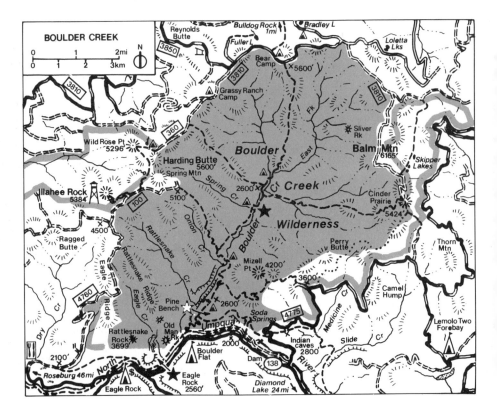

28

MOUNT THIELSEN

Location: 72 mi E of Roseburg, 80 mi NE of Medford
Size: 126 sq mi
Status: 86 sq mi designated wilderness (1984)
Terrain: Snowpeak, high forest
Elevation: 4260'–9182'
Management: Umpqua NF, Deschutes NF, Winema NF
Topographic Maps: Mount Thielsen Wilderness, PCT Central Oregon Portion (USFS)

The "Lightning Rod of the Cascades," Mount Thielsen's spire towers above the lakes, meadows, and high forests to the north of Crater Lake.

Climate

Snowfall from mid-October to April accounts for most of the area's 60 inches of annual precipitation. Most trails are snow-free by mid-June, but the Pacific Crest Trail may remain blocked until mid-July. Mosquitoes are numerous for about four weeks following snow melt.

Plants and Wildlife

Nearly pure stands of lodgepole pine blanket the lower areas, where the pumice and ash soils are extremely dry in summer. Nearly pure stands of mountain hemlock cover the higher elevations, where lingering snow provides summer moisture. Clark's nutcrackers, gray jays, and golden-mantled ground squirrels are everywhere abundant. Look for elk and red-headed pileated woodpeckers. Diamond Lake originally had no fish, but is now stocked to provide 3 million trout annually.

Miller Lake from the Pacific Crest Trail

Geology

A 5-foot-thick ground cover of lighter-than-water pumice rock remains as evidence that this area lay directly downwind of the cataclysmic explosion that created Crater Lake's caldera 7700 years ago.

Mount Thielsen, extinct for at least 100,000 years, was stripped to its central plug by the same Ice Age glaciers that carved the basins for Diamond Lake and Miller Lake. In 1965, after centuries with no glaciers at all, the peak was found to shelter two small moving ice masses on its northern flank.

Lightning strikes the Mount Thielsen's spire so often that carrot-shaped "lightning tubes" with glassy, brownish-green fulgurites of recrystallized rock form at the summit.

THINGS TO DO

Hiking

The most popular of the area's many viewpoint hikes is the Howlock Mountain Trail to Timothy Meadows. Starting from the horse corrals at North Diamond Lake, the route climbs through viewless forests for 3 miles before reaching the meadows along splashing Thielsen Creek. Here are good picnicking swales with wildflowers and glimpses of Thielsen's summit. However, it's worth climbing 2 miles farther along the creek for the astonishing view at Thielsen Creek Camp, where the peak looms like the Matterhorn.

Once at Thielsen Creek Camp, there are two tempting alternatives to simply returning via the same 5-mile route. It's only 2.6 miles farther to make a loop to the south, following the Pacific Crest Trail (PCT) to far-ranging views on the flank of Mount Thielsen before descending to Diamond Lake via the Mount Thielsen and Spruce Ridge Trails. On the other hand, spectacular alpine scenery also lies north of Thielsen Creek Camp, on an 8.1-mile return route that follows the PCT past serrated Sawtooth Ridge and broad Howlock Meadows before descending to Diamond Lake via Timothy Meadows.

Backpacking breaks these distances into shorter hikes. The only year-round water source on Mount Thielsen's flanks is Thielsen Creek; be sure to camp in the forest well away from the fragile clearings at Timothy Meadows or Thielsen Creek Camp, and build no fire.

Tipsoo Peak has a memorable view of Thielsen and Sawtooth Ridge. The quiet, 3-mile trail there from Wits End Road 100 gains 1600 feet in elevation. From the top, it's an easy scramble down loose cinders to the alpine meadows along the PCT.

Those who have already climbed to Cowhorn Mountain on the PCT from Windigo Pass (see area 25, Diamond Peak) might try three rarely visited viewpoint goals south of the pass. Tolo Mountain and Tenas Peak are both 5 miles; Windigo Butte's little cone is a 1.5-mile cross-country climb.

By far the most heavily used lakeside trails are several short routes beside Diamond Lake. Quieter, and just as scenic, is the 5-mile path around Miller Lake from the Digit Point Campground. From the same trailhead, try climbing 3.5 miles to a viewpoint on the PCT, where cliffs overlook Miller Lake. Another popular hike crosses the Cascade Divide 4 miles to forest-rimmed Maidu Lake. Reach the trailhead via Road 9772, which leaves Highway 97 at Chemult.

Backpackers and equestrians have several long-distance trip options. The PCT covers 29.4 miles from Windigo Pass to the North Crater trailhead beside Highway 138, on the National Park boundary. Also, a popular 8-mile segment of the North Umpqua River Trail climbs to Maidu and Lucille lakes from the Kelsay Valley trailhead.

Throughout the area, water sources are scarce. For solitude, carry water for a dry camp and strike off cross-country through the open, easily traversed forests.

Thousands of hikers climb—or nearly climb—Mount Thielsen each summer. Those without technical climbing experience must settle for the excellent view at the base of the near-vertical, 80-foot summit spire (even this goal is 5 miles away from Highway 138 and 3700 feet up). Follow the Mount Thielsen Trail from Diamond Lake, then hike south 0.3 mile on the PCT to where a track leads straight up the above-timberline scree slopes; pass the flank outcroppings of Red Rock and Black Castle on the left before heading for the southeast base of the summit pinnacle.

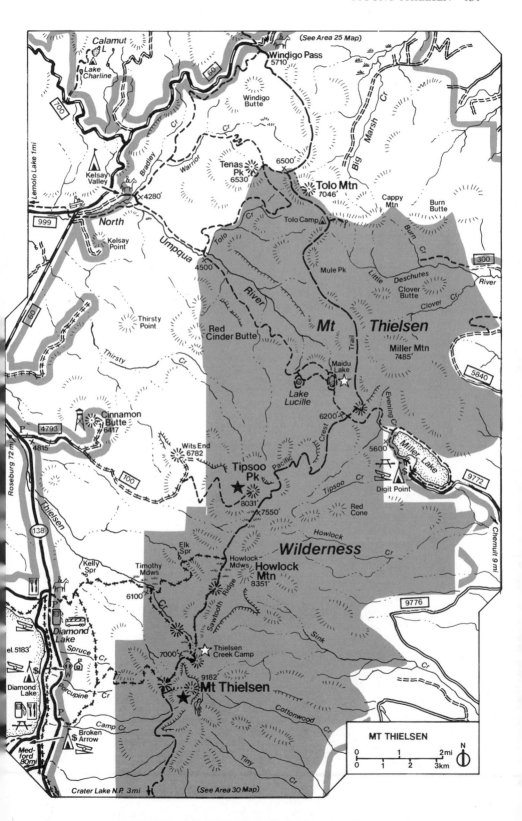

Hikers who don't want to risk scaling Mount Thielsen might consider climbing Mount Bailey instead; the broad, 8363-foot summit is on the opposite side of Diamond Lake, outside the wilderness. A 4.9-mile trail climbs 3100 feet from Bailey Road, a spur on the southwest part of the road around Diamond Lake.

Climbing

Mount Thielsen's summit pinnacle is a level I-3 climb from the southeast. A more difficult and extremely dangerous route to the summit, the III-5.7 McLoughlin Memorial, involves six rope lengths of technical work on rotten, east-facing cliffs, accessed via Thielsen Creek Camp.

Winter Sports

Resorts at North Diamond Lake and Lemolo Lake offer cross-country ski rentals and marked winter trails. All of the hiking trails between Diamond Lake and Mount Thielsen make good, if steep, cross-country routes. In addition, a nearly level trail heads south from Diamond Lake to the North Crater sno-park on Highway 138.

The fine view at Cinnamon Butte's lookout tower is 3 miles up from another Highway 138 sno-park. The reward for climbing 1600 feet on the lookout road's steady grade is a 2-mile downhill glide.

Boating

Diamond Lake and Miller Lake offer canoeing and sailing. Motors are permitted, but with a 10 mile-per-hour limit.

Mount Thielsen and Diamond Lake

29

ROGUE-UMPQUA DIVIDE

Location: 75 mi E of Roseburg, 56 mi NE of Medford
Size: 102 sq mi
Status: 52 sq mi designated wilderness (1984)
Terrain: High meadows, forested valleys, ridgetop rock outcroppings
Elevation: 2300'–6783'
Management: Umpqua NF, Rogue River NF
Topographic map: Rogue-Umpqua Divide Wilderness (USFS)

Atop a high divide west of Crater Lake, this relatively undiscovered area boasts alpine meadows, interesting rock formations, and small lakes.

Climate

Snow covers most trails from mid-November to mid-May. Annual precipitation is 50 inches; summers are dry.

Plants and Wildlife

The ridges feature showy Washington lilies and Indian paintbrush in June and ripe huckleberries in August. The bright red snow plant, a rare saprophyte, brightens the Fish Lake area as snow melts. Forests include sugar pine and ponderosa pine on the drier eastern slopes, true firs on the ridges, and Douglas fir on the western slopes. A parklike grove of old-growth incense cedars makes a nice stop along Road 800 north of the area.

Geology

The area belongs to the heavily eroded, 16- to 25-million-year-old Old Cascades. Glaciers broadened the valleys and left Buck Canyon, a mile-wide cirque. A massive landslide from Grasshopper Mountain dammed Fish Lake and created Fish Lake Creek Falls. Buckeye and Cliff Lakes nest atop the 6000-year-old slide.

THINGS TO DO

Hiking

Two trails lead to popular Fish Lake from Road 2840. This 90-acre lake, rimmed with meadows and mountain views, was named by a group of 1889 explorers who caught seventy fish there in an hour, using venison for bait. A 3-mile route to the lake ascends Fish Lake Creek through an old-growth forest and passes within earshot of an 80-foot waterfall. The shorter, less scenic Beaver Swamp Trail from Road 2840 loses 700 feet through a burned-over area to reach Fish Lake in 1.7 miles. Once at Fish Lake, it's tempting to add a 6.5-mile loop past Cliff and Buckeye lakes, with their close-up views of Grasshopper Mountain's cliffs. The view atop Grasshopper Mountain, 1.2 trail miles beyond Cliff Lake, makes another worthwhile side trip.

For a spectacular 13-mile loop hike from the Beaver Swamp trailhead, hike past Fish Lake on the trail up Highrock Creek (amid 10-foot-thick Douglas firs), turn left at a pass, and return on the Rocky Ridge Trail, a path lined with wildflowers, viewpoints, and rock pinnacles.

To reach these trailheads from Interstate 5, turn off at Canyonville, follow signs for Crater Lake 22 miles to Tiller, turn left onto South Umpqua Road (which becomes Road 28) for 23 miles, turn right on Road 2823 for 2.3 miles, head right on gravel Road 2830 for 1.7 miles, and turn left on Road 2840.

Colorful trailside sandstone cliffs highlight a 3-mile climb to the viewpoint at Anderson Mountain's former lookout site. To reach the trailhead at Falcon Creek, drive from Tiller up the South Umpqua Road 5 miles, turn right on Road 29 for 18 miles, veer right on Road 2947 for 2.5 miles, and then turn right on Road 300 for 3 miles.

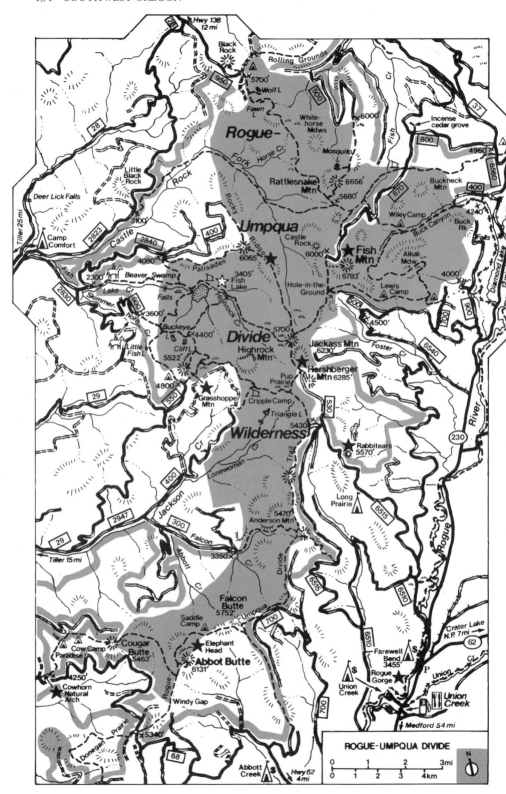

ROGUE-UMPQUA DIVIDE

0   1   2   3mi
0   1   2   3   4km

N

Elephant Head, a sheer-sided rock bluff on the shoulder of Abbott Butte, overlooks a high meadow fringed with true firs and quaking aspen. It's a 3.5-mile hike along the Rogue-Umpqua Divide Trail from the summit of Road 68. To find the trailhead from Medford, take the Crater Lake Highway north past Prospect 6 miles to a sign for Abbott Camp and turn left on Road 68 for 12.5 miles. To find the trailhead from Tiller, take South Umpqua Road 5 miles, turn right on Jackson Creek Road 29 for 12 miles, and turn right on gravel Road 68 for 16 miles.

A short car shuttle along Road 68 opens up another good hiking route down from Abbott Butte: the 6-mile, ridgetop Cougar Butte Trail. A stone's throw from this trail's end is Cowhorn Arch, an unusual volcanic formation.

Hershberger Mountain not only has a good view of its own, it is also just 0.5 mile from the trailhead for several day hikes. A nearly level 3-mile trail north to Hole-in-the-Ground (a high meadow basin) provides a close look at Fish Mountain, tallest point in the western Cascades. To the west of Hershberger Mountain, Grasshopper Mountain's viewpoint is 4.5 miles, past several meadows, the Cripple Creek shelter, and groves of huge Douglas fir.

A trip to the Rogue-Umpqua Divide can hardly be complete without a climb of Fish Mountain, the highest peak. Views range from Mount Shasta to the Three Sisters. From the end of Road 870, walk the trail 0.3 mile south to a crest, then scramble 0.5 mile up an open, trailless ridge to the summit. Another short route to the top starts at the end of Road 500 and crosses the meadow at Hole-in-the-Ground before tackling the trailless summit ridge.

To explore the high basins at the foot of Fish Mountain, try the 7-mile hike through Alkali Meadows and down Buck Canyon. June wildflowers in cow-trampled Alkali Meadows include pink kalmia. Plan a shuttle for this hike, driving one car from the starting point on Road 700 to the end of Road 400.

Whitehorse Meadows, in a pass overlooking the forests of Castle Rock Fork's broad valley, makes a good day-hike goal. From the north, a 2.3-mile trail to the meadows from Road 950 offers a side trip to Wolf Lake. Reach Road 950 via Road 28, which joins the North Umpqua Highway 138 near Eagle Rock.

Another day-hike route to Whitehorse Meadows begins at Road 870 within sight of Castle Rock's landmark crag, and traverses 4 miles around Rattlesnake Mountain. Take time to hike the steep side trail to Rattlesnake Mountain's summit (a fine viewpoint—with no rattlesnakes). The car shuttle distance between the Whitehorse Meadow's two trailheads is, alas, prohibitive.

Several trips require backpacking gear. One of the best is the 13-mile trail loop from Fish

Grasshopper Mountain from Buckeye Lake

Gray jay, or "camp robber"

Lake around the base of cliff-edged Highrock Mountain, hiking through a series of high meadows and scenic passes.

The area's best-known backpacking route, the Rogue-Umpqua Divide Trail, follows a ridgecrest the length of the wilderness—25 miles from Road 30, past Abbott Butte, Jackass Mountain, and Fish Mountain to Road 37—and even continues 8 miles beyond, to Garwood Butte.

The 45-mile Upper Rogue River Trail parallels Highway 230 from Prospect to the northwest corner of Crater Lake National Park. Don't miss the dramatic section (not shown on map) that starts 1 mile south of Union Creek at the Natural Bridge trailhead, where the river disappears into a lava tube, follows the river south for 3.5 miles to a crossing of Road 68 at Woodruff Bridge Campground, and continues another 4 miles to River Bridge Campground, passing Takelma Gorge along the way.

Climbing

Hershberger Mountain Road 6515 passes within 300 yards of the base of Rabbitears, a pair of 400-foot pinnacles first scaled in 1921. Both spires require level I-4 climbing skills.

Winter Sports

When snow levels are low, nordic skiing is easy on segments of the Upper Rogue River Trail. Try the 3.5-mile trail section north from the snowed-under Union Creek Campground, along the narrow, 50-foot-deep Rogue River Gorge.

For deeper snow, try unplowed Road 6560, at the 4000-foot level. Ski past Muir Creek Falls to Buck Canyon, below towering Fish Mountain. Advanced skiers with compass and survival gear can continue west on the wilderness trail system. Beginners can prowl the level meadows between Road 900 and Highway 230.

30

CRATER LAKE

Location: 64 mi E of Medford, 49 mi NW of Klamath Falls
Size: 280 sq mi
Status: National park (1902)
Terrain: Cliff-edged lake, high forest, pumice desert
Elevation: 3700'–8929'
Management: Crater Lake National Park
Topographic maps: Crater Lake (USGS, 25'); PCT Central Oregon Portion (USFS)

Oregon's famous national park sees half a million visitors annually, yet away from the paved rim road the trails are only lightly used. On an average summer night, only a dozen backpackers camp in the area's 259 square miles of wilderness backcountry. In fact, the heaviest backcountry use comes in winter, when the snow is excellent for ski touring.

Climate

Average annual precipitation is 66 inches, largely measured by melting the area's 44 feet of snowfall. Snow closes most trails and the rim road from mid-October to mid-June. The eastern portion of the rim road past Mount Scott seldom opens before mid-July.

Plants and Wildlife

Virtually all life in the area was destroyed by Mount Mazama's eruption 7700 years ago. The 600 species of plants and many animals here are evidence of ongoing repopulation. Forests, largely of lodgepole pine, have spread nearly everywhere but the Pumice Desert, where volcanic debris fell 200 feet deep. The Pumice Desert's cinder soil holds so little moisture that only occasional bunchgrass and dwarf lupine can live there.

Most, but not all, Cascade wildflowers have reestablished themselves along the lake's alpine rim. Gnarled whitebark pines clinging to the rim withstand the cliff edge's fierce storm winds because their branches are so supple they can literally be tied in knots. The dominant animal species of the rim appear to be cute golden-mantled ground squirrels and raucous, swooping Clark's nutcrackers, both of which aggressively encourage visitors to defy the park's ban on feeding wildlife.

Biologists theorize that the toads, garter snakes, and chipmunks living on Wizard Island migrated there overland when the lake was lower. The crayfish in Wizard Island's ponds were introduced by early visitors.

Visitors sometimes sight black bears. Though the bears generally avoid camps, hang all food 10 feet off the ground and 5 feet from a tree trunk at night.

Geology

Crater Lake fills the caldera of Mount Mazama, which collapsed after a cataclysmic eruption about 5700 B.C.

Mount Mazama first began to form 500,000 years ago, when neighboring Union Peak and Mount Thielsen were already extinct. At its height, Mount Mazama was a broad, 12,000-foot mountain the size of Mount Adams. Ice Age glaciers gouged its flanks with valleys (still visible as Sun Notch and Kerr Notch). Smaller volcanoes sprouted on its sides (Timber Crater, Red Cone, and Hillman Peak). Its slopes oozed thick lava flows (visible in cross-section as The Watchman, Llao Rock, and Cloudcap).

Then, in an eruption fifty times as massive as the 1980 Mount St. Helens blast, Mount Mazama suddenly exploded 14 cubic miles of pumice and ash into the sky, emptying its subterranean magma reservoir. Ash fell 10 feet deep at Klamath Marsh, and half an inch deep as far away as Saskatchewan. As the hollowed mountain collapsed, a glowing avalanche of pumice and

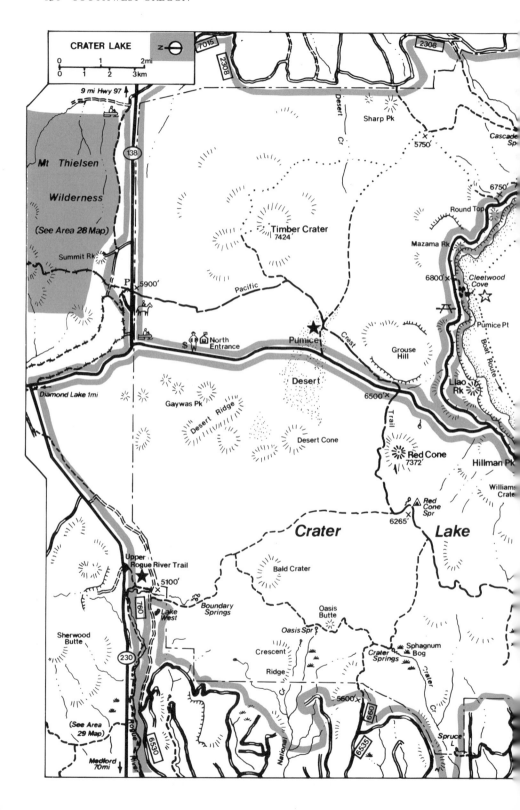

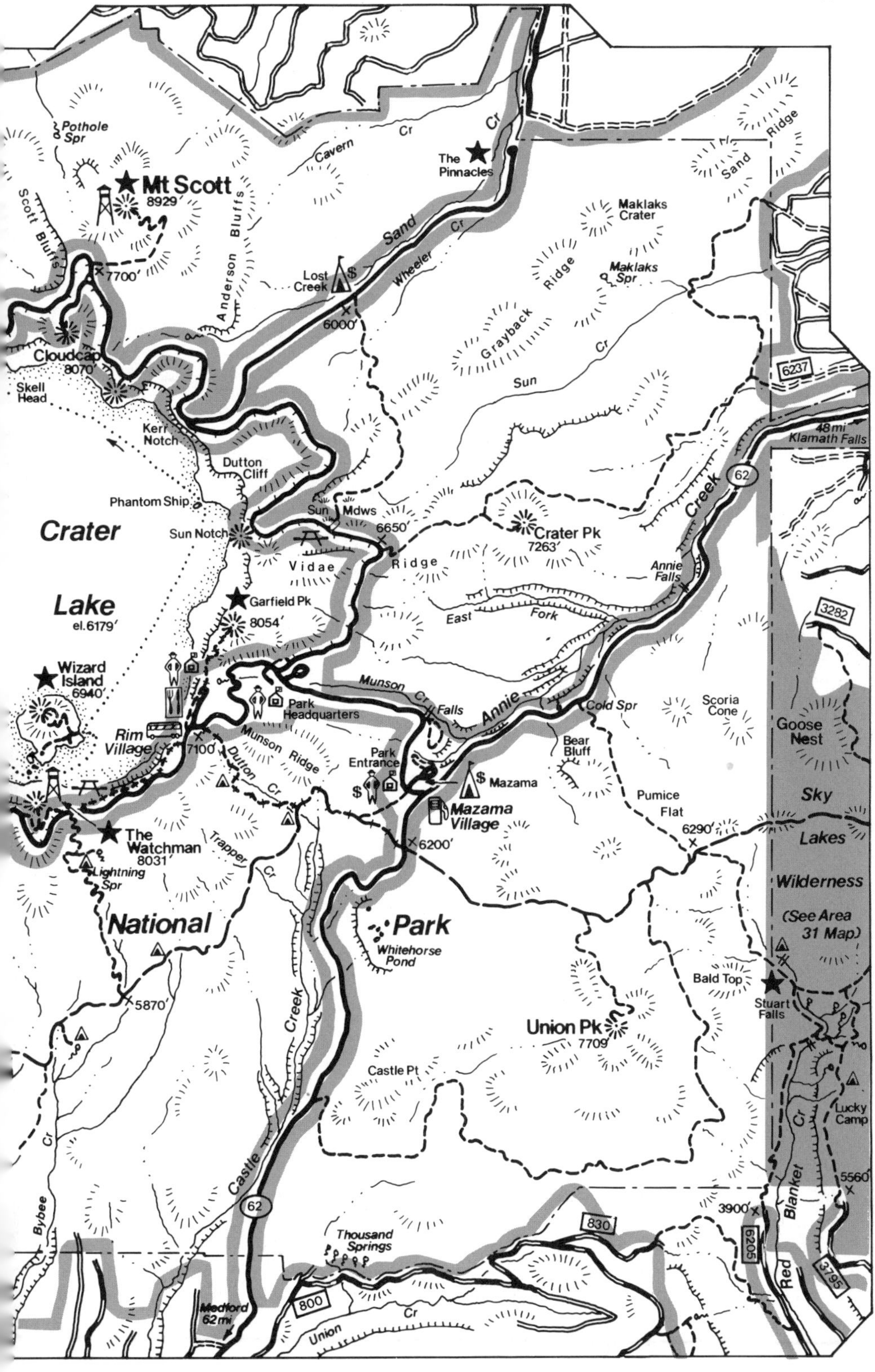

Pothole Spr

★ Mt Scott
8929'

Scott Bluffs

Anderson Bluffs

7700'

Cavern Cr

Sand

Wheeler Cr

★ The Pinnacles

Maklaks Crater

Grayback Ridge

Maklaks Spr

6237

48 mi
Klamath Falls

Cloudcap
8070'

Skell Head

Kerr Notch

Dutton Cliff

Phantom Ship

Lost Creek $
6000'

Sun

62

Creek

Crater
Lake
el.6179'

Sun Notch

Sun Mdws
6650'

Vidae Ridge

Garfield Pk
8054'

Crater Pk
7263'

East Fork

Annie Falls

3282

Wizard Island
6940'

Rim Village

7100'

Munson Ridge

Dutton Cr

Park Headquarters

Munson Cr Falls

Park Entrance

$ W

Annie

Cold Spr

Scoria Cone

Goose Nest

Sky

The Watchman
8031'

Lightning Spr

Trapper Cr

Mazama

Mazama Village

6200'

Bear Bluff

Pumice Flat

6290'

Lakes

Wilderness
(See Area 31 Map)

National

Park

Whitehorse Pond

Castle Creek

5870'

Bald Top

★ Stuart Falls

Union Pk
7709'

Castle Pt

Lucky Camp

5560'

Bybee Cr

62

Thousand Springs

830

3900'

Red Blanket Cr

3795

6205

Medford 62 mi

800

Union Cr

superheated gas raced down the slopes at freight-train speeds. Gas fumaroles in the fiery avalanche deposits welded pumice together around vertical vents; later erosion exposed these as pinnacles along Annie and Sand creeks.

Massive landslides promptly widened the caldera from 3 miles to 5 miles. Later, two cinder cones erupted on the caldera floor. Wizard Island's cone still rises 732 feet above the lake, but Merriam Cone was submerged as the caldera gradually filled with rain and snowmelt.

The deepest lake in North America, Crater Lake has no outlet but maintains its level by evaporation and seepage. The lake's 1932-foot depth and remarkable purity account for its stunning blue color.

THINGS TO DO

Hiking

Popular day hikes lead to viewpoints on the lake rim and nearby peaks. The little-used backcountry trail system is largely dry and viewless, but it's the best bet for backpacking since camping is prohibited within a mile of

The caldera's eastern rim and Mount Thielsen

the Rim Drive. In summer, free permits for backcountry camping can be picked up at the Rim Village Visitor Center or at the Steel Center along the south entrance road.

Other park rules: Pets are prohibited on all trails. Saddle stock are limited strictly to the Pacific Crest Trail (PCT); grazing is prohibited. Firearms and other hunting devices are forbidden. On the other hand, angling is permitted (no license required).

Only five hikes have views of the lake itself. Some of the best views are along the 1.7-mile trail switchbacking up 1000 feet from Rim Village to Garfield Peak, past alpine gardens of showy Davidson's penstemon, red Indian paintbrush, and spreading phlox.

Hikers with less time can take one of the 0.7-mile routes that climb 400 feet from the Rim Drive to a lookout tower amidst twisted whitebark pines atop The Watchman. The 2.8-mile Discovery Point Trail from Rim Village also leads to The Watchman.

Morning is the best time to scale Mount Scott for the farthest-ranging views in the park: from Mount Shasta to Mount Jefferson on a clear day. The 2.5-mile trail climbs steadily to the lookout on this geologically recent stratovolcano.

The park's most used trail (500 hikers a day) is a steep 1-mile path from the Rim Drive down to Cleetwood Cove, where two-hour guided boat tours of the lake depart on the hour between 10 A.M. and 4 P.M. from early July until early September. The really fun hike here, however, is to take the boat tour as far as Wizard Island, climb the 0.8-mile trail to its circular summit cone, then hike 2 more miles down to a quick, icy swim at one of the island's ponds. Just don't miss the last boat back to Cleetwood Cove at 4:30 P.M.

Craggy Union Peak lacks a lake view, but it commands a panorama of the rim peaks and of other Cascade summits. The 5.5-mile route there begins by following the PCT through a broad mountain hemlock forest south of Highway 62. Snow covers much of the route until mid-July.

Three other peaks make interesting hikes for those seeking respite from the rim's crowds. Plan a picnic to the wildflower meadow in the summit bowl of Crater Peak, a sometimes-rugged 2.5-mile hike from the southern tip of Rim Drive. For views of Mount Mazama's other flank (and Cascade peaks as far north as the Three Sisters), try scaling Red Cone. It's an easy, obvious

1.5-mile cross-country hike from a turnout on the park's north rim access road, 1 mile north of the Rim Drive junction.

A third cinder cone, Timber Crater, is too well forested to offer views. Carry water on the 4.6-mile route along abandoned roads from the Pumice Desert to the often snowy, flat summit—a crater filled to the brim by Mount Mazama's pumice. The final 0.5 mile is cross-country.

Those staying at the popular Mazama Campground won't want to miss three short loop hikes nearby. The 1.7-mile Annie Creek loop trail from the campground passes abundant wild-flowers and interesting gas-fumarole rock formations similar to those at The Pinnacles, in the park's distant southeast corner. Two miles farther up the south rim access road, the 1-mile Godfrey Glen loop trail follows a cliff edge past more pinnacle formations. And from the Park Headquarters, the self-guiding 0.7-mile Castle Crest wildflower garden nature-trail loop shows off the park's alpine flora.

Massive Boundary Springs, the sudden source of the Rogue River, is a 2.5-mile hike through riverside woods from the Crater Rim viewpoint, 6 miles west of Diamond Lake on Highway 230. The hike starts at the beginning of the Upper Rogue River Trail, a path that continues 45 miles downstream to Prospect.

Two trails connect the Rim Drive with the PCT and also lead to the most accessible backcountry camping. The 2.4-mile Dutton Creek Trail drops 1000 feet through viewless forest to a creekside wildflower display. The 4.1-mile Lightning Springs Trail passes a small water-fall after 1.5 miles, then becomes an abandoned forest road.

The PCT itself is uninspiring throughout the park: It is entirely viewless, with no water north of Red Cone Spring or south of Dutton Creek, and largely on abandoned roads. PCT hikers will want to consider hiking up Dutton Creek and along Rim Drive instead. To the north, a good alternate route leaves the PCT near Red Cone Spring, and heads for Boundary Springs (no camping permitted within a quarter mile). A side trip to study Sphagnum Bog's four carnivorous plant species will interest botanists with mosquito headnets and hip waders.

The area's prettiest waterfall is not within the park at all. It's 50-foot Stuart Falls, at the head of Red Blanket Creek's scenic glacier-carved valley, in the Sky Lakes Wilderness. Crater Lake visitors can hike there from the Highway 62's Cold Spring turnout on a dry, 5.4-mile route across forested Pumice Flat. But two shorter, more scenic trails reach Stuart Falls from the west, passing two-tiered Red Blanket Falls on the way. The nearly level, 4.6-mile Lucky Camp Trail route from Road 3795 is easiest, but remains blocked by snow until mid-July. The 4.2-mile trail from Road 6205 up Red Blanket Creek is snow-free a month earlier and passes through a stately low-elevation forest, but climbs 1500 feet.

To reach Stuart Falls' western trailheads, turn off Highway 62 at Prospect, taking Road 37 toward Butte Falls. Turn left off Road 37 in 1.1 miles to follow Road 6205 for 12 dusty miles to its end at the Red Blanket trailhead, or turn left off Road 37 in 6 miles to follow Road 3795 for 12 miles to its end at the Lucky Camp trailhead.

Winter Sports

Within the park, Highway 62 and its short spur to Rim Village are plowed in winter, allowing nordic skiers access to excellent tours on the snowed-under Rim Drive and surrounding terrain. Snowmobiles are out of earshot, restricted to the Diamond Lake area and the park's north access road. The lake itself is an unforgettable spectacle in winter.

The area's premier challenge, the 33-mile loop around the lake, is a two- or three-day excursion best attempted when winter's fiercest storms are over. The route is for experienced skiers and snow campers only. Road cuts and slopes can calve avalanches, but the most insidious danger is being lured too close to the rim, with its unseen cornice overhangs. By late spring, volcanic grit covers the snow, slowing progress and damaging skis. Permits are required for snow campers, winter camping is banned within a mile of the rim, and the Park Service recommends that ski parties carry radio telemetry beepers.

When choosing day trips and tours away from the Rim Drive, remember that scenic routes on steep slopes are prone to avalanches. Map, compass, and route-finding ability are essential in the flatter areas, where viewless forests hide landmarks.

31

SKY LAKES

Location: 36 mi NE of Medford, 22 mi NW of Klamath Falls
Size: 220 sq mi
Status: 177 sq mi designated wilderness (1984)
Terrain: Lake-dotted upland forests, peaks
Elevation: 3520'–9495'
Management: Rogue River NF, Winema NF
Topographic maps: Sky Lakes Wilderness, PCT Central Oregon Portion, PCT Southern Oregon Portion, Jackson Klamath Winter Trails (USFS)

Hundreds of lakes hide among the mountain hemlock forests on the Cascade crest between Crater Lake and Mount McLoughlin, the highest point in southern Oregon.

Climate

The heavy winter snowpack blocks most trails until mid-June, and the Pacific Crest Trail (PCT) until mid-July. Mosquitoes are so numerous after the snowmelt that headnets and zippered tents are advisable throughout July. Summers are dry, with occasional thunderstorms. Snows return in mid-October. Average annual precipitation is 55 inches.

Plants and Wildlife

The wilderness is heavily influenced by adjacent Upper Klamath Lake, which may shelter a half million birds at once during the October-November migrations. Bald eagles and osprey nesting near Klamath Lake's swamps commonly visit the high wilderness lakes. Pelican Butte is named for Upper Klamath Lake's white pelicans, unmistakable with their 9-foot wingspans.

The best time to view the teeming bird life on Upper Klamath Lake's marshy fringe is during the July and August nesting season, when a canoe put in at Rocky Point Resort (rentals available) enables birders to paddle 6 miles north up Crystal Creek, past red-necked grebes, white-headed woodpeckers, and possibly even sandhill cranes.

Sky Lakes' profusion of July mosquitoes coincides with a profusion of mosquito-pollinated wildflowers and tiny, mosquito-eating boreal toads.

In August the omnipresent huckleberry underbrush of the mountain hemlock forest sags with ripe fruit—especially along the Wickiup Meadow trail. By September the huckleberry leaves turn scarlet, filling the uplands with color.

Geology

Mount McLoughlin presents a smooth conical face toward Medford and Klamath Falls but conceals a craggy glacial cirque on its northern side. Strata exposed there show the mountain was once a tall cinder cone like nearby Pelican Butte, then erupted an armorlike covering of andesite, and finally lost its original summit when a glacier (since vanished) cut through its northern shell.

Other Ice Age glaciers scoured out most of the lake basins and gouged the deep, U-shaped valleys of the Rogue River's many forks. Narrow Alta Lake and Long Lake did not result from glaciers, however; they lie along a possibly active fault that extends through the Mountain Lakes Wilderness to California.

THINGS TO DO

Hiking

The area's most popular hike is also the most difficult: scaling 9495-foot Mount McLoughlin for a view of all southern Oregon. No technical equipment is required, only the stamina to gain 3900 feet in 4.9 miles and return.

From Road 3650 hike 1.4 miles to the PCT, where there's a short spur to Freye Lake. If the lake doesn't have a nice mountain reflection, turn back and try the climb in better weather. Otherwise, follow the ridgetop trail to a frustrating false summit at timberline. The true top's abandoned lookout foundations are another steep, trailless mile up a rocky ridge. Remember the route well; most search and rescue calls come for hikers who head south from the summit, missing the trail.

Other popular hikes prowl three clusters of forest-rimmed lakes: the Seven Lakes Basin, the Sky Lakes Basin, and the Blue Canyon Basin. Overused portions of some lakeshores are closed for rehabilitation, particularly near trails.

Trees bend under heavy winter snows.

Craggy Devils Peak towers above the Seven Lakes Basin—especially Cliff Lake, where swimmers can high dive from cliffs into deep water. An easy 4.7-mile trail to shallow Grass Lake from the Sevenmile Marsh trailhead on Road 3334 makes the entire lake basin accessible to day hikers, but it deserves a two- or three-day trip.

Backpackers to the Seven Lakes Basin won't want to miss the 6-mile loop trail over Devils Peak. Follow the PCT to a 7300-foot saddle, where a short, rugged spur trail heads for the peak's former lookout site and sweeping view.

Have another day to spend? Try an 8-mile loop to rock-rimmed Lake Ivern and slender Lake Alta. The route requires an easy 0.5-mile cross-country traverse between the Lake Ivern Trail and the Middle Fork Trail; follow a compass bearing northwest from the Bigfoot Spring spur trail turnoff. At Lake Ivern, be sure to take an easy 0.25-mile side trip due north to a 500-foot cliff overlooking the U-shaped canyon of the Middle Fork Rogue River.

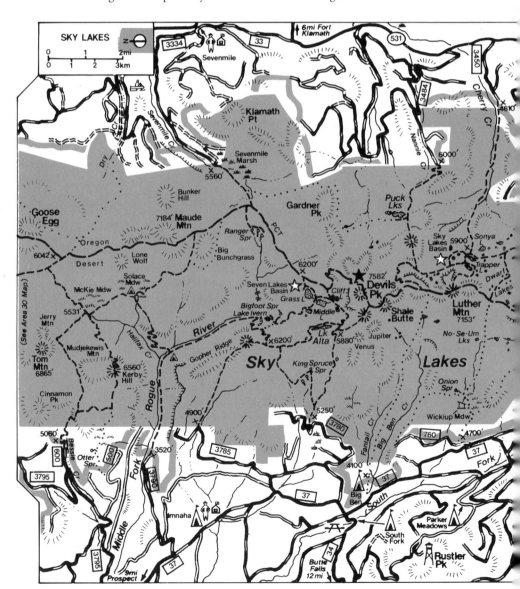

To reach the trailhead at Sevenmile Marsh, take Nicholson Road 4.3 miles west from Highway 62 at Fort Klamath, then continue on gravel Road 3334 to its end.

Less heavily used trails access the basin from the west. The shortest, a 5-mile path from Road 3780 to Cliff Lake, climbs 1600 feet over a ridge on its way. The longest, the 9.7-mile Middle Fork Trail from Road 3790 to Alta Lake, follows a splashing fork of the Rogue River through an old-growth forest with luxuriant, low-elevation greenery.

The Sky Lakes Basin makes up for a shortage of mountain views with an abundance of forest-rimmed lakes. The aptly named Heavenly Twin Lakes are an easy 2-mile day hike (one way) from the Cold Spring trailhead. It's worth the effort to continue on a 2-mile trail loop past deep Lake Notasha, swimmable Lake Elizabeth, and large Isherwood Lake. Another good extension to this day hike heads 2 miles north to scenic Trapper Lake, in a cluster of lakes with views of Luther Mountain's rocky ridge.

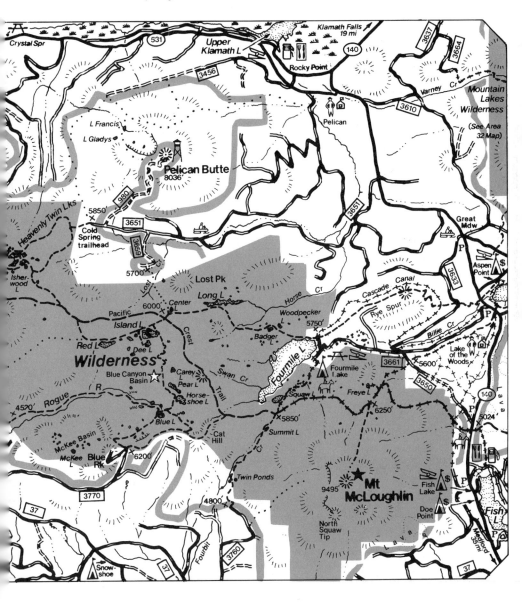

Two quieter trails also make good routes into the Sky Lakes Basin. The Nannie Creek Trail from Road 3484 passes large, swimmable South Puck Lake after 2.4 miles (a good day-hike goal for kids), then descends another 4.1 miles to Trapper Lake. The Cherry Creek Trail from Road 3450 arrives at that lake in 5.2 miles, but climbs 1300 feet, making the route more popular with equestrians than hikers.

Lakes in the Blue Canyon Basin offer reflections of Mount McLoughlin's snowy northern face. Island Lake, largest of the group, is a 2.4-mile day hike along the Lost Creek Trail from Road 3659. For a good swim, try nearby Dee Lake.

Day hikers can best reach the western lakes of this basin via the Blue Canyon Trail starting at Road 3770. It's 2 miles to deep, cold Blue Lake, with its cliff backdrop, and another 0.7 miles to Horseshoe Lake's peninsula. Trailside camps are closed here to allow the fragile flora to regrow. Best bets for solitude are off-trail hikes to Pear Lake and Carey Lake.

Fourmile Lake, popular with fishermen, is the starting point of several good day hikes. The 3.6-mile route to sinuous Long Lake visits several snag-filled bays of Fourmile Lake (with views of Mount McLoughlin) and passes wildflower meadows near pleasant Badger Lake. A 3.3-mile hike south of Fourmile Lake's outlet dam follows the sometimes-dry Cascade Canal then climbs Rye Spur to a viewpoint. From the Fourmile Lake Campground, the Twin Ponds Trail skirts shallow, grassy Squaw Lake, crosses the PCT, and descends to bouldery Summit Lake, a 2.9-mile trip.

Little-used trails in the north of this wilderness lead to McKie Meadow and Solace Meadow's cabin, both popular with equestrians. The 5.3-mile Tom and Jerry Trail to McKie Meadow from Road 600 offers a good cross-country side trip to the view atop Tom Mountain. An alternate route to McKie Meadow crosses Kerby Hill; it's steep, but features a spectacular view of the Middle Fork Rogue canyon.

The shortest route to Solace Meadow (6.3 miles) follows the Middle Fork Trail from Road 3790, then switchbacks up the Halifax Trail through a rapid succession of botanical zones.

The nearly viewless 49.7-mile segment of the PCT between Highway 140 and Highway 62 in Crater Lake National Park manages to avoid all lakes and water sources; be sure to detour into the three major lake basins. Also be sure to take the 0.6-mile side trip to Ranger Spring, a welcome oasis. The Oregon Desert, on the northern part of the PCT route, is a stark forest where only lodgepole pines and September mushrooms grow.

Cross-country hiking is easy and rewarding in all the upland lake basins, particularly in the McKee Basin near Blue Rock and in the glacial cirque on Pelican Butte—areas lacking maintained trails.

Winter Sports

Marked nordic ski trails radiate from several sno-parks along plowed Highway 140. Snowmobiles dominate snowed-under roads and are permitted on most nonwilderness trails (except the PCT and the Cascade Canal).

A good beginner tour off-limits to snowmobiles follows the Lake of the Woods shoreline 1.9 miles from Highway 140 to snowed-under Aspen Point Campground. Another easy route, with good views of Mount McLoughlin, begins at the Fish Lake Resort and loops 3 miles on marked roads and trails south of that lake.

The PCT offers routes both south of Highway 140, to viewpoints in the vast lava fields around nearby Brown Mountain, and north of the highway, where it climbs steadily 3.5 miles to Freye Lake's mountain view. A 1.5-mile trail connects the PCT with Fish Lake Resort, but a closer access to the PCT is the sno-park at the junction of Highway 140 and Road 3650.

Road 3650 and the parallel Cascade Canal provide a scenic, well-graded 9.7-mile nordic route from Highway 140 to Fourmile Lake. A shortcut to that lake, along Road 3661, is shared with snowmobiles but allows snow campers quickest access to the wilderness trail system beyond.

The area's most challenging ski tour, to the summit of Mount McLoughlin, should only be undertaken in perfect weather by groups familiar with avalanche danger areas.

Boating

Canoes and sailboats do well on Fourmile Lake, Fish Lake, and the marshy bays and creeks of Upper Klamath Lake; motorboats are limited to 10 miles per hour in these areas.

32

MOUNTAIN LAKES

Location: 38 mi E of Medford, 15 mi NW of Klamath Falls
Size: 45 sq mi
Status: 36 sq mi designated wilderness (1964)
Terrain: Forested buttes, lake basins
Elevation: 4700'–8208'
Management: Winema NF
Topographic map: Mountain Lakes Wilderness (USFS)

This pocket wilderness is large enough that some of its alpine viewpoints and forest-rimmed lakes are best seen on backpacking trips.

Climate

Late summer brings frequent thunderstorms, but most of the area's 40 inches of annual precipitation comes as snow, which blocks trails from early November to late June. Mosquitoes are numerous in July.

Plants and Wildlife

Bald eagles, osprey, and a variety of ducks from nearby Upper Klamath Lake frequent the high lakes. The dense forests below 7000 feet are chiefly droopy-topped mountain hemlock and prim, Christmas-tree-shaped Shasta red fir. At higher elevations, only gnarled whitebark pines survive. Their seeds are a primary food source for the area's raucous Clark's nutcrackers.

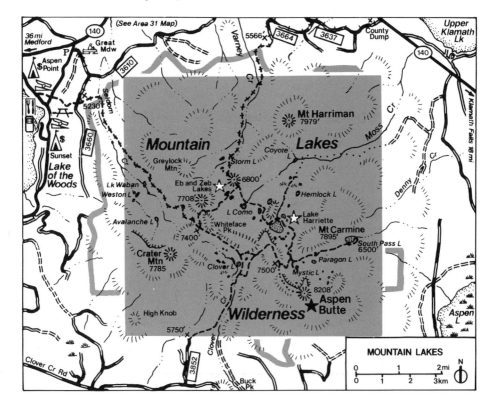

Harriette Lake

Geology

This roughly circular upland was once thought to be the eroded remnant of a collapsed 12,000-foot volcano similar to Crater Lake's Mount Mazama. However, the peaks here are actually a cluster of at least four overlapping volcanoes. Though glaciers have dissected them severely (Mount Carmine and Aspen Butte were once a single cone), they were probably never much taller than today. A feature of this volcanic hot spot is a swarm of faults running through the area, one of which aligned Seldom Creek's straight glacial valley.

THINGS TO DO

Hiking

Three trails climb to the 9-mile Mountain Lakes Loop, with its lakes and scenic passes. Because of the area's small size, permits are required for groups of more than ten, counting persons, saddle stock, and pack animals.

The most popular route into the wilderness is the Varney Creek Trail from Road 3664, which climbs among the creek's wildflowers (blooming in July) 4.6 miles to Eb and Zeb Lakes. These heavily visited, scenic, but shallow lakes are often warm enough for swimming.

Here most day hikers must turn around. Backpackers have more choices. Eastward, the Mountain Lakes Loop Trail heads 1.5 miles to very deep and very beautiful 40-acre Harriette Lake, passing Como Lake and shallow Silent and Zephyr lakes. Westward, the loop trail climbs 1 mile to a saddle, from which a 7708-foot summit with an excellent viewpoint is only a short cross-country hike away. Side trails from the 9-mile Mountain Lakes loop lead to seldom visited South Pass Lake, the Clover Lake basin, and the Hemlock Lake basin. Those ready for a grander cross-country viewpoint hike can head northeast from Eb Lake up a 2.5-mile ridge to Mount Harriman.

To find the Varney Creek trailhead, drive Highway 140 west of Klamath Falls 21 miles, turn south on Road 3637 for 1.7 miles, and turn left on Road 3664 to its end.

Another popular trailhead, on Road 3660 near Lake of the Woods, begins a 5.4-mile path up Seldom Creek's glacial valley to the Mountain Lakes Loop. After climbing 3.3 miles on this route, look for a spur trail to grassy Waban Lake, with its seasonal profusion of tree frogs.

A third path up to the Mountain Lakes Loop, the Clover Trail, is by far the shortest and least used. It reaches small Clover Lake from Road 3852 in 2.2 miles. Most hikers veer right at the 2-mile point, following the Mountain Lakes Loop to a ridgetop overlooking Harriette Lake. From here it's easy to strike off cross-country, following the alpine ridge up to the south past whitebark pines, dwarfed manzanita bushes, and showy Davidson's penstemons to Aspen Butte, whose summit view makes the strenuous 4.8-mile climb from Road 3852 worthwhile. Look for Crater Lake's rim peaks, Mount McLoughlin and Mount Shasta.

Backpackers hiking the 9-mile Mountain Lake Loop Trail may also want to explore the 1.7-mile spur trail eastward down a forested but increasingly arid glacial valley to large South Pass Lake.

Winter Sports

Nordic ski trips can begin from plowed Highway 140 either at the Great Meadow sno-park near Lake of the Woods or at the county dump near Upper Klamath Lake. Carry map, compass, and emergency gear; wilderness trails are not marked for winter use.

Great Meadow is a snowmobile center, but skiers leave noise behind when they leave Road 3660 for the Mountain Lakes Trail up Seldom Creek. Lake Waban, 4.5 miles from the sno-park, is a good goal.

From the county dump, skiers follow unplowed roads 3.5 miles to the Varney Creek trailhead. Eb and Zeb Lakes are a challenging 4.3-mile trek away.

33

SODA MOUNTAIN

Location: 13 mi SE of Ashland
Size: 50 sq mi
Status: Undesignated wilderness
Terrain: Steep, mostly wooded slopes
Elevation: 2300'–6091'
Management: Medford District BLM
Topographic maps: PCT Southern Oregon Portion (USFS); Siskiyou Pass, Soda Mountain, Parker Mountain, Hornbrook [California], Iron Gate Reservoir [California] (USGS)

The double cone of Mount Shasta stands high on the southern horizon from the slopes of Soda Mountain, where the Siskiyou Mountains and the Cascade Range meet.

Climate

Moderate snowfall blocks the Pacific Crest Trail (PCT) from about December to March or April. Annual precipitation varies from 40 inches in the upland forests to less than 20 inches on the dry, southern slopes, where summer temperatures can soar.

Plants and Wildlife

Soda Mountain stands at the apex of three biologic zones: the Cascades, the Siskiyous, and the high desert. Dark fir forests on the high, north-facing slopes resemble woods in the High Cascades. Droopy, canyon-bottom cedars and stiff-limbed manzanita brush remind one of the Siskiyous. Pungent sagebrush and juniper on the dry southern ridges belong to the Great Basin steppe.

The area is home to the showy Greene's mariposa lily (threatened in Oregon), though hikers are more likely to encounter trilliums and calypso orchids (in spring forests) or yellow-flowered rabbit brush (among fall sagebrush).

A large herd of blacktail deer from the Rogue Valley relies on the white oak grasslands of the lower southern slopes for winter browse. Other wildlife species include cougar, golden eagles, and quail.

Geology

Soda Mountain is a block of the Old Cascades, 16 to 25 million years old, wedged between the much older Klamath Mountains to the west and the much younger High Cascades to the east.

History

Pilot Rock's landmark basalt monolith once guided gold miners and trappers toward the Siskiyou Mountains' lowest pass. Train tracks built across Siskiyou Pass in 1887 filled the final gap in a rail line around the United States' perimeter. The area remained remote enough, however, to harbor Oregon's last known grizzly bear, the legendary, 8-foot-tall Old Reelfoot, which was shot near Pilot Rock's base in 1891. Later the D'Autremont brothers attempted a train robbery at Siskiyou Pass in 1923, murdering three men. They eluded a four-continent manhunt by camping under a deadfall tree beside Porcupine Creek.

THINGS TO DO

Hiking

Interstate 5 travelers can stretch their legs with a 1-mile forest walk on the Pacific Crest Trail to the cliffs and views at the base of Pilot Rock. From the Mount Ashland exit, follow old Highway 99 south under the freeway 2 miles, turn left on Pilot Rock Road 40-2E-33 for 2 miles, branch left at a quarry for 1.5 miles, and park at a saddle beside Porcupine Mountain, where a

gated side road joins on the right. Walk a few yards along this side road to the PCT crossing; for Pilot Rock, hike to the right.

For even better views of Mount Shasta, hike left on the PCT from the same trailhead 4 miles to Soda Mountain. A short access road leads from the PCT to the lookout tower (in use each summer) on the mountain's broad, alpine summit. The PCT continues north from Soda Mountain 1.5 miles through a dense old-growth forest before crossing Soda Mountain Road 39-3E-32.3. To reach this PCT trail-

Golden-mantled ground squirrel

head, take Highway 66 east of Ashland 15.6 miles, turn south just before Green Springs Summit, and follow the Soda Mountain Road 5 miles.

The best view of all is at Boccard Point's rocky promontory, an easy 0.2-mile walk from the end of Baldy Creek Road 40-3E-5. From the Ashland exit of Interstate 5, take Highway 66 east for 14.8 miles, turn right on Tyler Creek Road 1.5 miles, turn left on gravel Road 40-3E-5 for 7.5 miles to its end, and then hike south along the open, trailless ridge to the viewpoint.

Boccard Point also makes a good starting point for cross-country forays into the area's steep southern canyons. Trailless travel here is easiest through sagebrush and open grasslands along ridgetops, or along the creek's lush growth of moss and maples. Rock outcroppings and bands of nearly impenetrable scrub oak chaparral interrupt canyon slopes. Dutch Oven Creek's many small waterfalls make good goals.

Climbing

Pilot Rock's basalt tower offers seven mountaineering routes, including the scenic West Ridge (level I-5.3) and the South Face's broken basalt columns (rated II-5.6). The West Gully, a class 3 scramble route to the summit, is commonly used by technical climbers as a descent route. A pinnacle 200 yards southeast of Pilot Rock requires level I-5.7 skills.

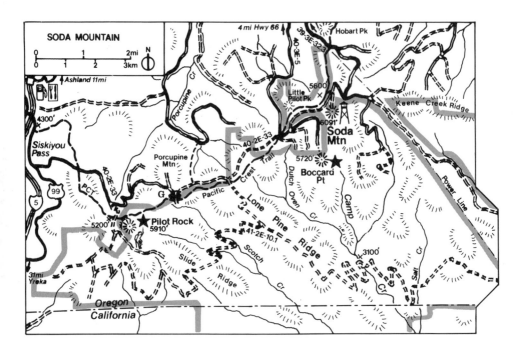

34

RED BUTTES

Location: 34 mi SW of Medford
Size: 130 sq mi total; 42 sq mi in Oregon
Status: 31 sq mi designated wilderness; 6 sq mi in Oregon (1984)
Terrain: Rocky buttes, forested ridges, small lakes
Elevation: 1300'–7055'
Management: Rogue River NF, Siskiyou NF, Klamath NF, Oregon Caves National Monument
Topographic maps: Red Buttes Wilderness, PCT Southern Oregon Portion (USFS)

Straddling the rocky crest of the Siskiyou Mountains, this little-visited area's trail system extends along view-filled ridges and subalpine meadows from the Pacific Crest Trail (PCT) to the Oregon Caves National Monument.

Climate

Snowfall closes high trails from about November to May. Summers are very dry. Annual precipitation measures 60 inches.

Plants and Wildlife

Expect signs of frequent wildlife on the trails: deer tracks, coyote scat, and palm-sized paw prints of cougar and bear. This is also a prime spot for Bigfoot fanciers; alleged sightings of ape men date to 1895. The Forest Service issued a special-use permit for a Sasquatch trap here in 1973.

The area teems with the unusual flora of the Siskiyous. Knobcone pines, resembling bumpy flagpoles, dot Figurehead Mountain. Droopy weeping spruce are common. Massive incense cedars, hollowed by fire, could serve as extra camping accommodations beside Sucker Gap's shelter. A loop trail from the Oregon Caves leads to Big Tree, one of Oregon's largest Douglas firs. Some of the world's southernmost Alaska cedars grow on Mount Emily, while the world's northernmost Baker's cypresses grow on Steve Peak, a quarter mile east of Miller Lake.

June brings wildflowers familiar from the alpine Cascades as well as Siskiyou novelties, including two delicate, pink *lewisia* species, best seen in Cameron Meadows or along the Fir Glade Trail to Azalea Lake.

Geology

Colorful rock cairns marking high trails here showcase these mountains' diversity; the rocks are up to 425 million years old (almost twenty times the age of the Old Cascades). Look for flat slate, shiny schist, green serpentinite, white marble, and speckled granite.

The ancient North American continent thrust westward here against the Pacific plate, jumbling up masses of sea-floor rock, including the red peridotite forming Red Buttes' twin peaks. The pressure of that collision also cooked limestone to marble, allowing later water seepage to create the white caverns of the Oregon Caves (now dripstone stalactites grow there at the swift rate of an

Siskiyou Crest from Figurehead Mountain with Red Buttes on the horizon at left

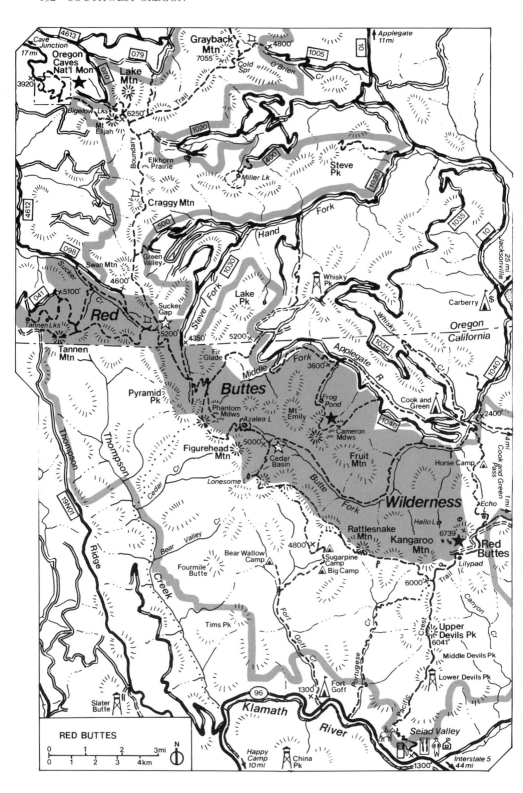

RED BUTTES

0   1   2   3mi
0   1   2   3   4km

N

inch per decade). Finally, hot granite intrusions melted out veins of mineral-rich quartz. Gold attracted swarms of prospectors in the 1850s. Mine tailings and washed-out, "hydraulicked" river bottoms remain.

THINGS TO DO

Hiking

Start with an easy 3.5-mile hike along the Pacific Crest Trail from Cook and Green Pass to aptly named Lilypad Lake, at the foot of Red Butte's double peak. Along the way take a short side trail to an overlook of Echo Lake, in a high basin. Have energy for a longer hike? From Lilypad Lake, it's a nearly level 2.6 miles to Upper Devils Peak and a look at the Klamath River 4700 feet below. For a view toward Oregon, turn off the PCT at Kangaroo Mountain and head west 2.5 trail miles to the cliff-edged pass atop craggy Rattlesnake Mountain.

In much of this wilderness, dry, south-facing slopes confound cross-country hikers with impenetrable chaparral tangles of manzanita, snowbrush, and stunted chinkapin. Open forests on northern slopes, however, invite trailless exploration. A top trip from Cook and Green Pass takes off from Echo Lake and circles Red Buttes' ruddy double peak, passing wildflower meadows, springs, and five scenic cirque lakes on a sometimes rocky 5-mile traverse, returning via the PCT.

To reach Cook and Green Pass from Medford, drive 31 miles southwest past Jacksonville, Ruch, and Star Ranger Station to the end of Applegate Reservoir. Trade pavement there for gravel Elliott Creek Road 1050, and after 1 mile, turn right on Road 1055 (roads not shown on map). An 8-mile climb reaches Cook and Green Pass and the PCT crossing.

Visit the wildflowers at Frog Pond and Cameron Meadows with a 6-mile loop hike from Road 1040. From the meadows, scramble up a ridge to the south for a good viewpoint. Planning a car shuttle between the two trailheads will save a final 2-mile walk along Road 1040 back to the car.

Sucker Creek Gap, at the junction of the east–west Siskiyou Mountains and the north–south Grayback Range, is a cool, grassy dale surrounded by impressive old-growth cedars. Hike there from the end of Road 1030 on a 3-mile trail through the deep forest along the splashing Steve Fork. An even shorter 1.4-mile route to the Sucker Creek Gap shelter takes off from the end of Road 098. From Cave Junction, head toward Oregon Caves for 14.5 miles, turn south on gravel Road 4612 for 9 miles, then turn right onto Road 098.

The swimmable Tannen Lakes, nestled in forest against a backdrop of Tannen Mountain's rockslides, are a popular day-hike goal. A gentle quarter-mile trail leads to the larger Tannen Lake from Road 041; East Tannen Lake is another mile along the Boundary Trail, a well-graded route that tempts hikers to continue to Sucker Gap. From Cave Junction or O'Brien, follow signs toward Happy Camp, but turn east at the Siskiyou summit on gravel Road 4812. After 4 miles branch to the right onto Road 041; the trailhead is 5 miles ahead.

Atop Lake Mountain, hikers can often spot both Mount Shasta and the Pacific Ocean. It's easy to combine a hike there with a visit to the renowned Oregon Caves, since the trail branches off from the National Monument's Cliff Nature Trail. At the 4-mile point, weary hikers can settle for a nice view atop lesser Mount Elijah. More energetic souls can side trip down to swim in the Bigelow Lakes.

Backpackers often head for Cedar Basin, a forested bowl featuring several swimmable lakes, June wildflowers, and views of rocky Figurehead Mountain. It's 6.5 miles to Cedar Basin's Azalea Lake from the Fir Glade trailhead. A 0.5-mile shoreline trail loops around the popular little lake, with separate camp areas designated for hikers and equestrians. Once at Cedar Basin, it's tempting to hike on to the rocky pass just south of Lonesome Lake for a look into the Klamath River country. Or climb Figurehead Mountain for views ranging from the western Siskiyous' Preston Peak to Mount Shasta and Mount McLoughlin. A good trail on Figurehead Mountain's northwest shoulder comes within a short cross-country ramble of the summit.

To reach the Fir Glade trailhead, drive to the end of pavement at the south end of Applegate Reservoir, 31 miles southwest of Medford. Take gravel Road 1040 for 5.8 miles (passing Cook

The Pacific Crest Trail at the foot of Red Buttes

and Green Campground) and turn left to continue on Road 1040 another 10.5 miles to the trailhead spur.

Several long-distance backpacking routes surpass the PCT here, with its grueling, 4700-foot ascent from Seiad Valley. The 18.3-mile Boundary Trail from Grayback Mountain to Tannen Lakes avoids the PCT's crowds.

Cook and Green Campground is the trailhead for two other excellent backpacking loops. A 12.5-mile trip climbs up the well-graded Cook and Green Trail to Cook and Green Pass, follows the PCT for 2 miles, then dives down past Echo Lake, back to the campground. But for the best sampling of this wilderness, take a 33.5-mile loop backpack from the campground past Cook and Green Pass, Red Buttes, Rattlesnake Mountain, and Cedar Basin, returning via the Butte Fork Trail.

35

KALMIOPSIS

Location: 33 mi SW of Grants Pass
Size: 672 sq mi
Status: 281 sq mi designated wilderness (1964, 1978); federal wild and scenic river
Terrain: Steep, rugged canyons, sparsely forested ridges, river rapids
Elevation: 240'–5098'
Management: Siskiyou NF
Topographic map: Kalmiopsis Wilderness (USFS)

Cut by the green-pooled Illinois River's rugged gorge, the Kalmiopsis is Oregon's largest but perhaps least visited forest wilderness. Seen from one of the dry ridgetop trails, jagged canyonlands spread like a vast sheet of crumpled paper. This is a land of torrential winter rains and blazing summer heat, of rare wildflowers and shy black bears.

Hikers should expect challenge as well as beauty on the steep trails. Boaters on the wild Illinois must prepare for ten churning class 4 rapids and the monstrous, class 5 Green Wall.

Climate

Heavy rains from October to May (100 to 150 inches) swell the rivers, making crossings difficult in spring. There are no bridges. Snow usually covers trails over 4000 feet from December through March. Afternoon temperatures often exceed 90°F in virtually rainless July and August.

Plants and Wildlife

Unusual species developed during the 50 million years that the Klamath Mountains were an island in the Pacific Ocean. Many of these species have survived because Ice Age glaciers left most of the area untouched. Plant collecting is prohibited.

Carnivorous pitcher plants resemble green baseball bats sprouting from boggy land. These plants make up for the area's poor soil by catching their own nutrients. A honey aroma lures insects into the plant's hollow stem, where tiny hairs prevent escape and enzymes reduce the catch to liquid. At springs look for brilliant blue gentian and white death camas.

Rare *Kalmiopsis leachiana* fills forests with pink blooms in June. This azalealike shrub, found only in and near the Kalmiopsis, is best seen at Bailey Mountain, Dry Butte, Gold Basin, and Taggarts Bar.

Forests are often Douglas fir and canyon live oak but include an odd mix of other species. Look for madrone, with peeling red bark, and chinkapin, with spiny fruit ("porcupine eggs"). Port Orford cedar and Brewer's weeping spruce, elsewhere rare, are common here.

Tail-twitching, orange Douglas squirrels scold hikers from trees. On rocky slopes, watch for western fence lizards, blue-tailed skinks, and the area's unaggressive rattlesnakes. Quiet hikers frequently surprise black bears foraging for sugar pine seeds, yellowjacket ground nests, or manzanita berries. The bears dislike dogs, but do all they can to avoid humans, typically climbing trees or fleeing on sight. Encourage this by wrapping smelly food tightly and hanging all food at night.

Geology

This portion of the Klamath Mountains was on the western shore of North America 200 million years ago when the continent began its present 1-inch-a-year westward drift. The movement buckled up masses of sub-seafloor rock and folded Siskiyou strata like taffy.

Today, outcroppings of sub-seafloor rock (red peridotite and shiny green serpentinite) are so infertile they visibly stunt vegetation; they also provide the traces of rare, heavy metals which account for the area's many gold-mining cabins and abandoned chrome mines.

The continent's westward drift also temporarily sheared off the Siskiyou Mountains, leaving

Gold miner's cabin on the Little Chetco River

them an island in the Pacific Ocean, much as Baja California has been sheared away from Mexico, or Vancouver Island from Canada. As proof of this, 45- to 90-million-year-old sea fossils are found on the eastern edge of the Klamaths. What's more, strata in the southern Klamaths match strata hundreds of miles away in the northern Sierras—as if the two ranges had been separated by a huge knife. The ancient strait has filled with sediment and volcanics from the Cascades.

Though new mining claims are prohibited in designated wilderness, recreational gold panning is allowed. To try, wash out heavy black sands gleaned from bedrock cracks in creekbeds in the Little Chetco River or Upper Chetco River area. Look for jasper along the Illinois River below Florence Creek.

THINGS TO DO

Hiking

The 27-mile Illinois River Trail over Bald Mountain is well graded and maintained. Nearly all other paths in the area, however, are steep, rocky miners' pack trails or bulldozed mining roads. Hikers may meet four-wheel-drive vehicles even in designated wilderness, since miners with valid pre-1984 claims have keys to the road gates.

A few other cautions: Beware of the shiny, autumn-red, three-leaved poison oak prolific at lower elevations. Vast brushfields of tough, red-limbed manzanita stymie most cross-country travelers. The danger of stumbling onto illegal marijuana plantations has declined from the 1970s and 80s, when off-trail hikers often encountered guarded marijuana patches near creeks and springs within a mile or two of trailheads.

The two most popular short hikes lead to cirque lakes high in the mountain forests: Babyfoot Lake in the east of the wilderness and Vulcan Lake in the west.

An easy, 1-mile trail through a designated botanical area reaches Babyfoot Lake from Road 140. Continue past the surprisingly green lake, follow a mining road south, and return along a view-filled ridgetop trail for a 3.5-mile loop hike. For even better views of the area's rugged canyonlands—and a glimpse of the distant ocean—head for Eagle Mountain or the abandoned lookout site atop Canyon Peak, both less than 4 trail miles from Babyfoot Lake. Reach the trailhead via Eight Dollar Mountain Road 4201, which branches off Highway 199 north of Cave Junction 5 miles.

Vulcan Lake is the same size as Babyfoot Lake (4 acres), but instead of being set in a lush forest, it fills a dramatic rock basin of stunted pines below broad Vulcan Peak. The red peridotite rock shores not only exhibit glacial scratch marks of interest to geologists; they also make ideal sunbathing spots for swimmers. A well-maintained 1.4-mile trail from the end of Road 1909 crosses a scenic ridge on its way to Vulcan Lake.

Other trails near Vulcan Lake make good day trips. The old lookout site atop Vulcan Peak, with views of the Kalmiopsis and the Pacific coast, is up a 1-mile trail (gaining 1000 feet). A mostly level 4-mile ridgetop route passes Red Mountain on its way to austere Chetco Lake. Another trail with views from an open ridgetop heads north 3 miles to Dry Butte's fields of *Kalmiopsis leachiana*. Trailhead access is from Brookings; turn off Highway 101 at the north end of the Chetco River bridge, follow the road along the Chetco River 16.5 miles, and then turn right on Road 1909 to its end.

Where trails exist at all along the Chetco River's rugged inner gorge, they generally traverse canyon slopes several hundred feet above the green-pooled stream. A day hike from the western edge of the wilderness samples one such trail, a 3-mile route from a spur of Road 360 to a ford and chilly swimming hole at Boulder Creek Camp. From there, hikers can climb an extra mile to a view of the Big Craggies from Lately Prairie, or else continue 3 miles along the Chetco River for a look up Tincup Creek's gorge. To reach the trailhead, drive 23 miles up the Chetco River from Brookings, turn off Road 1376 onto dirt Road 360 for a mile, then switchback onto spur Road 365.

Three popular day hikes begin near the McCaleb Ranch Boy Scout camp, on the Grants Pass side of the wilderness. The main attraction of the Fall Creek Trail is its first 0.5 mile, beginning

Galice 13 mi
Hwy 199 at Selma 5 mi
Hwy 199 6 mi
Briggs Cr
Red Dog Cr
Todd Cr
Oak Flat Launch Site
Store Gulch
Fall Cr
980'
McCaleb Ranch (Boy Scout)
Briggs Creek
Panther Cr
904'
River
Salmon Cr
Eagle Mtn
Whetstone Butte
Flat Top
Phillips Cr
York Butte
Labrador Cr
Castle Rock
Chetco Pass
3600'
Sourdough Flat
Slide Cr
Babyfoot Cr
Clear Cr
York Cr
Nome Pk
Granite Spr
5098'
Pearsoll Pk
Chinaman Hat
Trail
Pine Cr
Pine Flat
Boat Eater Rapids
1200'
2609'
Florence Cr
Klondike Cr
Granite Cr
Gold Basin
Granite Butte
Illinois
Illinois River
3850'
Bald Mtn
Sulphur Cr
Yukon Cr
Mt Billingslea
Taggarts Bar
Tincup Pk 4494'
Deadman Bar
Hayward Pk 4291'
Box Cr
Chetco Bar
Kalmiopsis
Mid Bald Prairie
4091'
Heather Mtn
Windy Camp
(See Area 36 Map)
Oak Flat Trailhead 4.3mi
Silver Cr
3460'
South Bend Mtn
3413'
Fawn Falls
Little Bald Prairie
The Green Wall Rapids
Tincup Pass
2500'
Chetco
Tincup Cr
Collier Bar
Submarine Hole
Little Green Wall
280'
2026'
Darling Cr
Lately Prairie
Rogue River 8 mi
Big Craggies
Fall Cr
300
480'
Horse Sign Butte
North Fk
Collier Cr
3124'
4621'
Hurt Cabin
River
South Fk
Mislatnah Cr
1400'
Game Lake
4300'
Green Craggie
Collier Butte
25
2512
700
390
675
642
4103
087
142
365
360
420
400
3680

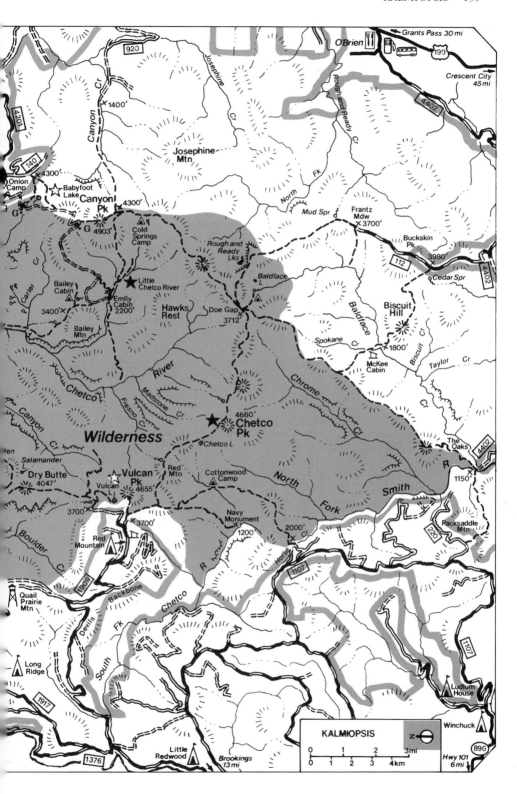

with a dramatic suspension footbridge over the Illinois River. For the two other hikes, drive up steep dirt Road 087 and park at Chetco Pass. From there, the view at Pearsoll Peak's cupola-style lookout tower, the highest point in the region, is a 2.3-mile walk up a rutted road-trail. Also from Chetco Pass, it's interesting to walk the mining road west, past mostly abandoned chrome mine camps at Sourdough Flat, 3 miles down to the Chetco River ford.

The popular 27-mile Illinois River Trail traverses wildflower-filled meadows on Bald Mountain's long crest, then descends through the wild Illinois River's remote inner gorge. Side trips to viewpoints at South Bend Mountain or to Collier Bar (a river ford passable from mid-June to November) can make the trip even more spectacular. Start at Briggs Creek, at the bumpy end of dirt Road 4103, and finish at a paved road 3 miles from Agness (see the map for area 36, Wild Rogue). Those who can't arrange the long car shuttle can catch a Rogue River mail boat (available May 1 to November 1) from Agness to bus connections in Gold Beach.

Backpackers with a yen for solitude and rugged beauty will find both in the vast interior of the Kalmiopsis. The premier trip is a 42-mile trail loop from Vulcan Lake past Dry Butte, Taggarts Bar, Emlly Cabin, Doe Gap, and Chetco Peak. Beware of dehydration, since trails follow dry ridges and canyon slopes. Carry plenty of water and study maps carefully for trailside springs and perennial streams.

Boating

Oregon's most difficult whitewater run, the Illinois River from Oak Flat to Agness, packs 156 rated rapids into 35 miles. The setting is a breathtakingly stark, trailless, 4000-foot-deep canyon. The brilliant green river is so clear that mossy boulders 30 feet underwater seem within reach.

Only very experienced river runners in kayaks, narrow inflatables, or portageable hard boats should attempt the Illinois, and then only in April or May when water levels range between 600 and 1400 cubic feet per second (gauged at the Kerby station). The lower water of early summer turns the run to a gamut of rock dodging and boat bashing. Higher water after heavy spring rains converts Boat Eater and the Green Wall to deadly maelstroms.

Start the three-day trip at the unmarked Oak Flat launch site 13 miles west of Selma where Road 4103 dips close to the river. A box here contains free, unlimited, self-issuing permits. Drift an easy 3 miles before coming to Panther Creek and the first of many rapids that must be scouted. The next 2 miles wallop boaters with seven increasingly powerful class 3 and 4 rapids, culminating with York Creek Rapids, a 4+ churner with an underwater shelf and tall standing waves in the preferred left channel.

Boat Eater Rapids, 3 miles downriver at the mouth of Pine Creek, funnels the river past a cabin-sized boulder into a roaring suckhole with a record of trapping every third or fourth craft it meets. Boaters usually camp immediately after this class 4+ trial.

Ten miles of swift but manageable water the second day out lead to the big stuff. It starts with class 4 Fawn Falls, down a 10-foot chute into a boulder obstacle course. Hardly 0.5 mile beyond, an ominous wall covered with green moss looms above the river, signaling all but the most athletic daredevils to the coming class 5 water.

The Green Wall Rapids drops boaters 50 feet in less than 300 yards. First comes a fast stretch of rocks and holes, then a drop through a barricade of truck-sized boulders, then another 12-foot cascade, and finally a possible crush against the wall itself.

Three-quarters of a mile farther, Little Green Wall's class 4 rocks hang up their share of boats. Whitewater is then nonstop for 2 miles to Submarine Hole's treacherous midstream boulder, which must be run on the left side (though this positioning requires strong rowing). Exhausted river runners will find no campsite for yet another 1.7 miles.

The third day is an easy drift to the Agness pullout on the Rogue River. The car shuttle between ends of the run totals 120 miles over several poor roads (Oak Flat to Grants Pass to Galice to Agness); if this route is closed by lingering April snow, plan on 150 miles via Crescent City and Gold Beach. Arrangements may be made by calling Whitewater Cowboys at (503) 479-0132.

36

WILD ROGUE

Location: 27 mi NW of Grants Pass
Size: 224 sq mi
Status: 56 sq mi designated wilderness (1978); federal wild and scenic river
Terrain: Steep, rocky, forested river canyon
Elevation: 140'–5316'
Management: Siskiyou NF, Medford District BLM
Topographic map: Wild Rogue Wilderness (USFS)

The irascible Rogue River, cutting through the mountains to the sea, is at times a string of sunny, green pools, lazily drifting past playful otter and circling osprey. But the river can also be misty mayhem, raging over Blossom Bar's boulders like a giant pinball course, swirling boats helplessly in The Coffeepot, and standing on edge in Mule Creek Canyon, a chasm so narrow boats sometimes bridge from wall to wall.

More than 10,000 visitors a year run the Rogue's famous whitewater. However, the beautiful, 47-mile Rogue River Trail is seldom crowded, and the rest of this river's rugged, 4000-foot-deep canyon remains virtually untrodden.

Climate

Toward the end of the reliably rainless, hot summers, river temperatures rise to 70°F, tempting swimmers but driving fish into cooler tributaries. Intermittent rains from September to May total 90 inches in the damp western end of the canyon but only 50 inches in the east.

Plants and Wildlife

It's easy to spot wildlife attracted to the river: deer, merganser ducks, otters, black bears (catching salmon), osprey (and their nests atop tall snags), great blue herons, kingfishers,

Rhododendron

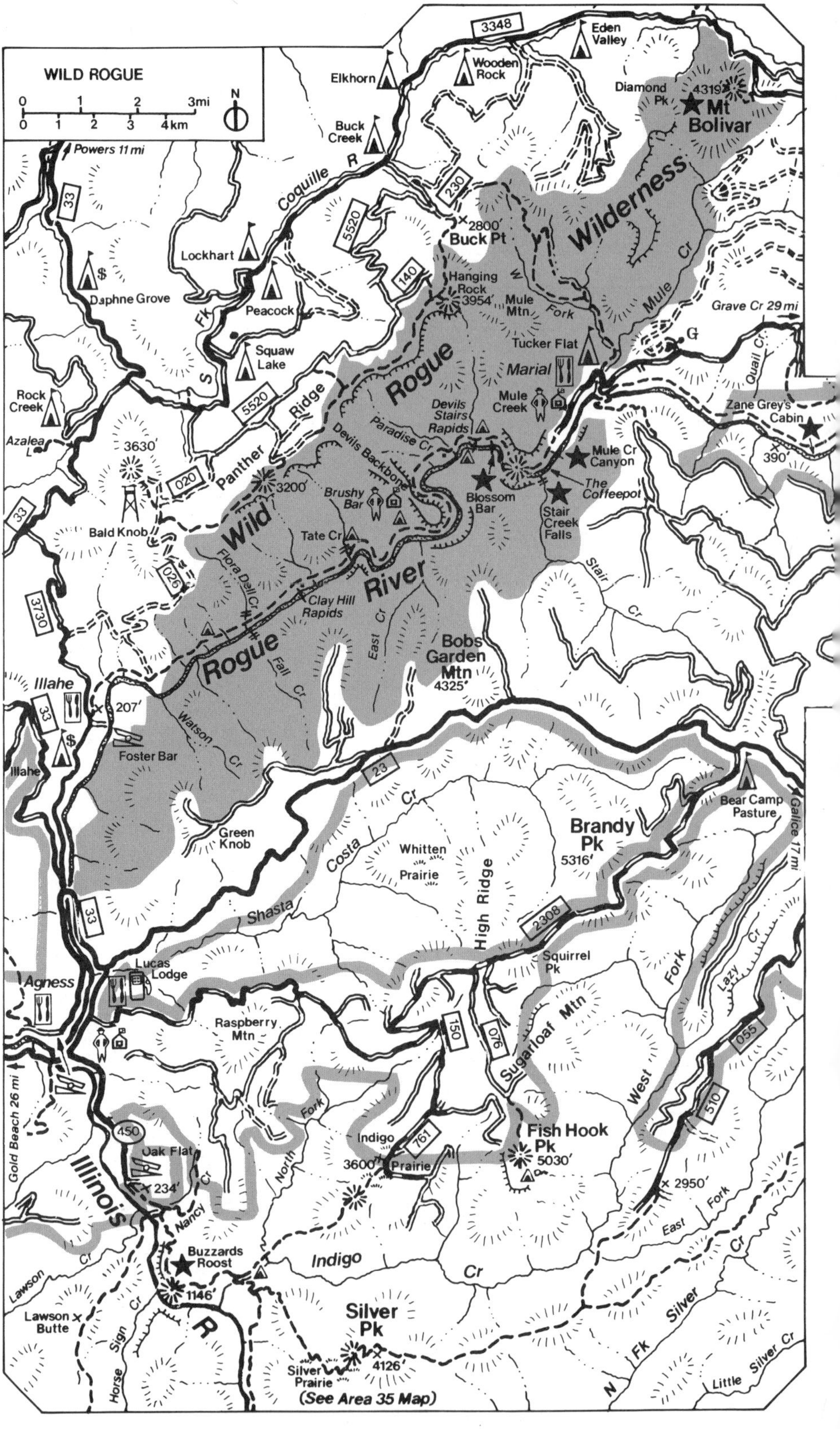

WILD ROGUE

0 1 2 3mi
0 1 2 3 4km
N

Powers 11 mi

Elkhorn

Wooden Rock

Eden Valley

Diamond Pk

4319'

Mt Bolivar

Buck Creek

3348

Lockhart

Coquille R

5520

230

Buck Pt
×2800'

140

Wilderness

Daphne Grove

Peacock

S Fk

Hanging Rock
3954'

Mule Fork

Mule Mtn

Grave Cr 29 mi

Mule Cr

Squaw Lake

Tucker Flat

Marial

G

Rock Creek

5520

Panther Ridge

Wild Rogue

Devils Stairs Rapids

Mule Creek

Zane Grey's Cabin

Azalea L

3630'

020

Paradise Cr

Devils Backbone

Mule Cr Canyon

390'

3200'

Brushy Bar

Blossom Bar

The Coffeepot

Bald Knob

026

Tate Cr

W

Stair Creek Falls

3730

Flora Dell Cr

Clay Hill Rapids

Rogue River

East Cr

Stair Cr

33

Rogue

Fall Cr

Bobs Garden Mtn
4325'

Illahe
×207'

Watson Cr

Foster Bar

23

Costa Cr

Bear Camp Pasture

Illahe

Green Knob

Whitten Prairie

High Ridge

Brandy Pk
5316'

Galice 17 mi

33

Shasta

2308

Squirrel Pk

Lazy Cr

Agness

Lucas Lodge

West Fk

055

Gold Beach 26 mi

Raspberry Mtn

150

076

Sugarloaf Mtn

510

North Fork

450

Fish Hook Pk
5030'

Oak Flat
×234'

Indigo Prairie
3600'

761

×2950'

Illinois R

Nancy Cr

Buzzards Roost
1146'

Indigo Cr

East Fork

Lawson × Butte

Lawson Cr

Sign Cr

Horse Cr

Silver Pk

Silver Prairie
4126'

(See Area 35 Map)

N Fk Silver Cr

Little Silver Cr

swooping cliff swallows (with mud nests on overhangs), and water ouzels. Try identifying the many tracks on the riverbanks each morning.

The river itself teems with salamanders, newts, and over 20 species of fish, including Chinook salmon, steelhead, rainbow trout, sturgeon, shad, carp, lamprey, sculpin, stickleback, and dace. Among Oregon rivers, only the Columbia provides a higher annual fish catch.

Hikers encounter scurrying lizards and blue-tailed skinks on the dry slopes. This is the northernmost habitat for the nocturnal ringtail, a tiny, big-eared relative of the raccoon once employed by miners to catch mice in mines.

The Douglas fir forests include lush red cedar and rhododendron in the west, but yield to canyon live oak and red-barked madrone in the more arid east. Brushfields of manzanita and chinkapin limit cross-country travel. May brings trailside blue iris and white beargrass blooms; expect blue lupine and California poppies in June.

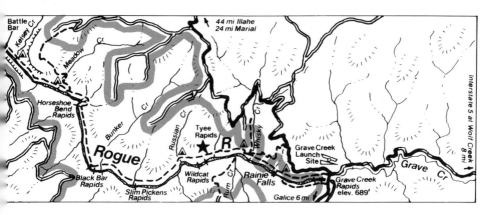

Geology

Tough, 150-million-year-old lava restricts the Rogue River through much of its lower gorge. A massive landslide visible just west of Whisky Creek briefly dammed 15 miles of the Rogue in the 1880s. Unusual kettle-shaped potholes in the riverbank rock, best seen near Clay Hill Rapids, form when floodwaters swirl pebbles in depressions, drilling them deeper.

History

The river's name comes from the Tututni and Takelma Indians, whom the early French trappers called *coquins* (rogues). Angered by a sudden influx of gold-hungry whites, the Indians massacred Rogue valley settlers in October 1855 and then retreated to this remote part of the river canyon for winter.

The next April, 536 U.S. cavalrymen tracked them to Battle Bar and traded fire across the river before turning back. A month later, Chief John's well-armed Indians besieged a smaller Army unit on a knoll at Illahe, where battle trenches are still visible. Relief troops from the east fled when Indians rolled rocks on them from a hillside near Brushy Bar, but soldiers from Gold Beach broke the siege. The Tututni and Takelma were transported north to the coastal Siletz Reservation.

In 1926, author Zane Grey bought a miner's cabin at Winkle Bar, where he fished and wrote his popular Wild West books. Few unguided parties ran the river until the 1930s, when boatmen dynamited boulders in the most difficult rapids. Slim Pickens Rapids and Blossom Bar dropped to class 3 and class 4 whitewater, respectively.

Until 1963, mules packed mail on the Rogue River Trail from Marial to Agness, where mail boats left for Gold Beach. Although pavement now extends up the canyon to Agness, jet-powered mail boats still make the run, carrying tourists.

THINGS TO DO

Hiking

The prime trip here is the 47-mile Rogue River Trail backpack from Illahe to Grave Creek; day hikers can sample scenic parts of the route. Because the sometimes rocky trail traverses steep slopes several hundred feet above the river, it is closed to horse use.

A 4.3-mile walk from Illahe to Flora Dell Creek's shady glen reaches a trailside waterfall that splashes into a swimmable pool. Those who drive the gravel road to Marial, at the Rogue River Trail's midpoint, can hike 2.1 miles downriver, past inspiring viewpoints of The Coffeepot and Stair Creek Falls to Blossom Bar, a good spot to photograph frantic boaters. East of Marial, Zane Grey's tiny log cabin lies 5.7 miles up the trail. And from the Grave Creek trailhead, a 3.3-mile walk passes 15-foot Rainie Falls on the way to Whisky Creek, where the BLM has preserved a historic 1880s mining cabin.

Hikers should be alert for yellowjackets, wood ticks, rattlesnakes, and prolific growths of head-high poison oak. Campers can expect nocturnal visits by the area's numerous black bears, particularly in the Brushy Bar–Clay Hill area. Here, bears have grown bold from finding easy meals in boaters' "bear-proof" cooler chests and hikers' backpacks. Hang all food at least 10 feet above ground and 5 feet from a tree trunk.

Lodges at Illahe, Clay Hill Rapids, Paradise Creek, and Marial offer meals and lodging by reservation. Scheduled daily jet boats take hikers from Gold Beach to the Clay Hill and Paradise lodges between May 15 and October 15, and to Lucas Lodge in Agness between May 1 and November 1.

Surprisingly few day hikers make the trip up from the primitive campgrounds on the Coquille River to several first-rate viewpoints on a ridgecrest high above the Rogue River. Two short hikes are tops here: a 1.5-mile path gaining 1200 feet up scenic Mount Bolivar, and a rhododendron-lined 1.7-mile trail from Buck Point to Hanging Rock (bring binoculars to spot rafters on Blossom Bar, 3600 feet below). For a longer trip, hike 10.5 miles along Panther Ridge from Buck Point to Bald Knob's lookout tower. Backpackers can tackle a 38-mile loop: hike from Illahe on the Rogue River Trail to Marial, climb to Buck Point on the newly reopened trail up the West Fork of Mule Creek, and return along Panther Ridge and Road 026.

The Illinois River Trail, south of Agness, offers an excellent 2.6-mile day hike (one way) to the craggy promontory of Buzzards Roost, with views in both directions along this green-pooled river's canyon. Backpackers will want to hike the entirety of the 27-mile Illinois River Trail (see area 35, Kalmiopsis). Those who can't arrange the required car shuttle can make a base camp at Indigo Creek for forays to the meadows and old-growth ponderosa pines in the rarely visited Silver Peak and Indigo Prairie areas, swept by fire in 1987.

One of the nicest day hikes in the area leads to 60-foot Silver Falls, in the narrow, fern-draped gorge of Silver Creek. Though this hike is not shown on the map, it's not difficult to locate. From Galice, drive 9 miles west on the paved Galice Timber Access Road to Soldier Camp Saddle and follow "Silver Creek" signs from there for 10 rough, badly rutted miles to the trailhead. Hike 1 mile to Silver Creek, and then rock-hop 0.3 mile upstream to the double waterfall.

Boating

The 40-mile wild stretch of Rogue River between Grave Creek and Illahe is Oregon's most famous and popular three-day whitewater trip.

Rafts, kayaks, and drift boats have hardly left the launch before they hit the spray of class 3 Grave Creek Rapids. Half an hour later the increasing roar of 15-foot-tall Rainie Falls warns boaters to *portage by lining craft down the shallow fish ladder on the right.* Large, well-constructed rafts of inner tubes sometimes succeed in running massive Rainie Falls, but such vehicles later often wedge side-to-side in Mule Creek Canyon or hang up on Blossom Bar's boulders.

Beyond the falls, pull in at Whisky Creek for a quarter-mile side trip to a well-preserved mining cabin. Downstream 1.2 miles, pull out again to scout class 4 Tyee Rapids. Keep to the far right to avoid a suckhole and then a house-sized rock. Promptly thereafter come class 3 Wildcat Rapids, with a submerged, spiny-backed rock known as The Alligator.

After passing the historic Rogue River Ranch Museum at Marial on the second day (or third, for slower drifters), boats accelerate toward class 4 Mule Creek Canyon, a chasm so narrow and turbulent that it's easy to lose an oar just when the need is greatest. After spring floods, scout from shore for logs jammed sideways. Past the canyon's final, dizzying Coffeepot comes Stair Creek's lovely side waterfall, a good swimming area.

Blossom Bar, 1.3 miles beyond, requires scouting from the right. Following this treacherous, class 4 boulder field are the Devil's Stairs, where the river drops 30 feet in a 300-yard series of chutes.

On the trip's final day, hike up to Tate Creek's shady waterfall pool, with a 25-foot natural slide of rock so smooth swimmers can zip down its chute *sans* suit.

Campers on the heavily used riverbars and creek benches must use stoves or bring their own firewood and metal fire pans. In summer, seek out solitude by camping away from side creeks with drinkable water; for these sites, carry drinking water or purify river water.

Perhaps the greatest challenge of the Rogue River is getting a permit to launch at all. For an average year's restricted season (June 1 to September 15), the Siskiyou National Forest issues 10,000 permits by lottery from 90,000 applications. For applications, write the Rand Visitor Center, 14335 Galice Highway, Merlin, OR 97532, or call (503) 479-3735. With or without permits, all boaters setting out between May 15 and October 15 must first check in at the visitor center in Rand, between Galice and Grave Creek.

Those who lose in the permit lottery can sign up for a commercially guided trip (at least $500) or join the mad rush of boaters during the free-for-all final weekends of September. A third alternative is to prepare for a trip in the off-season's iffy weather. By October, skies turn a misty gray and the river grows chilly, but solitude and empty campsites beckon. A few cautions: Winter high water can make the river too dangerous to run. And when snow closes the 55-mile car shuttle route's twisty mountain roads (usually from November to May), the only alternative is a 180-mile paved route via Crescent City.

Blossom Bar

37

GRASSY KNOB

Location: 51 mi S of Coos Bay, 9 mi E of Port Orford
Size: 39 sq mi
Status: 27 sq mi designated wilderness (1984)
Terrain: Rain forest–covered canyons and ridges
Elevation: 100'–2924'
Management: Siskiyou NF
Topographic maps: Father Mountain, Mount Butler, Sixes, Port Orford (USGS)

Fog drips from the tangled forest of this virtually trailless wilderness, where ridgetops provide surprising glimpses out to Cape Blanco's fringe of ocean islands.

Climate

Heavy winter rains push the average annual precipitation to over 130 inches. Summers are mostly sunny, since the area lies just inland of the coastal fog belt.

Plants and Wildlife

The rain forests here provide something precious in the heavily roaded southern Coast Range: pure, cold water. Close to 90 percent of the Sixes River's salmon spawn in Dry Creek and the South Fork Sixes River. Upriver clearcutting has pushed the Elk River's summer water temperatures to levels nearly fatal for fish, but Grassy Knob's small, shady creeks offer a cool retreat.

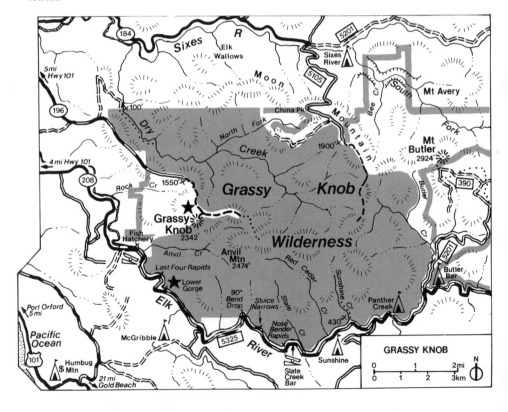

The Elk River near Sunshine Creek

Here rare, old-growth Port Orford cedar grow as much as 6 feet in diameter, with snaky limbs and characteristic white Xs on the underside of green leaf scales. Popular worldwide as a landscaping shrub, this fragrant cedar's small native range (five coastal counties) is shrinking rapidly. Japanese buyers pay as much as $10,000 for a single tree, since its wood is a close substitute for Japan's highly prized, and nearly extinct, hinoki cypress.

The *Phytophthora* root-rot fungus, accidentally introduced here from Portland nurseries in 1944, travels easily through groundwater, killing every Port Orford cedar in an infected drainage. Because the fungus can be carried in dirt on tire treads, the roadless side of Grassy Knob may be the wild Port Orford cedar's last stand.

Geology

Though largely hidden by forest, Grassy Knob's rocks consist of heavily folded and compacted sea-floor sediment scraped up the Klamath Mountains in the past 200 million years while that range slowly moved westward, overriding the Pacific plate.

History

A reconnaissance plane for a Japanese submarine dropped a 170-pound incendiary bomb into the forest between Grassy Knob and Dry Creek in 1942 in an attempt to start a fire. Alarmed rangers at the mountain's lookout tower radioed the Army Air Force. Because of confusion about the names of the nearby towns—Bandon and North Bend—U.S. fighters armed with antisubmarine depth charges streaked to the central Oregon town of Bend. Japanese pilot Nubuo Fujita landed his plane on pontoons, unbolted the wings, mounted the craft to his submarine's deck, and dived to safety.

However, the Japanese bomb failed to explode. Despite many searches, it has never been found.

THINGS TO DO

Hiking

The Grassy Knob Trail, converted to a 30-foot-wide gravel road in the waning months of the 1984 wilderness designation battle, is still the area's most interesting day hike. A barricade at the wilderness boundary keeps vehicles from this road's final 1.3 miles. The road is regrowing to forest so rapidly it is shown as trail on this map. Of interest are the plant succession in the road itself, the old-growth Douglas fir forest on either hand, and the view from Grassy Knob's former fire lookout site, a stone's throw from the road/trail's 0.3-mile mark. From road's end, a very roughly brushed-out trail route continues a mile to Anvil Mountain.

To drive to the Grassy Knob Trail from Port Orford, drive 4 miles north on Highway 101 and turn right on the Grassy Knob Road for 7 miles to the barricade.

Photographers looking for emerald green glens of waterfalls, autumn-red vine maple, and droopy Port Orford cedar will want to hike the passable cross-country route up misnamed Dry Creek or ford the shallow Elk River and explore the mossy canyons of Sunshine Creek or Red Cedar Creek. For views of the area's forested ridges, try the abandoned trail to Mount Butler from Road 390 or the abandoned road along Moon Mountain's ridgetop crest to a regenerating, square-mile clearcut within the designated wilderness.

Boating

The Elk River winds between narrow rock walls, alternating emerald green pools with lots of class 4 whitewater. Launch at unmarked Slate Creek Bar, 6.3 miles by road from the take-out point at the Elk River fish hatchery. Just 0.2 mile from the launch, beware of Nose Bender Rapids, especially in low water, when this 6-foot drop's rating increases from 3 to 4. Other class 4 rapids include Sluice Narrows, 90° Bend Drop, the scenic Lower Gorge, and Last Four Rapids.

To drive to the river, turn off Highway 101, 3 miles north of Port Orford. While driving to the launch site, scout the river for sweepers, the area's chief hazard.

38

OREGON DUNES

Location: Coos Bay to Florence
Size: 50 sq mi
Status: National recreation area (1972)
Terrain: Sand dunes, ocean beach, lakes, forest
Elevation: 0'–1000'
Management: Siuslaw NF
Topographic map: Oregon Dunes NRA (USFS)

Sea and sand lovers take note: Here one can backpack through an oceanfront Sahara, hang glide off the top of 400-foot dunes, or gallop on 45 miles of beach. Bird watchers can count 247 species where meandering creeks cross the sand. And hikers can explore the wind-rippled sand hills that inspired author Frank Herbert to write the science fiction classic *Dune.*

Climate

A marine climate brings cool summers and wet, mild winters. Summer fogs occasionally burn off by afternoon. Spring and fall see the most sunshine. Average annual precipitation hits 75 inches.

Plants and Wildlife

On the beach itself, watch the waves for harbor seals and the spouts of gray whales (December to May).

At creek mouths, bald eagles and huge egrets swoop for fish. Canada geese migrating on the Pacific Flyway stop to forage wild grains in the estuaries. Hundreds of elegant tundra swans winter in the south Siuslaw spit's sandy marshes. In all, it's possible to tally 118 species of aquatic birds, 108 species of songbirds, and twenty-one species of birds of prey.

Rarest of the coastal birds is the small, chubby western snowy plover, distinguished from sanderlings by its white shoulder yoke and its refusal to run piping along the beach's wet sand in search of food. Instead the plover finds sand fleas among driftwood and beach grass near creek mouths, where it also scoops out its shallow sand nest in plain sight. Off-road vehicles (ORVs) and nest-robbing crows have cut coastal plover populations to under 100, though about 900 birds of the same species eke out a living beside desert lake playas in southeast Oregon, where ORVs are also becoming a threat to their survival.

Plants and sand battle each other here on two fronts: To the east, winds shift the steep face of the high dunes 6 to 10 feet farther inland each year, burying forests alive. To the west, European beach grass (originally introduced to stabilize sand near developments) has spread along the entire beachfront, creating a 30-foot-tall foredune that blocks sand from blowing inland. Behind the foredune, winds have stripped a broad "deflation plain" of sand, allowing a succession of brush and trees to gain a foothold. The result: Forest is advancing on the high dunes from behind.

In the deflation plain behind the dunes, watch for the insect-eating sundew plant, which traps prey in its sticky drops of imitation dew. Among the alder and coast willow of the forest drainages, look for yellow skunk cabbage and eight of Oregon's fifteen salamander species. In the spruce and hemlock forests, admire white trilliums in March, 20-foot-tall pink rhododendrons in April, and chanterelle mushrooms in October.

Geology

Most of Oregon's coastline is too steep and rocky to collect much sand, but here winds have repeatedly pushed waves of dunes inland across a coastal plain. Each fresh onslaught of sand buries forests, and then new brush and trees sprout.

However, European beach grass stabilized a wall-like oceanfront foredune a half century ago,

Threemile Lake

blocking off the area's sand supply. The present high dunes are expected to run out of sand and stop their eastward march within 90 to 200 years. Since the stubborn European beach grass regrows when burnt or plowed, the Forest Service has experimented with breaching the foredune with bulldozers to set the dune-formation cycle in motion again.

The broad mud flats at the mouths of Oregon's coastal rivers are indirect products of the Ice Age. When enlarged polar ice caps converted much of the earth's water to ice, oceans dropped 300 feet and rivers cut their valleys deeper to match. When the ice melted 6000 years ago, the ocean rose into the widened river mouths. Sand and river silt have since converted these fjords to shallow estuaries.

History

The U.S. Army established Fort Umpqua on the Umpqua River spit in 1856 to watch over Indians of the Siletz Reservation to the north. After a visiting paymaster in 1862 found every officer, commissioned and non-commissioned, away on a hunting trip, the fort was permanently closed.

Before completion of a coast highway in the 1930s, stagecoaches traveled the hard sand beaches of low tide between Florence, Reedsport, and Coos Bay. This led to public ownership of all Oregon beaches under the Department of Transportation. Beaches are now park land.

THINGS TO DO

Hiking

Short forest trails lead to the open sand, where hikers can explore dunes, tree islands, and lakes without need of marked routes. Remember that walking in dry sand takes twice the time and energy of a hike on solid ground.

Off-road vehicles (ORVs) are allowed in about half of the area; the noise, tracks, and danger of speeding dune buggies reduce these zones' appeal to hikers. Beaches are subject to varying vehicle closure rules (see map) but warrant hiking regardless. The following hikes, listed from north to south, are outside ORV areas unless otherwise mentioned.

Swimmers at Cleawox Lake slide down a 100-foot sand dune into the clear water. This extremely popular lake borders both Girl Scout Camp Cleawox and Honeyman Park, a 382-unit state campground. While ORVs are banned near the south end of the lake, expect motor traffic when prowling over the dramatic dunes toward the area's interesting tree islands, Goose Pasture (a brushy bird-watching site), or the beach.

The short Siltcoos River meanders through campgrounds and dunes. A 0.5-mile, self-guided

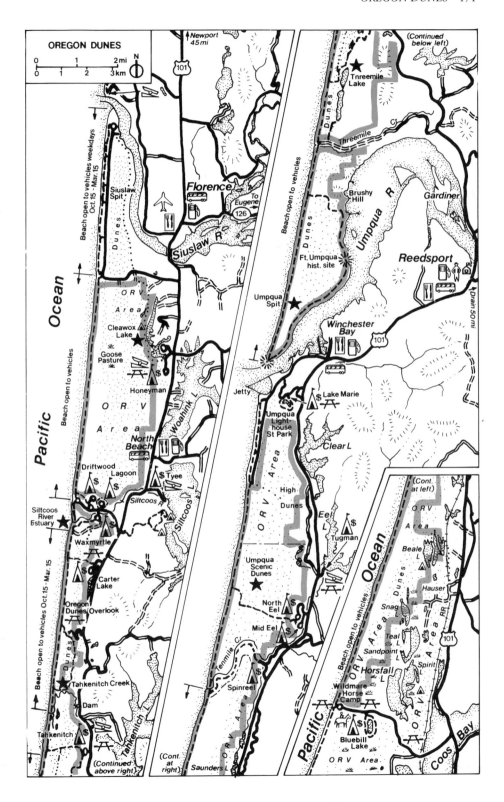

OREGON DUNES

0   1   2mi
0   1   2   3km

N

Newport 45 mi

(Continued below left)

Threemile Lake

Beach open to vehicles weekdays Oct.15 - Mar.15

Siuslaw Spit

Dunes

Florence

To Eugene

126

Siuslaw R

Threemile

Beach open to vehicles

Brushy Hill

Dunes

Umpqua R

Gardiner

Reedsport

Ft. Umpqua hist. site

Drain 50 mi

Ocean

ORV Area

Cleawox Lake

Goose Pasture

Honeyman

Umpqua Spit

Winchester Bay

101

Pacific

Beach open to vehicles

ORV Area

North Beach

Washink L

Jetty

Umpqua Lighthouse St Park

Lake Marie

Clear L

Driftwood

Lagoon

Tyee

Siltcoos R

Siltcoos

Siltcoos L

High Dunes

(Cont. at left)

ORV Area

Siltcoos River Estuary

Waxmyrtle

ORV Area

Eel L

Tugman

Beale L

Ocean

Hauser

Carter Lake

Umpqua Scenic Dunes

Snag

Oregon Dunes Overlook

North Eel

Teal L

101

Sandpoint

Beach open to vehicles Oct.15 - Mar.15

Dunes

Tahkenitch Creek

Mid Eel

Spirit

ORV Area Dunes

Pacific

ORV Area RR

Horsfall L

Dam

Tenmile C

Wildmare Horse Camp

Tahkenitch

Tahkenitch L

Spinreel

Bluebill Lake

(Continued above right)

(Cont. at right)

Saunders L

Ocean

Coos Bay

ORV Area

nature trail around Lagoon Campground visits an oxbow slough of the river. From Waxmyrtle Campground, a trail leads 1.5 miles along the river past open dunes to the beach. To make a pleasant 3.5-mile loop, wade the warm, knee-deep river at its mouth and return on a trail past Driftwood Campground.

Want a break from sun and sand? Hike 2 miles from Highway 101 through a cool, lush forest of ferns and Douglas firs to several primitive campsites on the shore of bulrush-lined Siltcoos Lake.

Marked by posts in the sand, a fun 4.9-mile loop trail through the dunes and along the beach to Tahkenitch Creek begins at the Oregon Dunes Overlook picnic area.

Some of the quietest and most spectacular sand landscapes lie between Tahkenitch Creek and remote Threemile Lake. From Tahkenitch Campground, a 6.2-mile loop trail climbs 2.7 miles along a forested ridge to backpacking campsites at the edge of the dunes overlooking Threemile Lake. The loop path then follows posts to the beach and runs north 1.5 miles before returning through the dunes.

Clams, huckleberries, dunes, and views lure hikers to the 6.5-mile-long Umpqua River Spit. For a scenic route to this vast sand peninsula, cross by boat from nearby Winchester Bay. Otherwise, park at the end of gravel on the Threemile Creek Road (100 yards short of the beach), hike south a mile on the beach, and follow a dune-buggy road inland to the dunes. Look for late August huckleberries on Brushy Hill; very low tides expose clamming mud flats along the Umpqua River below the hill. The long rock jetty at spit's end is a good spot to watch pounding waves and ocean-going ships.

An easy warm-up hike near Winchester Bay loops 0.5 mile around forest-lined Lake Marie at Umpqua Lighthouse State Park. Top the walk with a visit to the adjacent lighthouse.

ORVs dominate Oregon's tallest dunes, south of Lake Marie. Hikers bent on exploring these 400-foot sand mountains should watch for the red flags ORVs display atop 9-foot antennas; dune buggies often zip over blind dune crests.

The 280-foot Umpqua Scenic Dunes provide a 4-square-mile sand playground off limits to ORVs. A 2-mile trail from North Eel Campground leads through woods to the open sand and continues to the beach.

Beale Lake's scenic dunes, meadows, and isthmus make another good goal. Park at Hauser and hike along the railroad tracks 1 mile north to the lake.

Long-distance hikers can tramp the beach 23.7 miles from the tip of the Siuslaw Spit to the tip of the Umpqua Spit, but more interesting routes alternate beach hiking with dune exploration.

Throughout the Oregon Dunes, hikers should heed a few tips. Carry plenty of water. When hiking cross-country to the beach, mark the return route through the foredune with a stick in the sand. The open dunes have few landmarks, especially in the frequent fogs; when lost, simply *listen*—the sound of surf or traffic will point the way to the ocean or Highway 101. Camp well above the beach's driftwood line (night has its high tide too), and bring a sleeping pad (sand is rock-hard).

Equestrians often begin beach rides at Wildmare Horse Camp near Bluebill Lake Campground, though many other beach access points are also feasible.

Boating

The coastal dunes have dammed dozens of large, many-armed freshwater lakes. Sinuous shorelines make for interesting canoe paddling. Steady west winds provide first-rate sailing conditions but can create large waves on summer afternoons. Warm water makes windsurfing practical.

Cleawox Lake, with its steep sand-dune shore and long, narrow arms, is the most popular nonmotorized boating site. Launch at crowded Honeyman Park.

Most other lakes have sandless forest settings and shorelines of water lilies, sedges, and cattails. Tahkenitch Lake and 5-square-mile Siltcoos Lake are heavily used by fishermen for warm-water bass and easily caught yellow perch.

Hang Gliding

Reliable west winds and unobstructed landing sites make the 400-foot-tall High Dunes an excellent practice area. Hike 1 mile east from the last parking lot south of Winchester Bay on the jetty road. Watch for ORVs.

39

WASSEN CREEK

Location: 13 mi E of Reedsport
Size: 24 sq mi
Status: Undesignated wilderness
Terrain: Steep, densely forested creek valley
Elevation: 20'–1760'
Management: Siuslaw NF, Coos Bay District BLM
Topographic maps: Scottsburg, Smith River Falls, Deer Head Point, North Fork (USGS)

In this forgotten Coast Range valley, Wassen Creek splashes over stair-step falls and eddies against dark cliffs. Side streams tumble from steep slopes of sword fern and salmonberry. Rain drips from the great, drooping branches of age-old red cedar, Douglas fir, and western hemlock.

Adventurers exploring the creek's 14 miles of trailless, twisting canyon must follow paths blazed by elk and bear, or else hike the route of the canyon's cheery water ouzels: the creekbed itself.

Climate

Torrential winter rains boost annual precipitation to 90 inches. The dry summers are free of the coastal fog that socks in Highway 101 just a few miles west.

Plants and Wildlife

In the deep forest look for white trillium and yellow Oregon grape in early spring. Rhododendrons put out pink blooms in April. By early fall both blue and red huckleberry are ripe for picking.

Expect great blue herons and Pacific giant salamanders at Wassen Lake. In old-growth woods, watch for the red top-feathers of pileated woodpeckers and the dark eyes of silent spotted owls. Bald eagles soar above the creek canyon. Sea-run fish cannot leap the falls at the Devils Staircase, leaving the upper creek to small trout and bright red crawdads.

Geology

This part of the Coast Range began as mud-covered sea floor 50 million years ago. It lay directly in the path of the North American continent, which was crunching westward over the Pacific sea floor at the geologically speedy rate of an inch a year. However, a fracture in the Pacific floor lifted the Coast Range above the waves, where it became the western edge of the advancing continent.

As a result, Wassen Creek now flows over layers of weak sandstone and nutrient-poor, washed-out red clays that originated on the bottom of the sea. The area is roadless in part because road cuts in such soils send entire hillsides sliding toward the creek. Wassen Lake itself formed when a slump dammed the creek's headwaters about 150 years ago. Snags of drowned trees still stand in the 5-acre lake.

Falls on Wassen Creek

THINGS TO DO

Hiking

Though trailless, the valley's unusual solitude and beauty inspire cross-country exploration. Canyon slopes are too steep and rugged for bushwhacking, so plan to wear tennis shoes and wool socks, and wade along the creekbed itself. Wading is most pleasant in the warm weather of summer and early fall. Since the creek bottom is sandy but has some slippery mudstone, a walking stick is essential; hikers with packs will want two. Occasional parklike openings invite camping.

The easiest introduction to Wassen Creek is to visit Wassen Lake, a nice picnic spot. Rimmed with alder and old-growth conifers, the shallow lake teems with rough-skinned newts. Bushwhackers can circle the lake and prowl down the outlet creek.

Road access to Wassen Lake is entirely paved. Drive Highway 38 (between Reedsport and Drain); a quarter mile west of milepost 19 turn north on Wells Creek Road (BLM 22-9-7.0) for 2.3 miles. Then fork left onto paved Fern Top Road (BLM 21-9-32.0) for 3.3 miles, veer right on Wassen Lake Road (BLM 21-9-10.0) for 3.7 miles, and park at an unmarked pullout. Walk 100 yards down an old road to the left to the lake.

Only a handful of mortals have penetrated Wassen Creek's central canyon to visit the Devils Staircase, a series of five stair-stepped falls totaling 40 feet, with circular, greenish potholes large enough for swimming. For a bushwhacking route to Wassen Creek's central canyon, drive a mile north past Wassen Lake on the paved Wassen Lake Road, turn left on gravel Road 21-20-12.1 for 4 miles to Road 110, continue straight 1.7 miles, and then turn left on Road 119 to its end, avoiding smaller spur tracks. From here, walk out the ridge to find a trail paralleling the clearcut's edge. This rough path continues into the forest down to the creek. Hang a bright marker by the creek to help locate the route back to the car. Four trailless miles downstream is the Devils Staircase, but the trek is too rugged for a one-day trip.

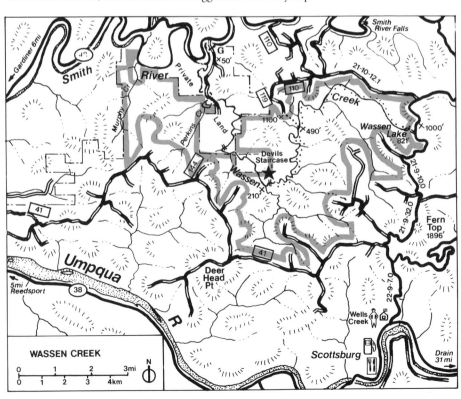

40

OREGON ISLANDS

Location: Along Oregon coast
Size: 1477 islands (1.2 sq mi)
Status: 56 islands (0.8 sq mi) designated wilderness and national wildlife refuge (1970, 1978)
Terrain: Small, wave-swept, rock islands
Elevation: 0'–327'
Management: Coos Bay District BLM, U.S. Fish and Wildlife Service
Topographic maps: Tillamook Head, Newport North, Cape Blanco, Cape Sebastian, and others (USGS)

Nesting seabirds and lolling sea lions crowd the nation's smallest and least accessible designated wilderness: surf-pounded islands scattered the length of Oregon's Pacific shore.

Climate

Wet, frost-free winters and cool, fog-shrouded summers push annual precipitation from 60 to 100 inches. Northwest winds bring fair skies; winter storms from the southwest batter the islands with 40-foot waves and high winds. Six- to twelve-foot tides submerge many rocks twice daily.

Plants and Wildlife

The islands' fascinating bird and sea mammal colonies are easily observed from mainland viewpoints, particularly with the aid of binoculars or a spotting scope.

From April to August, thousands of murres crowd the rocks to nest—the only time these black-and-white, loonlike birds visit land. Also in summer look for tufted puffins (with unmistakable, red-and-orange-striped bills) and their close relatives, the virtually neckless little auklets and murrelets.

When these birds leave for winter, other species arrive: long-necked loons, scoters (small sea ducks), and grebes (resembling clumsy, dark-backed swans). Year-round residents include five species of sea gulls and two kinds of black, crook-necked cormorants.

The brown dots one sees on these islands from a distance are often 600- to 2200-pound Steller's sea lions. Smaller harbor seals among the waves often watch humans with a curiosity rivaling our own. Also look for the spouts of gray whales, which pass here from December to February as they migrate toward Mexico, and from March to May as they return to Alaska. Sea otters, whose fur first brought regular European trade to these shores, were driven to extinction in Oregon by 1911. An attempt to reintroduce sea otters near Cape Blanco in 1970 failed.

Most islands support few plants beyond sea palms and bobbing kelp seaweed. Others are topped with brushy salal, twinberry, and stunted spruce. Seacliff stonecrop, a thick-leaved flower threatened in Oregon, is known only from these islands.

Best wildlife viewing sites are at the Yaquina Head lighthouse 3 miles north of Newport, on the Cape Meares Loop Road west of Tillamook, at Cape Kiwanda near Pacific City, at the state park on Cape Blanco, at Boardman State Park north of Brookings, and from the shore at Brookings itself.

In the few places where hiking on the islands is physically possible, access is strongly discouraged or prohibited to protect nesting species. Boats are allowed no closer than 200 yards to islands included in the federal wildlife refuge.

Geology

Wave erosion separated these islands' resistant rock from the softer rock of the mainland, much as tides reduce a sand castle to the pebbles that once topped its towers. All islands north of Bandon consist of tough, black basalt. The pillow-shaped fracturing of this basalt proves it

Sea anemones line a tide pool.

formed underwater, when lava squeezed between layers of sea-floor mudstone 20 million years ago. Subsequent faulting raised the sea floor, creating the Coast Range.

The islands south of Bandon are ten times older, belonging to the ancient Siskiyou Mountains. This fact doomed Bandon's landmark island, Tupper Rock. Composed of heavy, resistant Siskiyou blue schist, prized for use in seawalls, it was quarried to the ground and now forms Bandon's south jetty.

History

Two of Oregon's offshore islands have been inhabited. Sea lion bones and clamshells remain from an Indian camp on Zwagg Island beside Brookings. Dutch hermit Folker Von Der Zwaag, who moved to the island in 1889 with his dog Sniff, is remembered for the trolley he devised to retrieve fresh water from the mainland automatically.

A lighthouse built with great difficulty on Tillamook Rock in 1879 was abandoned in 1957. A Portland real estate consortium purchased the island in 1980, converted the building to a mausoleum, and has since been bringing in cremated remains by helicopter.

Though an estimated 2 million birds used Oregon's offshore rocks in 1940, their numbers have declined to fewer than 500,000 because of development and fishing along the coast.

Opposite: *The Imnaha River near Eureka Bar in Hells Canyon*

NORTHEAST OREGON

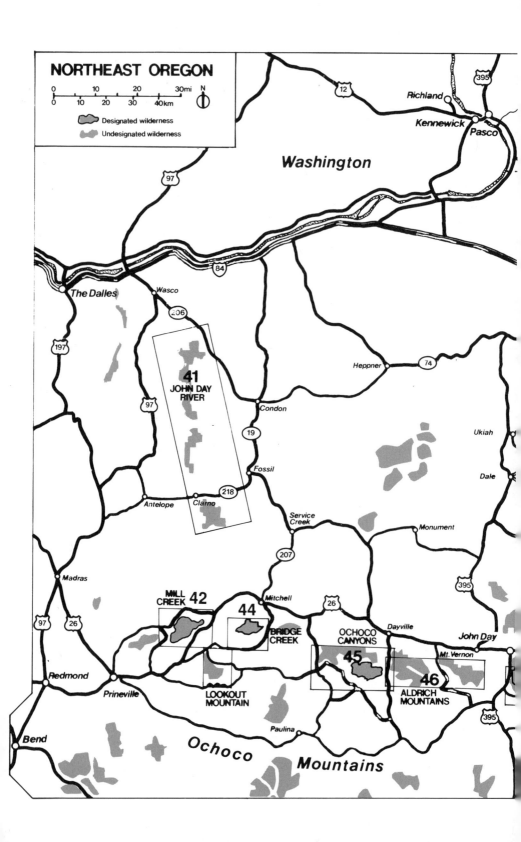

0   10   20   30mi   N
0   10   20   30   40km

Designated wilderness
Undesignated wilderness

Washington

Richland

Kennewick
Pasco

The Dalles
Wasco

Heppner

41
JOHN DAY
RIVER

Condon

Ukiah

Dale

Fossil

Antelope   Clarno

Service
Creek

Monument

MILL
CREEK 42

44

Mitchell

BRIDGE
CREEK

OCHOCO
CANYONS

Dayville

John Day

Mt. Vernon

Madras

45

46
ALDRICH
MOUNTAINS

Redmond

Prineville

LOOKOUT
MOUNTAIN

Bend

Paulina

Ochoco   Mountains

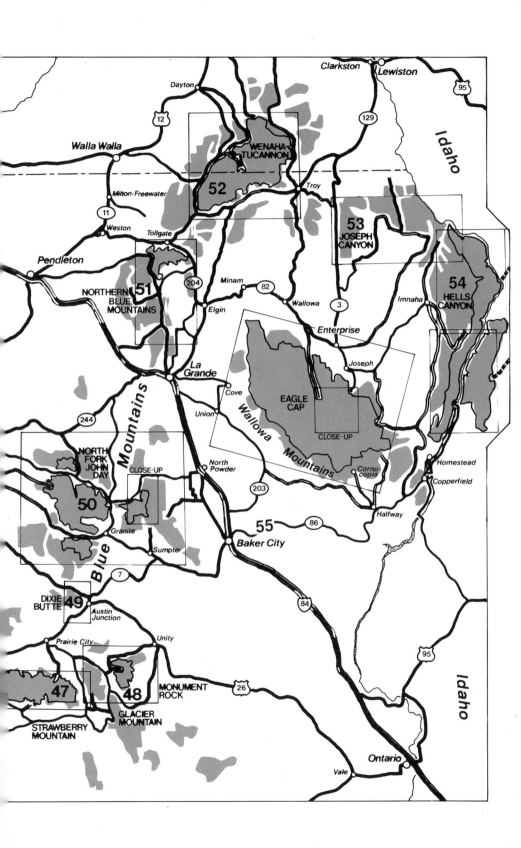

JOHN DAY RIVER

Location: 41 mi SE of The Dalles
Size: 93 sq mi
Status: Federal wild and scenic river
Terrain: Sagebrush canyonlands, river rapids
Elevation: 540'–3600'
Management: Prineville District BLM
Topographic maps: Muddy Ranch, Clarno, Chimney Springs, Bath Canyon, Shoestring Ridge, Horseshoe Bend, Indian Cove, Harmony, Esau Canyon (USGS)

Boaters on the uncrowded John Day River often float for a week through the winding, cliff-lined canyons without seeing more than a dozen people. Petroglyphs, fossils, and abandoned ranch houses make good goals for day hikes near the river.

Climate

The hot summers are virtually rainless; the freezing winters accumulate no snowpack. With just 10 inches of annual rainfall, this portion of the John Day only flows as a river because of precipitation in the distant Ochocos and Blue mountains.

Plants and Wildlife

The sagebrush steppe here features hedgehog cactus (blooms red in April) and matlike prickly pear cactus. Look for rare yellow hairy Indian paintbrush in May. Occasional junipers dot slopes, while creeks harbor wild rose, red osier dogwood, and snowberry.

Golden eagles and prairie falcons patrol the canyon skies. Canada geese, mergansers, goldeneyes, and green-winged teals paddle ahead of boaters. The river's salmon runs died in 1889 with construction of a since-demolished grist-mill dam. Steelhead trout, bullhead, and suckers remain. Smallmouth bass, introduced in 1971, thrive.

Hikers should be alert for scorpions and rattlesnakes, though chances are greater of meeting wild horses, mule deer, coyotes, and startled, partridgelike chukars.

Geology

Fossils from the Clarno Unit of the John Day Fossil Beds National Monument indicate this area was a coastal rain forest 34 million years ago. Primitive rhinoceroses and tapirs flourished alongside ferns and avocado trees.

The creation of the Cascade Range 16 to 25 million years ago not only dried up this area by blocking moisture from the sea, it also buried the landscape repeatedly with volcanic ashfalls, preserving skeletons of saber-toothed tigers and small, three-toed horses. The many layers of red, buff, and green volcanic ash form the "painted hills" visible on the west riverbank 4 miles north of Clarno. Vast floods of Columbia River basalt 13 to 16 million years ago capped the area with a rimrock of black lava; cliffs exhibit basalt's characteristic hexagonal pillars.

History

Numerous Indian house-pit sites and petroglyphs (painted rock carvings) testify to over 4500 years of human habitation along the river. From 1866 to 1930 white settlers built the remote riverside ranches whose abandoned buildings remain. Be sure to leave all homesteading memorabilia in place.

THINGS TO DO

Hiking

The area's only marked trails are two 0.25-mile interpretive nature paths at the picnic area of the John Day Fossil Beds National Monument near Clarno.

Spring Basin is a good spot to try cross-country hiking in the high desert. Wear sturdy shoes and carry water. From the basin's sagebrush plateau, climb to Horse Mountain's pinnacled viewpoint or explore the winding side canyons leading toward the John Day River (though the river's bank is private here). To reach Spring Basin from Clarno, drive 1.5 miles east on Highway 218, turn right onto a dirt road for 3 miles, park, and hike 2 miles up a BLM track to the east.

Walk up sandy-bottomed Rattlesnake Canyon between narrow rock walls, and then scramble cross-country up Amine Peak for one of the area's highest viewpoints. To reach the mouth of Rattlesnake Canyon, park in the same spot as for the Spring Basin hike, but then walk south along the riverside dirt road 5 miles.

Some of the area's finest cross-country hikes prowl the river's side canyons and bluffs in the BLM-owned land between Clarno and Cottonwood Bridge. Since the only public access to these remote lands is by boat, hikes must be planned in conjunction with float trips.

The John Day River at Rattlesnake Canyon

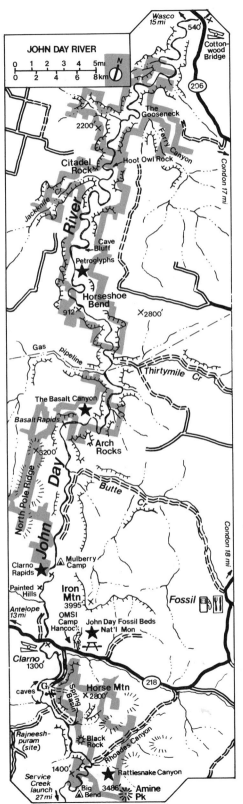

Climbing

The John Day Fossil Beds National Monument near Clarno offers several small blocks and towers, ranging from the level I-4 Steigomonster to the II-5.2-A3 Hancock Tower.

Boating

Plan for four lazy days by raft or three thrilling days by open canoe to drift the 70 scenic miles between Clarno and Cottonwood Bridge. Timing is critical, since this undammed river varies from an unnavigable maelstrom in winter to an unfloatable dribble in September. The river is technically runnable between 800 and 23,000 cubic feet per second (measured at the Service Creek gauging station), but expect the easiest levels (3000–7000 cfs) from April to July and again in November.

The river's wildest water, Clarno Rapids, begins 4.4 miles downstream from the Clarno Bridge launch site. This class 3, canoe-swamping rapid becomes a class 4 canoe-wrecker at water levels above 4000 cfs. Scout or portage on the left, remembering that Lower Clarno Rapids (class 2) lies just downstream. Beyond, however, the only serious whitewater is class 2+ Basalt Rapids, 15.9 miles from Clarno Bridge.

Expect good camping spots in The Basalt Canyon, a 4-mile-long gorge below Basalt Rapids. Then look back upriver to spot Arch Rocks' twin hoops atop a cliff. Just before Horseshoe Bend, watch the right bank for two wagons used in a 1928 movie here. Then, 1 mile past Horseshoe Bend, stop at Potlatch Canyon on the right to observe (but not touch) the cliff's Indian petroglyphs. Cave Bluff's river-level cavern makes a fun stop 3.5 miles farther downstream. Another 10 miles along are Hoot Owl Rock, an owl-shaped clifftop pillar, and Citadel Rock, a fortress-shaped palisade. Cottonwood Bridge is the last public takeout site before a falls and the tamed Columbia's backwaters.

Many who float the John Day launch 44 miles upriver from Clarno at Service Creek. The two- to three-day run to Clarno includes class 2 rapids located 6, 15, and 23 miles downriver from Service Creek.

42

MILL CREEK

Location: 20 mi NE of Prineville
Size: 27 sq mi
Status: Designated wilderness (1984)
Terrain: Forested upland valley
Elevation: 3725'–6240'
Management: Ochoco NF
Topographic maps: Steins Pillar, Whistler Point (USGS)

Mill Creek is a wholly preserved Ochoco Mountain valley with excellent forest trails, good rock climbing sites, and sweeping viewpoints. Considering that this valley lies just one hour's drive east of Bend, it's surprising Mill Creek is a little-known wilderness in a generally over-looked mountain range.

Climate

The area receives only 25 inches of precipitation annually, primarily as winter snow. Summers are dry and fairly hot. Late spring and fall are pleasant.

Plants and Wildlife

Mill Creek preserves one of the Ochocos' few remaining climax forests of ponderosa pine and bunchgrass. Wildfires traditionally cleared such forests of underbrush. However, biologists worry that decades of overzealous fire suppression have allowed an understory of Douglas fir to grow, enabling future fires to reach above the large ponderosa pines' fire-resistant trunks to their flammable crowns.

Livestock grazing limits most other native flora. Fauna include Rocky Mountain elk, mule deer, bobcat, cougar, and an occasional black bear.

Geology

The Ochoco Mountains formed as a string of coastal volcanoes 40 to 50 million years ago, before the Cascade Range existed. Twin Pillars remain as the plug of an eroded volcano. When the Ochoco volcanoes subsided and the Old Cascades roared to life 25 million years ago, massive ash deposits covered eastern Oregon, collecting in lakes and rivers. One such rhyolite ash deposit subsequently welded together to form the resistant tuff outcropping at Whistler Point. Look there, in the Ochoco Agate Beds off Road 27, for baseball-sized thunder eggs. The thunder egg, Oregon's state rock, forms when small cavities in the tuff fill with quartz and agate.

THINGS TO DO

Hiking

For a good day hike, take the trail from Wildcat Campground through an old-growth ponderosa pine forest along the East Fork of Mill Creek. The first 3.5 miles of this path are nearly level, but include several bridgeless crossings that require wading during the high waters of spring. To reach Wildcat Campground from Prineville, follow Highway 26 east 9 miles to Ochoco Reservoir, then turn left for 9 miles on Road 33.

For longer hikes, Wildcat Campground is nearly always the end point, since its elevation is 2000 feet lower than that of the wilderness's three other trailheads. A particularly scenic 8-mile trip down to Wildcat Campground begins at Bingham Prairie, off Forest Road 27, and passes the lichen-covered lava towers of Twin Pillars. Another popular 10-mile route starts at the White Rock Campground, on the shoulder of Wildcat Mountain. A third route to Wildcat Campground, from Whistler Point on Forest Road 27, is 13 miles.

Twin Pillars

Potential backpacking campsites are plentiful throughout. Only creeks named on the map are year-round water sources; all must be purified.

A new 2-mile trail to 400-foot Steins Pillar (shown in the lower left of the map) features views, flowers, and ponderosa pines. From Ochoco Reservoir, drive Road 33 for 5 miles and turn right on Road 500 for 2 miles to the trailhead at road's end.

Climbing

Twin Pillars are a pair of vertical-sided, 200-foot andesite plugs at 5500 feet, 1.5 miles from the Bingham Prairie trailhead. Though quite scenic and challenging (rated II-5.7), they are rarely climbed because of the proximity of the more challenging Steins Pillar. This 400-foot, overhanging spire of welded tuff, unscaled until 1950, offers routes from difficulty III-5.6-A3 to IV-5.7-A4.

Winter Sports

Ochoco Divide on U.S. Highway 26 offers good cross-country skiing and snowshoeing from January through March. The highway is plowed in winter, allowing access to unplowed roads along the eastern edge of the wilderness. View Point makes a scenic goal, 5 miles up Road 27.

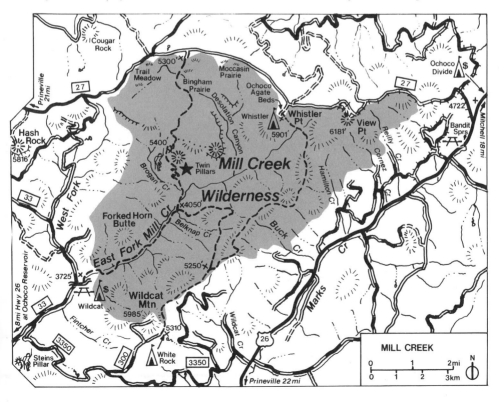

43

LOOKOUT MOUNTAIN

Location: 25 mi E of Prineville
Size: 26 sq mi
Status: Undesignated wilderness
Terrain: Forested ridges, grassy plateau
Elevation: 3793'–6926'
Management: Ochoco NF
Topographic maps: Lookout Mountain, Gerow Butte (USGS)

From the parklike meadows of Lookout Mountain's plateau, views stretch beyond the forested Ochoco Mountains to a string of High Cascades snowpeaks.

Climate

Winter snow accounts for most of the area's 30 inches of annual precipitation. Summers are dry and warm.

Plants and Wildlife

This is prime elk, wild horse, and mule deer range. Watch for herds in the high meadows during summer and in the cover of low-elevation forests during winter. Open, parklike forests of ponderosa pine invite cross-country travel, while wetter northern slopes host Douglas fir and larch (with scenic yellow needles in October). At the summit are subalpine fir and lodgepole pine.

Geology

A lava flow forms the flat top of Lookout Mountain. This basalt oozed from vents north of the John Day River about 25 million years ago, smothering most of the Ochoco Mountains. Outcroppings of older Ochoco rock in the valleys prompted an 1873 gold rush and some cinnabar mining.

THINGS TO DO

Hiking

Three routes reach the vistas atop Lookout Mountain. A 7.5-mile trail from the Ochoco Ranger Station picnic area climbs nearly 3000 feet along a rocky ridgeline, passing frequent viewpoints. An easier, newer 8-mile loop trail from the Independent Mine on Road 4205 passes a shelter (with a wood stove) just below the summit plateau. The third route to the top follows a ridgecrest from the end of Road 300.

To find the first of these trailheads from Prineville, drive 16 miles east on Highway 26; at a sign for Ochoco Creek turn right for 8 paved miles to Ochoco Ranger Station. For the second trailhead, turn right at the ranger station on Road 42 for 7 miles to Road 4205. For the third, take Road 42 a total of 12.5 miles and turn right on Road 300.

North of Road 42, the well-marked 7.5-mile Round Mountain Trail crests that peak's summit and descends to popular Walton Lake Campground.

Winter Sports

Cross-country skiers can drive up Road 42 to snow level and ski up the marked loop trail (shared with occasional snowmobiles) past the Independent Mine. The reward is great, for Lookout Mountain's high, 2.5-mile-long summit meadows have the Ochocos' best snow and superlative views.

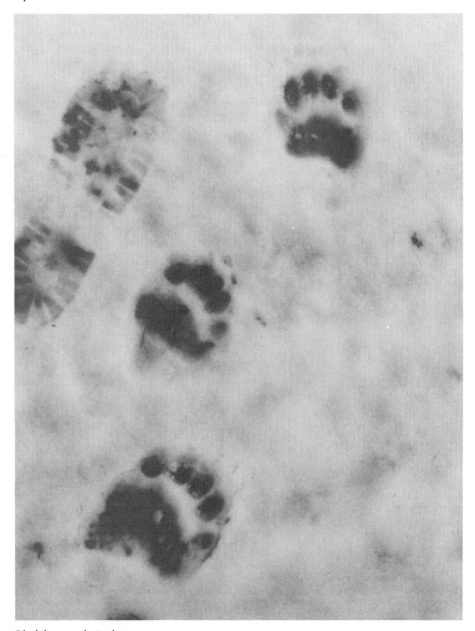

Black bear tracks in the snow

44

BRIDGE CREEK

Location: 39 mi E of Prineville
Size: 8 sq mi
Status: Designated wilderness (1984)
Terrain: Forested plateau, cliffs, slopes
Elevation: 4320'–6816'
Management: Ochoco NF
Topographic map: Mount Pisgah (USGS)

At the edge of the Ochoco Mountains' summit plateau, North Point's 600-foot cliff overlooks central Oregon and Cascade peaks from Mount Adams to the Three Sisters.

Bridge Creek's valley from the rim near East Point

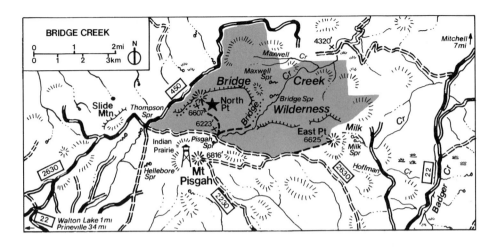

Climate

The area receives 30 inches of precipitation annually, primarily as winter snow. Summers are dry and hot.

Plants and Wildlife

Mixed conifer thickets of Douglas fir, true fir, and larch dominate the area, with bands of lodgepole pine and ponderosa pine. Clearings of sagebrush, bunchgrass, and sparse, gnarled mountain mahogany break up the plateau forests.

Mule deer and elk find good cover and browse here year round, but especially when hunting season drives them from roaded areas. Watch for prairie falcons, goshawks, and the large, red-headed pileated woodpeckers, which, because of their reliance on forest snags, are an indicator species for old-growth Ochoco forests.

Geology

North Point's cliff of pillar-shaped basalt columns is the edge of a lava flow capping most of the Ochoco crest. Vents north of the John Day River produced this lava about 25 million years ago.

THINGS TO DO

Hiking

The breathtaking view at North Point is an easy 1.2-mile walk up an old, closed jeep track from the Bridge Creek crossing of Road 2630 near Pisgah Spring. To reach the starting point from Prineville, follow Highway 26 east 16 miles, at a sign for Ochoco Creek turn right for 8 paved miles to Ochoco Ranger Station, continue straight on paved Road 22 for 8.5 miles, turn left on Road 150 for 0.5 mile, and turn right on Road 2630 for 7 miles (the last 2 miles are rough and rutted).

Conifer thickets stymie most off-trail hikers in this wilderness; however, frequent winds at North Point have stunted vegetation there, allowing easy and interesting cross-country hiking along the cliff edge for a mile on either side of the point. Bushwhacking becomes increasingly difficult—but possible with map and compass—for hikers intent on making a loop trip by continuing west to Thompson Spring, or along the cliff rim southeast to Bridge Creek.

East Point's rounded knoll offers lesser views; it's 1.5 miles along an arrow-straight jeep track from Road 2630.

The trail to Bridge Spring has been abandoned to the cattle that graze this sparse wilderness range each summer. Although the watershed is the domestic water supply for the town of Mitchell, Bridge Spring and Bridge Creek are usually churned to mud by hooves.

45

OCHOCO CANYONS

Location: 77 mi E of Prineville, 40 mi W of John Day
Size: 54 sq mi
Status: 21 sq mi designated wilderness (1984)
Terrain: Steep, forested canyons, sagebrush slopes, rocky creeks
Elevation: 2840'–6871'
Management: Ochoco NF
Topographic maps: Central Oregon (BLM); Aldrich Gulch, Wolf Mountain, Six Corners, Antone, Day Basin, Dayville (USGS)

Three major canyons, each with its own trail system and splashing creek, provide scenic examples of the Ochoco Mountains' remarkable transition from dense forests to sagebrush lowlands.

Climate

Summers are hot and dry. Snowfall from November to April brings the annual precipitation to a sparse 20 to 30 inches.

Plants and Wildlife

Water determines where there will be forest and where sagebrush will dominate in these steep mountains. Exposed ridgetops and sunny south slopes are brown and bald. Green swaths of forest cling to shady north slopes and fill the steep canyons like biological glaciers winding downhill to the arid lowlands, where all melts to brown again.

A hike through the forest reveals bands of lodgepole pine, ponderosa pine parklands, and dense thickets of Douglas fir and white fir. Spruce budworms have killed some of the Douglas fir. At creek's edge, expect an oasis of false Solomon's seal, coneflower, snowberry, wild gooseberries, and delicate twinflower.

Bear, coyote, mountain lion, deer, and elk are common year round. Watch for migratory cranes and geese passing overhead on their way to the Malheur Refuge to the southeast.

Geology

Black Canyon's winding, cliff-lined lower gorge, and the similar canyon of the adjacent South Fork John Day, resulted when these streams cut through the basalt lava that once flooded much of central Oregon. In Picture Gorge, 12 miles to the north, the John Day River has cut through no fewer than seventeen layers of this basalt. The lava, now characterized by rusty specks of weathered olivine, spread from vents north of Dayville as far as Idaho 16 million

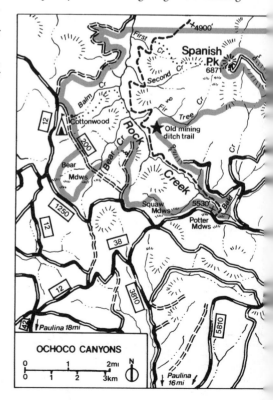

OCHOCO CANYONS

years ago. Nonetheless, this outpouring was dwarfed a few million years later by Oregon's next round of basalt floods, which filled much of the Columbia River Basin.

THINGS TO DO

Hiking

The 11.6-mile Black Canyon Trail descends along a rushing mountain stream to a narrow, cliff-walled gorge. Before starting out from the trailhead at Wolf Mountain, take a short side trip to the East Wolf fire lookout, a tall tree topped with a crow's-nest platform built in the early 1920s. No longer climbable, the lookout offers good views of Black Canyon from ground level.

Drive to Wolf Mountain from Prineville by turning right from Highway 26 a mile east of town. Follow a paved road 59 miles to a Y 4 miles past Paulina, keep left on paved Road 42 for 8 miles, turn right on Road 58 for a mile, turn left onto gravel Road 5810 for 10 miles, then take Road 5840 to the right 3 miles to the trailhead.

Where Black Canyon's gorge narrows on the final 2 miles of the Black Canyon Trail, the path crosses the chilly, 15-foot-wide creek twelve times; bring tennis shoes for wading. Likewise, there is no bridge at trail's end across the South Fork John Day to Road 47. This river is unfordable in high water January to March, but idles along only calf-deep in summer.

Three side trails also access Black Canyon: a 0.5-mile shortcut from Road 5820 to Owl Creek, a 4.5-mile route down from Mud Springs Campground to Big Ford, and a steep, 1.4-mile path from Big Ford to Seven Sixty Spring on Road 38.

Rock Creek's forested valley is steep, but the trail through it is not. Most of its 9 miles follow an almost perfectly level, abandoned ditch chiseled out of the canyon wall in the 1890s for gold mines once active north of here. Start at the Potter Meadows trailhead on Road 38, follow the mountain creek 2 miles, then begin the in-gully, out-ridge wanderings of the dry canal. At the 4-mile mark, the ruins of a log cabin at Fir Tree Creek make a good turnaround spot for day

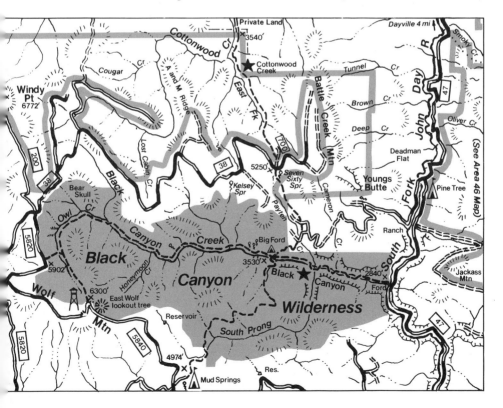

Black Canyon

hikers. Five miles beyond, the increasingly rough ditch trail ends abruptly at private land.

Cottonwood Creek meanders through the most isolated canyon of all. An often steep, 4-mile-long forest trail descends to the creek from spur Road 700 off Road 38. Downstream, the trail ends at an off-limits, private dirt road leading to the Mascall Ranch at Picture Gorge; upstream, 8 miles of creek await exploration by hardy bushwhackers.

Cross-country travel is easy enough in this wilderness along the many unforested ridges, but creek-bottom conifer thickets make for slow going. Two rugged but worthwhile bushwhacking routes connect with Rock Creek's otherwise dead-end ditch trail. One descends Balm Creek's canyon 1.5 miles from Cottonwood Campground to Rock Creek. The other begins at Spanish Peak, the area's highest and most spectacular viewpoint, and heads due west 2 miles, dropping almost 2000 feet along a ridge to the ditch trail at First Creek.

Winter Sports

Snowed-under ridgetop roads provide quiet routes for ski tours. Spanish Peak makes the most challenging and spectacular goal. Expect sufficient snow for skiing between December and March. Skiers must drive to snow level and park, for roads are rarely plowed.

ALDRICH MOUNTAINS

Location: 11 mi W of John Day
Size: 91 sq mi
Status: Undesignated wilderness
Terrain: Broad mountains, sagebrush slopes, forest
Elevation: 2649'–7363'
Management: Malheur NF, Prineville District BLM, Oregon Department of Fish and Wildlife
Topographic maps: McClellan Mountain, Big Weasel Springs, Aldrich Mountain S, Aldrich Gulch, Aldrich Mountain N, Dayville (USGS)

Fields Peak from the west

This little-known range between the Ochoco and the Strawberry mountains preserves two wild areas. In the west, the Aldrich Mountain lookout rises above the forests and sagebrush gulches of the Murderers Creek Wildlife Area. In the east, a dozen peaks with bare, 2000-foot-tall shoulders cluster about McClellan Mountain.

Climate

Most of the area's scant 20 annual inches of precipitation fall as snow from November to April. Hot summer afternoons may bring thunderstorms.

Dead Horse Mountain and Riley Creek gorge from a ridge near Packsaddle Gap

Plants and Wildlife

Bighorn sheep highlight the Murderers Creek Wildlife Area, between the South Fork John Day River and the Aldrich Mountain summit. Once hunted to extinction here, the wild sheep have increased to about sixty head since their reintroduction in 1978. They prefer Smoky Gulch and Oliver Creek's upper canyon. Sleek pronghorn antelope summer along Murderers Creek and winter in the north of the area. Elk rely on the timbered areas for winter cover, and mule deer come from as far as Strawberry Mountain for winter forage. Mountain lions, coyotes, rattlesnakes, meadowlarks, and mountain cottontails are also in the area. Bald eagles winter near Dayville.

Sagebrush, bunchgrass, juniper, and yellow-bloomed rabbit brush dominate the lower elevations and south-facing slopes. Douglas fir and white fir forests cling to north slopes and cap Aldrich Mountain. Near McClellan Mountain only the canyon bottoms are forested, with stately ponderosa pine and larch.

The Cedar Grove Botanical Area preserves a biological oddity: 60 acres of Alaska cedar, isolated 130 miles from other Alaska cedar stands. An easy 1-mile trail from Road 2150 leads to the grove.

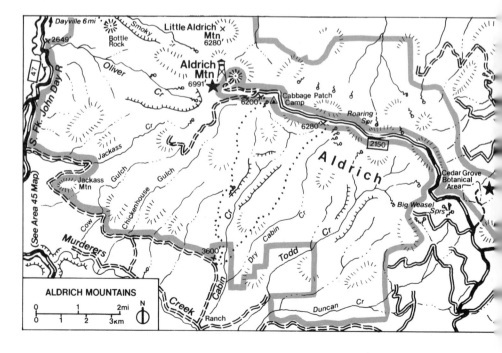

Geology

The Aldrich Mountains began as sea-floor mud and sand 150 to 250 million years ago. Though far from the ocean, their jumbled strata are typical of a coastal mountain range like the western Klamaths. One may conclude that before the Cascades and present Coast Range arose, Oregon's coastline ran diagonally from the Klamaths to the Blue Mountains, with the Aldrich Mountains as a seacoast ridge.

THINGS TO DO

Hiking

A well-graded 1.2-mile trail climbs to the area's highest point, Fields Peak, where views stretch across the John Day Valley to the Blue Mountains beyond. To find the signed trailhead, drive Highway 26 west of John Day 18 miles (or east of Dayville 13 miles), turn south onto Road 21 for 8 miles, turn left onto Road 2160 for 0.1 mile, and turn left onto Road 041 for 1.2 miles to its end.

Riley Creek's trail, in a wooded canyon between impressive, bare mountains, makes another good day hike. After 0.5 mile, hikers can either follow the creek cross-country to peer ahead into the creek's gorge, or follow steep trails up Riley Mountain or Dead Horse Creek to broader views. Drive Road 21 south from Highway 26 for 20 miles, then turn left on Road 2190 for 5 miles to the road's end and trailhead.

A topographic map, compass, and water are essential throughout the area, for trails are sometimes faint and many interesting routes are cross-country. This is particularly true on the steep, western flanks of Aldrich Mountain where wildlife observation is best. To spot bighorn sheep in winter, park on the South Fork John Day Road 47 between Smoky and Oliver creeks and hike cross-country up the ridge to an excellent viewpoint at Bottle Rock. In summer, start at Aldrich Mountain and hike down.

The area's newest, best-graded trail, around McClellan Mountain, is another place to spy bighorn sheep. On this path, it's 10.5 miles between the Fields Peak and Riley Creek trailheads. Side trips lead to viewpoints atop McClellan Mountain and Second Peak.

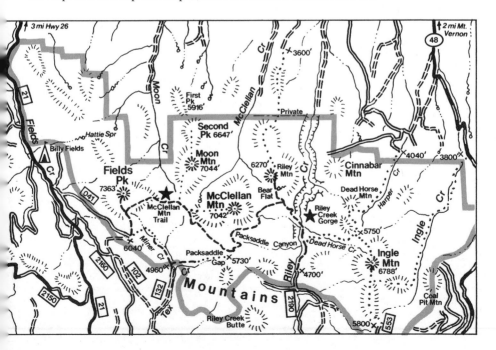

STRAWBERRY MOUNTAIN

Location: 4 mi SE of John Day
Size: 123 sq mi
Status: 107 sq mi designated wilderness (1964, 1984)
Terrain: Snowpeak, forest valleys, high meadows, lakes
Elevation: 3570'–9038'
Management: Malheur NF, Prineville District BLM
Topographic map: Strawberry Mountain Wilderness (USFS)

For a lesson in Eastern Oregon's diversity, visit the Strawberry Range. Above the John Day River's alfalfa fields, above an arid band of sagebrush and juniper, dense conifer forests rise past blue lakes, waterfalls, and alpine wildflowers to palisades of snow-draped crags.

Climate

Since most of the area lies over 6000 feet in elevation, snow closes trails from November to June and lingers across high passes until mid-July. Summers are fair and warm, with some thunderstorms and freezing nights. Snow flurries may interrupt October's typically cool, clear Indian summer. Annual precipitation measures 40 inches.

Plants and Wildlife

Five of the United States' seven major biologic zones are packed into this relatively small mountain range. Larch, the only native conifer to lose its needles in winter, spangles the high forests with autumn gold. Other trees include Engelmann spruce, white pine, Douglas fir, white fir, lodgepole pine, and ponderosa pine. The area's name derives from the wild strawberries rampant in mid-elevation forests; watch for their fruit in July and bright red leaves in October.

Bighorn sheep, reintroduced here after local extinction, now thrive on Canyon Mountain. Look for them up Sheep Gulch from Highway 395. Rocky mountain elk and mule deer summer here in profusion and seek shelter here during autumn hunting season. The Canyon Creek archery area, south and west of Indian Creek Butte, has been off-limits to firearms each fall since the 1930s. Other wildlife include black bear, coyote, mountain lion, bobcat, ground squirrels, and golden eagles.

Geology

The western half of the Strawberry Range is a chunk of sub–sea floor buckled up from the Pacific by the westward drift of North America 200 to 250 million years ago, before the creation of the Cascades and Coast Range made this an inland area. Canyon Mountain consists of reddish peridotite, greenish serpentinite, and crumbly brown basalt—all indicative of oceanic crust.

The eastern half of the Strawberry Range, beginning at Indian Creek Butte, consists of much younger volcanic rock. About 15 million years ago, volcanoes here spewed out immense amounts of ash and lava, burying the southern Blue Mountains. Rabbit Ears is the eroded plug of one vent. Above Wildcat Basin, colored ash deposits have weathered into scenic badlands.

Ice Age glaciers carved the many broad, U-shaped mountain valleys. They also left sandy moraines (visible in Indian Creek Canyon) and cirque lakes. Strawberry Lake formed when glacial ice retreated and the steep valley wall collapsed, blocking Strawberry Creek with a landslide.

History

Traces of gold in Canyon Mountain's peridotite launched a decade of intense placer mining in 1862, when Canyon City began as a tent town of 10,000 men. Pioneer Oregon poet Joaquin Miller lived and wrote in the boomtown during 1863–69.

Strawberry Lake

THINGS TO DO

Hiking

This compact mountain range features rugged alpine scenery and a thorough trail system with room for weeklong backpacking treks. Mountain lakes are rare in eastern Oregon, so the seven in this area are popular. To limit overuse, do not camp beside these small lakes, but do try the many scenic trails to less trodden meadows, ridges, and creek valleys.

From Strawberry Camp, a 1.2-mile uphill walk reaches Strawberry Lake with its photogenic backdrop of snowy crags. But save some film; another 1.1 miles up the valley Strawberry Falls cascades 40 feet onto boulders glowing with moss. Once at the falls, day hikers have at least three options: head back, ramble on another 0.6 level miles to a good lunch stop at Little Strawberry Lake, or tackle the climb to Strawberry Mountain's panoramic viewpoint. The climb makes for a demanding 6-mile hike from trailhead to summit and gains 3300 feet in elevation, but the trail grade is good and, after all, this is one of Oregon's tallest peaks. Get to the trailhead via Prairie City on Highway 26; turn south on Main Street and follow signs 11 miles to Strawberry Camp.

Slide Lake is another popular destination from the Strawberry Camp trailhead. It's 4.3 miles, with Little Slide Lake just a short distance beyond.

For a shortcut to the top of Strawberry Mountain, start at a trailhead on the southern side of the wilderness, 0.5 mile from the end of Road 1640 above Indian Springs Campground. From there, a 4.1-mile trail climbs just 1100 feet to the top. From a trailhead at the end of Road 1640, a good beginners' day hike ambles 1.3 miles to High Lake's scenic basin. Those who continue 1.8 miles past High Lake up a steep pass are rewarded with a view of Rabbit Ears and Slide Lake's glacier-carved valley. For an even broader view, hike cross-country from this pass up a cliff-edged ridge to Indian Springs Butte. To reach this trailhead, take Highway 395 south of John Day 10 miles, turn left on paved county Road 65 (which becomes Road 15) for 16 miles, turn left on Road 16 for 3 miles, and take gravel Road 1640 to the left; the trailhead is 11 miles uphill.

Wildcat Basin's July wildflowers make a good goal. Take the 2.4-mile trail up from Buckhorn Meadows, at the end of Road 1520. Follow Road 65 from Highway 395 for 10 miles, turn left on Road 1520, and follow it past the Canyon Meadows Reservoir.

Two uncrowded day-hike trails on the south side of the wilderness follow creeks to mountain lakes. One trail heads up Lake Creek to High Lake, and the other follows Meadow Fork past a waterfall to Mud Lake. Both routes are 4.2 miles one way. With a car shuttle, hikers can either combine the two hikes or else start out at the high-elevation Road 1640 trailhead and make the trip into an easy downhill romp. From Highway 395, take Road 65 for 16 miles, head left on Road 16 for 6.5 miles to Logan Valley, then turn left on Road 924 to Murray Campground. From there the Lake Creek trail begins 1.5 miles ahead at the end of Road 924; turn right from Murray Campground for 2 miles to reach the Meadow Fork trailhead at the end of Road 021.

The East Fork of Canyon Creek splashes through a stately forest in a deep canyon. Backpackers often take the trail along this stream when trekking to the higher country, especially to the small meadow and spring at Hotel de Bum Camp, 9 miles from the Road 812 trailhead. Day hikers will find the creekside path soothing, but may have trouble deciding when to turn back.

The Canyon Mountain Trail offers a different challenge. Blasted into the rugged upper slopes of the Strawberry Range, this route offers lots of scenery but very few campsites. For 15 miles between Dog Creek and Hotel de Bum there is only one reliable creek, and the flattest tent sites are in possibly windy passes. Still, the route's start makes a first-rate day hike, and it is the closest trail to Canyon City. Just take Main Street 2 miles uphill from Highway 395 and turn right for 2.5 miles on what becomes Road 333.

A complete circuit of the area's high lakes makes a fun two- or three-day backpacking trip. The 15-mile loop from the Road 1640 trailhead passes Strawberry Mountain, Strawberry Lake, Slide Lake, and High Lake. Add 2 miles if starting from Strawberry Camp. Allow time for side trips.

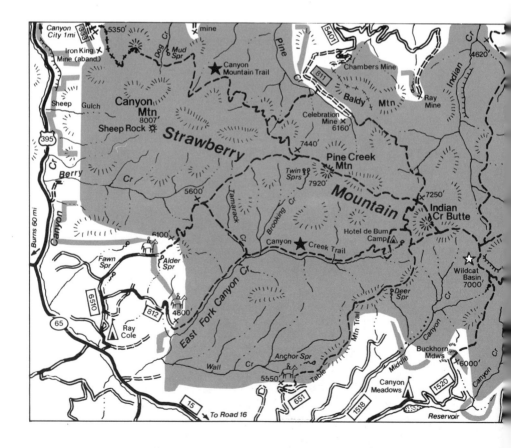

To really experience the Strawberries, try backpacking the entire length of the mountain range's crest. It's 42 miles, starting with the Skyline Trail's forested ridge in the east and ending with the Canyon Mountain Trail's rugged slopes in the west.

Winter Sports

There's plenty of winter snow in these mountains; the challenge is to get to it when most access roads are unplowed. When snow covers low elevations from January to March, one solution is to drive 15 miles south of John Day on plowed Highway 395 to the Starr Bowl winter sports area, with its network of snowmobile and ski trails among nonwilderness hills.

Another midwinter option is to park 2 miles up Canyon City's Main Street and ski Road 333 for 2.5 miles to the Canyon Mountain Trail. The first 2.4 miles of this trail are not too rugged, yet offer excellent viewpoints.

Paved Roads 14, 15, and 16 are also plowed, giving skiers access to excellent snow on the south and east sides of the Strawberry Mountain Wilderness. From the summit of Road 14 (elevation 5899 feet), ski up side Road 101 and the woodsy Skyline Trail. From Road 16 in Logan Valley (not shown on map), ski up side Road 1640. Snowed-under Indian Springs Campground is 8 miles along this road; adventurers can snow camp at Indian Springs and continue 7 miles to the summit of Strawberry Mountain itself.

Strawberry Lake in winter is a goal worth a journey. Expect snow to block the unplowed access road 2 to 8 miles short of the trailhead.

Some of the best snow, and best views, are atop Baldy Mountain. The access Road 5401, though unplowed, is seldom blocked by snow more than 2 or 3 miles before the Chambers Mine, where a spur climbs left to treeless upper slopes. Highway 26 joins the access road 6 miles east of John Day.

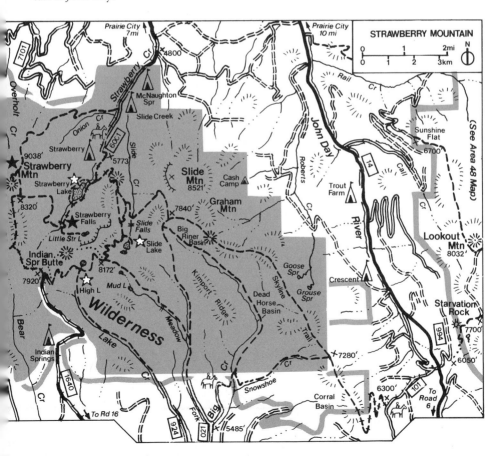

48

GLACIER MOUNTAIN AND MONUMENT ROCK

Location: 26 mi E of John Day, 52 mi SW of Baker City
Size: 91 sq mi, including Wildcat Creek area
Status: 31 sq mi designated wilderness (1984)
Terrain: Steep, forested canyons, open ridges
Elevation: 4300'–8033'
Management: Malheur NF, Wallowa-Whitman NF
Topographic maps: Monument Rock Wilderness (USFS); Bullrun Rock, Little Baldy Mountain, Deardorff Mountain (USGS)

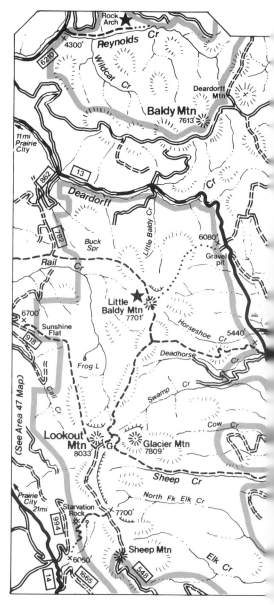

At the southernmost edge of the Blue Mountains, this area's alpine, once-glaciated ridges offer views across much of eastern Oregon. The canyon forests are dense enough to shelter the reclusive, bearlike wolverine.

Climate

The John Day valley funnels winter storms and summer thundershowers eastward to the mountain ridges here. As a result the area receives 40 inches annual precipitation, twice as much as the surrounding, arid lowlands. Expect snow to block trails over 6000 feet from November to May. Summer brings hot days and chilly nights.

Plants and Wildlife

A wolverine sighted west of Table Rock in 1980 provides rare evidence that this unusual animal still exists in Oregon. Named "skunk bear" for its habit of scenting uneaten food, and *Gulo gulo* (glutton glutton in Latin) for its diverse appetite, the wolverine resembles a small, bushy-tailed, gray-headed bear. Though only 18 to 42 pounds, its ferocity successfully drives coyotes, bears, and even mountain lions away from contested carrion.

Wolverines and mountain lions are among the few predators that dare to eat porcupines, a locally abundant species. Watch for porcupines during the day on low tree limbs (where they gnaw on bark and sleep), and at night in human campsites (where they eat sweaty backpack straps and fishing rod handles for the salt).

The unstocked Little Malheur River preserves a population of rare, red-banded trout. The area's seventy bird species include the creek-loving water ouzel and the red-headed pileated woodpecker.

Ponderosa pine and juniper sparsely forest the lowlands and dry south-facing slopes. Alpine meadows, June wildflowers, and spire-shaped subalpine fir top the high ridges. Thickets of mixed conifers crowd other areas.

Geology

Glacier Mountain, Lookout Mountain, and Little Baldy Mountain are glacial horns, their sides steeply scalloped by the U-shaped valleys of vanished Ice Age glaciers. That the equally high Monument Rock area shows so little of this scenic glacial topography remains a puzzle.

The rocks are mostly 15-million-year-old lava and ash from vents near Strawberry Mountain, but an outcropping of much older, more mineralized rock on Bullrun Mountain and Mine

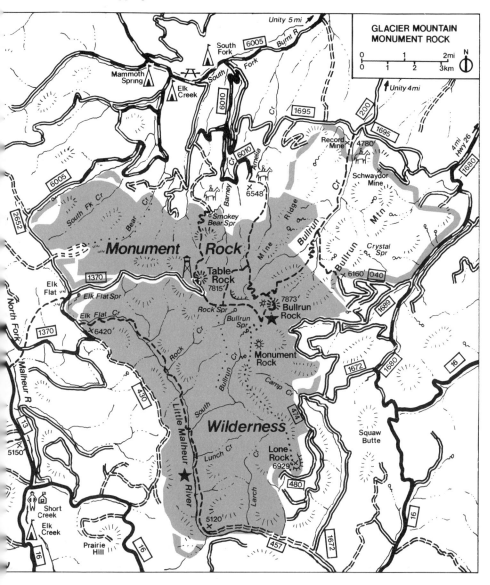

Ridge has spawned several small mines.

History

The lichen-covered 8-foot cylindrical stone monument atop Monument Rock may have been erected by pioneer sheepherders. The Snake Indians who once roamed here are not known to have built such megaliths, but did leave pictographs on a natural rock arch at Reynolds Creek.

The John Day Valley from Little Baldy

THINGS TO DO

Hiking

The area's high ridges feature easy trails to dramatic viewpoints. Even the road to the Lookout Mountain trailhead, dirt Road 548, provides thrilling views as it traces a narrow ridgeline from Sheep Mountain. From Road 548's gate, the tops of Lookout Mountain and Glacier Mountain are a half hour's hike away, but require some cross-country scrambling. A popular day hike continues past the gate on the abandoned road (now maintained as a trail) along the nearly level ridgeline 4 miles to Little Baldy Mountain's summit meadow, and the best view of the John Day valley.

Reach Road 548 from Prairie City by turning south on Main Street; drive 24 paved miles southeast on what becomes Road 14, turn left 1 mile past the road's summit onto dirt Road 1665 for 4 miles, then turn left on Road 548 to the trailhead.

The fire lookout tower at Table Rock is a good place to begin a visit to the Monument Rock area. After taking in the view, backtrack 0.5 mile down the lookout road and take a level, 2-mile stroll along an ancient dirt road to Bullrun Rock's 150-foot cliffs. A faint fork of the abandoned road winds close to Monument Rock and continues 4 miles to Lone Rock.

To reach the Table Rock lookout from Highway 26, drive west from downtown Unity up the South Fork Burnt River 16 miles following Road 6005, turn left on Road 2652 for 2 miles, and then take Road 1370 to the left. To reach the trailhead from Prairie City instead, turn south from Highway 26 on Main Street, follow a paved county road southeast 9 miles, turn left onto Road 13 for 12 miles, then take Road 1370 to the left.

Several streamside trails in deep forest offer cool retreats during summer's heat. The 2-mile path up Reynolds Creek traces this moss-banked, splashing stream well into its shady canyon. Explorers can visit the area's natural rock arch by leaving the Reynolds Creek Trail just after a major gulch appears on the left, 1.6 miles from the trailhead. Scramble 0.3 mile up a ridge to the left to a large basalt outcrop with the arch, some Indian pictographs, and a nice view of the valley. To get to the trailhead from Highway 26, take Prairie City's Main Street southeast 8 miles, then turn left on Road 6210 for 4 miles to the Reynolds Creek bridge.

A 7.5-mile trail follows the Little Malheur River from the end of Road 457 to the river's source at Elk Flat. The best day hike starts at the bottom and aims for a lunch stop near South Bullrun Creek. Beyond, the trail crosses the river four times, requiring log crossings or cold wades. Reach the trailhead via main Road 16; at the Little Malheur River bridge turn north onto Road 457.

Sheep Creek's trail has the advantage that day hikers who arrange a car shuttle can easily make the trip downhill. It's 6.5 miles from the Road 548 gate at Lookout Mountain to Road 13 at the bottom. In October the creek's broad glacial valley glows with bright orange quaking aspen and larch.

The Bullrun Creek Trail starts out with 2 easy miles of hiking in a steep-sided canyon, but then climbs 2000 feet in 3.5 miles up a ridge to Bullrun Rock. Drive to the trailhead from Highway 26 by heading west from downtown Unity on a paved road for 1 mile, then turning left onto gravel for 4 miles. Jog briefly to the right on Road 1695 to the trail.

49

DIXIE BUTTE

Location: 26 mi NE of John Day, 50 mi W of Baker City
Size: 19 sq mi
Status: Undesignated wilderness
Terrain: Forested butte and bench cut by creek valleys
Elevation: 4000'–7592'
Management: Malheur NF
Topographic maps: Bates, Dixie Meadow (USGS)

This prominent, cone-shaped butte overlooks a broad slope of pristine forest land, an island in an otherwise heavily roaded and logged portion of the Blue Mountains.

Climate

Snow blocks the Davis Creek Trail from about Thanksgiving to late April, the same period during which the Dixie Mountain Ski Area operates. The 30 inches of annual precipitation are chiefly snow. Summers are dry.

Winter fog on Dixie Butte

Plants and Wildlife

Mule deer and elk rely on the area for browse, and for cover during fall hunting season. Larch trees and creekside golden currant bushes provide orange foliage in October. The virtually unbroken forests are mostly Douglas fir and white fir, with some ponderosa and lodgepole pine.

Geology

Though shaped like a volcano, Dixie Butte was born of water. The peak's rocks are seafloor sediments buckled up by the Blue Mountains when they were a coastal range 200 to 250 million years ago. Lava flows from the Strawberry Mountains 15 million years ago covered the plateau below the Davis Creek Trail.

Dixie Butte from the Davis Creek Trail

History

Southern gold prospectors here during the Civil War christened Dixie Butte and (Jefferson) Davis Creek to spite the Union men who named the area's new county for Ulysses S. Grant.

THINGS TO DO

Hiking

The Davis Creek Trail contours 7 miles through Dixie Butte's forests. The creeks feature small log bridges, and elk often show themselves along the way. After the hike, plan to drive to the Dixie Butte lookout tower for an overview of the trail's route, as well as a bird's eye view of the snowy Strawberry Mountains across the John Day valley.

Winter Sports

The snowed-under roads looping through the foothills of Dixie Butte make ideal cross-country ski trails. Start at the Dixie Mountain Ski Area (warming hut, rope tow), and remember the route taken, since as many as six roads converge at intersections. In midwinter, park at Austin Junction for a nearly level, 3.2-mile jaunt along Road 2614 to icy Davis Creek.

The area's premier challenge is the 5.5-mile climb up Road 2610 to the summit's unmatched winter view. Beware of avalanche danger on steep roadsides.

50

NORTH FORK JOHN DAY

Location: 61 mi S of Pendleton, 13 mi W of Baker City
Size: 617 sq mi
Status: 190 sq mi designated wilderness (1984)
Terrain: Snowy mountain ranges, rugged river canyons, forested benchlands, cirque lakes
Elevation: 3356'–9106'
Management: Umatilla NF, Wallowa-Whitman NF, Malheur NF, Prineville District BLM
Topographic maps: North Fork John Day Wilderness (USFS); Anthony Lakes, Crawfish Lake, Bourne, Elkhorn Peak (USGS)

The largest wild area in the Blue Mountains, this sprawling complex of wilderness lands encompasses two entire mountain ranges—the craggy Elkhorns and the Greenhorns—as well as a major river, the North Fork John Day. Here roam a good share of the Blue Mountains' 52,000 elk and 150,000 mule deer.

Though separated by paved or well-graveled roads, each of the units of this wilderness has plenty of room for day hikes or long backpacking trips. Not to be missed are the Elkhorn Crest Trail's 24 miles of alpine scenery and the North Fork John Day River Trail's 25 miles of winding gorge. In addition, Anthony Lake offers a nordic skiing center with access to the wilderness in winter.

Climate

Snowfall is heaviest in the Elkhorn Mountains, where the Anthony Lake Ski Area usually operates from Thanksgiving to April 15. Snow blocks hiking trails over 7000 feet until early July; the lower part of the North Fork John Day River Trail clears of snow as early as April.

Crawfish Lake

Annual precipitation hits 45 inches in the Elkhorns, but drops to 20 inches in the western canyons. Summers are dry. October, though generally pleasant, may bring sudden snowstorms. Night temperatures can dip below freezing year round.

Plants and Wildlife

This is elk country, where 800-pound bulls with 5-foot-wide antlers bugle challenges to rival males each fall. More than twice as large as mule deer, elk bulls assemble harems of up to sixty cows during the August to November rut. In this season, listen at dawn or dusk for the bulls' bugles: snorts that rise to a clarinetlike whistle and end with several low grunts. Also look for saplings stripped of bark to mark territory, and elk wallows, small bogs dug by hooves and laced with urine as a bull's private orgy site.

Many of the area's deer and elk winter in the Bridge Creek Wildlife Area south of Ukiah, but others remain, able to survive in this high country's heavy snows by shifting daily between north- and south-facing slopes. The north-facing canyon slopes' dense conifer forests provide shelter from snow and wind. South-facing slopes are sparsely forested, allowing winds to expose the dried grass that elk rely on for food.

Summer hikers find bright green moss, shiny-leaved twinflower, and pink-bloomed prince's pine on the shady north slopes of canyons, while sunny south slopes feature wild strawberry and huckleberry on a dry floor of pungent ponderosa pine needles.

The highest of the alpine Elkhorn Mountains' rock-lined glacial lakes appear to have just been released from a glacier's grip; others have filled in to become marshy wildflower-filled meadows. Lower basins have grown over with subalpine fir and Engelmann spruce.

Dead and dying conifers throughout much of the area are evidence of the mountain pine beetle, which bores into pine bark, and the spruce budworm, which feeds on new needles of Douglas fir, grand fir, and spruce. Not all barren conifers are dead, however; larch normally

The upper portion of the North Fork John Day River Trail

sheds its needles for winter, spangling the forest with orange foliage each October.

Recovering from widespread dredging of stream gravels for gold 1920–54, the North Fork John Day River now provides spawning grounds for 70 percent of the John Day River's steelhead and 90 percent of its Chinook salmon. The fish runs, which peak in late August, help feed a population of bald eagles.

Geology

The granite and scrambled sedimentary rock here reflect the Blue Mountains' history as a volcanic range paralleling the coast 30 to 200 million years ago. Erosion has stripped away the old volcanoes, revealing the granite of their magma chambers. When magma cools slowly to form large-crystaled granitic rock, gold and silver collect along the rock's quartz veins—hence this area's colorful mining history.

Columbia River basalt flows buried the area about 15 million years ago and remain as rimrock on the western benchlands. Erosion stripped this lava from the Elkhorn and Greenhorn mountains when they later rose. Finally, Ice Age glaciers scalloped the ranges with scores of U-shaped glacial valleys.

History

Sumpter, Bourne, Granite, and Greenhorn are picturesque gold mining boomtowns from an 1862 gold strike. Ancient prospects, tailings, and a few small active mines dot hills near the towns, though the easy placer diggings are gone. An abandoned gold dredge near Sumpter once churned many valleys in these mountains to gravel wastelands. Part of the North Fork John Day River Trail follows an abandoned mining ditch once used to bring water to gold sluices.

THINGS TO DO

Hiking

The most popular day hikes explore the Elkhorn Mountains' alpine scenery. Anthony Lake, ringed with rugged peaks, is easily accessible from Interstate 84, making it the only destination in the entire area likely to be crowded.

For starters, take the 1-mile trail around Anthony Lake. A worthwhile 0.6-mile side trail skirts rugged Gunsight Mountain to Black Lake. Another easy side trail loops 1.8 miles from the south end of Anthony Lake, ascending Parker Creek to the Hoffer Lakes and returning down a ski area service road. From the Hoffer Lakes loop, however, the area's best view is just another 1.5 miles away and 1000 feet up; hike up the service road to a pass and keep left on a path up a craggy ridge to The Lakes Observation Point.

For an excellent sample of the high Elkhorns' scenery, take the 6.5-mile loop trail from Anthony Lake entirely around Angell Peak and Gunsight Mountain. The well-built path gains only 1400 feet along the way, passing views of Crawfish Meadow's basin and Dutch Flat Lake.

Other lakes make good goals. Pretty Crawfish Lake is 0.5 or 1.4 miles from Road 73, depending on the trailhead; from the lake, it's easy to bushwhack 1 mile due east along the inlet creek up to Crawfish Meadows' wildflowers. Van Patten Lake, in an alpine cirque, is a steep 1-mile hike from the defunct Little Alps Ski Area 2.5 miles east of Anthony Lake on Road 73; the hike begins up an old service road. Nearby, the 8.5-mile trail to Dutch Flat Lake ascends a gorgeous U-shaped glacial valley from Road 7307.

Three routes reach Cracker Saddle, a scenic flower-spangled pass in the heart of the Elkhorns that serves as the jumping-off point for high-country loops to Summit Lake or Lost Lake. Road 5505 to Cracker Saddle can be too rough even for four-wheel-drive vehicles; it's safer to stop at the mining ghost town of Bourne. Park in the ghost town where the road fords a creek to avoid a rickety bridge and walk the last 4 miles up to the saddle. A second route to Cracker Saddle, up North Powder River Road 7301, has been closed to cars by a washed out bridge. The prettiest route to Cracker Saddle, however, is from the north, following the Peavy Trail from the end of Road 380 up 1750 feet in 3.8 miles. For a spectacular 11.4-mile loop from the Peavy trailhead, climb to Cracker Saddle, take the Elkhorn Crest Trail north, and return on the steep, 3.3-mile Cunningham Trail.

NORTH FORK JOHN DAY

0 1 2 3 4mi
0   2   4   6km
N

244
Ukiah 12 mi
Interstate 84
at Hilgard 31mi
Frazier
Frazier
5226
Fly
Cr
5445
54
G
5448
4520'
Hidaway
5760'
Cr
075
Hidaway
Mdws
Lookout Cr
5160
52
Pearson
6300'
Tower Mtn
6850'
55
Gold
Dredge
5020'
North
5226
Squaw Cr
5293'
52
Hwy 395 at
Dale 6 mi
Winom Cr
Big
Creek
Winom
Butte
Meadow Cr
Forks
G
Log
Table
5225
5505
3356'
Big Cr
South Fork
Martin Cr
5480'
G
North Fork John Day
Fork
6080'
Packsaddle
Spr
Trout Cr
G
Hwy 395
at Dale
7 mi
5505
Lower
Cougar
Ryder Cr
Moon
Mdws
6000'
China
Mdws
10
5228'
Basin
Camp
North Fork
Silver Butte
6191'
Thorn-
burg
Mine
4600'
Upper
Cougar
Kelsay
Butte
Dixson Bar
Silver Spring
Crane Cr
1010
Glade Cr
3700'
John Day Trail
Gold mining
log cabins
Happy
Prairie
Bull
Prairie
6400'
Oregon
Gulch
3936'
Ford
Granite
Creek
1035
Desolation
Butte
6122'
Lake Cr
Rabbit
Butte
Granite Cr
Cr
Desolation
Howard Cr
Desolation
Day
Rabbit Cr
Sharp
Ridge
Jumpoff
Joe L
080
45
5700'
Lost Camp
5879'
Fremont
Powerhouse
13
21 mi Hwy 395
South Fk Desolation Cr
400
Olive
L
10
1310
Big
Olive Lake
Summit
Lost Mdw
5400'
Head o'
Boulder
Donaldson
Mine
Saddle
Lost Cr
Clear Cr
Ben Camp
635
Indian
Rock
7353'
Dupratt
Spr
7450'
Ben Harrison
Pk
Mountains
Cr
Greenhorn
Ben Camp
Spring
Galena
14 mi Hwy 7
Statler
Mine
Tempest
Mine
4559
8131'
Vinegar
Hill
Hwy 7
8 mi
4555
G
1010
Greenhorn
Wilderness
Wilderness

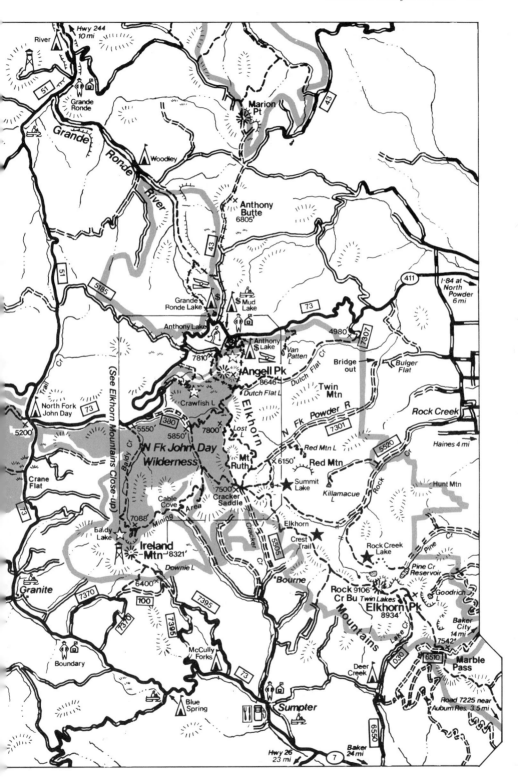

Rock Creek Lake fills a breathtakingly stark, treeless cirque, backed by the cliffs of the Blue Mountains' highest peak, 9,106-foot Rock Creek Butte. Both routes to this lake require 2400-foot climbs: the 3.5-mile trail from Road 5520 and the 2.5-mile path from Pine Creek Reservoir. Both trailheads can only be reached by high-clearance vehicles.

For a taste of the Elkhorn Crest Trail, start at Road 6510 atop Marble Pass and hike 4.1 miles along the ridge to the Lake Creek Trail junction. From there, switchbacks lead 1 mile down to Twin Lakes; more energetic souls can scramble up trailless Elkhorn Peak for a view of Baker and the distant Wallowa Mountains.

On the west side of the Elkhorns, a quiet 6.3-mile trail up Baldy Creek from Road 73 leads to Baldy Lake, overtowered by Ireland Mountain. For a path to Ireland Mountain's lookout tower, however, drive 11 miles west of Sumpter on Road 73, turn right on Road 7370 for a couple miles, and turn right on Road 100 for 0.3 mile to a sign, "Mount Ireland Trail ½ Mile." Since the road is blocked here, park and walk. The 3.5-mile trail climbs 1800 feet. A 1-mile side trip descends to Downie Lake.

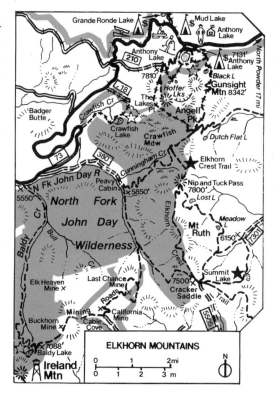

The Greenhorn Mountains, dotted with small, active mines, offer trails and old mining tracks among broad, subalpine summits. Start with the lovely 5.5-mile trail from the Olive Lake Campground past Upper Olive Lake's meadow and Saddle Camp to Dupratt Spring, in a scenic rocky pass between deep, glacier-carved valleys. For a 360-degree view, scramble 0.5 mile east to Ben Harrison Peak. For a loop, follow an old road-trail 2 miles northeast and fork left on a 3-mile path through Lost Meadow to a Road 10 trailhead, 2 miles from Olive Lake.

To explore more of the Greenhorn Mountains, park where Road 45 bridges South Fork Desolation Creek and hike the unofficial but surprisingly well maintained creekside path 6 miles to the head of that glacial valley. Or start at primitive Head o' Boulder Campground, just below Indian Rock's staffed lookout tower, and either follow the level Princess Trail 5 miles east to Dupratt Spring, or take the Squaw Rock Trail 4 miles north, descending Big Creek to Road 45.

The winding, 25-mile canyon traced by the North Fork John Day River Trail offers new vistas at every bend: forests plunging down 1000-foot slopes into the brawling stream, rustic log cabins among lodgepole pines, and towering rock outcroppings. Should the weather turn, even the private log cabins are left unlocked as emergency shelter (though many have rats and leaky roofs).

Day hikers can easily sample this impressive canyon trail at three points. The most popular route follows Granite Creek 3 miles from Road 1035 to a footbridge across the North Fork John Day and a meadow with a collapsed log cabin. At the canyon's eastern end, hikers starting from the North Fork John Day Campground can follow the river 3 miles to a bridge across rushing Trout Creek. At the canyon's western end, Road 5506 provides a third river-level access to the North Fork John Day River Trail.

Those unable to arrange a car shuttle for end-to-end backpacking trips along the Elkhorn Crest or North Fork John Day River Trails should consider several loop hike alternatives. An

18-mile, figure-eight-shaped loop from Anthony Lake follows the Elkhorn Crest Trail south to Cracker Saddle and returns via Lost Lake. A 31-mile loop from the Granite Creek trailhead climbs from Dixson Bar to Moon Meadows before returning via China Meadows and the upper portion of the North Fork John Day River Trail.

Climbing

The Elkhorn Mountains feature granite cliffs (rare in Oregon) up to 300 feet tall. Though scenic, the area lacks named routes and crowds of climbers because of its remoteness and the fact that all peaks have walk-up sides.

Winter Sports

The Anthony Lake Ski Area provides use of 10 kilometers of groomed nordic trails for a fee. Plowed Road 73, however, gives nordic skiers and snowshoers many other options.

Start with an easy 1-mile jaunt around Anthony Lake, with a side trip to nearby Black or Hoffer lakes.

Van Patten Lake, set in a narrow basin below Van Patten Ridge's cliffs, is a 1-mile climb from Road 73. Iced-over Crawfish Lake is another fun trip. Ski there cross-country from the top of the Anthony Lake ski lift or ski 4.5 miles along Road 73 (unplowed west of Anthony Lake) to spur Road 218 and a 1.2-mile route to the lake.

Take the Anthony Lake chairlift to start the dramatic, 6.5-mile loop around Angell Peak. Pass up this challenging trip if bad weather or avalanche danger threatens.

Boating

The North Fork John Day is not generally considered navigable through its wilderness portion due to boulders and low water levels. Raft and kayak trips on the North Fork commence at Dale and follow 40 miles of class 2+ whitewater to Monument.

Motorless boats are allowed on small, scenic Anthony Lake.

The "Bigfoot Hilton," a gold miner's shack along the North Fork John Day River at Trout Creek

51

NORTHERN BLUE MOUNTAINS

Location: 26 mi E of Pendleton, 9 mi NW of La Grande
Size: 233 sq mi
Status: 32 sq mi designated wilderness (1984)
Terrain: Plateaus cut by steep, partly forested canyons
Elevation: 2000'–6064'
Management: Umatilla NF, Wallowa-Whitman NF
Topographic maps: North Fork Umatilla Wilderness (USFS); Bingham Springs, Andies Prairie, Tollgate, Thimbleberry Mountain, Drumhill Ridge (USGS)

One of the roughest barriers confronting Oregon Trail pioneers in the 1840s, the northern Blue Mountains still harbor enough wilderness to challenge hikers and hide elk.

Climate

Autumns are renowned both for delightful Indian summer weather and surprise blizzards. Shade is at a premium during summer's heat, since less than half the area is forested. Annual precipitation—mostly winter snow—ranges from 30 inches in the arid canyons to 45 inches in the tablelands. Ski season at Spout Springs is from mid-November to mid-April.

Plants and Wildlife

Road building and logging have largely been confined to the area's plateaus, leaving wilderness in the steeply dissected canyonlands. There, only the relatively wet and shady north-facing slopes support forests (chiefly white fir). As a result, nearly every ridge offers a view to the south of forest and a view to the north of seemingly uninterrupted, dry grasslands, giving the illusion that one is always on the edge of a steppe.

The low-elevation creekbanks sprout lush foliage: sword fern, wild ginger, Oregon grape, yew, alder, wild cherry, stinging nettle, and snowberry. Look for beaver ponds and gnawed trees along the North Fork Umatilla. Expect to find boggy wallows made by bull elk along the North Fork Meacham and Five Points Creek.

Geology

The northern Blue Mountains do not resemble their southern cousins. Forty miles to the south, the Blue Mountains are craggy, granite peaks. Here the range consists of dissected basalt tablelands.

The difference is that when the Columbia River lava flows spread out from the Grande Ronde area 15 million years ago, they topped the southern Blue Mountains with a thin, easily eroded layer. Here, flow upon flow of lava buried the landscape 4000 feet deep. Even when subsequent uplifting allowed creeks to cut the leveled terrain into a jagged canyonland, the older rocks presumably below have still not been exposed.

History

This mountain range once divided the Cayuse and Nez Perce Indians. Lookingglass Creek commemorates Nez Perce leader Apash-wa-hay-ikt, dubbed Chief Lookingglass because he often carried with him a hand mirror.

The first white men here were crossing the continent to establish a fur-trading post at Astoria in 1812. In 1827 botanist David Douglas hiked to the Blue Mountain crest and found 4-foot-tall yellow lupine blooming—possibly the rare Sabine lupine, found only in these uplands.

In 1836, missionaries Marcus and Narcissa Whitman crossed the range on a primitive route now interpreted by the Forest Service as the Whitman Route: south of Mount Emily, across Five Points Creek and Meacham Creek, then down Horseshoe Ridge toward Walla Walla.

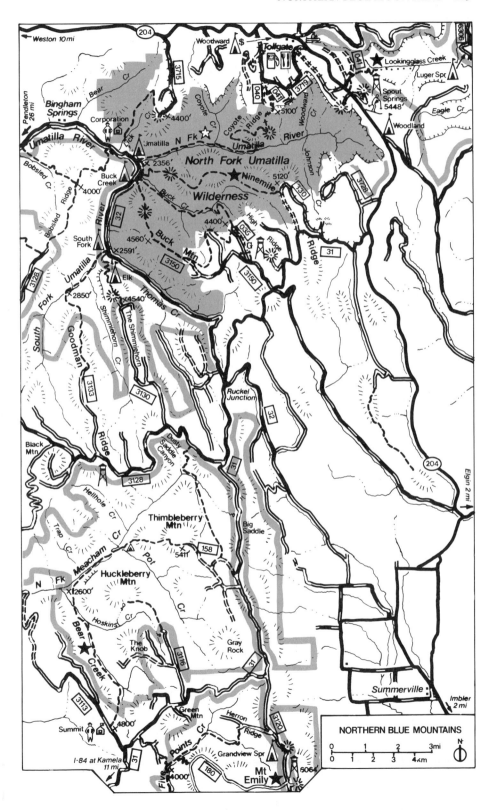

Marcus Whitman returned in 1843 leading a wagon train. Within five years, 9000 settlers had followed on what became the Oregon Trail, winching their wagons onto the tablelands west of La Grande to avoid the narrow, brushy canyon bottoms.

THINGS TO DO

Hiking

A cluster of campgrounds near the forks of the Umatilla River form the hub of eight radiating hiking trails. All of these paths gain some 2000 feet in elevation on their way to progressively higher and more compelling canyon viewpoints; however, the trails that follow creeks climb gently at first, while the ridge trails start out briskly. Two of the routes connect, making possible a dramatic 15-mile loop up Buck Creek, across the roaded tableland, and back down Buck Mountain's grassy ridge.

For other trails, up-and-back day hikes are in order. Those who wish to hike the trails only downhill must arrange car shuttles to the remote upper trailheads.

The most heavily trafficked trail follows the North Fork Umatilla River 3 miles from Umatilla Campground to a good picnic spot in an old-growth fir forest at the mouth of Coyote Creek. Here crowds thin out, for the trail, which had been nearly level, switchbacks 3 miles up grassy Coyote Ridge to Road 041 on Tollgate's plateau.

Several less crowded trails nearby also feature rushing streams. One traces the South Fork Umatilla River 2.3 miles before taking off up Goodman Ridge 1.5 miles to Road 3133. Another, the Lick Creek Trail, forks off from the North Fork Umatilla River Trail near its beginning, then contours past some canyon slope viewpoints before ascending Lick Creek's ravine. The upper trailhead at Road 3715 is 4 miles distant.

Of the four ridge trails near the Umatilla River campgrounds, the switchbacks up Ninemile Ridge climb with the gentlest grade. That route extends 7 miles to Road 330. As with all of the local ridgeline hikes, the first mile has most of the elevation gain while the remaining miles follow an open, view-filled crest with wildflowers (cat's ears, Indian paintbrush, balsamroot).

The 5.5-mile trail up Bobsled Ridge starts out with a few switchbacks that lessen its steepness. However, there are two ridge trails nearby that more closely resemble bobsled runs: the steep path up Buck Mountain and the (unmarked) very steep 1.5-mile Shimmiehorn Trail to Road 3130.

The area's largest roadless tract has been named Hellhole by the Forest Service—a name that misrepresents the area's lovely canyon scenery. For proof of this, try the trail down Bear Creek from the Summit guard station. The route gradually descends 6 miles through a cool, old-growth forest, then follows the clear North Fork Meacham Creek 2.5 miles to a grassy campsite at Pot Creek before climbing 3.5 miles to flat-topped Thimbleberry Mountain.

Mount Emily is not only the area's highest point, with a sweeping view across the Grande Ronde Valley to the Wallowa Mountains, it's also near the start of a quiet forest trail that's surprisingly close to downtown La Grande. Near the Mount Emily turnoff on Road 3120, follow Road 180 for 4 miles to the trailhead. The path switchbacks down 1 mile to Five Points Creek. Here, either head upstream 3.3 miles to a trailhead on Herron Ridge, or turn downstream, following the creek 5.5 miles to a ford and dirt road at Camp One, just 7 miles northwest of La Grande via backroads marked as the route of the old Whitman Trail.

For canyon solitude, try Lookingglass Creek. A good trail switchbacks 1.5 miles down from the Spout Springs area to the creek, but from there on, hikers are on their own.

Winter Sports

Highway 204, plowed in winter, provides nordic skiers with access to snowed-under roads on the tablelands fringing the North Fork Umatilla Wilderness. Expect competition from snowmobiles on routes near Tollgate. A good strategy is to head for canyon rim viewpoints, particularly the ones at the wilderness's upper trailheads. The trails themselves, especially the one on Ninemile Ridge, are also skiable for short distances. Turn back when they begin descending sharply to lands of less snow. Warm up at Spout Springs, a major winter center with three lifts, two day lodges, and a restaurant.

52

WENAHA-TUCANNON

Location: 50 mi N of Enterprise, 28 mi E of Walla Walla
Size: 363 sq mi total; 122 sq mi in Oregon
Status: 277 sq mi designated wilderness; 104 sq mi in Oregon (1978); federal wild and scenic rivers
Terrain: Steep, partly forested river canyons, dissected plateaus
Elevation: 1700'–6401'
Management: Umatilla NF
Topographic map: Wenaha-Tucannon Wilderness (USFS)

This huge canyonland on the Oregon-Washington border supports the nation's highest elk population density. The excellent trail network, popular with equestrians, has room for weeklong backpacking trips.

Climate

Snowfall from late November to April averages 8 to 12 feet at Oregon Butte and 1 to 2 feet along the Wenaha River. Trails to 4000 feet elevation clear of snow by early May, but higher routes may be blocked until June. August afternoon temperatures often exceed 100°F, while fierce winters bring weather as cold as –40°F and occasionally freeze the Grande Ronde River. Sudden snowstorms may interrupt autumn's cool, clear weather.

Plants and Wildlife

Elk dominate the area, but whitetail deer and big-eared mule deer are also plentiful. The herds move down from the mountains in winter to the Wenaha Wildlife Area, where the state supplies them with supplemental feed. These feeding stations are probably the best spot in Oregon to observe elk and deer. For a look at the herds, drive the road from Troy along Eden Bench from mid-January to late May.

Other mammals include the whistling marmot, Columbia ground squirrel, snowshoe hare, black bear, mountain lion, coyote, bobcat, and marten. Bald eagles winter along the Grande Ronde River. Chukar and grouse startle hikers by bursting out of trailside brush.

The trailside brush with elegant white berries is snowberry. When Lewis and Clark passed north of here they collected snowberry seeds and brought them to Thomas Jefferson, who delighted in the "very handsome little shrub" and presented a bush to Lafayette's aunt in Paris as a gift from America.

Old-growth cottonwoods, fir, and ponderosa pine line the Wenaha River. Sparse bunchgrass covers the steep canyons' dry, south-facing slopes. Dense mixed conifer forests cover other slopes and tablelands. Expect wildflowers in June and the beautiful red foliage of nonpoisonous sumac bushes in October.

Geology

This area was the main source of the Columbia River lava flows that buried the landscape from Utah to Astoria 15 million years ago with up to 5000 feet of basalt. For proof of this, look in the canyons, where stream erosion has cut deep into the old lava plain. Running vertically through the basalt layers are occasional, wall-like outcroppings of jointed rock, looking almost like stacked cordwood. These are dikes, formed when the lava oozed up from the earth and squeezed into cracks on the way.

The distinctive red layers between rimrock levels are old soil horizons, indicating that thousands of years of forests had time to grow between lava eruptions.

History

The name Wenaha is Nez Perce, for this was once the *ha* (domain) of Wenak, a Nez Perce chief. Similarly, the Imnaha River to the east was the *ha* of Chief Imna.

WENAHA - TUCANNON

0   1   2   3mi
0   1   2   3   4km
N

Dayton 11 mi
18 mi Dayton
Tucannon 34 mi Hwy 12
Tucannon

Touchet R
46
64
G

Panjab
4712
2970
Panjab Trailhead
3100'
4713
Turkey Cr
Indian Corral 5600
4608
Meadow Cr
5600'
Tepee
Oregon Butte 6401
Godman
5640
Rainbow Cr
Danger Pt
Wenaha-
Ski Bluewood
Ski Lift
46
West Fk Butte Cr
East Fk
Huckleberry Spr
3000'
300
Buck Ridge
5680'
Twin Buttes
Box Canyon
Weller Butte 5640
Tucannon
Burnt Flat
Cr
5400'
Mill Cr
Table Rock 6250'
Paradise Ridge
Butte Cr
Indian
North Fork
Sawtooth Ridge
Beaver Cr
5144'
Grizzly Bear Ridge
Washington
Oregon
5680'
Slick Ear Cr
Wilderness
Milk Cr
Round Butte
Rock Cr
4300'
65
Shoofly Cr
Trapper Cr
Wenaha
River
Wenaha Forks
2800'
Big Hole Canyon
6217
G
Squaw Springs
Elk Cr
Mosler Spr
62
Walla Walla 24 mi
64
Jaussaud Cr
4960'
Elk Flats
Squaw Cr
Reser Cr
Bone Spr
South Fork
Cougar Canyon
Bear Cr
S Fk Walla Walla R
Mottet
4740'
6415
Timothy Spring
Lookout Mtn 5229'
Grande
Box Canyon
6401
62
10 mi Tollgate
6413
Jubilee Lake
Elgin 24 mi

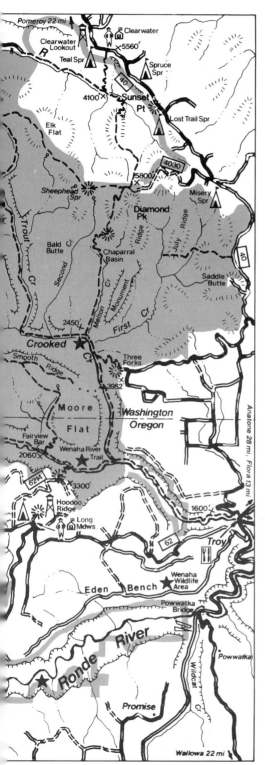

THINGS TO DO

Hiking

Part of the wonder of this area is its enormity. Even day trips open vistas of seemingly endless canyonlands, wild rivers, and rugged ridges.

Troy (population 58) offers the only river-level trailhead on the Oregon side. Start here for a 6-mile walk up the Wenaha's arid, winding canyon to the footbridge and broad gravel bar at the mouth of Crooked Creek. Troy can be reached year round by gravel road from Boggan's Oasis, Washington, which is 32 miles south of Lewiston on Highway 129. To get to Troy from Enterprise, take Highway 3 north to the ghost town of Flora (the road is icy in winter), then take a steep gravel road 13 miles west to Troy.

A good way to sample the area's rugged scenery is to hike from a canyon rim down to one of the rivers. Of the many possible routes, here are three that are neither too steep nor too long: The Hoodoo Trail switchbacks 2.2 miles from Road 6214 to a narrow part of the Wenaha River's chasm near Fairview Bar, losing just 1300 feet. A 3.5-mile route from the Three Forks trailhead loses 1600 feet on its way to Crooked Creek. And finally, those who prefer a longer, gentler trail through forest might try the 5-mile path from the Elk Flats Campground down 2100 feet to Wenaha Forks. The canyon-bottom flat at Wenaha Forks features big cottonwoods, snowberry, and gravel bars.

Other day trips follow ridgelines to high viewpoints. Start at Indian Campground on Road 64 for a 3.4-mile walk to Round Butte and a view down the length of the Wenaha River; the final 0.25 mile to the summit is cross-country. A different day trip climbs to the fire lookout on Oregon Butte, the wilderness's highest point. The view is well worth the 2.2-mile hike from Tepee Campground.

Trailheads on the southwest side of the wilderness are best reached via Walla Walla or Tollgate. From Walla Walla, take Highway 12 east 3 miles and turn right onto paved Mill Creek Road, which becomes Road 65. From Tollgate, located on Oregon Highway 204 halfway between Weston and

The town of Troy from the Wenaha River trailhead

Elgin, take gravel Road 64 for 11 miles to the popular Jubilee Lake Campground, shown on the map.

Much of the vast backcountry can only be reached by overnight trips. Don't miss the 31.3-mile Wenaha River Trail from Timothy Spring Campground to Troy. This well-maintained route requires no major fords. The Forest Service's elaborate footbridge across the North Fork Wenaha, left high and dry when that fork changed course, has been replaced by a log conveniently felled by beaver.

Of the many possible loop trips, here are three suggestions for exploring the wilderness's interior: An 18.2-mile route begins at the Twin Buttes trailhead on Road 300, follows Grizzly Bear Ridge's mesa to the Wenaha River, then returns to Twin Buttes via Wenaha Forks and Slick Ear Creek. For a 29.2-mile loop, start at Diamond Peak, follow the ridge to Indian Corral, descend Trout Creek and Crooked Creek, then return via the trail up Melton Creek. A spectacular 41-mile loop visits Oregon Butte, Moore Flat, Crooked Creek, and Indian Corral; one can get to this loop from any of the eastern trailheads.

Just west of the Wenaha-Tucannon area, the South Fork Walla Walla River rushes through Box Canyon, a rocky gorge where stream-loving water ouzels dip and sing. At one point the popular trail here is a mossy ledge lapped by the river and overtowered by basalt cliffs. Day hikers can reach Box Canyon by switchbacking down 1800 feet in 2.3 miles from Mottet Campground on a good trail; cross the footbridge at Reser Creek and amble downstream a mile or two into the canyon. Backpackers can start at the head of the South Fork Walla Walla Trail at Road 65 and continue 18 miles to either of two trailheads. One is at the end of the South Fork Walla Walla Road (13 miles west of Milton-Freewater); the other climbs to a spur road 0.5 mile northwest of Target Meadows Campground, near Tollgate.

Winter Sports

The best access to winter snow is via Dayton, Washington. Take Fourth Street to plowed Road 64 and the Ski Bluewood ski area. From there, ride the lift to the canyon rim and set out on snowshoes or cross-country skis. Snowed-under Roads 46 and 300 provide well-defined, nearly level ridgetop routes with views into the North Fork Wenaha River canyon. The trail along narrow Buck Ridge stays level for 2 miles (then descends dangerously). Another tour from Road 46 climbs slightly for 2.5 miles to Burnt Flat's plateau.

Boating

The Grande Ronde River winds through a 2400-foot-deep canyon of steep forests and interesting basalt formations. Canoeists can navigate the river except in April to June's high water, which kayakers often prefer. Low water grounds most craft in September.

The run begins at Minam on Highway 84, follows the Wallowa River 8.5 miles to Rondowa, then continues down the Grande Ronde River 28.5 miles to Powwatka Bridge, 8 miles south of Troy. All rapids in this section can be scouted by boat. The most serious of these is the (class 3) Minam Roller, 1.5 miles below the Minam put-in.

From Powwatka Bridge, boaters can continue 26 miles to Boggan's Oasis (on the Enterprise-Lewiston highway), and then another 26 miles to Heller's Bar on the Snake River. In low water The Narrows, below Boggan's Oasis, poses a class 4 hazard.

53

JOSEPH CANYON

Location: 20 mi N of Enterprise
Size: 39 sq mi
Status: Undesignated wilderness
Terrain: Steep, sparsely forested canyon
Elevation: 2400'–4920'
Management: Wallowa-Whitman NF
Topographic maps: Table Mountain, Roberts Butte, Sled Springs (USGS)

Birthplace of the Nez Perce Indian leader, Chief Joseph, this stark canyon features the same kind of awe-inspiring scenery as the larger, but less easily accessible Hells Canyon nearby.

Climate

The canyon's wildflowers bloom and the bunchgrass greens April to June. In summer, temperatures top 100°F. Fall is dry, infrequently interrupted by brief snowstorms. Winter temperatures remain below freezing for weeks at a stretch. Highway 3, though plowed of snow, is often icy and treacherous from December to March. Annual precipitation is an arid 15 inches.

Plants and Wildlife

The canyon's sides are corrugated with steep gulches; forest grows on north-facing gulch slopes and bunchgrass grows on dry south-facing slopes. The result is the distinctly stripy vegetative cover popular with elk, who need to shift between shelter and grazing areas, especially in winter.

A forest fire in 1986 performed the maintenance work traditionally reserved for wildfire here: clearing out deadfall, brush, and mixed conifer thickets while leaving the old-growth ponderosa pine intact.

Joseph Creek

Bring binoculars to distinguish raptors in flight: golden and bald eagles, goshawks, Cooper's hawks, and sharp-shinned hawks. All of these nest here, as do blue grouse, ruffed grouse, and chukars. Joseph Creek and its tributaries provide spawning grounds for salmon and steelhead.

Geology

This canyon exposes some of the state's most interesting basalt formations. The area was a major source of the colossal Columbia River basalt flows 15 million years ago. Not only are dozens of horizontal basalt flows visible in cross-section, but basalt dikes show as vertical stripes, formed when the upwelling lava squeezed into cracks. The basalt has eroded into cliffs, caves, and crags, including domed Haystack Rock.

When the land here began to rise about 13 million years ago, creeks swiftly cut canyons into the lava plain, following the areas' north–south fault lines.

History

Chief Joseph, leader of the Wallowa band of the Nez Perce, was born in a cave along this portion of Joseph Creek. The original 6.5-million-acre Nez Perce Reservation of 1855 included Joseph Canyon. A divisive 1863 treaty left the tribe with only a small tract of land in Idaho. The Wallowa band refused to sign the treaty or to recognize it. President Grant upheld their right to the Wallowa valley and Joseph Canyon in 1873, but under mounting pressure from settlers, the Army in 1877 ordered the Indians to leave, setting in motion the Nez Perce's famous, ill-fated march toward freedom in Canada.

THINGS TO DO

Hiking

Begin with a visit to the Joseph Canyon viewpoint on Highway 3. West of the highway stretches an unassuming plain of forest and wheat fields, while to the east the land suddenly falls away into a gaping, 2100-foot-deep chasm.

The Davis Creek Trail offers the gentlest route into this canyonland. The trail begins 9 miles south of the Joseph Canyon viewpoint (or 20 miles north of Enterprise) at a Highway 3 road-side parking area marked only by an outhouse. Walk north on dirt Road 170, keeping right at junctions to find the 1.7-mile trail down Davis Creek, whose long, V-shaped valley forms a ma-

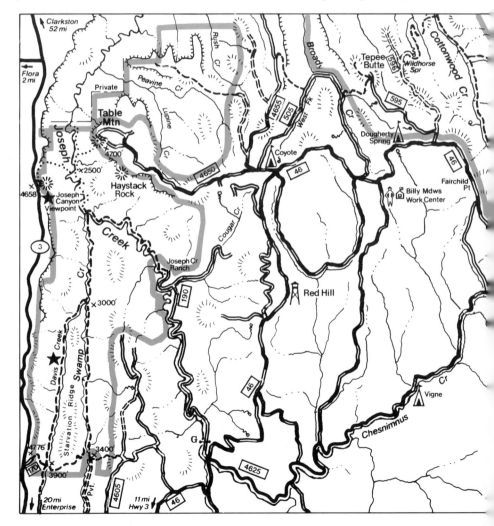

jor branch of Joseph Canyon. Day hikers can lunch along Davis Creek and return. Backpackers will want to continue north to Joseph Creek (12 miles from this trailhead) and allow a day to prowl the deeper canyon there before returning, perhaps via Swamp Creek and the connector trail over Starvation Ridge. Cattle share these trails.

Adventurers with good shoes and sound knees can hike to the bottom of the Joseph Canyon in just 2 miles by following the steep, abandoned Wilder Trail down from the Joseph Canyon viewpoint on Highway 3. To avoid the cliffs below the viewpoint, first hike north along the canyon rim 0.2 mile, then descend a rounded ridge past the remains of a log cabin. The faint trail heads southwest halfway down and is easy to lose.

At the bottom, another unmaintained route follows the winding creek through its cliff-edged gorge—a narrow oasis of green shaded by noble ponderosa pines. Bring creek-wading sneakers, for the cold, calf-deep creek crosses the narrow canyon often. Private land blocks creek bushwhackers 2.3 miles downstream from the Wilder Trail terminus and 6.8 miles upstream at the Joseph Creek Ranch.

The grassy edge of Table Mountain's forested plateau affords a sweeping view of the entire canyon and the distant Wallowa Mountains. Haystack Rock provides an easy cross-country goal across the grassy slopes from Road 4650.

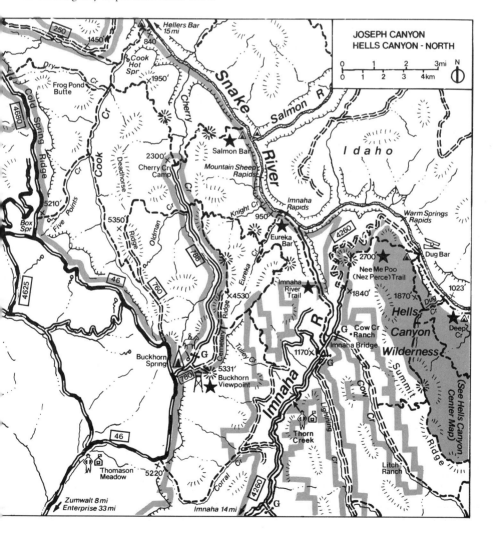

HELLS CANYON

Location: 80 mi E of Baker City, 36 mi E of Enterprise
Size: 761 sq mi
Status: 336 sq mi designated wilderness (1975, 1984), federal wild and scenic rivers, national recreation area
Terrain: Immense unforested chasm, whitewater river, forested tablelands, snowpeaks, lakes
Elevation: 840'–9393'
Management: Hells Canyon National Recreation Area
Topographic maps: Hells Canyon NRA, Wild and Scenic Snake River (USFS)

The deepest river gorge on earth, Hells Canyon inspires awe for its sheer size. From the gentle wildflower meadows on its rim, this chasm gapes like the ragged edge of a broken planet. Basalt rimrock and stark, treeless terraces alternate downward toward a tiny curve at the bottom: the brawling whitewater of the mighty Snake River, over a vertical mile below. And stacked 9000 feet high on the Idaho rim loom the crags of the snowy Seven Devils Mountains.

Climate

Two different climates prevail here at once: Heavy snows drape the alpine rim from November to May or June, while the relatively balmy, but much more arid canyon bottom receives less than 10 inches of precipitation in an entire year. Summer temperatures often hit a sweltering 100°F along the river but remain in the 70s on the rim, where nights can freeze in any season. Spring and fall are pleasant in the canyon.

Plants and Wildlife

Bring binoculars to spot big-eared mule deer and herds of up to 100 elk from miles away in this open canyonland. Also watch for mountain goats, with shaggy coats and spike horns, and bighorn sheep, with curling horns. The black bears in Hells Canyon are a distinctive cinnamon brown. This is the only site in Oregon with a recent sighting of a wolf.

Birds include great blue herons and nonmigrating geese, enticed to year-round residency by the river's mild climate.

The Snake River itself provides rare habitat for giant white sturgeon up to 12 feet long. Sea runs of salmon and steelhead died forever from the entire upper Snake River system when the Idaho Power Company built the Hells Canyon, Oxbow, and Brownlee dams in 1958–64 with inadequate fish-passing facilities. The company has since built a hatchery on the Rapid River in an attempt to perpetuate Snake River strains of fish in the free-flowing Salmon River system.

In April and May the canyon slopes glow green with bunchgrass. Flowers include tiny pink phlox and prickly pear cactus. In June red Indian paintbrush and yellow desert parsley carpet the alpine meadows interspersed with forest along the rim. The canyon turns brown in summer, but balsamroot brightens river benches with miles of little sunflowers. Summer is the only likely time to spot rattlesnakes. By October most gulches flame with the beautiful scarlet leaves of (nonpoisonous) sumac bushes. Sumac's relative, poison oak, grows on a few riverbanks.

Geology

This enormous chasm did not exist as recently as 15 million years ago, for Columbia River basalt now found on the widely separated Oregon and Idaho rims has been shown to be part of a single, 15-million-year-old lava flow.

Surprisingly, Hells Canyon was not carved by the Snake River. The ancestral Snake flowed across southern Oregon to the sea. When Great Basin faulting lifted large chunks of eastern Oregon about 13 million years ago, the Snake backed up, creating a lake over most of southern

Idaho. Meanwhile, north–south fractures from the Great Basin faults allowed Columbia tributaries to cut deeply into the new northern Oregon uplands, carving the parallel canyons of the Imnaha, Salmon, and an unnamed creek that dead-ended in Hells Canyon. When this unnamed creek cut its canyon to the edge of the huge lake in Idaho, the waters suddenly poured northward to the Columbia, and the Snake River raged into Hells Canyon.

The canyon cuts through 4000 feet of Columbia River basalt to expose the older surface below. This light gray rock, forming the Snake's rugged Inner Gorge, consists of jumbled sedimentary and volcanic strata laid down on the sea floor 200 million years ago, then scraped up into an ancient coastal range by the westward-moving continent.

At first it seems puzzling that the tablelands bordering Hells Canyon slope upward to the canyon's edge. However, the Earth's crust floats on a molten mantle. When the creation of Hells Canyon removed some 500 cubic miles of rock here, the crust floated upward like an emptied gravel barge. This in turn caused the river to cut the canyon still deeper. The Seven Devils Mountains, between the vast, empty canyons of the Salmon and Snake, have bobbed highest of all.

Ice Age glaciers ground out the many lake basins in the Seven Devils Mountains and rounded the valleys of the Imnaha River, Rapid River, and upper Granite Creek.

Prickly pear cactus along the Snake River

History

Pit-house depressions along Tryon Creek testify to ancient habitation, as do petroglyphs at Willow Bar and elsewhere. Vandalism by pottery- and basket-seekers threatens study of the estimated 160 to 200 archaeological sites in the canyon. Even arrowheads and old bottles are federally protected.

Nez Perce Indians under Chief Toohoolhoolzote established domination of the canyon by obliterating a Shoshone village at Battle Creek. In 1877, U.S. Army negotiators trying to convince Oregon Nez Perce to move to a small Idaho reservation took Toohoolhoolzote hostage. Sullenly, the Wallowa band's Chief Joseph led 400 Indians and several thousand head of cattle and Appaloosa horses toward the reservation. The tribe marched down the Imnaha River and managed to cross the Snake in flood stage. A 3.7-mile portion of the amazingly rugged route they followed is preserved as the Nee-Me-Poo (Nez Perce for "the real people") Trail. A shootout near the reservation, however, sent the tribe on a four-month tactical retreat, ending with defeat just 30 miles short of permanent sanctuary in Canada.

Hells Canyon frustrated explorers seeking a navigable river route west, notably an 1811–12 overland expedition to Astoria. Once, in 1870, a full-sized steamboat built on the upper Snake River ran the canyon downriver, but lost 8 feet of its bow in the process.

A copper and gold strike at Eureka Bar in 1900 brought regular steamboat service from Lewiston to the mouth of the Imnaha River. A 125-foot ship winched herself up the river with the aid of giant iron rings still visible in the cliffs above Wild Goose and Mountain Sheep rapids. The ship lost power on a 1903 run, drifted backward into Mountain Sheep Rapids, bridged the 62-foot-wide canyon there, and broke in half. Visible at Eureka Bar are remains of the steamboat landing and a huge, never-completed ore mill.

In 1887, a group of seven Idaho cowhands robbed and murdered thirty-two Chinese gold miners panning river gravel at Deep Creek. Chinese numerals still mark the wall of the miners' crude rock shelter. The robbers buried their loot at the scene; one vial of gold dust turned up there in 1902.

Homesteaders built hardscrabble ranches in the canyon bottom during 1910–30. The Forest Service has acquired most of the abandoned ranches and has restored the Kirkwood Ranch's clapboard ranch house and log bunkhouse as a museum of that era.

THINGS TO DO

Hiking

Nearly all of the trails crisscrossing this huge, open canyonland provide shake-your-head-in-wonder viewpoints. The area is so remote, however, that trailheads require long drives on poor roads. Many of the rugged trails involve wearying elevation gains of up to 6000 feet. And expect that rarely used paths (not described here) will be faint and hard to follow.

Several lookout towers reachable by car provide good starting points. Most popular is Hat Point, the area near the middle of the Oregon rim. Day hikers can savor views of the Seven Devils from wildflower meadows along the start of the trail switchbacking down from Hat Point. Drive Highway 82 to Joseph, then continue 30 miles to pavement's end at Imnaha (general

Hell's Canyon from the trail below Buckhorn Viewpoint

store, no gas). Hat Point is an hour and a half beyond Imnaha on a 24-mile, one-lane gravel road.

Buckhorn Viewpoint, on the northern part of the Oregon rim, overlooks the jumbled canyonlands at the mouths of the Imnaha and Salmon rivers (see the map for area 53, Joseph Canyon). To drive to Buckhorn Point, take Highway 82 south from Enterprise 3 miles, turn left on Crow Creek Road for 6 miles, turn right on Zumwalt Road for 34 miles, and turn right on Road 780 for 1 mile. For the best view, however, drive past the lookout tower a mile or two until Road 780 becomes too rough for cars, then hike out Cemetery Ridge.

The most popular viewpoint on the Idaho side is the Heavens Gate lookout tower, close to the Seven Devils' crags. From Highway 95 at Riggins, Idaho, take gravel Road 517 for 17 miles to the trailheads at Seven Devils Lake and Windy Saddle, then drive north 1.5 miles to the lookout.

Only a few hikes in the area are short enough and level enough to qualify as day trips. Two of the most accessible begin at the south end of the canyon near the Hells Canyon Dam. A 1-mile river trail from the Hells Canyon Creek boat-launch site (just past the dam) reaches Stud Creek before the path is stopped by cliffs. Farther south, a 4.8-mile path follows the Oregon shore of Hells Canyon Reservoir from Copper Creek (not shown on map) to campsites at Leep Creek; north of Leep Creek the shore trail is blocked by a rockslide, but energetic hikers might tackle a 9-mile loop up McGraw Creek to an old cabin instead. To find these trailheads from Baker City, take exit 302 of Interstate 84, and drive 70 miles east on Highway 86 to the bridge at Copperfield. The boat-launch trailhead is 28 paved miles north on the Idaho side of the river, while the Copper Creek trailhead is 9 gravel miles north on the Oregon side.

Another three easy trails are in the north end of Hells Canyon. These begin with a grueling 20-mile drive north of Imnaha on rough gravel Road 4260 (see the map for area 53, Joseph Canyon). There, from the Imnaha Bridge at Cow Creek Ranch, a delightful 4.5-mile trail follows the raging Imnaha River through a cliff-edged defile to the Snake River at Eureka Bar's mile-long gravel beach. Here, prowl the ruins of Eureka's gold mill and watch boats run Eureka Rapids.

The Nee-Me-Poo Trail, tracing Chief Joseph's route, begins 2 miles past the Imnaha Bridge on Road 4260. This 3.7-mile path climbs 900 feet to the excellent view at Lone Pine Saddle before descending to Dug Bar.

Road 4260 ends at Dug Bar, but the last 8 miles of road (past Imnaha Bridge) are too rough for trailers. From Dug Bar a 3-mile portion of Oregon's Snake River Trail leads to Deep Creek's bar, where an old Chinese miners' camp overlooks the Snake River and cliffs. A return loop route climbs 900 feet over bluffs.

Pittsburg Landing, the only road access to the middle of Hells Canyon, is the start of the Idaho shore's popular Snake River Trail. An up-and-back day hike along the trail's first 5 miles penetrates the narrows opposite Oregon's easternmost point and reaches the museum at Kirkwood Ranch. To drive to the trailhead from Highway 95 at White Bird, Idaho, take gravel Road 493 for 16 miles to Upper Pittsburg Landing.

Backpacking or horseback trips are needed to reach most of the trails in this enormous wilderness. Maximum group size is eight people and sixteen head of stock. Keep in mind that open fires are banned within 0.25 mile of the Snake River. Fragile streambank and lakeshore areas see such heavy use that visitors are advised to keep campsites and stock 200 feet away from water.

The commercial jet boats roaring up and down the river detract from the wilderness atmosphere but provide backpackers with an alternative to dusty trailheads. For about $85 per person, any of three jet-boat outfitters will take backpackers from Lewiston to the Idaho shore at Pittsburg Landing or Johnson Bar and back. Prices from Pittsburg Landing to Johnson Bar are about $25. The short run from Hells Canyon Dam to Wild Sheep Rapids (where hikers can join either the Idaho or Oregon Snake River trails) costs about $20. Most outfitters operate only from Memorial Day to September 15 and require reservations. For names and schedules, contact the Clarkston office of the Hells Canyon National Recreation Area, P.O. Box 699, Clarkston, WA 99403; (509) 758-0616.

The Idaho Snake River Trail is not only spectacularly scenic, it's nearly level for 35 miles from its start at Pittsburg Landing to its end at Brush Creek, 3 miles short of the Hells Canyon

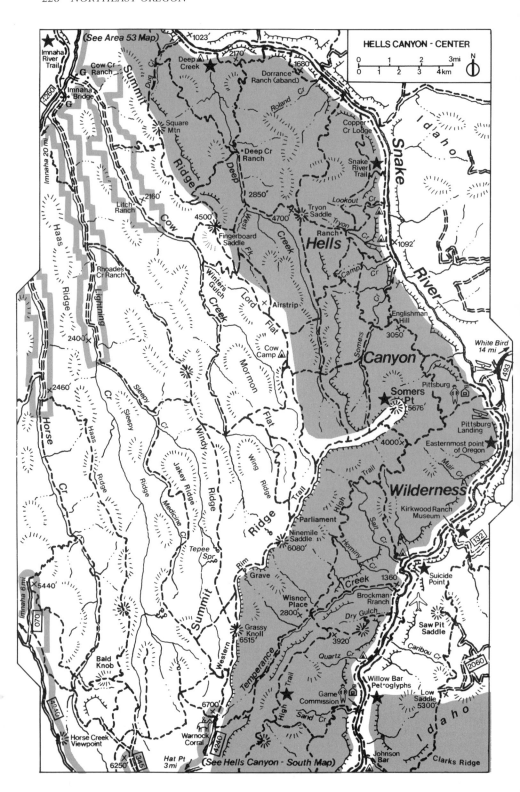

HELLS CANYON - CENTER

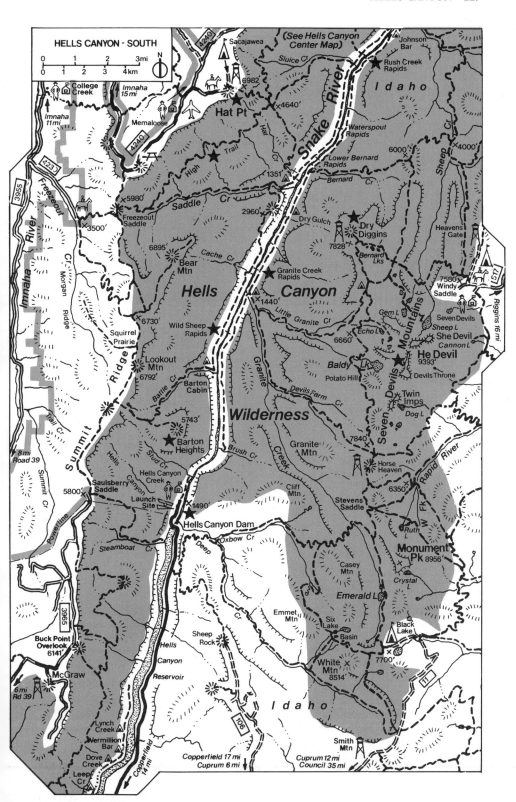

Dam. At Suicide Point, the trail has been blasted from sheer cliffs nearly 500 feet above the river. Four major side trails climb 6000 feet into the Seven Devils Mountains, increasing the options for longer treks.

The Oregon shore's Snake River Trail is equally scenic, but longer (56 miles from Dug Bar to Battle Creek), and climbs sharply away from the river on four occasions. Side trail options abound. Most notable are the route up Dry Gulch to the High Trail, trails from Sluice Creek and Saddle Creek to Hat Point, the Saddle Creek Trail to Freezeout Saddle, and the Battle Creek Trail to Saulsberry Saddle.

The Western Rim Trail hugs the plateau edge. Somers Point's remote view is 14 miles (mostly on an old road) from the Warnock Corral trailhead north of Hat Point. South of Hat Point, the Summit Ridge Trail continues another 13.5 miles from Road 4240 to Saulsberry Saddle. Side trails lead to photogenic Snake River vistas atop Bear Mountain and Barton Heights. To reach the Saulsberry Saddle trailhead from Joseph, drive toward Imnaha 8 miles, turn right onto Road 39 for 31 paved miles, then turn left onto Road 3965 for 16 miles to its end, passing the McGraw lookout tower and several Hells Canyon viewpoints along the way.

The High Trail zigzags through the canyon halfway up, passing grassy slopes, stands of big ponderosa pines, and tumbling creeks. Try a portion of this route for variety on a longer trek, or hike along this rugged bench the length of the canyon: 63 miles from the Freezeout Creek trailhead to Dug Bar, via Freezeout Saddle, Englishman Hill, Tryon Saddle, and Deep Creek.

Private land blocks access to trailheads along Cow Creek and Lightning Creek. For permission to pass the gates here, contact Jack McClaren of the Cow Creek Ranch near Imnaha Bridge.

There are those who swear the best canyon view is at Dry Diggins in Idaho and the most scenic loop hike circles the Seven Devils Mountains. A 25-mile trip combines the two. From Road 517 at Windy Saddle, a 7-mile trail to the lookout tower at Dry Diggins dips 1000 feet crossing Sheep Creek's glacial valley. Continue south to the less spectacular Horse Heaven lookout. Return to Windy Saddle along the range's east face. The trail passes only the Bernard Lakes, but worthwhile side trails climb to Sheep, Echo, Baldy, and Cannon lakes.

Boating

Huge canyon scenery and several huge rapids make the Snake River a popular float trip. Plan on two to eight days from the boat ramp below Hells Canyon Dam, depending on whether the goal is Pittsburg Landing (32 miles), Hellers Bar at the mouth of the Grande Ronde River (79 miles), or Asotin, Washington (104 miles). Be forewarned that all the big whitewater thrills jam into the first 17 miles below the dam. *For this stretch, ranger-issued permits are required from the Friday before Memorial Day through September 15.* Self-issuing permits suffice for the slower water below. For permit reservation information, call (509) 758-1957.

Wild Sheep Rapids, 6 miles below Hells Canyon Dam, can easily flip 18-foot rafts. This class 4 whitewater, the longest on the river, concludes with big diagonal waves that must be run head-on. Two miles beyond lie Granite Creek Rapids, where a large submerged rock in the river's center creates a variety of unpredictable class 4 turbulence, which is class 5 at high flow levels.

Lower Bernard Creek Rapids, at river mile 12 below the dam, is a 6-foot, class 4 drop that washes out in high flows. Beyond it 1.3 miles, Waterspout Rapids develops a class 4 suckhole, especially at low levels; better scout it. The final rapids requiring scouting is Rush Creek, at river mile 16, with a boat-hungry, class 4 hole on the Idaho side.

This is no river for open canoes or rafts under 12 feet, though jet boats and rafts with up to thirty passengers are allowed. The National Recreation Area provides toilets and tables at thirty-nine heavily used river-bench campsites (camping is not allowed at the Hells Canyon Dam). Each year landing beaches grow smaller as upriver dams silt in, blocking the supply of fresh sand. Open campfires are banned within 0.25 mile of the river. Bring camp stoves or use fire pans that contain all fire and ashes. There is no firewood along the river.

The Snake is runnable year round, with 70°F water and low flows in summer, chilly water and some squalls in fall, cold weather in winter, and very challenging high water in spring.

EAGLE CAP

Location: 7 mi S of Enterprise, 21 mi E of La Grande
Size: 715 sq mi
Status: 560 sq mi designated wilderness (1964, 1972, 1984)
Terrain: Snowpeaks, high lakes, alpine meadows, valley forests
Elevation: 2700'–9845'
Management: Wallowa-Whitman NF
Topographic map: Eagle Cap Wilderness (USFS)

This wilderness in the Wallowa Mountains encompasses Oregon's largest single alpine area. Here are wildflower meadows and ice-bound lakes. Of the twenty-nine mountains in Oregon over 9000 feet tall, seventeen are here. Presiding at the hub of eight radiating valleys rises 9595-foot Eagle Cap.

Climate

The wettest area east of the Cascades, the Wallowas collect up to 100 inches of precipitation each year. Heavy winter snows close most trails from about the end of October to the start of July. Snowdrifts cling to high passes into August, but the lower Minam River Trail clears of snow as early as April. High water from snowmelt can make river fords difficult in May and June.

Mosquitoes can be thick in lake basins throughout July, when wildflowers are at their peak. Come prepared for brief afternoon thundershowers in July and August. September often brings clear Indian summer weather with freezing nights.

Ice Lake and, at right, the Matterhorn

Plants and Wildlife

Rocky Mountain bighorn sheep, reintroduced here in 1971 after local extinction, now number about thirty. In winter bring binoculars to spot them on the slopes above the Lostine River near Pole Bridge picnic area. In spring they lamb on high ledges, where the young's only predators are golden eagles. In summer these curly-horned sheep range into the high country, where males butt heads during the November rut. Also watch for the area's twenty spike-horned mountain goats that winter on Sacajawea Peak. Easier to find, however, are mule deer; many winter on the moraines of Wallowa Lake.

The little, round-eared "rock rabbits" whistling warnings to each other from the Wallowas' alpine rockslides are pikas. These cute, industrious animals clip and sun-dry large piles of grass and wildflowers, then store them in tunnels under rockslides, where the pikas winter without hibernating. One of their few predators here is the weasel-like marten, which likewise does not hibernate. The marten may travel 15 miles a night through treetops in pursuit of squirrels.

Chipmunks and cinnamon-colored black bears are numerous enough that food must be hung at night for safe-keeping. Campers also report nighttime visits from porcupines that chew fishing rod handles and sweaty backpack straps for their salt.

Wallowa Lake attracts geese, ducks, and occasional tundra swans in winter. Summer bird watchers can watch for the rare Wallowa gray-crowned rosy finch. Known chiefly from just three locations—Glacier Lake, Petes Point, and a tarn near Tenderfoot Pass—this finch feeds on numbed insects that have fallen onto high snowfields. Its winter home remains a mystery.

July brings an impressive show of wildflowers to the area's many alpine meadows, most notably at the Bonny Lakes south of Aneroid Mountain. Buttercups, yellow monkey flower, and purple elephanthead brighten wet areas, while drier fields host blue lupine, aster, scarlet gilia, bluebells, and heather.

Douglas fir and lodgepole pine dominate the forests. The twisted trees at timberline are whitebark pine and limber pine, both sporting five-needle clusters and limbs so flexible they can literally be tied in knots. Limber pine, identified by its longer cones, grows nowhere else in Oregon but the Wallowas.

Geology

The predominantly granite Wallowas have been called America's Little Switzerland, and in fact resemble the Alps geologically.

Many of the Wallowas' jumbled strata began as sea-floor sediment. Green stones forming the peaks directly south of Wallowa Lake are 250-million-year-old metamorphosed sea-floor basalt. The stunning white marble and contorted limestone of the Matterhorn and Marble Mountain began 200 million years ago as compacted seashells. Dark outcroppings are usually slate and shale: 150-million-year-old sea-floor mud.

All this rock was buckled up from the Pacific by the advancing North American continent and then cooked by magma bubbling up from below 100 million years ago. The magma cooled slowly to form granite. Next, erosion must have nearly leveled the mountain range, for Columbia River basalt flows 15 million years ago successfully blanketed the entire area with lava. Shortly afterward, Great Basin faulting lifted the Wallowas as much as 5000 feet above the surrounding plain, allowing stream erosion and glaciers to strip the basalt from most of the range. Basalt rimrock still tops ridges along the lower Minam River.

Ice Age glaciers ground out U-shaped valleys and basins for the area's fifty-eight named lakes. The last major glacial advance left the smooth moraines that dam Wallowa Lake on three sides. Today eastern Oregon's only glacier, tiny Benson Glacier, survives near Glacier Lake.

History

The Wallowa band of Nez Perce occupied a winter village on the site of the present Wallowa Lake State Park until their flight in 1877 under Chief Joseph. The names of Joseph and his U.S. Army adversary, General Howard, now grace opposing mountains across Wallowa Lake. A lakeside cemetery contains the grave of Joseph's father, the elder Chief Joseph.

The 1885 boomtown of Cornucopia produced $15 million in gold before its mines closed in 1941.

THINGS TO DO

Hiking

Ninety percent of all visits by horseback riders and hikers begin at just three adjacent trailheads: Wallowa Lake State Park, Hurricane Creek Campground, and Two Pan Campground. As a result, trails in this central area are crowded, camping space is tight, and some lakeshores are roped off as restoration sites. For solitude, skip the Lake Basin. The Wallowas have four other lake clusters and 400 miles of quieter trails.

Scenic Wallowa Lake offers only a few paths short enough for day hikers. For an easy panoramic view, ride the gondola to the top of Mount Howard; from there, hike the open ridge (no trail needed) 2.5 miles up to 9447-foot East Peak. To avoid the gondola fare, climb the nearby trail to Chief Joseph Mountain instead. It's 7 miles to the base of the peak's summit cliffs, with vistas of Wallowa Lake all the way. The classic day hike from Wallowa Lake, however, is the dusty, 6-mile climb to the rustic log cabins at beautiful Aneroid Lake.

Chimney Lake is one of several good day-hike goals from dirt Road 8210 south of Lostine. The popular, 4.4-mile route from Lillyville Campground to Chimney Lake climbs 2500 feet; it's worth continuing another mile to Hobo Lake in order to scramble to the view atop 8831-foot Lookout Mountain. Another option is to take a fork of the trail to Chimney Lake and cross a pass to less-visited John Henry Lake in Wilson Basin, 6.5 miles from Road 8210. Nearby, the switchbacking 4-mile trail from Shady Campground up to Maxwell Lake is also quiet. And popular trails from Two Pan Campground, at the end of Road 8210, lead to large Minam Lake in 5.7 miles and to a view of Eagle Cap across the East Lostine River's beautiful meadows in just 2.8 miles.

For a look at the vast canyonlands in the northwest of the wilderness, climb the steep, 2-mile trail from Road 8250 to Huckleberry Mountain's former fire lookout site. Or, farther west, take the much gentler 5-mile trail from Bear Wallow Spring to Standley guard station's 1932 cabin; the best canyon views are a mile beyond, to the south. Drive to Bear Wallow Spring via Road 8270, which leaves Highway 82 a mile east of Minam.

Day hikers can sample the lower Minam River's rugged, V-shaped canyon by hiking down the canyon's side 3.5 miles from Rock Spring on Road 62. A second, once-popular trailhead to the lower Minam River was at Meads Flat. A locked gate now blocks the private road there, but equestrians can still reach the trailhead by riding up the river itself 7 miles from the Highway 82 bridge at Minam.

On the south side of the Wallowas, the Mule Peak lookout offers a view extending to the Blue Mountains. A steep 7.4-mile loop trail from Road 600 includes the 3200-foot climb to the lookout.

The headwaters of Eagle Creek fan out in U-shaped valleys to nearly a dozen lakes in different high mountain bowls. From West Eagle Meadow on Road 77, hike 4.9 miles to Echo Lake. The trail gains 1700 feet elevation (a gentle climb by Wallowa standards); Traverse Lake is 1.6 miles beyond and another 500 feet up.

Eagle Lake, in a spectacular cirque rimmed by 9000-foot peaks, is 6.7 trail miles from Boulder Park on Road 7755, almost too far for a day trip. Closer goals from the same trailhead include Lookingglass Lake (6.2 miles), Bear Lake (5.8 miles), Culver Lake (5.2 miles), and Heart Lake (4.3 miles). Elevation gains to these timberline pools average 2300 feet.

The eastern edge of the Wallowa Mountains is also uncrowded. A nearly level path follows the rushing Imnaha River from Indian Crossing Campground on Road 3960; Imnaha Falls provides an ambitious 6.3-mile destination. To reach the trailhead from Joseph, drive 8 miles toward Imnaha, turn south on Road 39 for 28 miles, then turn right on Road 3960 for 9 miles to its end.

Most hikers headed for the wildflower fields at Bonny Lakes trudge up the long, crowded Aneroid Lake Trail. However, the 4.5-mile trail up Sheep Creek from Road 100 is shorter and only climbs 900 feet on its way to the lakes (Road 100 is too rough for passenger cars). Looking for an even less visited wildflower patch? Try McCully Basin, 5.5 miles up from a spur of Road 3920.

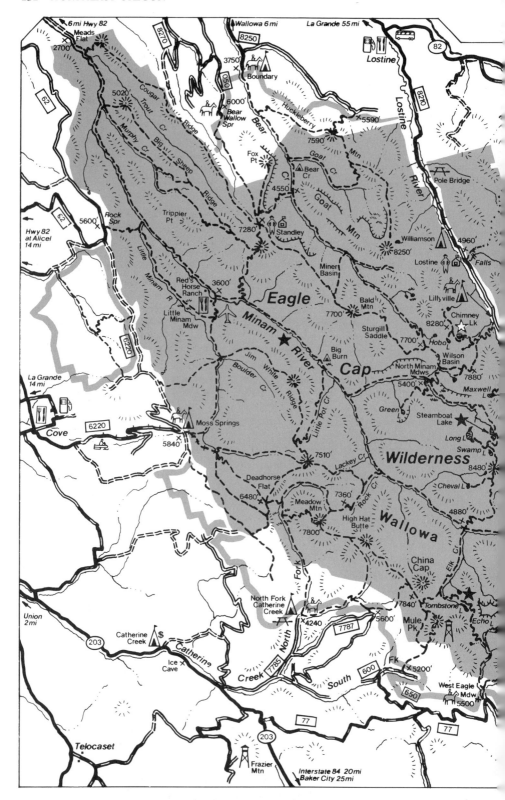

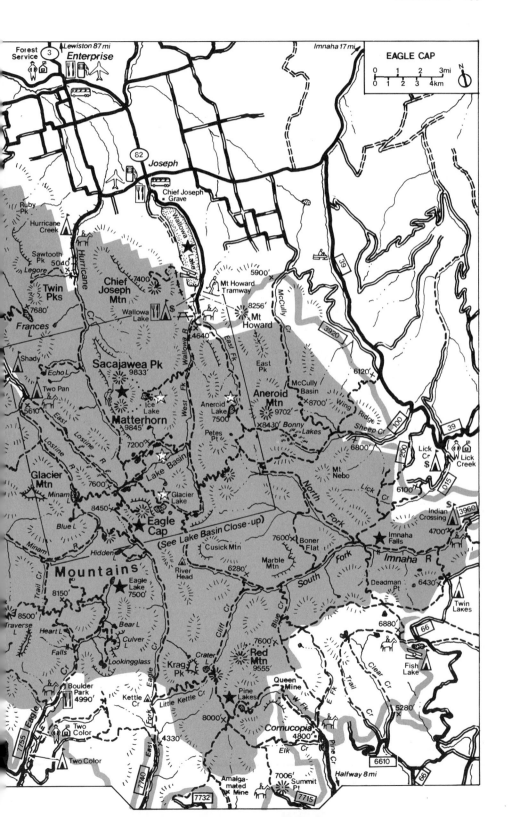

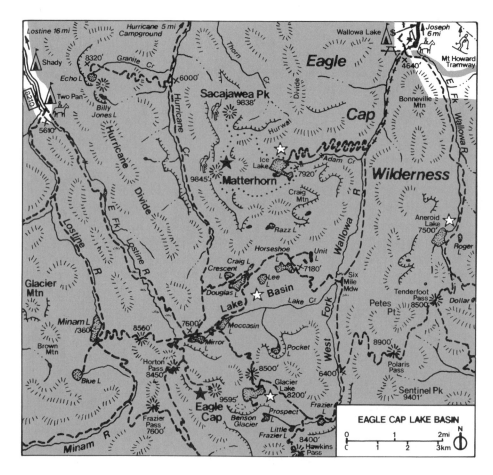

Backpackers and equestrians in the wilderness should note camping is banned within 200 feet of any lake. Stock cannot be grazed or confined within 200 feet of lakes. Group size is limited to six in the Lake Basin and twelve elsewhere in the wilderness. Campers are not allowed to cut firewood from standing trees, alive or dead. Downed firewood is scarce; bring a camp stove.

The most popular goals for overnight trips are the fragile lakes overtowered by the Matterhorn and Eagle Cap. Before taking the trail south from Wallowa Lake to this spectacular high country, however, consider that there are no trailside camping sites for 8 or 9 uphill miles. Camping and stock grazing are banned at Six Mile Meadows on the West Fork Wallowa River. At Ice Lake (7.9 miles) and Horseshoe Lake (9 miles), most level, wooded ground is closed for restoration. Expect to search away from trails or lakes for a low-impact campsite.

Ice Lake is a scenic timberline base for hikers scaling Oregon's sixth and seventh tallest mountains, the Matterhorn and Sacajawea Peak. Though high enough to warrant caution, the route from the lake gains only 1900 feet and requires no special gear or use of hands. A ridge between peaks allows ambitious hikers to reach both summit viewpoints on the same trip.

Stark, island-dotted Glacier Lake climaxes an 11.8-mile trail ascending the West Fork Wallowa River past Six Mile Meadow, through a rocky gorge, and past Frazier Lake. For a scenic 27-mile loop trip, continue north from Glacier Lake across a pass with a sweeping view and return through the Lake Basin.

Eagle Cap is not the area's tallest peak, but its summit view is unsurpassed, and a register box at the top immortalizes those who make the trip. A 2.5-mile trail leads there from Mirror Lake, which in turn is 6.5 miles from the Two Pan Campground trailhead.

Climbers on the Matterhorn in the Eagle Cap Wilderness

To appreciate the enormity of the Matterhorn's 1800-foot, west-facing marble cliff, hike up Hurricane Creek 7.5 miles to the mountain's base, or, better yet, climb to Echo Lake across the valley for a bird's-eye view. The lake is 8.3 miles from the trailhead near Hurricane Campground; the final 3 miles are steep.

Frances Lake fills an alpine valley in the midst of bighorn sheep country, where open slopes tempt hikers to scramble up nearby 9000-foot peaks. The 9.1-mile trail from Road 8210 gains 3200 feet before dropping 800 feet to the lake.

Steamboat Lake and North Minam Meadows highlight an uncrowded region of peaks, lakes, and winding glacial valleys. An 11-mile route from Two Pan Campground climbs 2900 feet, then drops to Steamboat Lake, with its ship-shaped rock formation. North Minam Meadow's mile-long pasture lies 5.5 miles beyond. The quickest route back to civilization from the meadows climbs through Wilson Basin and descends to Lillyville Campground (11.8 miles).

River-sized Bear Creek drains the northwest corner of the wilderness. An 18.5-mile trail loop from Boundary Campground follows the river, ascends Goat Creek, and returns along Huckleberry Mountain's alpine ridgecrest of flowers and views.

Want to track a river to its source? Take the Minam River Trail 46 miles to Blue Lake's alpine cirque. The rugged lower canyon is V-shaped; higher up, the valley is heavily forested and cut to a U shape by vanished glaciers. Privately owned Red's Horse Ranch offers meals, accommodations, and a bridge 9.9 miles into the wilderness from the Rock Spring trailhead on Road 62.

The closest trailhead to Interstate 84, Moss Springs Campground is the starting point for a relatively gentle, 20.4-mile trail loop along the forested Little Minam River valley and alpine Jim White Ridge. Drive to Moss Springs via the town of Cove and Road 6220.

From North Fork Catherine Creek Campground nearby, a more strenuous 18-mile loop heads up the creek past a large, privately owned meadow, climbs to Meadow Mountain's view, then returns via a timberline pass on High Hat Butte's shoulder.

Part of the appeal of scenic Tombstone Lake is the difficulty of getting there. It's roughly 9 miles from any of the three closest trailheads, and all routes cross high passes.

Start at Cornucopia, a rustic, semiabandoned mining boomtown, for the 7.1-mile hike to Pine Lakes. Walk the closed road up the West Fork of Pine Creek to the Queen Mine's ore tramway. A footbridge there leads to the trail proper. Some antique mining machinery remains at the alpine lakes. For a loop trip, continue south around Cornucopia Peak to Elk Creek (16.4 miles in all), or head north past Crater Lake around 9555-foot Red Mountain (26.7 miles). To drive to Cornucopia from Baker City, take Highway 86 east from Interstate 84 to the town of Halfway and follow signs north.

Climbing

Although all peaks have walk-up sides, granite cliffs provide technical challenges in Yosemite-like rock. The Matterhorn's 1800-foot marble west face is the toughest of all. Winter ascents of the Matterhorn and Sacajawea can be undertaken with snowshoes or even skis from Ice Lake.

Winter Sports

A good warm-up jaunt for nordic skiers traverses the snowed-under park and shore of Wallowa Lake at the end of plowed Highway 82. Nearby, the trail up the West Fork Wallowa River is gradual enough for skiers, but the Chief Joseph Mountain Trail has more viewpoints. For the best view of all, ride the Mount Howard gondola to the 8256-foot summit and ski 2.5 miles up to East Peak.

Those hoping to spot mountain goats or bighorn sheep can park at snow level on the roads up Hurricane Creek or the Lostine River and continue on skis. Check with the Forest Service for avalanche danger; Hurricane Creek won its name from the swaths of broken trees left not by windstorms but by snowslides.

A ski trip from the snowmobile loading point on Road 6220 near Cove climbs the road 4 miles to Moss Springs Campground, then continues on trail 2 miles to the Little Minam River. The road portion gains 1600 feet; the trail drops 400.

Opposite: *The Lower Owyhee River at the Hole in the Ground*

SOUTHEAST OREGON

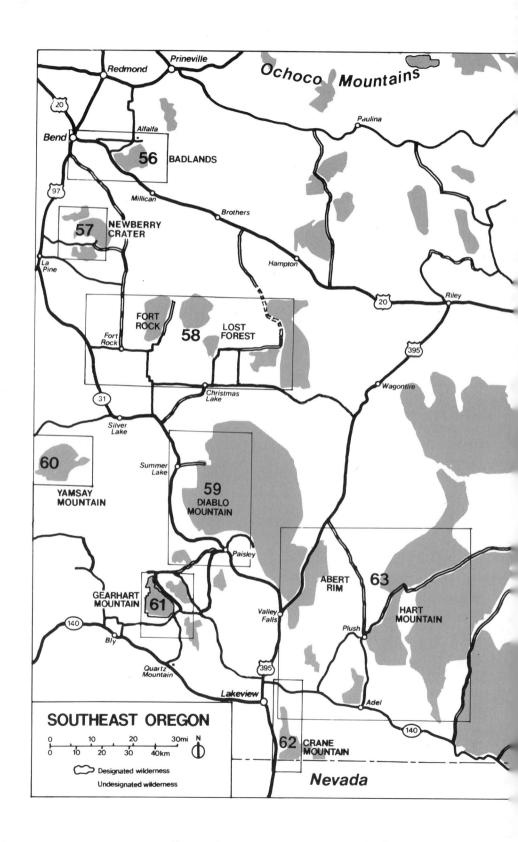

Ochoco Mountains

Prineville

Redmond

Paulina

20

Alfalfa

Bend

56 BADLANDS

97

Millican

Brothers

57 NEWBERRY
CRATER

La
Pine

Hampton

FORT
ROCK

Fort
Rock

58 LOST
FOREST

20

Riley

395

Christmas
Lake

Wagontire

31

Silver
Lake

60

YAMSAY
MOUNTAIN

Summer
Lake

59
DIABLO
MOUNTAIN

Paisley

ABERT
RIM

63

GEARHART
MOUNTAIN

61

Valley
Falls

HART
MOUNTAIN

140

Bly

Plush

Quartz
Mountain

395

Lakeview

Adel

140

SOUTHEAST OREGON

0	10	20	30mi	N
0	10	20	30	40km

⌒ Designated wilderness

Undesignated wilderness

62 CRANE
MOUNTAIN

Nevada

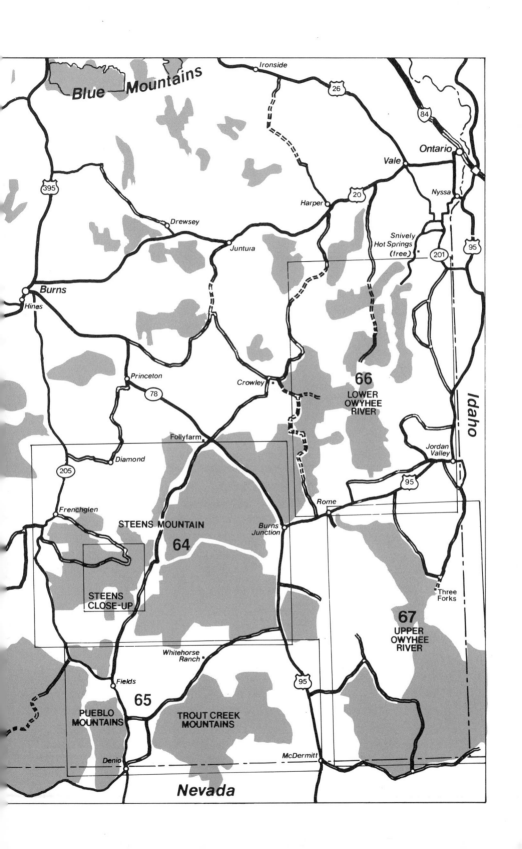

56

BADLANDS

Location: 10 mi E of Bend
Size: 50 sq mi
Status: Undesignated wilderness
Terrain: Juniper-forested lava plain, sandy basins, dry river gorge
Elevation: 3400'–3865'
Management: Prineville District BLM
Topographic maps: Alfalfa, Horse Ridge, Millican, Horse Butte (USGS)

Just 10 miles from sprawling Bend, but a world apart, this maze of lava formations, ancient juniper trees, and hidden sandy basins is a little-known wilderness retreat.

Climate

Cold, windy winters give way to pleasant spring weather as early as March. Summers are hot and dry, but fall arrives cool and clear. Annual precipitation is just 12 inches.

Plants and Wildlife

An old-growth forest of scenic, gnarled juniper dots these rugged lava lands, increasing the feeling of isolation by blocking most long-range views. Sagebrush adds its pungent desert smell. Bright yellow and orange lichens encrust many rocks. Watch for mule deer, lizards, and signs of bobcat. Evening brings bats from lava tube caves.

Geology

This basalt lava flow's rugged ridges and caves formed when molten rock continued to move beneath the flow's hardened crust. During the wetter climate of the Ice Age, a since-vanished lake in the Fort Rock–Lost Forest area spilled north across the lava here to the Crooked River, leaving narrow cuts and smoothed water channels along Dry River's bed. Pumice and ash dusted the lava repeatedly from eruptions at distant Mount Mazama (Crater Lake) and Newberry Crater. This ash, plus windblown sand, created the area's sandy openings.

THINGS TO DO

Hiking

The best cross-country exploration routes begin along Highway 20 or the dirt road on the area's southern edge. It's particularly fun to find and follow the 30-foot-deep chasm of the long-extinct Dry River, where petroglyphs in "riverside" caves remain from wetter ages. Elsewhere,

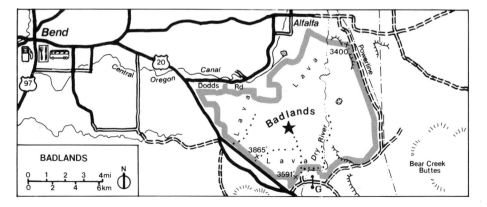

Cave along the Dry River

hikers can climb up craggy basalt ridges for views, photograph 200-year-old junipers, hunt for lava caves, or head for the interior of the area in search of secluded, sandy openings—excellent campsites for high-desert study.

Bring good boots for the rough rock and plenty of water (there is none here at any time of year). Also pack a compass; the lack of landmarks in this level, forested lava land can be disorienting. The occasional, overgrown ruts of old, meandering roads offer little guidance.

57

NEWBERRY CRATER

Location: 23 mi S of Bend
Size: 51 sq mi
Status: National volcanic monument
Terrain: Forested peaks, high lakes, lava flows, cinder cones
Elevation: 4750'–7984'
Management: Newberry National Volcanic Monument
Topographic maps: Paulina Peak, East Lake, Lava Cast Forest, Fuzztail Butte (USGS)

Oregon's newest national monument houses the remnants of an ancient volcano, Mount Newberry, which collapsed in Crater Lake fashion to form Newberry Crater (a 5-mile-wide caldera) and the Paulina Mountains (the caldera's ragged rim). Unlike Crater Lake, however, this caldera features two large lakes, two obsidian flows, eight popular campgrounds, and a trail around the entire, roadless rim.

Climate

Patches of snow remain in the campgrounds and ice still fringes the lakes when crowds arrive for the opening of fishing season here in late May. Snow blocks the higher Rim Trail until July. By August all streams are dry except Paulina Creek. Winter snows, commencing again in November, account for most of the area's 15 to 30 inches of annual precipitation.

Plants and Wildlife

A lodgepole pine forest covers almost the entire area. Big ponderosa pines grow at lower elevations. The woods harbor wildlife typical of both the Cascades and the high desert, though raucous gray jays and inquisitive golden-mantled ground squirrels seem prevalent. The state stocks East Lake and Paulina Lake with 300,000 trout annually.

Geology

This volcanic hot spot marks the western end of the Brothers Fault Zone, a line of recent eruptive centers running from here to Idaho. This major fault, and the jumble of Great Basin

East Lake from the rim at Cinder Hill

faults south of it, resulted from the North American continent's shearing collision with the Pacific sea-floor's plate. Oregon is being stretched diagonally, and lava is leaking through the ensuing cracks.

The remains of the Newberry volcano form one of Oregon's most massive and least noticed mountains. Countless thin basalt lava flows stack here into an enormous shield shape 25 miles in diameter and 4000 feet above the surrounding plain. From the highways at the mountain's perimeter, however, the overall silhouette seems low. The hundred parasitic cinder cones dotting the mountain's flanks look like molehills in a giant's garden.

After the Newberry volcano had been built of basalt, the magma became richer in silica, causing more violent eruptions of pumice. Hollowed by explosions and massive lava outpourings, the volcano collapsed inward. Eruptions continued inside the caldera; two obsidian flows and the 6700-year-old Central Pumice Cone have separated Paulina and East lakes.

At the Lava Cast Forest, a fluid basalt flow surged through a stand of large trees, then ebbed, leaving the trees encased with lava up to the flow's highest level. The trees burned, but their lava shells retain even the checked pattern of the wood.

THINGS TO DO

Hiking

A paved 1-mile interpretive trail loops through the Lava Cast Forest. The road there joins Highway 97 just opposite the turnoff to Sunriver.

Another short nature trail, this one inside the Paulina Mountains' caldera, begins on Road 21 a mile east of Chief Paulina Campground. The paved 0.5-mile path climbs a staircase to the top of a huge, glassy obsidian flow with views across the caldera to the distant Three Sisters. For a better overview of this spectacular flow, drive 0.5 mile farther on Road 21, park on the right, and take a trail that climbs 900 feet in 3.6 miles to a viewpoint atop the caldera rim. From there, the obsidian flow looks like dark chocolate cake dough poured into a gigantic pan.

Don't miss the easy 7.5-mile trail around Paulina Lake. The circuit passes two campgrounds on the north shore accessible only by boat or trail, a beach with underwater warm springs, and an obsidian flow on the northeast shore.

Two fun, short hikes climb to views atop the rims of little cinder cones: a 1.5-mile loop path from Little Crater Campground at Paulina Lake, and a 0.7-mile trail from Road 21 to the horseshoe-shaped rim of The Dome.

A lovely 8.6-mile trail follows Paulina Creek from Paulina Lake's outlet down to the Ogden Group Horse Camp (not shown on map), located on Road 21, 2.8 miles from Highway 97. Either end of this trail makes for an easy day hike: walk the lower 2.8 miles (open year round) up to a 20-foot waterfall at McKay Crossing Campground, or hike the trail's topmost section 0.3 mile down to 100-foot Paulina Creek Falls.

Gravel Road 500 climbs to the area's most popular view and highest point, Paulina Peak. Here the vista extends from the peaks of the Cascades to Fort Rock in the high desert. A dusty 2-mile path from the top drops 1500 feet to another trailhead on Road 500.

The 21-mile Rim Trail passes several other viewpoints—all less crowded than Paulina Peak, and all within range of day hikers. Head north from Paulina Lake Lodge on this trail for tree-framed glimpses of Paulina Lake. At the 4-mile mark, make an easy cross-country side trip to the summit of North Paulina Peak for a view of Bend and possibly even Mount Adams.

Those who prefer to climb less for their views can join the Rim Trail at the 7009-foot-level, where it meets Road 21 above East Lake. From this pass, head north along the broad, nearly level rim top, or cross Road 2127 and hike the narrow, up-and-down rim west toward Paulina Peak, 5.9 miles away.

Hikers here must carry water, and backpackers must plan on dry camps. Cross-country travelers will find solitude and unobstructed hiking outside the caldera area. The most interesting goals on the mountains' flanks are the dozens of small cinder cones, many of which have summit craters.

Winter Sports

Clear weather, dry snow, and plowed access make these mountains attractive to snowshoers and nordic skiers despite the presence of snowmobiles. Two methods work to avoid the noisy snow machines: visit on a weekday, or steer clear of their favored haunts (the snow-covered humps of the Big Obsidian Flow, the road up Paulina Peak, and the lakeshores).

From the uppermost sno-park on Road 21, follow the snowed-under road 2.5 miles to the Paulina Lake Lodge, open year round. Explore the lakeshore or head north up the Rim Trail for viewpoints. Don't miss icy Paulina Creek Falls, 0.5 mile below the lake.

If Road 21 is heavily trafficked, three much quieter, parallel routes also lead to the lake. Just north of Road 21, a snowed-under dirt road follows powerlines to the lodge. Still further north (across Paulina Creek) is the Paulina Creek Trail. And a ski trail just south of Road 21 also climbs to the lake.

Boating

Paulina Lake and East Lake are both large enough for sailing and scenic enough for rowing or canoeing. Sail over the hotsprings near the southeast shore of East Lake. Squalls and choppy water can appear quickly. Motors are allowed with a 10-mile-per-hour limit.

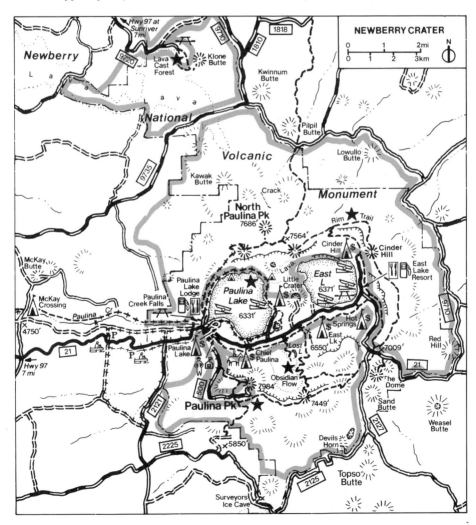

58

FORT ROCK AND LOST FOREST

Location: 64 mi S of Bend
Size: 263 sq mi
Status: Undesignated wilderness
Terrain: High-desert plain, lava beds, sand dunes
Elevation: 4290'–5585'
Management: Lakeview District BLM
Topographic maps: Cougar Mountain, Sixteen Butte, Fox Butte, Hogback Butte, Crack in the Ground, Fossil Lake, Sand Rock, Moonlight Butte, Mean Rock Well (USGS)

The high desert here is full of curiosities: Oregon's largest inland sand dunes, Fort Rock's imposing citadel, Hole in the Ground's enormous crater, Crack in the Ground's fissure, a "lost" forest of ponderosa pine, and three large lava beds.

Climate

Studies of tree rings in the Lost Forest show the current, bleak 9 inches of annual precipitation has been the average here for over 600 years. A foot of snow may fall in the very cold months of December and January. In July and August, afternoon heat can be withering. Clear skies are the rule.

Plants and Wildlife

The Lost Forest's puzzle is how a 5-square-mile stand of ponderosa pine thrives in a sagebrush steppe with barely half the rainfall usually required for such stately trees. There are no other ponderosas for 40 miles. The answer is that during the wetter climate of the Ice Age, pines grew throughout southeast Oregon. This relict grove survives where rainfall collects in windblown sands underlain by the impermeable hardpan of an ancient lake bed. Oregon's largest juniper, with a trunk 18 feet around, is also in the Lost Forest.

More than a century of intense cattle grazing cleared the high-desert savannah of its original grassy cover, allowing sagebrush and juniper to spread. Ungrazed "islands" within lava flows here provide a rare glimpse of ungrazed bluebunch wheatgrass and other hard-pressed native species.

Bald eagles winter here, relying on mule deer that die during harsh weather. Many local and migratory birds gather at Cabin Lake Campground's spring; a public blind there provides first-rate bird-watching. Throughout the area, bobcats and coyotes hunt jackrabbits, cottontails, and kangaroo rats.

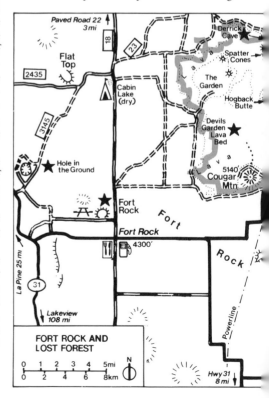

Fort Rock

Geology

The fresh-looking volcanism here is a by-product of an east–west fault zone extending from Newberry Crater to Jordan Craters near Idaho. When the Ice Age brought heavier rains, a 170-foot-deep lake collected in the Fort Rock and Christmas Lake valleys. Eruptions during that time met surface water and exploded in blasts of steam and rock, leaving rimmed craters, or *maars*. Mile-wide Hole in the Ground looks like a meteorite crater, but is actually a maar. Fort Rock, another explosion crater, lay in water deep enough that waves eroded its once-sloping rim to sheer, 320-foot-tall walls. Maars at Flat Top and Table Mountain later filled to the brim with basalt.

Bones preserved at Fossil Lake reveal this enormous Ice Age lake attracted camels, elephants, horses, and a profuse bird population of flamingos, gulls, and cormorants. Winds have collected

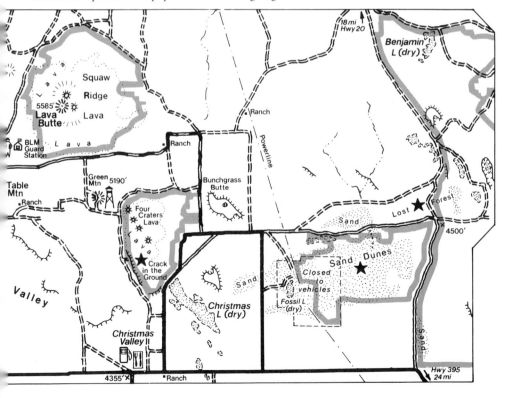

the vanished lake's sands into miles of dunes as tall as 60 feet near Fossil Lake.

Most of the Devils Garden Lava erupted from a low, U-shaped vent in the extreme northeast of the flow. When the basalt's crust hardened, lava flowed on underneath, leaving lava tubes, such as Derrick Cave. South of Derrick Cave, a line of small vents formed many circular spatter cones 5 to 30 feet across and two larger cones, the 400-foot-wide Blowouts. The soupy, pahoehoe lava of this flow left a relatively smooth surface with ropy wrinkles. In the south of the flow, collapsed lava tubes left sinuous depressions and circular dips that filled with pumice from the eruption of Newberry Crater 1900 years ago.

Both the Squaw Ridge Lava Bed and the Four Craters Lava Bed consist of much more rugged, blocky lava. Crack in the Ground, at the edge of the latter flow, is a 2-mile-long tension fissure.

History

Archaeologists here rocked the scientific world in 1938 with the discovery of seventy-five sandals over 9000 years old, pushing back estimates of man's arrival in North America. The sandals, woven from sagebrush bark, were found in Cow Cave, in a bluff just west of Fort Rock. Flourishing wildlife at the area's once-huge Ice Age lake apparently attracted early hunters. Artifacts found in caves on nearby Cougar Mountain date back 11,900 years.

THINGS TO DO

Hiking

From the Fort Rock State Monument picnic area, walk below the rock's imposing outer walls to observe the wave-cut terraces and cliff-swallow nests there, or explore the "fort's" open center for penstemon wildflowers and views across the valley. In the evenings watch for owls leaving perches on the eastern rim.

The Lost Forest and nearby sand dunes offer easy and rewarding cross-country hiking. In the Lost Forest, climb a small basalt outcropping near the forest's center for a look around, hike to the forest's eastern edge to see the sand dunes encroaching there, or photograph artistically gnarled juniper trees. Then trek southwest into the dunes' vast Saharan landscape to let the kids romp in the sand. To reach the area, drive east 8 miles on paved road from Christmas Valley's general store, turn left on a paved road 8 miles to a T intersection, and take a dirt road right another 8 miles. Dune buggies make the eastern dunes hazardous on Memorial Day or Labor Day weekends.

Crack in the Ground is a 2-mile-long basalt slot 10 to 70 feet deep and often so narrow that it is bridged by boulders. Winter ice remains in its depths year round. Drive 8 miles north of Christmas Valley to the crack's northern end, then hike south; the first mile is well traveled. North of the crack, energetic hikers can cross a rugged lava flow to four prominent cinder cones.

The Devils Garden Lava Bed attracts both hikers and volcanologists. From the dirt road at the flow's northeast corner, hike to the flow's main vent, a row of spatter cones, and Derrick Cave. Bring lanterns, warm clothes, and hard hats to explore this lava tube. Above ground again, hike a mile southwest of Derrick Cave over rough lava to reach Little Garden, an old lava dome island in the fresher basalt flow.

To visit an even longer lava tube, drive 6 miles north of Cabin Lake Campground and turn left on Road 22 for 1.2 miles to a sign for 1000-foot South Ice Cave (not shown on map).

For an overview of the smoother, southern part of the Devils Garden flow, make the short climb up Cougar Mountain. Then head north from that summit across the lava to find small sandy openings and desert solitude.

The highest point and best view in the area is atop Lava Butte, 3 miles from a road over the extremely rugged Squaw Ridge Lava.

Hikers should carry plenty of water. Fort Rock and Cabin Lake Campground have the only public sources of drinking water. All lakes and streambeds are dry. Wear sturdy boots when hiking on the area's sharp, rugged lava flows. Expect dirt roads to be badly rutted, slow, and unsigned. Side roads can be confusing, and after a rain, mud can stop even four-wheel-drive vehicles.

59

DIABLO MOUNTAIN

Location: 73 mi S of Bend, 49 mi N of Lakeview
Size: 757 sq mi
Status: Undesignated wilderness
Terrain: High-desert rimrock, brush-covered sand, alkali flats
Elevation: 4130'–6145'
Management: Lakeview District BLM, Oregon Department of Fish and Wildlife
Topographic maps: Diablo Peak, Ana River, South of Ana River, Loco Lake, Sharp Top, Bull Lake, St. Patrick Mountain (USGS)

From this fault-block mountain's 1800-foot eastern cliff, views extend across high-desert hills and salt lake beds to distant Cascade peaks. Birdlife thrives at Summer Lake's refuge.

Climate

July and August afternoons top 100°F. Intensely cold, December and January bring light snows. Spring and fall are pleasant. Annual precipitation is a scant 9 inches.

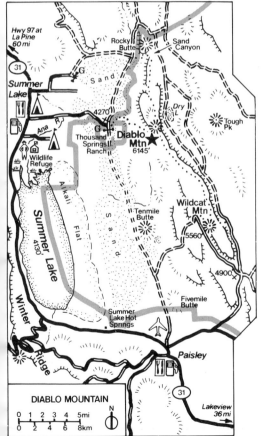

Plants and Wildlife

Marshes north of Summer Lake attract bald eagles and tundra swans in winter, migratory species in spring and fall, and white pelicans, Canada geese, and sandhill cranes in summer. The best bird-watching is in March and April.

Unusually salt-tolerant plants, including three spiny shrubs—greasewood, shad scale, and hopsage (blooms brilliant orange in July)—survive in Summer Lake's vast alkali flats. Sagebrush dominates Diablo Mountain, but May brings wildflower shows of yellow, orange, and red paintbrush.

Bobcats are common in uplands, but they're shy. Bighorn sheep were reintroduced in 1990. Watch for sage grouse and flocks of western bluebirds. Raptors nest in rimrock.

Storm-gnarled juniper tree on Diablo Mountain

Geology

Great Basin faults left the impressive, east-facing scarps of Winter Ridge and Diablo Mountain. Summer Lake, with no outlet, is the salty remnant of a 40-mile-long Ice Age lake.

THINGS TO DO

Hiking

From the Wildlife Refuge Campground on the Ana River, walk Summer Lake's marshland dikes to spot birds and muskrat.

Diablo Mountain's breathtaking, 1800-foot cliff deserves an overnight trip, but a 5.5-mile (one way) day hike also reaches the summit. Drive east from the Summer Lake store 7 miles to a fenceline. Hike east and north around the fenceline to the peak.

Wildcat Mountain is the best viewpoint in the south, a 1-mile cross-country hike from either of two dirt roads. In the north of the area, drive past the area's only brushless dunes to the base of Rocky Butte, then explore cliff-rimmed Sand Canyon.

Western fence lizard

60

YAMSAY MOUNTAIN

Location: 87 mi S of Bend, 75 mi NE of Klamath Falls
Size: 40 sq mi
Status: Undesignated wilderness
Terrain: Forested mountain, canyons, streams
Elevation: 5840'–8196'
Management: Fremont NF, Winema NF
Topographic maps: Yamsay Mountain, Gordon Lake (USGS)

Like a misplaced High Cascades peak, this solitary 8196-foot cone rises from the ponderosa pine forests 40 miles due east of Crater Lake.

Climate

Snow caps Yamsay Mountain from November to May. Summer and fall are pleasant, with the hottest days cooled by afternoon thundershowers. Annual precipitation tops 40 inches.

Plants and Wildlife

Lodgepole pine thickets cloak much of the mountain, with meadows and parklike ponderosa pine groves in creek canyons. Above 7000 feet the forests include mountain hemlock, white fir, and weather-gnarled whitebark pine.

Geology

Like Newberry Crater to the north, Yamsay Mountain is a shield volcano, but its cliff-rimmed crater was formed by ice, not fire. An Ice Age glacier on the shady north face gouged the craterlike cirque and Jackson Creek's canyon.

History

Klamath Indians called this mountain *Yamsi,* the north wind, and believed it the home of *Kmukamtch,* a supreme deity who sometimes took the weasel-like form of Marten.

THINGS TO DO

Hiking

The Fremont Trail climbs 16.3 miles from Silver Creek Marsh Campground to a top-of-the-world view on Yamsay Mountain. The path's lower 4 miles (to Road 3038) make a nice day hike, following a fork of Silver Creek through a canyon full of old-growth ponderosa pine. For a

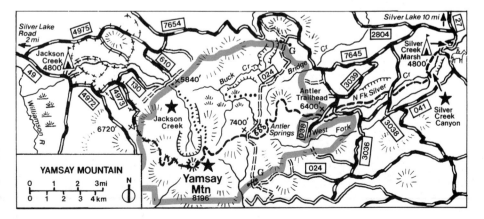

Old-growth ponderosa pines along the Fremont Trail

backpack trip, take the path's upper 9 miles from the Antler trailhead on Road 038 up a broad ridge to the summit. Antler Springs, 0.2 mile off the trail along closed Road 024, offers a logical camp stop. Cross-country explorers can strike off from the springs to find the idyllic meadows in Buck Creek's basin.

For these hikes, drive Highway 31 a mile west of the town of Silver Lake, turn south onto Road 4-11 (which becomes Road 27), and follow signs for Silver Creek Marsh Campground or the Antler trailhead.

On the west side, a road once led to a lookout tower on Yamsay Mountain's summit. With the tower gone, the abandoned road has become an alternate trail to the top, climbing 3.4 miles from the end of Road 4973.

Though trailless, Jackson Creek's open forests and creekside meadows invite bushwhacking—especially along the 4-mile section from Road 130's crossing to the creek's forks in a bowl-shaped cirque below the summit cliffs.

To find westside hiking routes, drive Highway 97 to the Klamath Forest Wildlife Refuge sign near milepost 228, turn east on the Silver Lake Road for 21 paved miles, and turn right on Road 49 for 5 miles to Jackson Creek Campground.

Winter Sports

Jackson Creek Campground, accessed by plowed Road 49, is a winter nordic ski center with 25 miles of marked trails. For starters, ski 1.4 miles up Jackson Creek on a snowed-under road, cross the creek, and climb east 0.8 mile to a viewpoint of Yamsay Mountain. Loop routes return either along the north rim of Jackson Creek's canyon or south through ponderosa pine woods. The area's toughest goal is Yamsay Mountain's summit, 8.7 miles from the Jackson Creek Campground and 3400 feet up.

61

GEARHART MOUNTAIN

Location: 36 mi NW of Lakeview, 66 mi E of Klamath Falls
Size: 72 sq mi
Status: 35 sq mi designated wilderness (1964, 1984)
Terrain: Forested ridges, cliffs, valleys
Elevation: 5700'–8364'
Management: Fremont NF
Topographic maps: Gearhart Mountain Wilderness, Fremont National Forest Visitors Map (USFS); Coleman Point, Coffeepot Creek, Lee Thomas Crossing, Cougar Peak (USGS)

Picturesque cliffs and rock domes top this long, low-profile mountain. Nearby, Dead Horse Rim and Coleman Rim feature cliff-top viewpoints and stately stands of old-growth ponderosa pine. Throughout, lush meadows dot high, once-glaciated valleys.

Climate

Summer days shine clear and seldom hot in this forested upland. Be prepared for possible afternoon thunderstorms and frosty nights. Snow blocks the Gearhart Mountain Trail's crest from November to mid-June. Snow covers Dead Horse Rim, Coleman Rim, and most roads from early December to the end of April. Winters can be extremely cold. Annual precipitation ranges from 35 inches at Gearhart Mountain to 20 inches in the lowlands.

Plants and Wildlife

The rare, parklike stands of ponderosa pine here survive wildfire well. Because old-growth ponderosas lack low branches, fires burn brush and grass without reaching the trees' crowns. Ponderosa bark, which turns orange after a century or more in the sun and develops a pleasant vanilla smell, features a jigsaw-puzzle surface that flakes off during fires to remove heat from the trunk.

The smaller, denser lodgepole pines burn easily in forest fires, but reseed profusely because their cones open after a fire's heat. Many lodgepole pines have been killed by mountain pine beetles, making room for white pine, and at high elevations, supple-limbed whitebark pine. Lodgepoles have two needles to a cluster, while ponderosas have three and other local pines five.

Mammals here include mule deer, black bear, coyotes, and porcupine. Listen for little, round-eared pikas whistling from their rockslide homes.

Geology

Both Gearhart Mountain and Dead Horse Rim began as shield-shaped volcanoes built of many thin basalt layers. The older of the two, Gearhart Mountain may once have stood 10,000 feet high. Erosion uncovered the resistant lava which forms its summit cliffs, The Dome, and Haystack Rock. Ice Age glaciers scooped out the impressive U-shaped valleys of Gearhart Creek, Dairy Creek, and Dead Horse Creek.

Coleman Rim's cliff is the scarp of a fault block, like most cliff-edged mountains in the Great Basin.

THINGS TO DO

Hiking

From the north end of the popular, well-graded Gearhart Mountain Trail, an easy 3-mile hike reaches often-crowded Blue Lake and a view of the long, low mountain 4.4 trail miles beyond. To drive to the trailhead from Paisley (on Highway 31 between Lakeview and Summer Lake), take Mill Street west from town 1 mile, turn right onto gravel Road 3315 for 20.5 miles, turn left on paved Road 28 for 0.5 mile, turn right on gravel Road 3411 for 6 miles, turn left on Road 3372 for 1.5 miles, and turn right on Road 015 to its end.

From the south end of the Gearhart Mountain Trail, day hikers starting at Lookout Rock's tower sometimes stop at The Dome, 3 miles in. However, the cliffs, views, and meadows become increasingly spectacular for the next 2.8 miles, from The Dome to the trail's high point below Gearhart Mountain's summit cliffs. To reach the trailhead from Paisley, drive west of town on Mill Street (which becomes paved Road 33) for 19 miles, turn left on Road 28 for 2 miles, turn right on Road 3428 for 8 miles, switchback to the left on Road 34 for 5 miles, then turn right on Road 012 to its end.

On a clear day, hikers atop Gearhart Mountain's summit can spot Steens Mountain, the Three Sisters, and even Mount Lassen. Take the trail from Lookout Rock 4.8 miles to a pass,

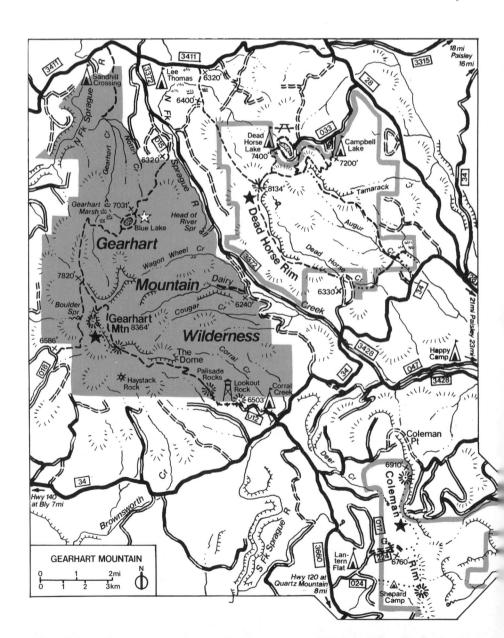

then hike the trailless but easily followed open ridge another mile to the top. No special gear or use of hands is required.

The Boulder Spring Trail offers a quiet shortcut to Gearhart Mountain's high country. This 2.7-mile route climbs from a ponderosa pine forest at Road 018 to a trail junction on the peak's shoulder, passing the meadows at Boulder Spring on the way. To reach the trailhead from Bly (between Klamath Falls and Lakeview), take Highway 140 a mile east of town, turn north for 0.5 mile on a county road, turn right on Road 34 for 4 miles, turn left on Road 335 for 1.5 miles, and turn right on Road 018 for 7 miles.

Dead Horse Rim

Dead Horse Rim, though nearly as tall as Gearhart Mountain, sees much lighter use. For a 1.5-mile warm-up hike here, take the trail between Campbell Lake and Dead Horse Lake campgrounds. Connecting trails switchback up to the rim's 8134-foot summit. The shortest route to the top, however, is the 1.7-mile path beginning at the west end of Dead Horse Lake. After soaking in the view at the rim's high point, hikers can explore trails along the forested ridgecrest 4.3 miles south to a Weyerhaeuser road or 4.5 miles north to Road 3411.

Cross-country hiking is easy in the area's open forests; bring a compass and topographic map. At Gearhart Mountain and Dead Horse Rim, strike off from established trails to follow ridges or find meadows in high creek basins. Old trails at Dairy Creek and to Gearhart Creek from Road 3411 provide good starts. Likewise, cross-country hikes are the way to explore Coleman Rim's interesting ridgecrests, ponderosa pine forests, and meadows. Two routes lead to Coleman Rim from the primitive Lantern Flat campsite on Road 024. Either drive 0.7 mile past Lantern Flat on Road 024 and hike east through aspen-filled meadows (known as Shepard Camp), or drive north from Lantern Flat 0.7 mile on Road 017 and hike abandoned Road 224 east to meadows along the rim.

Backpackers can hike the entire 12.1-mile Gearhart Mountain Trail or simply spend a few days in the high country exploring from a base camp. Firewood is scarce and fire danger often high; bring a camp stove. Saddle stock are only allowed within 200 feet of open water in the designated wilderness for watering, loading, or travel on trails.

Winter Sports

Though none of the roads in the area is plowed in winter, cars can usually drive from Lakeview or Bly to the Corral Creek Campground (elevation 5960 feet) by early April. From there, ski or snowshoe 2 miles up to the Lookout Rock tower and another nearly level mile to Palisade Rocks.

Boating

Small craft do well on 0.5-mile-long Dead Horse Lake and smaller Campbell Lake; no motors allowed.

62

CRANE MOUNTAIN

Location: 5 mi E of Lakeview
Size: 60 sq mi
Status: undesignated wilderness
Terrain: Forested fault-block mountain, high meadows
Elevation: 5200'–8454'
Management: Fremont NF
Topographic maps: Crane Mountain, Crane Creek (USGS)

The highest point in south-central Oregon, Crane Mountain lifts its sudden scarp above the sagebrush flatlands and shore marshes of vast Goose Lake.

Climate

Very cold winters whiten the mountain's crest by late November; the snow lingers to late May. Summer temperatures are pleasantly mild. Despite 40 to 60 inches of average annual precipitation, blue skies predominate.

Plants and Wildlife

May and June bring wildflower displays to the high meadows covering much of this long mountain. Expect Indian paintbrush, aster, balsamroot, clarkia, penstemon, phacelia, yarrow, and spreading phlox. In fall, white-barked quaking aspen brighten the gulches with brilliant orange leaves. Evergreen trees range from spire-shaped subalpine fir at the highest elevations to mountain mahogany on dry slopes and tall ponderosa pine in lower forests.

Hikers may spot mule deer, jackrabbits, porcupines, and coyotes. Goose Lake's tremendously varied bird population, which peaks during spring and fall migrations, includes pelicans, herons, tundra swans, geese, and many ducks. Bald and golden eagles soar above the mountain and lake during winter.

Geology

Great Basin faulting has chopped much of southeast Oregon into broad valleys and blocky mountains. The huge fault scarp forming Crane Mountain's abrupt western cliffs continues north 40 miles to Abert Rim. Once-level basalt layers have been hoisted 3700 feet to the top of Crane Mountain, exposing underlying John Day rhyolite tuff on the mountain's western flank. Rock hounds find agate nodules and thunder eggs in this rhyolite layer east of Highway 395.

Quaking aspen

The optimistically named Highgrade Mining District uncovered small amounts of gold-bearing quartz in the basalt flows capping the southern end of Crane Mountain. The find still puzzles geologists; basalt is usually a hopeless place to look for gold.

Older residents in the area recall when Goose Lake drained via the Pit River to the Sacramento. Irrigation has since lowered the lake, leaving it landlocked and increasingly saline.

THINGS TO DO

Hiking

Start with an overview of the area from a former lookout site on Crane Mountain's crest. Dirt Road 015 leads there but is rough for passenger cars; consider parking at the junction with gravel Road 4011 and walking the final 2.2 miles. Just before Road 015's end, the Crane Mountain Trail branches south. This scenic, 8.7-mile route, with views from Mount Shasta to Steens Mountain, parallels the rim's edge into California. The highest point on Crane Mountain is a mile south along this trail and a short scramble west.

A newer section of the Crane Mountain Trail heads north from Road 015. It begins 0.8 mile below the end of Road 015 and switchbacks down the ridgecrest past Red Peak, meeting dirt roads at the 3-, 6-, and 8-mile marks. Equestrians can follow the signed Crane Mountain Trail farther north, largely along roads, another 20 miles to a trail junction for paths down Crooked Creek and past Twelvemile Peak (see area 63, Abert Rim and Hart Mountain).

The high meadows and open forests lend themselves to cross-country exploration. One rugged route follows a bench on the western face of Crane Mountain from Kelley Creek to Cogswell Creek.

Winter Sports

The Warner Mountain Ski Area operates a T-bar lift and day lodge from mid-December to mid-March, depending on snow conditions. The area serves as a base for cross-country ski trips south on snowed-under roads toward Crane Mountain.

63

ABERT RIM AND HART MOUNTAIN

Location: 25 mi NE of Lakeview, 93 mi SW of Burns
Size: 718 sq mi (including Drake Peak and Fish Creek Rim)
Status: Undesignated wilderness; 430 sq mi national wildlife refuge
Terrain: High-desert block mountains, ephemeral lakes
Elevation: 4237'–8405'
Management: U.S. Fish and Wildlife Service, Lakeview District BLM, Fremont NF
Topographic maps: Lake Abert South, Little Honey Creek, Crook Peak, Drake Peak, Hart
  Lake, Warner Peak, Campbell Lake, Flagstaff Lake, Priday Reservoir, Adel, Guano Lake,
  Alger Lake, and 14 other maps (USGS)

Pronghorn antelope and bighorn sheep here roam the edges of the nation's tallest fault-scarp cliffs. Marshes at the Warner Lakes attract pelicans, cranes, and swans. In the uplands, sagebrush plains stretch to the horizon.

Poker Jim Ridge and the Warner Lakes

Climate

As upland snow melts from March to May, dry lakes fill and mud may close some dirt roads. Wildflowers bloom in May and June. July and August afternoons can top 100°F, though nights are cool. Fall brings mild days and frosty nights. Sub-zero snowstorms close the Plush-Frenchglen road and Highway 140 east of Adel periodically between December and March. Blue sky presides 300 days a year in this region of only 9- to 20-inch annual precipitation.

Plants and Wildlife

Graceful pronghorn antelope browse sagebrush throughout the area. North America's swiftest animals at up to 65 miles per hour, they flash their white rumps and release a musk when alarmed to flight. The Hart Mountain National Antelope Refuge reports an average of about 2000 head; most winter in Nevada.

Overhunting and domestic sheep diseases drove bighorn sheep to extinction in Oregon by 1915. Twenty of the curly-horned sheep reintroduced at Hart Mountain from British Columbia in 1954 multiplied with such success that animals have since been trapped here and released at many southeast Oregon locations. About 450 now live on rimrock ledges from Hart Mountain to Poker Jim Ridge, with smaller herds on the cliffs of Fish Creek Rim and Abert Rim.

Warner Lakes' marshes sustain elegant egrets, awkward white pelicans, eared grebes, ruddy ducks, geese, and many other birds. Visit in March or April for the spectacular spring migrations.

Bald eagles, golden eagles, and prairie falcons nest in rimrock ledges; Fish Creek Rim averages four aeries per mile. Ask refuge employees for the best spots to watch sage grouses perform their peculiar strutting, puffing, gurgling courtship displays at the crack of dawn from mid-March to mid-May.

Twelve species of sagebrush grow here. Silver sage graces alkali playas. In rich soils, big sagebrush reaches 15 feet tall with 8-inch-diameter trunks. Near big sage, expect profuse displays of paintbrush, larkspur, buckwheat, and sage buttercups in spring. The low sagebrush of rocky, high elevations protects different spring flowers: bitterroot, crag aster, and goldenweed. Rarest plants in the area are salty Lake Abert's endangered Columbia watercress, South Abert Rim's delicate blue-leaved penstemon, and Guano Creek's threatened Crosby's buckwheat.

In fall, quaking aspens in rim gulches turn stunning yellow and orange. Small groves of ponderosa pine, remnants of a vast Ice Age forest here, survive near Hart Mountain's Blue Sky campsite and on Abert Rim east of Valley Falls. The snowier Warner Mountains about Drake Peak support fir forests.

Geology

Though history records no major earthquakes here, the rocks do. Very fresh-looking fault scarps at Abert Rim, Poker Jim Ridge, Hart Mountain, and Fish Creek Rim show that blocks of earth have shifted 2400 feet vertically, leaving plateaus and gaping lake valleys. The landscape here must have been mostly flat 10 million years ago, for Steens Mountain basalt flows of that age cover all these disjointed rims. Hot springs and the Crump Geyser suggest ongoing crustal activity.

The Ice Age brought rain instead of ice to this warm region. Lake levels rose about 200 feet, unifying the Warner Lakes and connecting Lake Abert with Summer Lake (see area 59, Diablo Mountain). Beaches of these once-huge lakes remain as gravel terraces on valley edges near Plush and along Poker Jim Ridge. Now even Lake Abert and Hart Lake run dry in lean years.

Jasper, agate, and opal have been found on Hart Mountain's western face. The wildlife refuge allows collection of 7 pounds of rocks per person.

History

Northern Paiute Indians sailed these lakes on rafts of bundled bulrushes to hunt ducks and gather eggs in disposable cattail baskets. Petroglyphs remain at Hart Lake, Colvin Lake and the southern tip of Fish Creek Rim. Caves in the rimrock overlooking Guano Lake may have been occupied in the Ice Age. All artifacts are federally protected.

THINGS TO DO

Hiking

There are few marked trails, but rim edges, creeks, and ridges offer abundant natural pathways in this open landscape.

Drive slowly along the gravel road from Plush toward the Hart Mountain refuge, watching with binoculars for birdlife in the Warner Lakes and for bighorn sheep on the eastern cliffs. An interpretive center is planned for Hart Lake, with a nature trail and wildlife-viewing blind. A short, all-accessible trail to Swamp and Mugwump lakes is also in the works. Where the road crests Poker Jim Ridge, hikers can follow the rim northwest for views across the often dry lakes below. Backpackers can hike the rim 12 miles to Bluejoint Lake.

At the refuge's Hot Springs Campground, relax in the hot springs' 104°F natural pool. Purifiable drinking water is a mile down the road at Valet Spring.

Hiking routes radiate from this campground. Follow Rock Creek 5 miles downstream to the refuge headquarters, passing beaver ponds along the way. Or hike 4 miles northwest onto the plateau at the head of Willow Creek to visit a bighorn sheep corral and get an impressive rim-edge view of Flagstaff Lake.

Warner Peak, the refuge's highest viewpoint, makes a good goal for day hikers (or backpackers headed on to Hart Mountain's plateau). Since the jeep track nearest to Warner Peak's eastern cliffs is impassable to most cars, it's best to start either on the road a mile south of Hot Springs Campground or at the Blue Sky campsite near Guano Creek's scenic ponderosa pine grove. From either point the summit is 4 miles away and 2000 feet up. A third, more challenging route to Warner Peak is to hike up Degarma Creek's scenic canyon from the Warner Lakes' valley floor.

Permits are required to camp anywhere in the refuge except Hot Springs Campground. It's best to obtain these from the Lakeview office (Box 111, Lakeview, OR 97630; 503-947-3315). The headquarters at the refuge is often unstaffed. The refuge also bans off-road vehicle travel, hang gliders, excessive noise, and destruction of live plants; firearms are restricted. Mountain

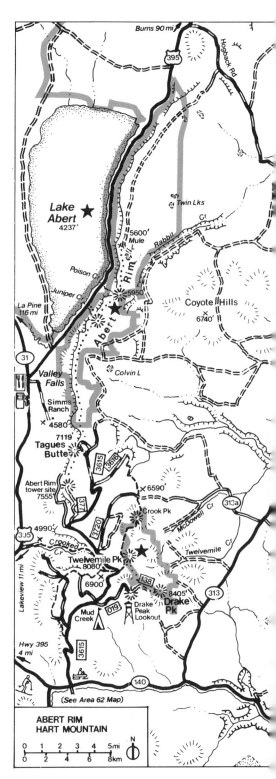

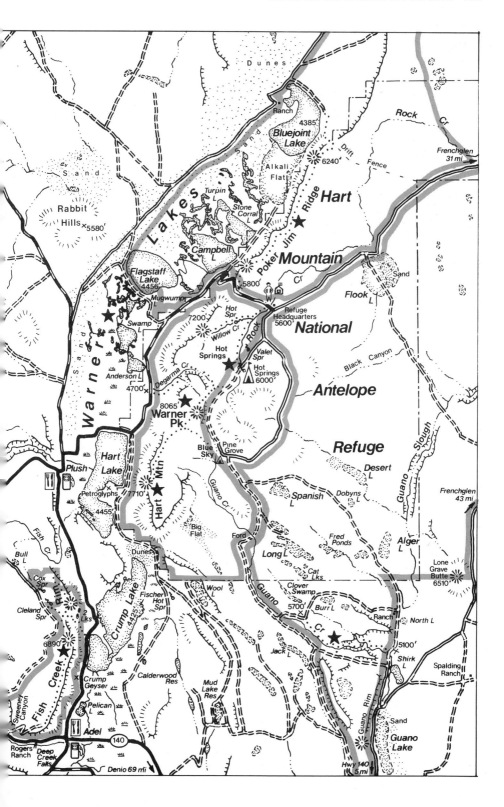

Lake Abert from the rim above Poison Creek

bikes are permitted only on established roads.

Abert Rim's stark face may look unhikable, but a little-known 2-mile scramble route from Highway 395 takes hikers right to the top. Park at the "watchable wildlife" parking area at the southern end of Lake Abert and climb beside Juniper Creek to a breathtaking overlook of alkali-fringed Lake Abert, 1700 feet below. From the top, it's easy to follow the rim 3 miles north to a spring and ancient, rock-walled Paiute hunting blind on the rimrock above Poison Creek. For an 11-mile backpack, trek Abert Rim south from Juniper Creek to the hang gliding launch site atop Tagues Butte, a good place to leave a shuttle car.

For a break from sagebrush bushwhacking, try the newly built trail system through fir forests and quaking aspen groves of the Drake Peak area. Three trail routes converge at the South Fork Crooked Creek trailhead on paved Road 3615. To the north, a delightful trail skirts grassy, rounded Twelvemile Peak and Crook Peak before crossing Road 3720 at the 7.2 mile mark. To the west, a 6-mile trail descends Crooked Creek's canyon, dropping 2000 feet to a spur of Highway 395. To the southwest, a third trail follows a roaded, logged rim toward Crane Mountain (area 62).

For the best overview of the half-dozen peaks surrounding the once-glaciated basins of Twelvemile and McDowell creeks, drive to the Drake Peak lookout (which is not on Drake Peak), take spur Road 138 a mile east, park, and then hike along an open ridge another mile to Drake Peak's real summit.

Little-known Fish Creek Rim raises its cliffs 2400 feet above the Warner Lakes, providing a view across 5 miles of thin air to Hart Mountain. The best routes for cross-country exploration follow the rim's edge or else descend through a break in the rimrock 3.5 miles from Cleland Spring to the Plush-Adel highway at Crump Lake. Drive to the upper rim by taking paved Road 313 north from Highway 140 for 12 miles; turn right on a rough dirt road for 8 miles, then park and hike east.

Guano Creek is a misnamed oasis. Park at the creek crossing north of Shirk Lake and hike up this green-banked stream as it meanders between low rimrock walls. From Adel, drive 21 miles east on Highway 140, and then take a dirt road 13 miles north.

On all hikes, carry plenty of water. After spring all lakes and streams are dry or undrinkable due to salinity or cattle pollution. Also, dirt roads shown as dashed lines on the map may be impassable for passenger cars; inquire locally.

Boating

In wet years, the Warner Lakes feature 300 miles of canoe routes. Of particular interest are the sinuous waterways linking Campbell Lake with a primitive campsite at Turpin Lake, as well as routes linking Mugwump, Swamp, and Anderson lakes.

Hang Gliding

Abert Rim's 2000-foot west scarp faces the west wind, and thermals off Lake Abert make 20-mile flights along the length of the rim possible. To find the launch site at Tagues Butte from Highway 140, drive 21 miles north on Road 3615, turn left at the second entrance to loop Road 032, and after 0.8 mile take a 0.5-mile spur through a gate.

Land on the west side of the road to Simms Ranch, avoiding guarded private land along adjacent Highway 395.

64

STEENS MOUNTAIN

Location: 63 mi S of Burns
Size: 1293 sq mi (including Alvord Desert and Sheepshead Mountains)
Status: Undesignated wilderness
Terrain: Snow-capped fault-block mountain, glaciated canyons, desert playas, sagebrush hills
Elevation: 4025'–9733'
Management: Burns District BLM, Vale District BLM
Topographic maps: Alvord Desert, Steens Mountain to Alvord, Steens Mountain to Page Springs, Page Springs to Diamond (Desert Trail Association); Fish Lake, Wildhorse Lake, Alvord Hot Springs, and 33 other maps (USGS); Steens Mountain (non-topographic, BLM)

Landmark for all of southeast Oregon, 50-mile-long Steens Mountain looms snowy and sudden a vertical mile above the Alvord Desert's stark alkali flats.

Huge U-shaped gorges dissect the western flank of Steens Mountain's 9733-foot-tall plateau. Rushing western streams lead to the Donner und Blitzen River, which winds through a rimrock-lined canyon on its way to the bird-rich marshes of the Malheur National Wildlife Refuge. The vast, treeless Sheepshead Mountains stretch to the northeast, a jumble of sagebrush ridges and dry lake beds.

Cross-country hiking routes and a 77-mile segment of the Desert Trail lead to the popular uplands of Steens Mountain and dozens of lesser-known attractions.

Climate

A sign at the foot of the Steens Mountain Loop Road notes, "Storm area ahead. Weather may change from clear to blizzard in a few minutes. No shelters available." Winter snow and gates block access to the Steens' uplands from about mid-November to the first of July. However, summer on the mountain is generally cool and clear with freezing nights. Prepare for thundershowers and possible July mosquitoes or gnats. Avoid trees and high places during lightning storms. To check Steens' weather conditions before a visit, call the BLM's Burns office at (503) 573-5241.

April, May, and June are pleasant below 6000 feet elevation, with abundant wildflowers and water. In these months, the Alvord Desert and other playas may become lakes. July and August bring blazing heat to lower elevations, with little or no shade. Fall is cool but bone dry; the Sheepshead Mountains and many other areas will have no water. December to February, fiercely cold winds rake the region.

Annual precipitation drops from 40 inches on Steens Mountain to just 7 inches in the Alvord Desert, Oregon's driest spot.

Plants and Wildlife

Five life zones band the mountain. Above 8000 feet, expect bunchgrass, colorful rock-encrusting lichens, and a blaze of August wildflowers. Steens paintbrush, moss gentian, a dwarf blue lupine, and showy Cusick's buckwheat grow atop Steens Mountain and nowhere else in the world. In high cirques, look for bleeding heart, shooting star, bitterroot, buttercup, and wild onion. A herd of over 200 bighorn sheep also likes these cirques; watch for them from the East Rim overlook.

Quaking aspen groves dot the 6500–8000-foot zone, with flashing leaves in summer and orange foliage in fall. Look for (but do not deface) the bawdy graffiti Basque shepherds carved in the aspen's white bark near old camps in Little Blitzen Gorge and Whorehouse Meadows. Beldings ground squirrels and marmots thrive here, as do July flowers: Clarkia, monkey flower, and prairie star.

Juniper and low sagebrush dominate between elevations of 5500 and 6500 feet. Listen at dawn for sage grouse strutting and puffing in courtship displays from March to mid-May. Wild horses and antelope run here, especially on the benchlands west of Blitzen Crossing. Jackrabbits, coyotes, and rattlesnakes are common. May brings blooms of penstemon, buckwheat, and (in the Stonehouse Creek area) rare Biddle's lupine.

Below 5500 feet, tall sagebrush rules. Watch for young burrowing owls standing about their ground holes in June. At small, multientranced burrows, listen for the thumping of long-tailed kangaroo rats scolding within. The kit fox, once thought extinct in Oregon, still hunts the southern Sheepshead Mountains by night. Lizards abound.

Alkaline playas such as the Alvord Desert are virtually devoid of life, but salt-tolerant species cling to their sandy fringes: bright green greasewood bushes, leafless orange iodine bush, salt grass, and spiny shad scale. Silver sage covers other dry lake beds, such as Follyfarm Flat. Spadefoot toads emerge en masse from the ground after rains. Antelope ground squirrels scamper even in summer heat, shaded by their curled white tails.

Huge flocks of migrating birds—snow geese, lesser sandhill cranes, tundra swans, and pintails—begin arriving at the Malheur National Wildlife Refuge in late February. The spectacle peaks from mid-March to mid-April. Greater sandhill cranes nest in April, when migrant curlews, avocets, and stilts arrive. Songbirds pass through in April and May. By June grass is so tall at the refuge that birds are more often heard than seen. Watch for muskrats in the refuge's canals, and porcupines and great horned owls in streamside willow thickets.

Since creeks here have had no outlet to the sea for millennia, unusual fish species have evolved, including redband trout and the Catlow tui chub. Wildhorse Lake, Mann Lake, and Juniper Lake have been stocked with rare Lahontan trout.

Geology

All rocks here are volcanic; there are layers of dark basalt lava and light rhyolite ash. When this rock erupted about 15 to 20 million years ago, it covered most of southeast Oregon 4000 feet deep, leveling the landscape. Nonetheless, the eruptions here were smaller than the massive Columbia River basalt floods in northeast Oregon. And the Steens basalt is different, in that it is often full of big feldspar crystals.

Then North America's shearing collision with the Pacific crustal plate stretched Oregon diagonally, shattering southeast Oregon into north–south-aligned basins and ranges. Steens Mountain rose entirely in the past 5 to 7 million years, while the Catlow Valley and Alvord Desert fell. The Sheepshead Mountains consist of smaller rims and basins. Hot springs indicate continuing fault movement.

The Ice Age brought increased rain as well as snow. A lake filled the Alvord Basin 200 feet deep all the way to Coyote Lake, but found no outlet. Glaciers formed on Steens Mountain, gouging five U-shaped canyons 2000 feet deep. The canyons only left fingers of the original Steens plateau intact, and at Rooster Comb and Kiger Notch the glaciers breached even these rims.

When the Ice Age was drawing to a close about 10,000 years ago, eruptions along the Brothers Fault Zone produced rugged, fresh-looking basalt flows at Diamond Craters (north of Diamond) and the Saddle Butte Lava Field.

Today, look for smooth bedrock polished by glaciers at the head of Big Indian Gorge. Along Pike Creek and Little Alvord Creek, exposed ash formations contain thunder eggs, agates, and petrified wood. And in desert basins, note where wind has stripped the ground to "desert pavement," fields of pebbles stained brown by "desert varnish," a crust of oxides.

History

Seminomadic Northern Paiute Indians lived in brush lean-tos and caves in this area, relying chiefly on jackrabbits for meat and fur. Peter Skene Ogden led beaver trappers to the area's creeks in 1825–29. Army Major Enoch Steen, who named the mountain in the late 1860s, battled the Paiutes, exiling Indians to reservations at Yakima and later Burns.

Pete French built a cattle empire here during 1872–97; his P Ranch near Frenchglen is now owned and maintained by the Malheur Wildlife Refuge. By 1901, Basque and Irish shepherds

The east face of Steens Mountain

were grazing over 140,000 head of sheep on Steens Mountain, obliterating once-lush grass-lands. Domestic sheep were banned from public land on the mountain in 1972, but cattle still range all public lands—even the delicate wildlife refuge.

THINGS TO DO

Hiking

The area's most spectacular views are just a short walk from the Steens Mountain Loop Road. Drive this rugged route up from Frenchglen 23 miles and hike a 0.5-mile spur road to an overlook of colossal Kiger Gorge and Kiger Notch. Walk another 0.5 mile north along the rim; at that point, a very steep scramble trail descends 1400 feet to the valley floor.

Next, drive 3 miles farther along the Loop Road and walk a spur road 0.4 miles to the East Rim's breathtaking vista of the Alvord Desert. Then, from the same parking spot on the Loop Road, hike south on a gated road 2.5 miles to the Steens' highest point, with Wildhorse Lake in a gaping canyon below. A very rough trail drops 1300 feet down to the lake.

The Desert Trail traversing Steens Mountain is not a specific footpath but rather a general corridor marked by cairns. Hikers must pick their own route through the open, generally tree-less terrain. A topographic map and compass are essential. To see the most, plan to backpack. Since dead sagebrush is the only firewood, bring a camp stove.

In the Steens uplands, follow the Desert Trail and its alternate routes through any of four

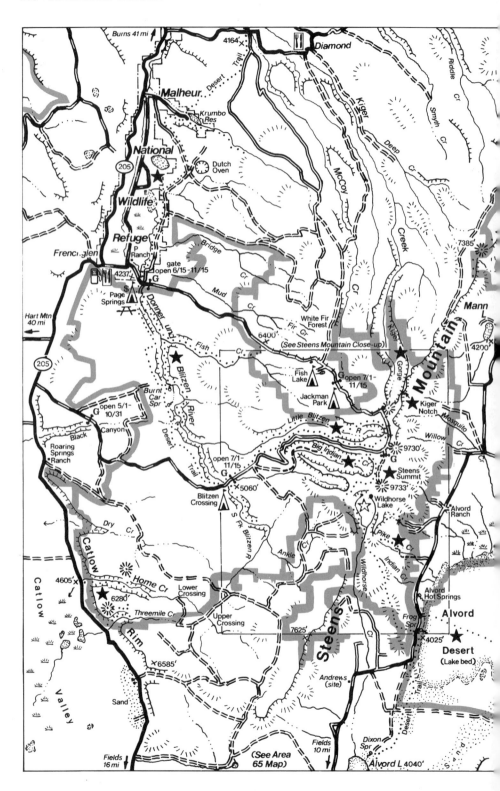

Burns 41 mi
4164' ⛏ Diamond
Malheur.
Krumbo Res
National
Dutch Oven
205
Wildlife
Refuge
French glen
P Ranch
Bridge
gate open 6/15-11/15
4237'
G
Page Springs
Cr
Mud
Cr
White Fir Forest
Fir Cr
6400'
(See Steens Mountain Close-up)
Hart Mtn 40 mi
205
Fish Cr
Fish Lake
open 7/1-11/15
Jackman Park
Blitzen River
Burnt Car Spr
open 5/1-10/31
G
Black
Canyon
Roaring Springs Ranch
Donner und
Desert
Trail
open 7/1-11/15
G
Little Blitzen
R
Big Indian
Cr
9730'
G
Steens Summit
9733'
Wildhorse Lake
Kiger
Gorge
7385'
Mann L
4200'
Mountain
Kiger Notch
Mosquito
Willow
Cr
Cr
Alvord Ranch
Blitzen Crossing
× 5060'
S Fk Blitzen R
Dry
Cr
Ankle
Cr
Pike
Cr
Indian Cr
Alvord Hot Springs
4605' ×
Catlow
Home Cr
Lower Crossing
6280'
Threemile Cr
Upper Crossing
7625'
Steens
Wildhorse
Cr
Frog Spr
Alvord
× 4025'
Desert
(Lake bed)
Catlow
Rim
× 6585'
Sand
Valley
Andrews (site)
Fields 16 mi
Fields 10 mi
(See Area 65 Map)
Dixon Spr
Alvord L 4040'
Desert
Kiger
Deep
Cr
McCoy
Creek
Cr
Riddle Cr
Smyth Cr
Desert Trail

Follyfarm (site)

Burns 66 mi

4100'

STEENS MOUNTAIN

0 1 2 3 4 5mi N
0   2   4   6   8km

Burnt Flat

Oriana Flat

5200'

6330' X

Tencent

Renwick Canyon

Lava

Squaw Cr

Fifteen Cent

4600' Small Butte

Ryegrass Cr

Saddle

Butte

78

L a v a

Squaw L

Heath Lake (dry)

6289'

Lake Ridge Res

L a v a

Juniper

South

Johnny Cr

Heath C

Stonehouse Peak

Palomino Cr

Palomino

Stonehouse Cr

Sheepshead Mountains

Palomino Hills

X 5225'

5005'

Sulfur Spr X

Coffin Butte

Table Mtn 6060'

Bone Spr

Jordan Valley 46 mi

Burns Junction

West Pk 6068'

Mickey Basin

Wildcat Cr

4300'

Bone C

Flat Top Mtn 4575'

Mickey Butte

6294'

Creek

4100'

Mickey Hot Springs

S a n d

Cr

95

5384'

Crooked

S a n d

Coyote Lake (dry) 4040'

X 4555'

4800'

Big Sand Gap

Whitehorse Ranch 6 mi

(See Area 65 Map)

Whitehorse Ranch 8 mi

Winnemucca 101 mi

colossal gorges. Expect wildflowers, plenty of springs, scenic quaking aspen, and waterfalls. Start the 9-mile route along the Little Blitzen River either at the steep trail down from Wet Blanket Springs, or at the canyon mouth (park on the Steens Loop Road at a curve 3.5 miles from Blitzen Crossing and traverse a slope north). Brush slows hikers in the canyon's lower mile.

Begin hikes up Big and Little Indian canyons from the Steens Loop Road, too. Drive 2 miles east of Blitzen Crossing and turn right on Big Indian Canyon Road; it's 2.2 miles to the gated trailhead, but the road is so rough that visitors with passenger cars should park and walk. From the gate, it's 10 miles via either canyon to the Steens Loop Road near East Rim Viewpoint, but only confident hikers should attempt to scramble up the rugged headwalls of these canyons.

A 15-mile section of the Desert Trail traverses impressive Wildhorse Canyon on the way from the Steens Loop Road to Frog Spring, on the Fields-Follyfarm road. Side trips explore the alpine basins of Wildhorse and Little Wildhorse lakes.

The Donner und Blitzen River cuts a 400-foot-deep, rimrock-lined canyon through the sagebrush tablelands south of Page Springs Campground. The Desert Trail route parallels this canyon across the tableland. It's rougher but more interesting to hike up the brushy canyon bottom from Page Springs. Expect to wade occasionally. Fish Creek's brushy side canyon is also worth exploring.

North of Page Springs, the Desert Trail follows Malheur Wildlife Refuge backroads. Camping is banned on refuge lands, as are horses, open fires, swimming, and rock collecting.

The east side of Steens Mountain also offers interesting day hikes and overnight trips. Check the gas gauge before driving the Fields-Follyfarm road to the Alvord Desert. If the desert lake bed is dry, hike out onto the cracked, alkali surface a few miles to experience this remarkably empty playa and to admire the view of snowy Steens Mountain. Better yet, camp in the desert, continue to the greasewood-covered sand hummocks of the far shore (7 miles distant), prowl Big Sand Gap's canyon, and climb to the rimrock viewpoints nearby.

For this and other desert hikes, do not travel in midsummer heat, carry a gallon of water for each day, and bring a hat or cloth for shade. Expect roads shown by dashed lines to be passable only by four-wheel-drive vehicles.

Conclude a visit to the Alvord Desert with a relaxing soak in Alvord Hot Springs, at an easily visible shack 100 yards from the Fields-Follyfarm road. The Alvord Ranch owns the springs but allows the public to use the site. Reward this courtesy by keeping the area free of litter.

Driving north from the Alvord Desert, choose one of Steens Mountains' steep eastern canyons to explore on a day hike. Pike Creek and Little Alvord Creek are favorites, with waterfalls, rugged rock narrows, wildflowers, and views of the desert playa below. Start hiking at the end of the dirt roads leading up these creeks. Rocks and streamside brush make these cross-country hikes rough. Expect to detour uphill to the right several times to circumvent creekside cliffs.

Mickey Hot Springs features shifting steam vents, mud pots, and turquoise "glory pools" as hot as 210°F. Walk about this harsh area and nearby playa, or climb treeless Mickey Butte for a bird's-eye view of Steens Mountain.

The Sheepshead Mountains are the most barren and forbidding-looking hills in Oregon. And therein lies their secret charm. For even when spring fills the creeks and fires the sagebrush slopes with wildflowers, there are no crowds in this huge world of hidden canyons, cliffs, and valleys. To sample this range, hike 2 miles east from Fifteen Cent Lake (on the Fields-Follyfarm road) through a canyon to hidden Heath Lake's playa, and scale an unnamed rim nearby for a view. To see more, backpack south from Follyfarm Flat at Highway 78, hike up Renwick Canyon, follow the high rim of the Sheepshead scarp, descend North Heath Creek's canyon, and return to Follyfarm—23 miles in all.

Try these other utterly uncrowded scenic areas for hiking:

The far northern end of Steens Mountain. Hike north from Stonehouse Peak's castle-shaped rock along a 7000-foot rim or explore the lakes and aspen groves near perennial Squaw Creek.

Catlow Rim. Walk up the canyons of Threemile Creek or Home Creek between sheer, 1300-foot walls and hike to a rim-edge overlook of Catlow Valley and distant Hart Mountain.

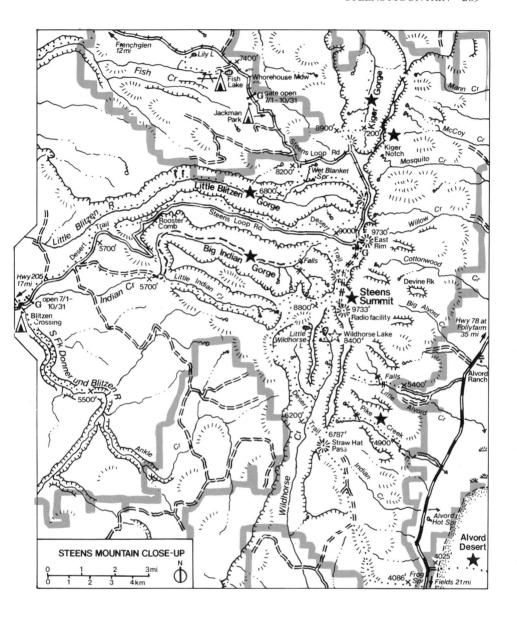

STEENS MOUNTAIN CLOSE-UP

0   1   2   3mi

0   1   2   3   4km

N

Coyote Lake. Devotees of pure desert delight that this desolate playa is even more remote than its Alvord Desert twin.

Runners compete each August on Oregon's highest 10-kilometer course, the Steens Rim Run from Fish Lake to the 9730-foot East Rim. Record time is 47 minutes.

Winter Sports

Powder snow and far-ranging winter vistas are plentiful on Steens Mountain's crest, but difficult access and treacherous weather stop all but the most accomplished snow campers from skiing or snowshoeing there. Sudden whiteouts and freezing winds can occur in any month. Arrange with the Burns District BLM office (503-573-5241) to pick up a snow-gate key. In April, expect snow to block the road at least 3 miles before Fish Lake.

65

PUEBLO MOUNTAINS AND TROUT CREEK MOUNTAINS

Location: 105 mi S of Burns, 100 mi N of Winnemucca
Size: 641 sq mi
Status: Undesignated wilderness
Terrain: Fault-block mountains, creek canyons, desert flats
Elevation: 4040'–8634'
Management: Burns District BLM, Vale District BLM
Topographic maps: Pueblo Mountains, Alvord Desert (Desert Trail Association); Chicken Spring, Little Whitehorse Creek, Doolittle Creek, Oregon Canyon Ranch, Van Horn Basin, Ladycomb Peak, and 16 other maps (USGS)

South of the desolate Alvord Desert, the Pueblo Mountains surprise hikers with high-meadow basins nestling against snowy crags. In the Trout Creek Mountains, a dozen creeks have cut scenic, rimrock-lined canyons into a high tableland.

Climate

In the Pueblos, snow blocks the Desert Trail from November to late May. Wildflowers peak in June. July and August are only hot in the lowlands. Sudden storms bring lightning and occasionally even snow in summer.

In the Trout Creek Mountains, the snowpack melts in early May and wildflowers appear in May and June. Cattle grazing July 1 to September 15 diminishes mid-summer appeal. Fall is cool and dry.

Annual precipitation, just 7 inches in the lowlands, creeps to 25 inches in the Trout Creek Mountains and 15 in the Pueblos.

"Glory pools" at Borax Hot Springs, with Pueblo Mountain on the horizon

Plants and Wildlife

Unusual fish have evolved here, cut off from the sea for millennia. The 90°F alkaline hot springs at Borax Lake support their own species: the 2-inch-long Borax chub. Trout Creek is named for its redband trout, while Willow and Whitehorse creeks contain Lahontan cutthroat trout, a federally listed threatened species. Many of the streams are closed to fishing; obey signs.

Sagebrush and bunchgrass dominate, but willow and quaking aspen turn streams into linear oases. On open slopes, mountain mahogany develop elongated tree crowns, a result of browsing below and shearing winds above.

Wildflowers in meadows include blue lupine, sunflowerlike balsamroot, phlox, and the showy Bruneau mariposa lily. In dry areas, look for delicate penstemon and pink bitterroot. Along creeks expect tall larkspur, mint, and 3-foot-tall bluebells.

In the Trout Creeks, Oregon Canyon is a veritable museum of rare and endangered wildflowers: red buttercup, Lemmon's onion, two-stemmed onion, and bristle-flowered collomia. The Pueblos' Cottonwood Creek harbors one of the northernmost populations of Mormon tea, a green, leafless bush used to brew a mild stimulant. Oregon's only long-flowered snowberry bushes grow along Fifteenmile Creek.

Beavers work virtually every stream in the Trout Creek Mountains. Bighorn sheep live in the Pueblos, but mule deer are more often sighted. Partridgelike chukars by the hundreds cluck in lower canyons of the Pueblos. Listen for the California quails' three-syllable call, the western meadowlarks' territorial songs, and the omnipresent Brewers sparrows. Watch for sage grouse and prairie falcons.

Geology

Steens basalt lava and ash buried all of southeast Oregon 15 to 20 million years ago. Great Basin faulting then hacked the flattened landscape into block-shaped, tilted plateaus such as these two ranges. Fault scarps here have exposed the older rock beneath the basalt. Granite, greenstone, and schists along the eastern base of the Pueblos and in canyons of the western Trout Creek Mountains contain gold, copper, and mercury.

Two enormous, violent volcanoes on faults in the Trout Creek Mountains collapsed about 14 million years ago, leaving 15-mile-wide, Crater Lake–style calderas. The lakes filled with sediment and breached their rims. Willow Creek and McDermitt Creek now drain the two basins. A long arc of cliffs between Disaster Peak and the head of Oregon Canyon marks the McDermitt Caldera rim.

History

The 1860s Pueblo Mining District gave the range its name. Look for stone-cabin ruins in Denio Canyon and along the Pueblos' Willow Creek. Mining continues in Denio Basin.

The Rose Valley Borax Company once shipped 400 tons of borax a year from Borax Lake to Winnemucca via sixteen-mule-team wagons. The Nature Conservancy now leases the lake to protect its ecosystem.

Whitehorse Ranch, headquarters for John Devine's cattle empire during 1869–89, remains a showplace of the old West.

THINGS TO DO

Hiking

The popular Desert Trail route parallels the Pueblo Mountains' crest for 22 miles from Denio to Fields. Day hikers can sample the route at Denio Canyon and from the Domingo Pass Road near Roux Ranch. Backpackers can take side trips to the 8634-foot summit of Pueblo Mountain (southeast Oregon's second-highest point) or along the cliff-edged ridge to the west. Other side routes ascend Cottonwood Creek, Colony Creek's canyon meadows, and Van Horn Creek's narrow, rugged gorge.

In the Pueblos, forty-eight cairns mark the cross-country route of the Desert Trail. Although each rock pile is within sight of the last, it's still easy to miss the cairns; topographic map and compass are essential. All other hiking routes are unmarked, but the open terrain invites cross-country travel, and cattle trails simplify most canyon routes. Water sources can be found only in the high Pueblos and along major streams in the Trout Creek Mountains; always carry a gallon per day. Sagebrush is the only firewood.

Borax Lake makes a fascinating day-hike goal. Park at Soap Lake amid brush-covered sand dunes and fields of Apache teardrops (wind-polished obsidian). Hike a mile to Borax Lake, passing a sod house and rusting borax vat, and then continue 2 miles north along a string of algae-colored hot springs, turquoise "glory pools," and steam vents, to alkaline Alvord Lake's sandy shore.

For a desert challenge, hike the Desert Trail 25 miles across sagebrush flats from Fields to the Alvord Desert (see the map for area 64, Steens Mountain). The Steens, Pueblos, and Trout Creek mountains look deceptively near all the way. Avoid midsummer's blazing heat. The only water source is Dixon Spring, 14 miles from Fields.

In the Trout Creek Mountains, hikers often begin excursions from base camps at Mud Spring or Chicken Spring. From Mud Spring, hike east 2 miles to an overlook of 1600-foot-deep Oregon Canyon. Many possible routes lead to the bottom. Backpackers can prowl Oregon

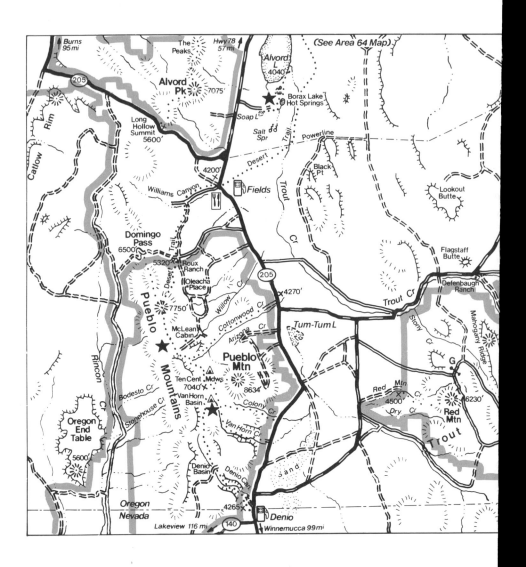

Canyon Creek's forks and botanize. Less difficult access to this canyon requires permission to cross the Echave Ranch downstream.

Whitehorse Creek's many-branched canyon lies 1 mile west of Mud Spring. Pick one of many routes down through breaks in the rimrock and explore side canyons for beaver dams, waterfalls, and colonnades of spire-shaped rock formations.

From Chicken Spring, drive south 5 miles to McDermitt Creek and hike up the North or South Fork to high meadows amid extensive stands of quaking aspen. From there, backpackers can continue 15 miles down Little Whitehorse Creek's winding, rimrock-lined canyon.

Orevada View, this range's highest area, is an 8506-foot plateau overlooking cone-shaped Disaster Peak and four states. The 4-mile cross-country route across the plateau skirts private land at Sherman Field.

Winter Sports

Fierce winter weather limits skiing or snowshoeing in the Pueblo Mountains to experts. By late March, snow level is typically at 5600 feet, but winds have sorted things into icy slopes and awkward drifts.

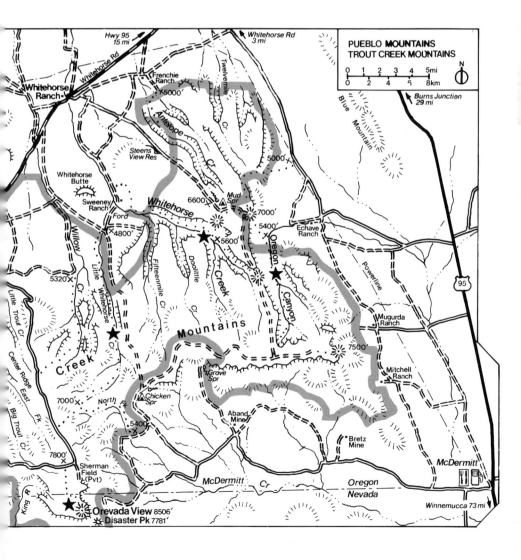

LOWER OWYHEE RIVER

Location: 40 mi S of Ontario, 104 mi E of Burns
Size: 606 sq mi (including Jordan Craters)
Status: Federal wild and scenic river, undesignated wilderness
Terrain: Cliff-lined desert river, colored rock formations, lava
Elevation: 2670'–6000'
Management: Vale District BLM
Topographic maps: Pelican Point, Rooster Comb, Diamond Butte, Jordan Craters N and S, The Hole in the Ground, Rinehart Canyon, Lambert Rocks, Owyhee Butte, and 25 other maps (USGS)

Whitewater boaters on this desert river drift into a remote world of towering stone canyons, wild rapids, cliffside caves, and rock pinnacles. Hikers can follow the canyon too, or investigate the colored crags of The Honeycombs. Nearby, Jordan Craters Lava Bed features spatter cones and Coffeepot Crater.

Climate

Blue sky and frosty nights predominate from April to June, but even in this popular season the desert climate can bring surprise snow flurries or 100°F heat. July and August are too hot for travel, but autumn's coolness again allows hiking. The very cold winter brings only light snows to this region of just 11 inches annual precipitation.

Plants and Wildlife

One hundred fifty wild horses and 200 bighorn sheep roam the rock gulches east of Owyhee Reservoir; in the winter they're joined by an average of 850 mule deer. Commonly sighted smaller wildlife include lizards, rattlesnakes, and white-tailed antelope ground squirrels.

The river and reservoir attract 150 species of songbirds and numerous waterfowl. Bald eagles come to hunt these birds and usually stay until the reservoir is drained for winter. Another good birding spot is Batch Lake, a cluster of marshy potholes amid the Jordan Craters lava. Look for white pelicans, sandhill cranes, and egrets.

Sagebrush dominates here, though juniper survive atop the tallest peaks, and gnarled hackberry trees hug some river benches. The only pine trees, at last count, were forty-nine ponderosas on a ridge south of Leslie Gulch. The ashy soils of this area have produced a wealth of rare wildflowers. Ertter's grounsel, Packard's blazing star, MacKenzie's phacelia, Owyhee clover, two species of milk vetch, and grimy ivesia are known chiefly from Leslie Gulch. A new penstemon was identified in the early 1980s north of Dry Creek Buttes.

Geology

Erosion carved the colored badlands and rock pinnacles here from compacted volcanic ash deposits as much as 2000 feet thick. Sandwiched throughout this immense ash layer are resistant basalt lava flows also 15 to 20 million years old. This volcanic activity may have dammed the ancestral Snake River, for the ash's stripy strata indicate lake bed deposition.

The old basalt now forms a rimrock cap at Table Mountain, Red Butte, and many other places. The partially welded ash of The Honeycombs contains weak spots that have eroded into caves, ledges, and honeycomblike indentations. Paleontologists unearthed horse, bear, camel, and antelope fossils from ash near Red Butte. Succor Creek State Park allows amateur collecting of thunder eggs, agates, and petrified wood from ash deposits there.

Coffeepot Crater and Lava Butte vented the Jordan Craters Lava Beds within the past 9000 years. Look for lava tubes and spatter cones near these two source vents. The relatively smooth,

The Honeycombs

ropy surface of these pahoehoe-style lava flows has been jumbled by pressure ridges, cracks, domes, and collapsed caves. Jordan Craters sits atop the Brothers Fault Zone, source of a string of recent eruptions across southeast Oregon.

History

Cave campsites, petroglyphs, and arrowheads indicate humans have lived along the Owyhee River for 12,000 years. Defacing petroglyphs or removing cultural artifacts is a federal crime. The name Owyhee, a 19th-century spelling for Hawaii, commemorates two Hawaiians hired by early beaver trappers and killed here by Indians in 1819. Fish runs on the Owyhee died when the Owyhee Dam was built in the 1930s. The reservoir now teems with black crappies; the river supports sparse catfish, suckers, and carp.

THINGS TO DO

Hiking

Boats provide a good way to reach many hiking areas. While drifting the Owyhee north of Rome, stop at Chalk Basin to spend a day exploring the colored rock formations and delicately fluted cliffs there. Not far downstream, stop at a huge, river-level cave near Whistling Bird Rapids and hike up a sandy-bottomed gulch past rock narrows and dry waterfalls to Hoot Owl Spring. From the same base camp, another good cross-country hike climbs up 1300 feet in elevation to the canyon rim and Iron Point, practically overhanging the river.

From the Owyhee Reservoir, hikable sandy washes lead to The Honeycombs, an area of gulches lined with sculpted pinnacles. The formations are most concentrated north of Carlton Canyon, but extend to Three Fingers Gulch and Leslie Gulch. Rugged passes provide routes between canyons.

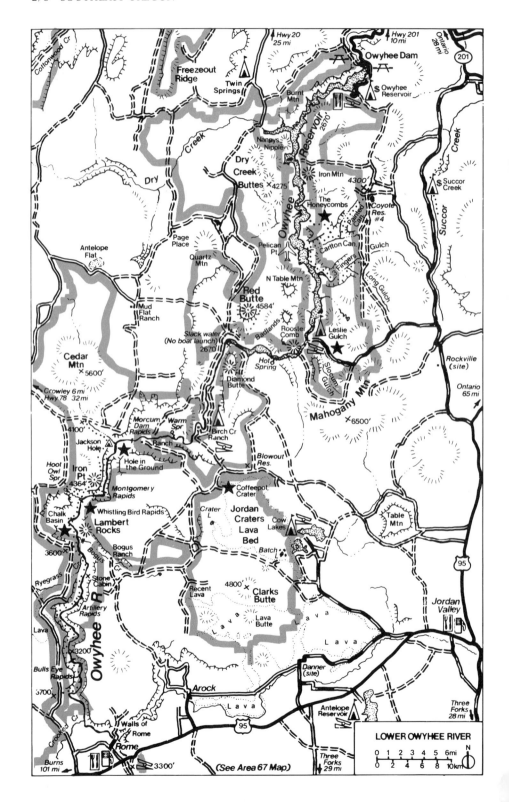

Cottonwood Cr.

Hwy 20
25 mi

Hwy 201
10 mi

Ontario
28 mi

201

Owyhee Dam

Freezeout
Ridge

Twin
Springs

Burnt
Mtn

Owyhee
Reservoir

$

Nannys
Nipple

Dry
Creek
Buttes ×4275

Iron Mtn
4300'

4300'

$ Succor
Creek

Dry

Succor Creek

Owyhee Reservoir 2670

The
Honeycombs

Coyote
Res.
#4

Page
Place

Pelican
Pt.

Carlton Can.

Fingers

Gulch

Antelope
Flat

Quartz
Mtn

N Table Mtn

Long Gulch

Mud
Flat
Ranch

Red
Butte
×4584'

Badlands

Rooster
Comb

Leslie
Gulch

Rockville
(site)

Cedar
Mtn
×5600'

Slack water
(No boat launch)
2670

Hot
Spring

Slocum Gulch

Ontario
65 mi

Crowley 6 mi
Hwy 78 32 mi

Diamond
Butte

Mahogany Mtn
×6500'

4100'

Morcum
Dam
Rapids

Warm
Spr.

Birch Cr.
Ranch

Ranch

Jackson
Hole

Blowout
Res.

Hoot
Owl
Spr.

Iron
Pt.
×4364'

Hole in
the Ground

Coffeepot
Crater

Table
Mtn

Montgomery
Rapids

Chalk
Basin

Whistling Bird Rapids

Crater
L.

Jordan
Craters
Lava
Bed

Cow
Lakes

Lambert
Rocks

95

3600'×

Bogus
Ranch

Batch
L.

Jordan
Valley

Ryegrass

Bogus Cr.

Stone
Cabin

Recent
Lava

4800'
×

Clarks
Butte

Artillery
Rapids

Lava
Butte

Lava

Lava

Owyhee R.

×3200'

Bulls Eye
Rapids

Lava

Danner
(site)

Arock

3700'×

Lava

Antelope
Reservoir

Three
Forks
28 mi

Burns
101 mi

Walls of
Rome

Crooked Cr.

Rome

×3300'

95

(See Area 67 Map)

Three
Forks
29 mi

LOWER OWYHEE RIVER

0 1 2 3 4 5 6mi

0 2 4 6 8 10km

N

From the south end of Owyhee Reservoir, climb to viewpoints at Rooster Comb and Red Butte. Between these lies a colorful badlands of rounded hills.

No boat? Then drive to these hikes. A dirt road (accessible only in dry weather by high-clearance vehicles) heads north from Rome, coming within a 2-mile walk of scenic Chalk Basin, and within 4 miles of Iron Point. Another route (also for high-clearance vehicles) leads to within a 4-mile hike of Jackson Hole, where Lower Owyhee Canyon is deepest and grandest. Turn off Highway 78 at Follyfarm Junction, 66 miles east of Burns. Take the gravel Crowley Road 25 miles and turn right, through a gate, onto an unmarked dirt road. After 8 very rough miles the track becomes impassable for vehicles. Continue 1 mile on foot, then hike a cattle trail down a gulch to the river.

The scenic road to Leslie Gulch is marked with "Leslie Gulch–Succor Creek National Back Country Byway" signs. For a short walk from the Leslie Gulch Campground, hike 2 miles up Slocum Gulch's narrow canyon. Or drive 3 miles east and walk 1 mile up colorful Juniper Gulch.

The main part of The Honeycombs' canyonland is trickier to find overland. Drive south from Ontario 32 miles on Highway 201, turn right onto the dirt Succor Creek Road for 6 miles, turn right onto an unmarked dirt road for 6 miles, take a fork to the right for 2 miles, and then take a left fork for another 2 miles to the watering tank labeled number 4. From here hike west on a jeep track 2 miles to the head of Painted Canyon. The farther one hikes down this canyon, the more dramatic it becomes.

Wear sturdy boots to explore Jordan Craters' lava land. Coffeepot Crater is the most popular day-hike goal, though Batch Lake's wildlife and Lava Butte's lava tubes are also of interest.

Backpacking? Spend a few days exploring The Honeycombs, or else prowl the Owyhee's rim from Jackson Hole to Chalk Basin. From Chalk Basin it's possible to hike 24 miles south along the trailless riverbank toward Rome; hike up to the road before hitting private land at Crooked Creek.

On all hikes, bring plenty of water. Pure water sources are limited to infrequent springs along the Owyhee River. A U-shaped tent peg helps tap these dribbles, but by late summer many are dry.

Boating

First floated in 1953, the 55-mile stretch of Owyhee River between Rome and the reservoir has become a popular four- to six-day trip. Intermediate-level rafters and kayakers generally portage or line through the class 4 rapids (Whistling Bird, Montgomery, and Morcum Dam). Caution is important, for losing a boat on this very remote desert river means trouble. Boaters must register at the launch site or the BLM office in Vale. Commercial boaters need special permits.

Upstream snowmelt makes the river runnable only in March and May (kayaks sometimes run until mid-June); bring gear for cold weather. Also carry a day's supply of drinking water, for springs are few. Motors are banned on the river.

First serious whitewater comes 11.5 miles down from the Rome launch site: class 3 Bulls Eye Rapids. Nineteen miles beyond, stop on the left to scout or portage Whistling Bird Rapids. A slab of canyon wall has tumbled into the river here on the right, forcing boaters hard left. Two miles downstream, Montgomery Rapids provides a class 4 drop at a sharp right riverbend. The last major hurdle comes 7 miles farther along, where an abandoned rock dam partially blocks the river. In low water, line boats on the left. In high water, experts can also run Morcum Dam's middle.

Owyhee Reservoir's slack water at mile 55 leaves boaters 11 miles to paddle (four hours for rafts) to the Leslie Gulch ramp. An alternative is to take boats out at the staffed campground at the historic Birch Creek Ranch, although driving there requires a high-clearance four-wheel-drive vehicle.

Canoes and sailboats can do well on the reservoir despite competing powerboats and strong winds. Shoreside campsites abound.

UPPER OWYHEE RIVER

Location: 105 mi SE of Burns
Size: 750 sq mi
Status: Federal wild and scenic river, undesignated wilderness
Terrain: Sheer-walled river canyons, whitewater, sagebrush tablelands
Elevation: 3300'–6500'
Management: Vale District BLM
Topographic maps: Three Forks, Whitehorse Butte, Skull Creek, Indian Fort, Dry Creek, Scott Reservoir, Drummond Basin, No Crossing, and 23 other maps (USGS)

Oregon's wildest whitewater river cuts a dramatic, 1000-foot-deep slot through the sagebrush tablelands where Oregon, Idaho, and Nevada meet. Drift boaters here pass cliffside caves and hot springs on their way to raging Widowmaker Rapids. Hikers either follow the branching canyon's arid rims or trace the canyon bottoms, wading when streams careen between sheer cliffs.

Climate

In March and June, when the river is high enough to be run, prepare for unpredictable weather: balmy blue sky, freezing nights, searing heat, or even snow. After a rain, dirt roads may be impassably muddy—especially the final mile to Three Forks. May and June are best for hiking in the uplands. Plan canyon-bottom hikes for September or October, when streams are low and fordable. Avoid the freezing winds of winter or the scorching heat of July and August. Annual precipitation is just 11 inches.

Plants and Wildlife

Watch for kingfishers and water ouzels along the water's edge, fat chukars in the side gulches, and raptors nesting in the rimrock: golden eagles, buteos, and prairie falcons. Sage grouse, jackrabbits, and rattlesnakes are more numerous here than anywhere else in Oregon. Pronghorn antelope and mule deer are common.

Sagebrush and bunchgrass dominate this treeless terrain. Plant life in the canyons remains pristine, for cliffs restrict most cattle grazing to the uplands. Phlox and evening primrose provide delicate flowers in spring. Rabbit brush and sunflowerlike balsamroot bloom yellow in fall.

Geology

During immense volcanic eruptions 15 to 20 million years ago, rhyolite ash exploded from vents and basalt lava spread across this entire area. Later, as the land gradually rose, the Owyhee River cut downward, exposing the orange welded ash layers and black basalt flows in canyon walls.

THINGS TO DO

Hiking

Three Forks, a remote ford near the confluence of three major Owyhee River branches, serves as a base for cross-country exploration of this trailless canyonland. Before setting out, put on boots that can get wet.

Start with a 1.3-mile hike up the main Owyhee River, wading across a tributary and following part of an old military wagon road. A hot springs with swimmable rock pools, 2 miles upriver, is on private land.

Next, put the wet boots back on and try walking up the North Fork's streambed a few miles into that river's inner gorge, where calm, wall-to-wall water reflects the towering canyon above. For a more rugged day hike, explore the Middle Fork's slotlike canyon 3 or 4 miles up from its

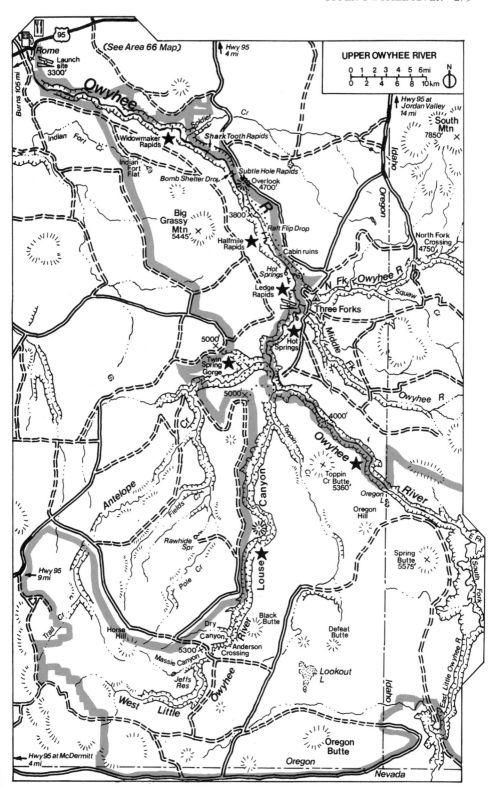

Kayakers prepare for whitewater

mouth. The Middle Fork may stop flowing altogether by fall, but leaves deep, wall-to-wall pools that require chest-deep wades.

Streamside cliffs and swift water prevent hikers from following the main Owyhee riverbank downriver from Three Forks. However, it's possible to hike atop the canyon rim all the way to Rome. The 40-mile route requires few detours (Soldier Creek is the only major side canyon to circumvent), but has no water.

Drive to Three Forks either via dirt Three Forks Road (which joins Highway 95 about 18 miles east of Rome) or on the partly paved State Line Road from Jordan Valley. Both routes are marked as the Soldier Creek Watchable Wildlife Loop. The 5-mile spur road descending the canyon to Three Forks is the only rough section for passenger cars.

Antelope Creek and the West Little Owyhee River both have long, deep, scenic, and very remote canyons. Cross-country hikers following these canyon bottoms must wade some pools and boulder-hop across a few rockslides, but they can discover towers, caves, columns, chutes, and colored rock walls. There is no easy way to access these canyons from Three Forks. With a four-wheel-drive vehicle you can cross the North Fork bridge and the Middle Fork ford, drive 3 miles up to the tablelands, turn right, and negotiate a maze of bad roads 5 miles to a 600-foot cliff overlooking the mouth of the West Little Owyhee River. But only serious adventurers are likely to find their way down to the alluring canyon's mouth.

A better road accesses the upper portion of the West Little Owyhee River's canyon. Turn east off Highway 95 at a gravel road 40 miles south of Burns Junction. Follow the road 15 miles, and then turn right for 20 additional miles to Anderson Crossing. From here the canyon extends 30 miles downstream.

Boating

The 39 miles of Owyhee River between Three Forks and Rome provide one of the most challenging and scenic runs in the state. Boaters must register at the put-in or at the BLM office in Vale. Commercial boaters need special permits. The run can only be made in March or June. Possible cold weather and cold water in these months make hypothermia a danger; wet suits or dry suits are advisable.

Just 1.5 miles below the deceptively calm waters of the Three Forks launch site, the rushing, narrow chutes of Ledge Rapids leave many a boater swimming through a rugged, 0.25-mile-long rock garden. Scout this class 4+ whitewater carefully (from the left side); there is no easy way out of this remote desert canyon for those who have lost their boat.

Bitterroot

Nine miles beyond Ledge Rapids, stop at a sharp right bend to scout Halfmile Rapids ahead. This class 4+ rapids begins with rocks jutting into the current on the right and continues with a full 0.5 mile of rough water. After only a 100-yard lull, boaters face Raft Flip Drop's big wave (class 3-4).

Subtle Hole (class 3+), at river mile 15 below Three Forks, is longer than Raft Flip Drop. Bomb Shelter Drop (class 3) follows immediately; pull left in order to stop at the interesting cave below it. Three miles beyond, two rocks in midstream mark the start of Shark Tooth Rapids (class 3).

Class 5+ Widowmaker Rapids, at river mile 21.5, must be portaged by all but daring experts in medium-length rafts. Part of this fall's treachery is that it is preceded by 0.5 mile of class 3 rapids. Begin a difficult portage on the right before the river ahead disappears between huge boulders. This chute, sometimes briefly mistaken for the Widowmaker itself, is actually a class 3 drop that fills boats with water, making them unmanageable at the brink of Widowmaker's 10-foot waterfall immediately ahead.

Another, less frequented Owyhee River whitewater run begins near the town of Owyhee, Nevada, and follows the South Fork Owyhee to Three Forks.

APPENDIX A: STATE TRAIL PLAN

A network of existing and proposed long-distance trails links many of Oregon's wild areas. Four trail routes cross the entire state. Other routes follow rivers or serve as connectors between Oregon's population centers and the longer trail routes.

The Pacific Crest Trail and routes east of the Cascades are open to both hikers and equestrians. However, all long-distance trails west of the Cascade summit (except the North Umpqua River Trail) are for hikers only.

The Pacific Crest Trail (PCT) follows the Sierra Nevada and Cascade Range on a 2638-mile route from Mexico to Canada. Although the PCT's last gap (in California) wasn't completed until 1992, the 424-mile Oregon section was finished in 1987. Begun in the 1920s as the Oregon Skyline Trail, the route was one of two trails authorized by Congress in the 1968 National Trail Systems Act. Today the well-marked route, built with a wide tread and gentle grade, has become so popular that sections near highway trailheads may be quite dusty by late summer. Snow closes much of this high-elevation trail from mid October to early July.

The Oregon Coast Trail (OCT), now 80 percent complete, utilizes the open sands of Oregon's publicly owned beaches for much of its 360-mile route between Washington and California. Forested trail segments lead hikers over headlands. Gray cedar posts mark completed sections of this all-season route, notably the northernmost 64 miles from Fort Stevens (on the Columbia River) to Garibaldi (near Tillamook).

The Desert Trail (DT), crossing Oregon's southeast corner, explores high-desert mountain ranges, rimrock canyons, and wide-open landscapes where sagebrush dominates. Rock cairns mark the trail's general route, allowing travelers to pick their own way through the open terrain. Trail markers and published trail guides define the completed 150-mile section between Denio on the Nevada border and Highway 20 east of Burns.

The Desert Trail Association, cooperating with the Bureau of Land Management, proposes continuing the trail as far as Mexico and Canada. The planned route south would traverse Nevada to connect with an existing southern Californian portion of the Desert Trail. The route north would briefly join the New Oregon Trail in the Blue Mountains, and then crosses Hells Canyon and Idaho to follow the Continental Divide National Scenic Trail to Canada.

The New Oregon Trail (NORT), 57 percent complete, follows the crests of four mountain ranges on its 1300-mile route from Oregon's westernmost point at Cape Blanco to the state's easternmost point in Hells Canyon. The NORT connects the trans-state Oregon Coast Trail and Desert Trail, and follows a portion of the Pacific Crest Trail. The route, first hiked end to end by William L. Sullivan in 1985, also incorporates two earlier long-distance trail proposals: the Ochoco Trail and the Blue Mountain Trail.

Nearly all of the existing trail segments of the NORT traverse wild areas, and are thus included in this book. Hikers can fill trailless gaps by following logging roads and highway shoulders, although the route is still unmarked. Snow blocks high portions of the mountain ranges in winter.

The Columbia Gorge Trail leads from the Portland area through the Columbia Gorge, where it crosses the Pacific Crest Trail. Hikers can currently follow the route 25 miles from Sheppards Dell State Park (near Bridal Veil Falls) to Starvation Creek (near Viento State Park). Weather rarely closes this low-elevation route, even in winter. Plans would extend the route west to

Mount Hood from the Timberline Trail near Cairn Basin

Troutdale, in order to join the 40-Mile Loop around Portland. The proposed Chinook Trail would extend the Columbia Gorge Trail east to The Dalles, cross the Columbia River to Washington, and return to Vancouver along the gorge rim via Three Corner Rock and Silver Star Mountain.

The 40-Mile Loop began as a 1910 proposal to link Forest Park trails with a 40-mile route encircling Portland. Growth of the city has lengthened the mapped loop to 140 miles, but the trail's original name remains. Currently hikable throughout, the loop connects existing trails in more than 30 parks (notably the Wildwood Trail in Forest Park and the Marquam Trail in Council Crest and Marquam Nature Parks) with a variety of sidewalk and roadside routes.

The Clackamas Trail will eventually link the Portland area to the PCT near Mount Jefferson. The plan would utilize the abandoned Portland Traction Railroad corridor from Gresham to Boring, as well as the existing 7.8-mile Clackamas River Trail, the 4-mile Riverside Trail, the 5-mile Rho Ridge Trail, and the 4.4-mile Red Lake Trail to the PCT at Olallie Lake.

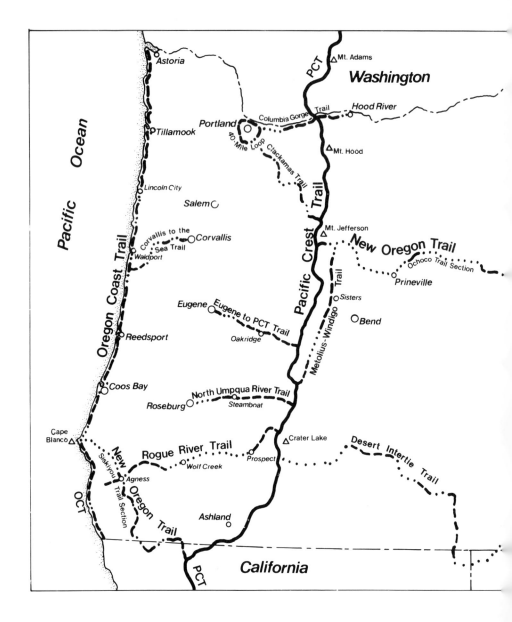

The Corvallis to the Sea Trail currently offers only 15 miles of completed trail, including the Corvallis-Philomath bike path, a trail at Marys Peak, and trails in the Drift Creek Wilderness. The proposed 105-mile route would cross the Coast Range entirely on public land to connect with the Oregon Coast Trail at Cape Perpetua. Eventually, a connecting horse trail from Cape Perpetua would continue as far south as the Smith River.

The Eugene to PCT Trail, 74 miles long, is about 80 percent complete, and is currently hikable from Lowell to the PCT (at Bobby Lake, near Waldo Lake). The completed portion follows forested ridges usually free of snow from June to November. Volunteer trail-building efforts proceed on the remaining valley-bottom route that would continue past Mount Pisgah to join the Eugene-Springfield riverside bike path.

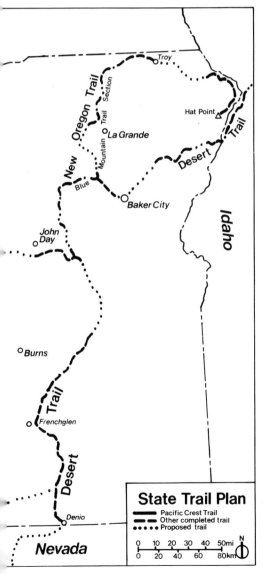

The North Umpqua Trail provides 78 miles of completed trail along this forested and often cliff-lined river from its headwaters at Maidu Lake in the Mount Thielsen Wilderness. The completed section extends from the Pacific Crest Trail past Steamboat to Idleyld Park. Volunteers propose continuing construction downriver 23 miles to Roseburg.

The Rogue River Trail consists of two widely separated sections. The popular Lower Rogue River Trail extends 47 miles from Grave Creek to Illahe, traversing the rugged Wild Rogue Wilderness. The little-known Upper Rogue River Trail climbs 45 miles from Prospect to the northwest corner of Crater Lake National Park. A proposal to connect the two trail segments suggests a nonriver route through Wolf Creek.

The Metolius-Windigo Trail features a completed, 45-mile path through central Oregon's pine forests. The route primarily attracts equestrian use and serves as a low-elevation alternative when the nearby, high-elevation PCT is blocked by snow.

The trail crosses Highway 20 at Indian Ford, 5 miles northwest of Sisters. To the north of Highway 20, the path skirts Black Butte and follows Green Ridge, overlooking the Metolius River. To the south, the trail continues as far as Three Creek Lake, near Broken Top. A Forest Service proposal would eventually extend the route south to join the Pacific Crest Trail in the Mount Thielsen Wilderness.

The Desert Intertie Trail will link the Desert Trail with the PCT, crossing Yamsay Mountain and incorporating the Fremont Trail (22 miles complete) and the Crane Mountain Trail (34 miles complete).

APPENDIX B: MANAGING AGENCIES

UNITED STATES FOREST SERVICE (USFS)

Pacific Northwest Regional Office
319 SW Pine St.
Portland, OR 97208
(503) 326-3644

Columbia Gorge National Scenic Area
902 Wasco Ave.
Hood River, OR 97301
(541) 386-2333

Deschutes National Forest
1645 E Highway 20
Bend, OR 97701
(541) 388-2715

Fremont National Forest
524 N "G" St.; P.O. Box 551
Lakeview, OR 97630
(541) 947-2151

Malheur National Forest
139 NE Dayton St.
John Day, OR 97845
(541) 575-1731

Mt. Hood National Forest
2955 NW Division St.
Gresham, OR 97030
(503) 667-0511

Ochoco National Forest
P.O. Box 490
Prineville, OR 97754
(541) 447-6247

Rogue River National Forest
P.O. Box 520
Medford, OR 97501
(541) 776-3600

Siskiyou National Forest
200 NE Greenfield Rd.
Grants Pass, OR 97526
(541) 479-5301

Siuslaw National Forest
4077 SW Research Way
Corvallis, OR 97333
(541) 757-4480

Umatilla National Forest
2517 SW Hailey Ave.
Pendleton, OR 97801
(541) 276-3811

Umpqua National Forest
2900 NW Stewart Parkway
Roseburg, OR 97470
(541) 672-6601

Wallowa-Whitman National Forest
P.O. Box 907
Baker, OR 97814
(541) 523-6391

Willamette National Forest
P.O. Box 10607
Eugene, OR 97440
(541) 687-6522

Winema National Forest
P.O. Box 1390
Klamath Falls, OR 97601
(541) 883-6714

BUREAU OF LAND MANAGEMENT (BLM)

Oregon State Office
825 NE Multnomah
Portland, OR 97208
(503) 231-6274

Burns District
HC 74-12533, Highway 20 W
Hines, OR 97738
(541) 573-4400

Coos Bay District
1300 Airport Lane
North Bend, OR 97459
(541) 756-0100

Eugene District
2890 Chad Dr.
Eugene, OR 97401
(541) 683-6600

Lakeview District
1000 9th St. S
Lakeview, OR 97630
(541) 947-2177

Medford District
3040 Biddle Rd.
Medford, OR 97501
(541) 770-2200

Prineville District
185 E 4th St.
Prineville, OR 97754
(541) 447-4115

Salem District
1717 Fabry Rd.
Salem, OR 97306
(503) 399-5646

Vale District
100 Oregon St.
Vale, OR 97918
(541) 473-3144

*Sawmill Falls on the Little North Santiam River,
near Opal Creek*

OTHER AGENCIES

Confederated Tribes of the
Warm Springs Indian Reservation
Natural Resources Department
P.O. Box C
Warm Springs, OR 97761
(541) 553-1161

Crater Lake National Park
P.O. Box 7
Crater Lake, OR 97604
(541) 594-2211

Crooked River National Grassland
2321 E 3rd St.
Prineville, OR 97754
(541) 447-4120

Hells Canyon National Recreation Area
88401 Highway 82
Enterprise, OR 97828
(541) 426-4978

Nature Conservancy
821 SE 14th
Portland, OR 97214
(503) 230-1221

Newberry National Volcanic Monument
(Fort Rock Ranger District)
1230 NE 3rd
Bend, OR 97701
(541) 388-5674

Oregon Caves National Monument
19000 Caves Highway
Cave Junction, OR 97523
(541) 592-2100

Oregon Department of Fish and Wildlife
2501 SW 1st Ave.
Portland, OR 97207
(503) 229-5403

Oregon Dunes National Recreation Area
855 Highway Ave.
Reedsport, OR 97467
(541) 271-3611

Oregon State Parks and Recreation Division
1115 Commercial St. NE
Salem, OR 97310
(503) 378-6305

U.S. Fish and Wildlife Service
P.O. Box 111
Lakeview, OR 97630
(541) 947-3315

APPENDIX C: TOPOGRAPHIC MAP PUBLISHERS

Bureau of Land Management (BLM)
P.O. Box 2965
Portland, OR 97208
(503) 231-6281

The Bureau of Land Management publishes several topographic maps for $1 each: the Lower Deschutes River, the Lower John Day River, and Central Oregon. In addition, the BLM's planimetric maps can be extremely useful in eastern Oregon, both for driving the maze of dusty tracks near roadless areas and for hiking within the roadless areas themselves. The Steens Mountain Recreation Lands map ($1) covers Steens Mountain, the Alvord Desert, the Pueblo Mountains, and most of the Sheepshead Mountains and Trout Creek Mountains. Other areas in eastern Oregon are covered best by the BLM's 30-minute quadrangle series ("Blue Line Quads"); these sixty-six black-and-white maps, scaled 1 inch to 1 mile (1:63,360), cost $2 each and cover an area 25 miles wide by 34 miles long. All BLM maps show public and private land ownership.

Desert Trail Association
P.O. Box 589
Burns, OR 97720

This nonprofit association organizes hikes, distributes a monthly newsletter (*Desert Trails*), and publishes topographic maps of the Desert Trail route. The maps include detailed notes for following the trail route, but are broad enough to cover alternative hiking terrain. The five maps available in Oregon so far (more are planned) cover the Pueblo Mountains, the Alvord Desert, Steens Mountain, the Donner und Blitzen River, and the Malheur Wildlife Refuge. Price is $3, postpaid.

Geo-Graphics
18860 SW Alderwood Dr.
Beaverton, OR 97006
(503) 591-7635

This publisher offers high-quality topographic maps of popular Cascades wilderness and winter sports areas. The Mount Hood Wilderness map ($6) covers the Mount Hood Wilderness at a scale of 1:24,000 on the front, and the Columbia, Badger Creek, and Salmon-Huckleberry wildernesses at a scale of 1:100,000 on the back. The Mount Jefferson Wilderness map ($5.95 on plain paper, $7.95 on waterproof paper) covers the peak itself at 1:30,000 and the rest of the wilderness at 1:62,000. The Three Sisters Wilderness map ($5) covers the entire Three Sisters Wilderness and half of the Mount Washington and Waldo Lake wildernesses at a scale of 1:70,000. The Mount Washington Wilderness map ($5.95) covers that area at 1:30,000. Other topographic maps cover the winter sports areas at Santiam Pass ($4.75) and Willamette Pass ($3). Postage is free for mail orders over $15; otherwise add $1. The maps are also available at many bookstores and outdoor stores in northwest Oregon and Bend.

Green Trails
P.O. Box 1272
Bellevue, WA 98009

Green Trails publishes 15 topographic maps for Oregon, covering the Northern Oregon Cascades at a scale of 1:69,500. These frequently updated maps each cover about 12 by 18 miles, showing trails, cross-country skiing routes, and other recreational data. The maps are available in many outdoor stores in northwest and north-central Oregon, but can also be ordered direct from the publisher. Up to four maps cost $2.25 each, postpaid; five or more cost $1.95, postpaid. Orders of less than ten maps are folded and mailed. Orders of ten or more are shipped flat via UPS.

Imus Geographics
P.O. Box 161
Eugene, OR 97440
(503) 344-1431

Imus Geographics publishes a high-quality topographic map of the Diamond Peak Wilderness. The map is available in many outdoor stores or can be ordered by mail for $5.95 apiece, postpaid. Maps are shipped folded unless otherwise requested.

United States Forest Service (USFS)
P.O. Box 3623
Portland, OR 97208
(503) 221-2877

The U.S. Forest Service publishes convenient topographic maps for designated wilderness areas under their management, generally at a scale of 1:62,500. However, maps are not complete for most of the areas designated since 1979, and the completed maps often exclude adjacent roadless areas. The USFS also offers special topographic maps covering the Pacific Crest Trail through Oregon, trails in the Columbia Gorge, and winter ski trails in certain areas. Finally, nontopographic recreation maps cover each of the thirteen National Forests in Oregon, showing major roads, most trails, and other data at a scale of 1:126,720. All of these maps are priced from $1 to $2.50. District offices generally stock all the maps, while ranger stations only keep maps of local interest on hand.

To keep track of the latest Forest Service roads, try the $3 District Transportation maps. Most of the National Forest's fifty-seven Oregon ranger districts offer copies of these frequently updated maps to the public on request. Often topographic, always awkwardly large, the maps attempt to show every Forest Service road and trail at a scale of 1:62,500.

United States Geological Survey (USGS)
Box 25286
Denver Federal Center
Denver, CO 80225
(303) 236-7477

The U.S. Geological Survey has completed its effort to produce topographic maps for all of Oregon in its 7.5-minute series, a format that shows great detail but can be unwieldy for large areas (in Oregon 1 minute is approximately 0.8 mile). Unless otherwise noted, the USGS maps recommended in the area descriptions are in this series. The older 15-minute series maps, though larger, date from the 1950s and do not show many newer roads. USGS maps with a 1:250,000 scale span 100 miles but show insufficient detail for most uses.

USGS topographic maps are available at a few outdoor stores and bookstores, but maps can also be ordered direct. The 7.5-minute and 15-minute maps cost $2.50 postpaid; the 1:250,000 series maps and special 25-minute Crater Lake map cost $4 postpaid. Send the map name, state, and series type along with full payment. The USGS ships maps rolled. They do not accept telephone orders, but will send a free state index map on request.

Many university and large city libraries in Oregon stock all Oregon USGS topographic maps and allow them to be checked out or photocopied.

APPENDIX D: SELECTED BIBLIOGRAPHY

PLANTS AND WILDLIFE

Arno, Stephen, and Ramona Hammerly. *Northwest Trees*. Seattle: The Mountaineers, 1977.
Ferguson, Denzel and Nancy. *Oregon's Great Basin Country*. Bend: Maverick Publications, 1978.
Hitchcock, C. Leo, and Arthur Cronquist. *Flora of the Pacific Northwest*. Seattle: University of Washington Press, 1973.
Horn, Elizabeth. *Wildflowers 1: The Cascades*. New York: Touchstone Press, 1972.
Jolley, Russ. *Wildflowers of the Columbia Gorge*. Portland: Oregon Historical Society, 1988.
Matthews, Daniel. *Natural History of the Cascades and Olympics*. Portland: Portland Audubon Society, 1988.
Niehaus, Theodore F. *A Field Guide to Pacific States Wildflowers*. New York: Houghton Mifflin, 1976.
Pandell, Karen, and Chris Stall. *Animal Tracks of the Pacific Northwest*. Seattle: The Mountaineers, 1981.
Peterson, Roger Tory. *A Field Guide to Western Birds*. New York: Houghton Mifflin, 1961.
Ross, Charles R. *Trees to Know in Oregon*. Corvallis: Oregon State University Extension Service, 1975.
Ross, Robert A., and Henrietta L. Chambers. *Wildflowers of the Western Cascades*. Portland: Timber Press, 1988.
Taylor, Ronald J., and Rolf W. Valum. *Wildflowers 2: Sagebrush Country*. New York: Touchstone Press, 1974.
Whitaker, John O., Jr. *The Audubon Society Field Guide to North American Mammals*. New York: Knopf, 1980.
Whitney, Stephen R. *A Field Guide to the Cascades & Olympics*. Seattle: The Mountaineers, 1983.

GEOLOGY

Alt, David D., and Donald W. Hyndman. *Roadside Geology of Oregon*. Missoula: Mountain Press Publishing, 1978.
Baldwin, Ewart M. *Geology of Oregon*. Eugene: University of Oregon Bookstore, 1992.
Chronic, Halka. *Pages of Stone: Geology of Western National Parks and Monuments, Vol. 2*. Seattle: The Mountaineers, 1986.
Harris, Stephen L. *Fire & Ice: The Cascade Volcanoes*. Seattle: The Mountaineers, 1980.

HISTORY

Ashworth, William. *Hells Canyon*. New York: Hawthorn Books, 1977.
Brogan, Phil F. *East of the Cascades*. Portland: Binfords & Mort, 1964.
McArthur, Lewis A. *Oregon Geographic Names*. Portland: Western Imprints, 1982.
Sullivan, J. Wesley. *Jam on the Ceiling*. Eugene: Navillus Press, 1987.
Williams, Chuck. *Bridge of the Gods, Mountains of Fire: A Return to the Columbia Gorge*. Seattle: The Mountaineers, 1980.

HIKING AND BACKPACKING

Ambler, Julie, and John Patt, eds. *Guide to the Middle Santiam and Old Cascades*. Corvallis: Marys Peak Group, Sierra Club, 1981.
American Outdoor Safety League. *Emergency Survival Handbook*. Seattle: The Mountaineers, 1984.

Angels Rest, at the western end of the Columbia Gorge

Bernstein, Art. *76 Day-Hikes Within 100 Miles of the Rogue Valley.* Grants Pass: New Leaf, 1987.

Doan, Marilyn. *Hiking Light.* Seattle: The Mountaineers, 1982.

George, Tony. *The Mount Jefferson Wilderness Guidebook.* Salem: Solo Press, 1983.

————. *The Olallie Scenic Area Guidebook.* Salem: Solo Press, 1983.

Hardesty Mountain Study Group. *Hiking the Hardesty Wilderness.* Springfield: Hardesty Mountain Study Group, 1981.

Hart, John. *Hiking the Great Basin.* San Francisco: Sierra Club Books, 1981.

Henderson, Bonnie. *Best Hikes With Children in Western and Central Oregon.* Seattle: The Mountaineers, 1992.

Jones, Philip N., ed. *Columbia River Gorge: A Complete Guide.* Seattle: The Mountaineers, 1992.

Lilja, Irene and Dick. *Siuslaw Forest Hikes.* Albuquerque: Heritage Associates, 1990.

Lowe, Don and Roberta. *50 Hiking Trails: Portland & Northwest Oregon.* New York: Touchstone Press, 1986.

————. *35 Hiking Trails: Columbia River Gorge.* New York: Touchstone Press, 1988.

Ostertag, Rhonda and George. *Day Hikes from Oregon Campgrounds.* Seattle: The Mountaineers, 1991.

————. *50 Hikes in Oregon's Coast Range & Siskiyous.* Seattle: The Mountaineers, 1989.

————. *100 Hikes in Oregon.* Seattle: The Mountaineers, 1992.

Plumb, Gregory A. *A Waterfall Lover's Guide to the Pacific Northwest.* Seattle: The Mountaineers, 1989.

Prater, Yvonne, and Ruth Mendenhall. *Gorp, Glop & Stew: Favorite Foods From 165 Experts.* Seattle: The Mountaineers, 1982.

Schaffer, Jeffrey P. *Crater Lake National Park and Vicinity.* Berkeley: Wilderness Press, 1983.

Schaffer, Jeffrey P., and Bev and Fred Hartline. *The Pacific Crest Trail, Vol. 2: Oregon and Washington.* Berkeley: Wilderness Press.

Spring, Ira, and Harvey Manning. *Northwest Trails.* Seattle: The Mountaineers, 1982.

Sullivan, William L. *Blue Mountain Trails.* Eugene: Navillus Press, 1990.

————. *100 Hikes in the Central Oregon Cascades*. Eugene: Navillus Press, 1991.

————. *100 Hikes in Northwest Oregon*. Eugene: Navillus Press, 1993.

United States Forest Service. *A Guide to the Kalmiopsis Wilderness*. Siskiyou National Forest, 1985.

Wellborn, Sherry, ed. *Oregon Coast Range Wilderness*. Corvallis: Siuslaw Task Force, 1980.

Williams, Jerold. *Afoot in Lane County*. Eugene: Calapooya Books, 1989.

Williams, Paul M. *Oregon Coast Hikes*. Seattle: The Mountaineers, 1985.

Wood, Wendell. *A Walking Guide to Oregon's Ancient Forests*. Portland: Oregon Natural Resources Council, 1991.

CLIMBING

Graydon, Don, ed. *Mountaineering: The Freedom of the Hills*. Seattle: The Mountaineers, 1992.

Thomas, Jeff. *Oregon High: A Climbing Guide*. Portland: Keep Climbing Press, 1991.

————. *Oregon Rock: A Climber's Guide*. Seattle: The Mountaineers, 1983.

Watts, Alan. *Climber's Guide to Smith Rock*. Portland: Chockstone Press, 1992.

WINTER SPORTS

Brady, Michael. *Cross-Country Ski Gear*. Seattle: The Mountaineers, 1983.

Gilette, Ned, and John Dostal. *Cross-Country Skiing*. Seattle: The Mountaineers, 1988.

Lund, John W. *Southern Oregon Cross Country Ski Trails*. Klamath Falls: Lund, 1987.

Newman, Doug, and Sally Sharrard. *Oregon Ski Tours*. New York: Touchstone Press, 1973.

Prater, Gene. *Snowshoeing*. Seattle: The Mountaineers, 1988.

Vielbig, Klindt. *Cross-Country Ski Routes of Oregon's Cascades*. Seattle: The Mountaineers, 1984.

BOATING

American Outdoor Safety League. *Boater's Safety Handbook*. Seattle: The Mountaineers, 1982.

Campbell, Arthur. *John Day River Drift and Historical Guide*. Portland: Frank Amato Publications, 1980.

Jenkinson, Michael. *Wild Rivers of North America*. New York: Dutton, 1981.

Jones, Phil. *Canoe Routes: Northwest Oregon*. Seattle: The Mountaineers, 1992.

Quinn, James M. *Handbook to the Illinois River Canyon*. Waldport: Education Adventures Inc., 1979.

————. *Handbook to the Rogue River Canyon*. Waldport: Educational Adventures Inc., 1978.

Willamette Kayak and Canoe Club. *Soggy Sneakers: Guide to Oregon Rivers*. Corvallis: Willamette Kayak and Canoe Club, 1986.

INDEX

Note: **Bold face** indicates major wild areas. *Italic* page numbers refer to maps.

M

Macduff Mountain 109, *110*
Macks Canyon Campground 87, *88*
Maiden Peak *117*, 118
Maidu Lake 130, *131*
Maklaks Mountain *122*
Malheur National Wildlife Refuge 264, *266*
Mann Lake 264, *266*
Marble Pass 210
Marial 164, *164*
Marie, Lake *171*, 172
Marilyn Lakes 114, *117*, 119
Marion Lake *59*, 60, 62
Marion Mountain *59*, 60
Matterhorn 229, *233*, 234, *235*, 236
Matthieu Lakes *65*, 67
Maupin 88
Maxwell Butte *59*, 60
Mazama Campground *139*, 141
Mazamas 31
McArthur Rim 105, *106*, 113
McCaleb Ranch (Boy Scout) 157, *158*
McClellan Mountain 195
McCully Basin 231, *233*
McDermitt *273*
McDowell Creek *260*, 262
McGraw Creek 225
McIntyre Ridge 37, *38*
McKenzie Bridge *110*
McKenzie Pass *65*, 66, 67
McKenzie River 64, *110*
McKie Meadow *144*, 146
McLennan Mountain *110*
McLoughlin, Mount 142, *145*
McNeil Point 31, *33*
McQuade Creek Trail *71*, 73
Meacham Creek, North Fork *213*, 214
Meissner Sno-park 113
Melakwa Lake Scout Camp *64*
Menagerie Wilderness *68*, 68–71
Metolius Breaks **93–96**
Metolius River *93*, 94
Metolius-Windigo Trail 285
Mickey Hot Springs *267*, 268
Middle Santiam Wilderness *71*, 71–74
Middle Sister 113
Midnight Lake *117*, 119, 121, *122*, 123
Mill Creek Wilderness 184–186, *185*
Miller Lake 130, *131*, 132
Minam Lake 231, *233*, 234
Minam River 231, *232*, *233*, 236
Mink Lake *107*, 108, *111*
Minto Lake 61
Mirror Lake (Mount Hood) 37, *39*
Mirror Lake (Wallowas) 234
Mizell Point 128
Monkey Face 96, 97, 98

Monon Lake 54, 55
Monument Rock Wilderness 200–203, *201*
Moolack Mountain *116*
Moose Lake *68*, 70
Moraine Lake 105, *106*, 108
Moss Springs Campground *232*, 236
Mount Hebo 78–80
Mount Hood Wilderness 29–36, *33*
Mount Jefferson Wilderness 56–63, *59*
Mount Thielsen Wilderness 129–133, *131*
Mount Washington Wilderness 63–68, *64*, *65*
Mountain Lakes Wilderness 147–149
Mowich Lake *59*, 61
Mule Creek Canyon *162*, 164
Multnomah Falls 25, *26*
Multorpor Meadows 35
Murderers Creek 194
Muskrat Lake *116*

N

Nannie Creek Trail *144*, 146
Nasty Rock *50*, 52
Nee-Me-Poo Trail *221*, 223, 225
Nesmith Point 25, *26*
New Oregon Trail (NORT) 282, *284*
Newberry Crater 243–246, *245*
Niagara Falls *78*, 79
Nick Eaton Ridge 25, *27*
Ninemile Ridge *213*, 214
North Falls 48
North Fork John Day Wilderness 205–212, *209*
North Fork Umatilla Wilderness 212–215
North Point 189
North Sister 113
North Umpqua River *128*
North Umpqua River Trail *284*, 285
Northern Blue Mountains 212–215
Nose Bender Rapids *166*, 168

O

Oak Flat Launch Site *158*, 160
Oak Springs Rapids 88
Obsidian Trail 105
Obsidian trailhead *106*
Ochoco Canyons 190–193
Ochoco Divide 185
Ochoco Ranger Station 186
Odell Lake *117*, 121, *122*, 123
Olallie Butte *54*, 55
Olallie Lake 53, 55
Olallie Lake Scenic Area 53–56, *54*
Olallie Mountain 109, *110*
Olallie Ridge 109
Olallie Trail 109, *110*
Old Baldy 37, *38*
Old Cascades *68*, 68–71
Olive Lake Campground 210
Oneonta Gorge 24, 25, *26*

About the Author

William L. Sullivan began backpacking in Oregon at the age of six and has been in love with adventure ever since. At seventeen he left high school to study at remote Deep Springs College in the California desert, where his duties included milking cows by hand. He went on to earn a B.A. in English from Cornell University and an M.A. in German from the University of Oregon. He and his wife, Janell Sorensen, bicycled 3000 miles through Europe, studied two years at Heidelberg University, and built a log cabin by hand on Oregon's Siletz River.

In 1985, Sullivan backpacked 1360 miles across the state—from Oregon's westernmost point at Cape Blanco to the state's easternmost point in Hells Canyon. His journal of that two-month solo trek, published as *Listening for Coyote*, was a finalist for the Oregon Book Award in 1989.

A freelance writer since 1980, Sullivan has written seven books. He and Janell live in Eugene with their children Karen and Ian.

About the Oregon Natural Resources Council

The Oregon Natural Resources Council (ONRC) is Oregon's largest conservation network. A nonprofit, tax-exempt corporation, the ONRC is composed of over eighty-five local and statewide conservation, sporting, education, business, and outdoor-recreation organizations and more than 3000 individual members. The Council addresses major conservation and natural-resource-management issues facing Oregon's forests, rivers, rangelands, and coast. Wilderness protection, especially through legislation, has been a premier organizational priority and is viewed as vital for both environmental and economic purposes. With a full-time staff of twenty, including regional field coordinators who live and work in each corner of Oregon, the ONRC's strength is its strong and active grass-roots citizen network of volunteers. The Council coordinates public involvement in Oregon conservation issues at the agency-planning level, represents its members in court, and lobbies with them directly at the State Legislature and in Congress. Its educational programs provide information and assistance to all members of the public interested in management of Oregon's lands, waters, and natural resources.

The ONRC is a publicly supported educational, scientific, and charitable organization dependent upon private donations and citizen support. It receives no government funding. Memberships and contributions are tax-deductible.

Main Office
522 SW 5th, Suite 150
Portland, OR 97204
(503) 223-9001

Western Regional Office
1161 Lincoln St.
Eugene, OR 97401
(541) 344-0675

Central Oregon Field Office
16 NW Kansas St.
Bend, OR 97701
(541) 382-2616

South Central Field Office
P.O. Box 667
Chiloquin, OR 97624
(541) 783-2206

THE MOUNTAINEERS, founded in 1906, is a nonprofit outdoor activity and conservation club, whose mission is "to explore, study, preserve, and enjoy the natural beauty of the outdoors...." Based in Seattle, Washington, the club is now the third-largest such organization in the United States, with 15,000 members and five branches throughout Washington State.

The Mountaineers sponsors both classes and year-round outdoor activities in the Pacific Northwest, which include hiking, mountain climbing, ski-touring, snowshoeing, bicycling, camping, kayaking and canoeing, nature study, sailing, and adventure travel. The club's conservation division supports environmental causes through educational activities, sponsoring legislation, and presenting informational programs. All club activities are led by skilled, experienced volunteers, who are dedicated to promoting safe and responsible enjoyment and preservation of the outdoors.

The Mountaineers Books, an active, nonprofit publishing program of the club, produces guidebooks, instructional texts, historical works, natural history guides, and works on environmental conservation. All books produced by The Mountaineers are aimed at fulfilling the club's mission.

If you would like to participate in these organized outdoor activities or the club's programs, consider a membership in The Mountaineers. For information and an application, write or call The Mountaineers, Club Headquarters, 300 Third Avenue West, Seattle, Washington 98119; (206) 284-6310.

Send or call for our catalog of more than 300 outdoor books:
The Mountaineers Books
1001 SW Klickitat Way, Suite 201
Seattle, WA 98134
1-800-553-4453